The Cambridge Companion to
Modern British Culture

British culture today is the product of a shifting combination of tradition and
experimentation, national identity and regional and ethnic diversity. These
distinctive tensions are expressed in a range of cultural arenas, such as art, sport,
journalism, fashion, education and race. This Companion addresses these and
other major aspects of British culture and offers a sophisticated understanding
of what it means to study and think about the diverse cultural landscapes of
contemporary Britain. Each contributor looks at the language through which
culture is formed and expressed, at the political and institutional trends
that shape culture and at the role of culture in daily life. This interesting and
informative account of modern British culture embraces controversy and debate
and never loses sight of the fact that Britain and Britishness must always be
understood in relation to the increasingly international context of globalisation.

MICHAEL HIGGINS is Director of the Journalism and Creative Writing
programme at the University of Strathclyde, Glasgow.

CLARISSA SMITH is Senior Lecturer in Media and Cultural Studies in the School
of Art, Design and Media, University of Sunderland.

JOHN STOREY is Professor of Cultural Studies and Director of the Centre for
Research in Media and Cultural Studies, University of Sunderland.

CAMBRIDGE COMPANIONS TO CULTURE

The Cambridge Companion to
Modern British Culture

Edited by
MICHAEL HIGGINS
CLARISSA SMITH
and
JOHN STOREY

CAMBRIDGE
UNIVERSITY PRESS

University Printing House, Cambridge CB2 8BS, United Kingdom

Published in the United States of America by Cambridge University Press, New York

Cambridge University Press is part of the University of Cambridge.

It furthers the University's mission by disseminating knowledge in the pursuit of education, learning and research at the highest international levels of excellence.

www.cambridge.org
Information on this title: www.cambridge.org/9780521683463

© Cambridge University Press 2010

First published 2010

A catalogue record for this publication is available from the British Library

Library of Congress Cataloguing in Publication data
The Cambridge companion to modern British culture / edited by Michael Higgins,
Clarissa Smith, John Storey.
p. cm. – (Cambridge companions to culture)
Includes bibliographical references and index.
ISBN 978-0-521-86497-8 – ISBN 978-0-521-68346-3 (pbk.)
1. Great Britain–Intellectual life–20th century. 2. Great Britain–Social life
and customs–20th century. 3. Popular culture–Great Britain–History–
20th century. 4. Great Britain–Social conditions–20th century. 5. Great Britain–
Civilization. I. Higgins, Michael, 1967– II. Smith, Clarissa. III. Storey, John,
1950– IV. Title. V. Series.
DA110.C253 2010
941.082–dc22
2010023745

ISBN 978-0-521-86497-8 Hardback
ISBN 978-0-521-68346-3 Paperback

Contents

Contributors

JANE ARTHURS is Professor of Media and Cultural Studies and Head
of Culture, Media and Drama, at the University of the West
of England, Bristol. Her publications in feminist cultural
studies and contemporary television include *Television and
Sexuality: Regulation and the Politics of Taste* (2004) and the edited
collection *Crash Cultures* (2002), as well as work on post-feminist
drama for the journal *Feminist Media Studies*.

ELLIS CASHMORE is Professor of Culture, Media and Sport at
Staffordshire University and is a regular media commentator
on sports culture and ethics. His most recent books include
Celebrity/Culture (2006), *Making Sense of Sports* (4th edn, 2005),
Beckham (2nd edn, 2004) and *Tyson: Nurture of the Beast* (2004).

DAVID CRYSTAL is Honorary Professor of Linguistics at the University
of Bangor. He read English at University College London, then
held university posts at London, Bangor and Reading before
becoming an independent scholar in 1984. The author of many
books on linguistics and English language studies, he is best
known for his two *Cambridge Encyclopedias*: of *Language* (1997) and
of *The English Language* (2003). An autobiographical memoir, *Just a
Phrase I'm Going Through*, was published in 2009.

CAROLINE EVANS is Professor of Fashion History and Theory at Central
Saint Martins College of Art and Design within the University of
the Arts, London. She is the author of *Fashion at the Edge: Spectacle,
Modernity and Deathliness* (2003) and co-author of *The London
Look: Fashion from Street to Catwalk* (2004), *Fashion and Modernity*
(2005), *Hussein Chalayan* (2005) and *The House of Viktor & Rolf* (2008).

ALEX GOODY is Senior Lecturer in Twentieth-century Literature at Oxford Brookes University. Her research interests cover the relationships between modernity, technology, culture and gender, and current projects include a forthcoming book on technology, literature and culture. Goody is author of *Modernist Articulations* (2007).

MICHAEL HIGGINS is Director of the Journalism and Creative Writing programme in the Department of English Studies at the University of Strathclyde in Glasgow. He has published numerous articles covering such areas as political communications, celebrity culture, news discourse and national identity. He also serves as co-convenor of the Media and Politics Group of the Political Studies Association. Higgins's most recent book is *Media and Their Publics* (2008).

KEN JONES is Professor of Education at Goldsmiths, University of London. He has written *Education in Britain* (2003) and co-authored *Schooling in Western Europe: The New Order and its Adversaries* (2008). He is currently working on a book about the survival or re-emergence of radical educational traditions in the twenty-first century and is co-editing a reader on 'creative learning'.

MICHAEL MANGAN is Professor of Drama at Exeter University. He has also worked as a playwright, a director, a literary manager, a dramaturg and an actor. His primary research interests lie in the area of theatre and society, and he has published a wide range of books, articles and papers on the subjects of theatre and gender, Shakespeare and Renaissance theatre, theatre and cultural history, applied theatre and contemporary British theatre. His most recent monograph is *Performing Dark Arts: A Cultural History of Conjuring* (2007).

TARIQ MODOOD is Professor of Sociology, Politics and Public Policy and the Founding Director of the Centre for the Study of Ethnicity and Citizenship at the University of Bristol. He is a regular contributor to the media and to policy debates in Britain, was awarded an MBE for services to social sciences and ethnic relations in 2001 and was elected a member of the Academy of Social Sciences in 2004. His most recent books are *Multiculturalism: A Civic Idea* (2007) and, as co-editor, *Secularism, Religion and Multicultural Citizenship* (2009).

VALERIE REARDON is Senior Lecturer in Media at University College Plymouth St Mark and St John as well as a practising fine-art photographer. She has written extensively for *Art Monthly*, and her articles on the aesthetics, meanings and uses of art appear in such journals as the *Journal of Feminisms and Art* and the *Journal of Media Arts and Cultural Criticism*.

CLARISSA SMITH is Senior Lecturer in Media and Cultural Studies at the University of Sunderland. Her research and publications focus on the expanding sexual sphere for heterosexual women: its institutional practices, representational strategies, uses and meanings. Smith has published in a variety of journals and edited collections, including *Sexualities* and the *European Journal of Cultural Studies*, and is author of *One for the Girls: The Pleasures and Practices of Reading Women's Porn* (2006).

JOHN STOREY is Professor of Cultural Studies and Director of the Centre for Research in Media and Cultural Studies at the University of Sunderland. He has published widely in cultural theory and cultural history. His latest book is called *Culture and Power in Cultural Studies* (2010).

JOHN STREET is Professor of Politics at the University of East Anglia. His main research is on the relationship between politics and popular culture and mass media. He is the author of *Mass Media, Politics and Democracy* (2001), *Politics and Popular Culture* (1997) and *Rebel Rock: The Politics of Popular Music* (1986). He is a member of the editorial group of the journal *Popular Music* and of *The Cambridge Companion to Rock and Pop* (co-edited with Will Straw, 2001).

SARAH STREET is Professor of Film at the University of Bristol. Her most recent books are *Transatlantic Crossings: British Feature Films in the USA* (2002), *The Titanic in Myth and Memory* (co-edited with Tim Bergfelder, 2004), *Black Narcissus* (2005) and *Queer Screen: The Queer Reader* (co-edited with Jackie Stacey, 2007). Her latest book, *Film Architecture and the Transnational Imagination: Set Design in 1930s European Cinema*, is co-authored with Tim Bergfelder and Sue Harris (2007).

JOHN TOMANEY is Professor of Regional Development and Director of the Centre for Urban and Regional Development Studies (CURDS) at the University of Newcastle upon Tyne, Professor of Regional Studies at Monash University in Melbourne, Associate Director of the UK Spatial Economics Research Centre (SERC) and an Academician of the (UK) Academy of Social Science. He has published over 100 books and articles on questions of local and regional development including *Local and Regional Development* (2006) and has undertaken research projects for, among others, UK Government and Research Councils, the European Commission, the Organisation for Economic Co-operation and Development and local and regional governments and private sector and voluntary organisations in the UK and elsewhere.

PATRICIA WAUGH is Professor of English at Durham University. She has published widely in the field of twentieth-century fiction, literary theory and literature and intellectual history. Her most recent books are *Revolutions of the Word* (1997) and *Literary Criticism and Theory: An Oxford Guide* (2006). She is currently completing two books: *Beyond the Two Cultures: Literature, Science and the Good Society* and the *Blackwell History of British Fiction, 1945–Present*.

SHEILA WHITELEY is Professor of Popular Music at the University of Salford. Her interests include the relationships between popular music, sexualities and gender, as well as between popular music and hallucinogenics. Her books include *Women and Popular Music: Sexuality, Identity and Subjectivity* (2000) and *Too Much Too Young: Popular Music, Age and Identity* (2003).

The Formation of Modern British Culture

Chronology of key events

1707	The Act of Union between the parliaments of England and Scotland.
1708	Merger to form the Honourable East India Company, to facilitate imperial trade.
1775–83	American War of Independence.
1776	Publication of Adam Smith's *The Wealth of Nations*.
1785	Foundation of *The Times* newspaper in London.
1793–1802	French Revolutionary Wars.
1803–15	Napoleonic Wars.
1811	Publication of the debut *Sense and Sensibility* by Jane Austen.
1819	The Peterloo Massacre, in St Peter's Fields, Manchester.
1832	Reform Act, to increase parliamentary representation in cities and to extend voting rights on the basis of the control or ownership of land.
1836	Charles Dickens's first novel, *The Pickwick Papers*, is published.
1838	The formation of the Chartist movement, demanding the right to vote for men over twenty-one, annual parliamentary elections, the abolition of property qualification for MPs, payment for MPs, vote by secret ballot and equal electoral districts.
1855	The repeal of the Stamp Act on the cost of newspapers.

1867	The Second Reform Act, extending the vote to male householders.
1870	The Elementary Education Act, providing for free education for all children between five and thirteen years of age.
1884	Third Reform Act, equalising voting rights across urban and rural areas and limiting constituencies to one Member of Parliament.
1898	The acquisition of the 'new territories' of Hong Kong on a ninety-nine-year lease.
1900	The formation of the Labour Party.
1914–18	The First World War.
1918	The Representation of the People Act, giving votes to women and removing property qualifications for men.
1921	Marie Stopes opens birth-control clinic in London.
1922	The establishment of the BBC.
1926	The General Strike.
1928	The Representation of the People (Equal Franchise) Act, lowering the voting age for women to equal that for men.
1939	The outbreak of the Second World War.
1942	Publication of the Beveridge Report, calling for a welfare state.
1945	The end of the Second World War.
1945	Election of a Labour government, led by Clement Attlee.
1948	The arrival of the ship *Empire Windrush* at Tilbury, carrying first immigrants from the West Indies.
1948	Withdrawal from India and partition of the former colony into India and Pakistan.
1954	The Television Act, establishing an independent television network.
1956	The emergence of Lonnie Donegan and skiffle music.
1956	The Suez Crisis.
1957	The formation of the Campaign for Nuclear Disarmament.
1959	The Obscene Publications Act.
1960	D. H. Lawrence's *Lady Chatterley's Lover*, unedited.
1960	The first episode of soap opera *Coronation Street*.
1960	Defeat in the Commons of the Private Members Bill to relax laws on homosexuality.
1961	Birth-control pill made available to 'all women'.

1962	The Beatles release their first single for the Parlophone label.
1962	*That Was the Week That Was* political satire first shown on BBC television.
1963	Equal Pay Act passed in the USA.
1965	The Beatles play at the Shae Stadium in New York.
1966	The England football team win the World Cup.
1967	Sexual Offences Bill legalising homosexual sex in private for consenting adults over the age of twenty-one.
1967	The formation of the far-right political party the National Front.
1967	The switch of the BBC Radio's Home, Light and Third Services to Radios 1, 2, 3 and 4.
1968	Enoch Powell's 'Rivers of blood' speech, attacking immigration.
1970	First Glastonbury Festival (originally Pilton Festival) held at Michael Eavis's Worthy Farm; Tyrannosaurus Rex were the headline act.
1970	Equal Pay Act passed in Britain.
1975	Sex Discrimination Act promoting equality of opportunity between men and women.
1976	Race Relations Act, incorporating the earlier acts of 1965 and 1968, prohibiting discrimination on the grounds of race, colour, nationality, ethic and national origin.
1977	The Silver Jubilee of Queen Elizabeth II.
1977	The formation of political movement the Anti-Nazi League.
1979	Election of a Conservative government, led by Margaret Thatcher.
1981	New Cross Fire: arson attack on a house party in London killed eighteen young black partygoers.
1981	Riots in Toxteth, a district of Liverpool, and Brixton, a district of London.
1981	Marriage of Prince Charles and Lady Diana Spencer.
1982	The Falklands Conflict.
1982	Launch of Channel 4 as a second commercial broadcaster.
1983	Provisional IRA bomb outside Harrods department store in London kills six and injures ninety.
1984–5	The Miners' Strike.

1984	Provisional IRA bombing of the British Cabinet at the Grand Hotel in Brighton.
1985	Live Aid concert.
1985	English football hooliganism prompts indefinite Union of European Football Associations ban.
1985	Riots in Brixton, Toxteth and Peckham. Lord Scarman cites poverty and racial discrimination as causes of rioting.
1986	British and French plan construction of Channel Tunnel.
1987	Third term for Margaret Thatcher and the Conservative Government.
1987	Fire kills thirty-one people at the King's Cross underground station.
1988	Terrorist bomb destroys Pan Am Flight 103 over Lockerbie, Scotland.
1988	The publication of Salman Rushdie's *The Satanic Verses* and subsequent fatwa.
1988	Passing of the Local Government Act including Section 28 requiring that local authorities 'shall not intentionally promote homosexuality or publish material with the intention of promoting homosexuality'. Eventually repealed in Scotland in 2000 and in the rest of the UK in 2003.
1989	Sky TV first satellite channel in UK.
1989	Hillsborough Football Stadium disaster.
1989	Church of England Assembly votes to allow ordination of women priests.
1990	Restoration of diplomatic links between Britain and Argentina.
1990	Poll Tax riots.
1990	Margaret Thatcher resigns as leader of Conservative Party. John Major becomes Prime Minister.
1990–1	Participation in the Gulf War, against Iraq.
1991	IRA launch bomb attack on Downing Street.
1992	UK opts out of Maastricht Treaty.
1992	Queen Elizabeth II's *annus horriblis*.
1992	Launch of English football's Premier League.
1992	General Election returns John Major as Prime Minister and the Conservative Government for its fourth term.
1993	Murder of black teenager Stephen Lawrence.

1994	Church of England ordination of women priests.
1994	Official opening of the Channel Tunnel connects the UK to mainland Europe.
1994	The election of Tony Blair as Labour leader and development of 'New Labour'.
1994	British Government meet with Sinn Féin.
1994	Launch of National Poetry Day.
1995	Diana, Princess of Wales, interviewed by Martin Bashir for the BBC.
1996	Reconstruction of Shakespeare's Globe Theatre opened.
1996	IRA bombing of Manchester.
1997	The election of a Labour government led by Tony Blair.
1997	Publication of J. K. Rowling's *Harry Potter and the Philosopher's Stone.*
1997	IRA declares a ceasefire.
1997	The Sensation exhibition of Young British Artists.
1997	The formal handover of Hong Kong to the Chinese Government.
1997	The death of Diana, Princess of Wales, in a car crash in Paris.
1998	Good Friday Agreement is signed, bringing peace to Northern Ireland and cessation of IRA bombing campaigns in mainland Britain.
1998	Human Rights Act.
1999	The formation of a devolved Scottish parliament and Welsh assembly.
2000	Ken Livingstone becomes Mayor of London in the UK's first direct mayoral election.
2000	Opening of Tate Modern art gallery.
2000	Sven-Goran Eriksson is made first foreign manager of English football team.
2000	Channel 4 broadcasts first series of reality TV production *Big Brother.*
2000	Race Relations Amendment Act establishing statutory duty on public bodies to promote race equality.
2001	Tony Blair and New Labour secure second term in government.
2001	Participation in the US-led invasion of Afghanistan.

2001	Foot and Mouth crisis.
2002	Hutton Inquiry into death of David Kelly and BBC reporting.
2002	Channel 4 soap opera *Brookside* ends after twenty-one years.
2002	Anti-Terrorism Crime and Security Act.
2003	Participation in the invasion of Iraq and a second Gulf War.
2003	UK entry to the Eurovision Song Contest receives *nul points*.
2004	Hunting Act bans hunting with hounds.
2004	Civil Partnerships Act legalises same-sex union.
2005	Freedom of Information Act.
2005	The '7/7 Bombings' in London.
2005	General election returns Labour Party with reduced majority.
2005	Relaunch of BBC's sci-fi series *Dr Who*.
2006	Gordon Brown becomes Prime Minister after Blair steps down.
2007	*Celebrity Big Brother* 'race row'.
2007	UK Borders Act.
2007	Wettest summer since records began.
2008	Criminal Justice and Immigration Act receives royal assent.
2008	Financial crisis leads to 'credit crunch' and the nationalisation of a number of large banks.
2009	The release of the expenses claims of Members of Parliament, many of which are excessive, provokes a national media scandal on standards in public life, and prompts the introduction into law of a Parliamentary Standards Bill to police future Members' allowances.
2010	General election produces a hung parliament in which no party has an overall majority, with the Conservatives as the largest single party.

MICHAEL HIGGINS, CLARISSA SMITH AND JOHN STOREY

Introduction: modern British culture: tradition, diversity and criticism

What does it mean for us to study a national culture? As we will see in the pages to come, it means looking across and reflecting upon a range of the practices and activities that contribute towards the shared experience of community and 'nation'. In part our endeavour calls upon an understanding of the various cultural and political institutions within which culture is organised and regulated, but, perhaps even more, it demands we comprehend something of the transience and excitement of everyday experience. In Britain, cultural activities are shaped by their histories and their traditions, but they also have a dynamic relationship with the present. A comprehensive account of British culture should therefore be alert to the forces that give living, thinking and playing in Britain form and character, while presenting an enthusiastic account of how this national culture changes along with the population and the world at large.

The Cambridge Companion to Modern British Culture offers just such an introduction to culture in twenty-first-century Britain. It brings together seventeen critical and insightful essays by some of the leading academics in British intellectual life. The subjects and issues the chapters cover are purposively varied, reflecting the diversity and debates that circulate in discussions of modern British culture. What emerges is a dynamic collection that brings together a number of aspects of living in and thinking about British culture. This is, therefore, a *Companion* designed to provide a fascinating and informative overview of modern British culture. However, the reader will also learn that British culture is not singular. Like most modern national cultures it is characterised by diversity and difference.

The Companion captures this diversity in two ways. First, it includes chapters that reflect a broad range of the forms of interests, activities and pursuits that come under the rubric of 'culture'. These include the daily practices discussed in David Crystal's chapter on language and Clarissa Smith's on sex. There are also examples of those activities that express the relationship between the realms of the person and the state, such as Ken Jones on education and John Street on politics. The majority of the chapters present critical overviews of individual cultural realms: Sarah Street (cinema), Patricia Waugh (fiction) and Alex Goody (poetry), Mick Mangan (theatre), Jane Arthurs (television), Valerie Reardon (art), Caroline Evans (fashion), Ellis Cashmore (sport), Sheila Whiteley (popular music) and Michael Higgins (newspapers). Second, in a manner designed to build on and complement those chapters dedicated to cultural forms and practices, the collection also explores how 'culture' needs to be seen within a network of difference and a hierarchy of social relations. The themes of diversity and difference highlighted by John Storey and developed in John Tomaney's chapter on regions, as well as the chapter by Tariq Modood on ethnicity, provide critical interpretations of the various factors and mechanisms that direct contemporary British life.

Aside from its divisibility into nations, ethnicities and regions, what is also exceptional about Britain and British culture – a commonly cited point of distinction between Britain and many other Western democracies – is its retention of an informal but nevertheless pervasive system of social class. The influence of social class is easily recognisable in British culture, as David Crystal's discussion of the link between accent, dialect and social belonging demonstrates. Of course, it is far too simplistic to draw from this that Britain has none of the characteristics of a meritocracy. Yet it remains the case that while much media coverage is devoted to those figures in British civil and civic life that come from working-class backgrounds – businessman Lord Alan Sugar and former Deputy Prime Minister John Prescott are two prominent examples of this – the higher reaches of the formidably powerful British Civil Service tend to be staffed by those educated at the medieval English universities of Oxford and Cambridge and drawn from the middle and upper classes.

However, even as aspects of British cultural life remain in place, a broader appreciation will see Britain as a state characterised by change. Indeed, those turning to contemporary Britain as an object of study may well be struck by the fact that the country is in a period of transformation, almost crisis. Much of the mass media in Britain reports on shifting population patterns that reflect immigration first from the former colonies of the Caribbean and South-East Asia, and then from the accession states to the European Union. The UK itself has altered its political structure, with Wales and Scotland forming devolved parliaments and establishing a relative autonomy within the British political framework. All too often, the assumption is that the very notion of 'Britain' is under threat like never before. Yet, as John Storey and Tariq Modood show, external influences have often guided the development of the British state and national sense of itself. As a collection of islands, Britain has always been and continues to be a diverse cultural mix.

The capacity of British culture as a whole to engage with a shifting social and ethnic environment is helped by a journalistic, intellectual and scholarly resolve to reflect critically on the implications of Britain's national culture and its imperial past. In an important sense, the critical traditions exemplified in this *Companion* are as integral to British culture as the artefacts and practices they describe. Indeed, in order to fully understand the political underpinnings of much of the British cultural landscape, it is important to understand this tradition of highlighting and criticising the role of culture in fostering social inequality in British culture.

Britain operates as an alliance between relatively autonomous nations. At present, the bureaucratic category of 'the United Kingdom of Great Britain and Northern Ireland' – the phrasing that appears on the passport of any British subject – comprises England, Northern Ireland, Scotland and Wales. This is a geographically complex arrangement. Whereas England, Scotland and Wales are on the largest island of 'Great Britain', Northern Ireland is part of the neighbouring island of Ireland along with the independent Republic of Ireland. In terms of 'state' identity, what John Storey refers to in Chapter 1 as the idea of Britain, this stems from a mixture of political alliances, including a 1707 union between the English and Scottish parliaments. Recent decades have shown how these arrangements of state are subject to rapid change. The period since 1999, for example, has seen devolved parliaments and legislative assemblies set up in Northern Ireland, Scotland and Wales, amid discussion in both Northern Ireland and Scotland over the distribution of powers between parliaments and even the integrity of the British Union. It is important to note that while the form and extent of identification with the nations of Britain are fluid, each has maintained a coherent and viable cultural identity.

Resilient and powerful as the national identities contained within the bureaucratic state of Britain may be, the modes of identification within Britain are not confined to the internal nations and are also expressed in keenly held regional identities within and across the composite nations.

In the opening chapter, John Storey presents a critical account of what it 'means' to be British. Nationality, he argues, is an important part of the networks of signification we call culture. To share a national culture is to interpret the world, to make it meaningful and to experience it as meaningful, in recognisably similar ways. Signification is, therefore, fundamental to our sense of national belonging. Britishness, like any other national identity, is a body of meanings with which we learn to identify. Moreover, it is a body of meanings that seems natural and replete with common sense. For the British traveller abroad, so-called 'cultural shock' may happen when his or her sense of what is 'natural' (i.e. British) is suddenly confronted by another nationality's sense of what is 'natural', when his or her British 'common sense' is suddenly challenged by the 'common sense' of another national culture.

Since culture is bound up in regimes of influence and definition that are subject to shift, so culture itself is in continual development. This is apparent in David Crystal's clear and convincing account of language change in contemporary Britain. As Crystal points out, languages are continually changing. There are occasions in which this change is dramatic. The Norman Conquest, for example, had an enormous impact on English spelling and vocabulary. Similarly, during the Renaissance, the number of words borrowed from other European languages more or less doubled the number of English words in use. Mostly language change is slow and generally unnoticed; however, as Crystal observes, we are now living through a period of 'rapid and widespread language change'. Crystal's chapter specifies what lies behind an interesting episode for language and British culture. According to Crystal, a range of diverse factors, including the social, economic and technological, have conspired to make the past two decades extremely important ones for the evolution of language in Britain.

The acceleration of change that we see in language in Britain is also reflected in education, as Ken Jones observes in his chapter on the culture of schooling. Jones also joins with Crystal in acknowledging the international influences on cultural change. Until the late twentieth century, Jones writes, school education in Britain was organised within clearly defined national boundaries. Over the past twenty years, however, this has changed completely, as the influences of international bodies have begun to weigh on the British school system. Jones explains how the Organisation for Economic Co-operation and Development – a worldwide body dedicated to the imposition of the free market – unites with the various policy initiatives of the European Union to confront British schools with the challenges of contributing to a new global 'knowledge economy'. With particular focus on the English experience, Jones explores how education has responded to this new global policy agenda. He outlines the terms of the relationship between government and curriculum design and how this arrangement impacts upon the dominant ways of understanding the social and economic purpose of education in contemporary Britain.

In his chapter on changes in political communications, John Street also shows how cultural change in Britain is best viewed within the broader international context. In Britain, as in many other Western liberal democracies, the realm of politics appears to be drawing upon many more of the resources of popular culture than ever before. He charts this shift to the emergence in the late 1950s of television as a major tool of election campaigning. These developments in electoral strategy set in place a new industry dedicated to the refashioning of politics for a mass-media audience, and these practices of 'marketing politics' have subsequently spread from the exceptional periods of election time to the everyday routine of daily press briefings and policy announcements. Street discusses those perspectives that see this popularisation of politics as the contamination of the British public realm, as well as those that make the positive case that political discourse in Britain is simply being rendered more accessible. The extra factors that Street highlights, though, include the expansion of political activism amongst popular British cultural figures, such as musicians, added to an increasing media competence of the British electorate in 'reading' political communications in a critical way. In other words, it is arguably the case that the more that political discourse moves into the broader British cultural realm, the better equipped the electorate is to interpret the issues in their own terms.

John Tomaney's chapter notes the marginalisation of ideas of 'the regional' in learned writing, and it should be clear to us that this oversight has been an unfortunate one. As Tomaney demonstrates, it is important to understand regional culture if we are to have a full appreciation of the variations and particularities that go into the make-up of British culture. He argues that the North cultivates a particular 'structure of feeling' based around notions of masculine forms of working-class belonging, framed within a regionally contingent sense of 'authenticity'. It is a key component of the narrative of the 'English North' that such qualities of endeavour and sincerity reside there rather than in the South. However, it has always been necessary to see these regional identities as constituents within British culture, even as they operate in an oppositional relationship to the metropolitan centre.

Sarah Street's chapter is also concerned with a sense of belonging. Dividing British cinema into thematic categories: nostalgia, youth culture, ethnicity and asylum, and place, space and identity, Street shows how recent films have explored social inequalities and notions of community using heightened realism and stylistic energy such that the films combine 'a local address with a more global sensibility', opening up British cinema to international audiences. Although the 'fairy-tale' existence of the privileged denizens of *Notting Hill* (dir. Roger Michell, 1999) and *Four Weddings and a Funeral* (dir. Mike Newell, 1994) remain a feature of British film, titles such as *Trainspotting* (dir. Danny Boyle, 1996), *28 Days Later* (dir. Danny Boyle, 2002), *Last Resort* (dir. Pawel Pawlikowski, 2000) and *My Son the Fanatic* (dir. Udayan Prasad, 1997) challenge any notion of an homogeneous British film culture, given that their 'environments of displacement and alienation' contrast sharply with the 'heritage' prettiness of Merchant Ivory films. Street emphasises the dynamic use of tradition in British film.

In her chapter on contemporary British fiction, Patricia Waugh explores the redrawing of the maps of British fiction and the contributions of contemporary authors, who, in their explorations of identity and the politics of gender, race, sexuality and ethnicity, have catapulted British fiction out of its inwardness and timidity. Galvanised by what Waugh describes as a 'Thatcher effect', British fiction launched its own critiques of the greed and individualism of the 1980s political scene and finally deposed the domestic novel to install new kinds of writing from the margins and from the experiences of 'the migrant'. Contemporary British fiction encompasses an impressive array of modes of storytelling from the allegorical and experimental to the traditional, but what unites much of it is a shared determination to cross 'boundaries' of convention, ethnicity and social belonging.

Alex Goody's chapter argues that far from being an archaic form of expression, contemporary British poetry articulates a vibrant and youthful challenge to the traditional power structures of language and literature, energised, as it is, by Black British poets as well as the regional cadences of Scottish and Welsh poetry. The ambivalences of identity are central concerns of British poetry's 'hybrid voice'. Such poetry explores the many possible roots and routes of 'belonging' in contemporary Britain. This energy is also found in poetry that explores and reworks sexual and gender identifications. British poets cross multiple boundaries, of science and myth, technology and art, past and present, sensual and logic in innovative ways that challenge all claims that 'British poetry is dead'.

In his discussion of British theatre, Michael Mangan begins with the recognition that drama is widespread in Britain. Its most popular forms of exhibition are television, film and radio. Although Mangan's focus is on live theatre, he is aware that any attempt to maintain a clear division between live and recorded performance is very complicated indeed. Mangan's chapter presents a critical map of the many places where these collide and influence each other. Although live theatre may no longer be the hegemonic mode of theatrical performance it still has a significant role to play. As he explains, the immediate cultural relevance of theatre stretches back to the productions of ancient Athens, 'celebrating' and 'defining' society. In ways complementary to other realms of national cultural expression, live theatre in Britain intervenes in the social and cultural environment as well as giving it expression.

The particular role of television in what is argued to be a cultural era of abundance is discussed in Jane Arthurs' chapter. She writes that globalising forces have had a significant impact on the mixed system of public service and commercial provision that had previously defined British broadcasting. As the driving ethos behind television production changes from the Reithian 'giving the public what they need' to the more consumerist 'what they want', Arthurs tells us, television continues to occupy a role as educator and improver of the British populace. Arthurs examines the role of the citizen-consumer in relation to these changes and the rhetorical purposes this figure fulfils in debates about content, regulation and competition. Even if television's ideological role may be changing, Arthurs concludes, within institutional and regulatory debates it retains its central place as 'a window on the world'.

Just as Arthurs emphasises the economic pressures behind the development of television policy, so it is necessary to keep sight of the relationship between even the most socially conscious cultural activities and the needs of commerce. Valerie Reardon's chapter takes a critical view on the art 'movement' credited with the reinvention of London as a significant cultural capital. In her discussion of 'young British artists' (YBAs), Reardon explores the ways in which art myths are born and their importance to individual artist's commercial success and to wider political and cultural agendas. The transition of the political scene from Thatcherite individualism to the regeneration of 'New Labour' provided a space, she argues, in which a new art avant-garde could flourish, founded, as it was, in the shared principles of publicity, opportunism and metropolitan savvy. Although the term 'YBA' spanned a very disparate group of artists, it became synonymous with the marketing of brand Britain. Reardon's chapter explores the intersections between politics and hard-nosed economics, the promulgation of notions of nationhood in the seemingly 'transcendent' sphere of the Arts.

The Britishness of British fashion, as Caroline Evans demonstrates in her chapter, is traditionally defined from outside, by American, European and Japanese consumers keen to purchase the innovative, individual and often eccentric outfits designed by names such as McQueen and Westwood. What is understood as 'British' or more often, 'English' style is a playful use of images of tradition and history as 'stylistic and iconographic indices of British identity' rather than anything solidly British. Evans argues that British fashion's strong profile and distinctive identity in the global marketplace is the result of a seemingly democratic mix of multicultural diversity, sub-cultural identities and style from the British streets, together with the creative input of its designers and retailers. Sartorial codes and styles of dress in Britain have been used to signal opposition to dominant culture, often allied with musical genres in ways that Evans suggests are peculiarly British. The class and ethnic dynamics of sub-cultural style have been essential to the development of British street styles and to the British reputation as 'more creative but less commercial than fashion in any other country'. With its further links to the British art-school tradition, fashion in Britain is eclectic and often revolutionary; even as its economic presence is comparatively small, its influence is felt across the globe.

In his chapter on contemporary sport in Britain, Ellis Cashmore acknowledges the capacity of sport to drive changes in dominant modes of social representation and gender relations, although always in parallel with an increasingly powerful commercial ethos. Through the conduit of sport, such factors as gender, race and ethnicity temporarily cede their importance to the spectacle of individual and team excellence and to an overall national sporting interest. Yet understanding the modern history of sport in Britain involves coming to terms with an internal contradiction. As Cashmore explains, there is, on the one hand, the Corinthian ideal of amateurism, most readily associated with the upper classes and the tradition of public-school sports. According to these values, 'competition itself was a respectful order in which players exerted themselves unsparingly' with a view to improving the self rather than merely defeating one's opponents. This sits in contrast with the rise of the professional players from the late nineteenth century onwards and the surrender of sport to competitiveness and business interests. Cashmore describes how sport has shifted to the very centre of British culture, in the main through its transformation from a pastime to an industry. The defining philosophy of modern sport, the demand to 'strive for success', has helped replace class-based authority with the force of the commercial imperative.

In any prolonged study of culture, it is easy to lose sight of the broader meaning of culture as also concerned with ordinary behaviour as much as with art and learning. In keeping with this fuller understanding of culture, Clarissa Smith explores an area of life normally excluded from collections on national culture, the nation's sexual pleasures and behaviours. Smith's discussion ranges across the multiple sites, political, popular and private, where sexuality is debated and practised. She does not argue for a peculiarly British sexual character but rather tries to show how, far from being a matter of personal choice or private interest, sex is of significant importance in modern British culture, a site of regulation, improvement and social engineering as well as a source of considerable angst and entertainment.

Also concentrating on the way in which popular culture is mediated, used and experienced, Sheila Whiteley's chapter focuses on British popular music, in particular the rise and fall of Britpop in the final decade of the twentieth century. Whiteley's analysis includes an insightful discussion of the ways in which popular music is often used to articulate notions of national identity and how such applications inevitably exclude as much as they include. Writing as a feminist popular musicologist, and using Glastonbury (Britain's foremost popular music festival) as a case study, Whiteley also explores the relationship between gender and genre. Her general position is to present popular music as the outcome of a negotiated series of relations of power and influence, as she teases out important aspects of the significance of popular music in contemporary Britain: the 'hidden agendas' behind its production and consumption, as well as those means of representing the self that music helps to cultivate.

Michael Higgins begins his chapter on British newspapers by acknowledging the importance of newspapers to Britain's sense of its political and cultural identity. He argues that the notion of the press as a 'fourth estate of the realm' situates the industry as representative of the British population against the institutions of power and privilege. Although the press have never lived up to the rhetoric of this demanding tradition and are currently suffering from declining print sales, Higgins argues that newspapers remain important as socio-political identifiers and as a means of reproducing established political and class-based social groupings. Higgins's argument resonates with that of John Street, such that it appears that the politics of newspapers are motivated as much by target markets as an attachment to political ideologies. Higgins suggests that these divisions in the newspaper market extend beyond the conventional one between popular and quality newspapers and include various factors of political party allegiance and identification with particular, shifting social groupings and politically significant categories.

Tariq Modood presents a compelling analysis of religious equality and secularism in multi-faith Britain. As he explains, Britain has long been a multi-faith society in which the dominant Anglican Church has had to compete with other versions of Christianity. Throughout the twentieth century, and mostly through processes of migration, significant additions to Britain's religious plurality have included Jews, Hindus, Muslims and Sikhs. Although, as Storey indicates in an earlier chapter, these patterns are at the very core of British culture and its development, Modood points to the elasticity of those discourses of prejudice that are exercised against ethnic minorities in Britain. In Modood's assessment, prejudice has the capacity to redirect itself towards various and new forms of migrant, ethnic and religious belonging. Indeed, the shifting character of Britain's population has meant that prejudicial conduct and systems of behaviour prove capable of eluding even the most robust anti-discrimination legislation.

Together, the chapters collected here present the reader with an interesting and informative account of modern British culture, an account that never loses sight of the fact that Britain and Britishness must always be understood in relation to the increasingly international context of globalisation.

1
_____

Becoming British

Introduction

Although the Greeks and the Romans used versions of the term 'Britain' to describe the islands and their Celtic inhabitants, it only became the name of a nation in the early eighteenth century. While it is true that the seeds of this invention can be found in earlier periods (the incorporation of Wales in 1536, James I of England being also James VI of Scotland in 1603), Britain was itself invented in 1707 by the Act of Union that united England and Scotland. Between 1801 and 1921 Ireland was added and the title changed to the United Kingdom. Following the division of Ireland in 1921 the name changed again, becoming the United Kingdom of Great Britain and Northern Ireland.

In her 1992 book *Britons*, Linda Colley details how the new invention had become firmly established by the time Victoria came to the throne in 1837. The Act of Union was itself followed by, for example, the composition of the unofficial British national anthem, 'Rule Britannia' in 1740, the official national anthem, 'God Save the King/Queen' in 1745 and the designing of the national flag, the Union Flag in 1801. She argues that conflict with France was perhaps the most significant factor in the formation of British self-identity: 'It was an invention forged above all by war. Time and time again, war with France brought Britons, whether they hailed from Wales or Scotland or England, into confrontation with an obviously hostile Other and encouraged them to define themselves collectively against it.'[1]

Conflict with France allowed a version of Britishness to be superimposed over a range of internal differences. In other words, war encouraged a movement from passive awareness of nation to active support for it. In doing this, it also encouraged a certain overshadowing of internal differences, especially those of social class. But war with France was not the only significant factor in this process. Also driven by war, the building of the British Empire in North America, Africa, India and Australia, I would argue, was an even more important factor in producing a shared sense of Britishness.

Traditionally, national identity has often been understood as something coherent and fixed, an essential quality of a group of people that is guaranteed by the 'nature' of a particular territorial space. However, although identities are clearly about 'who we think we are' and 'where we think we came from', they are also about 'where we are going'. National identities are always a narrative of the nation becoming; as much about 'routes' as they are about 'roots'. In other words, nations are never only ever invented once: invention is always followed by reinvention. History is full of examples of where powerful national figures and national institutions have engaged in creating new symbols, new ceremonies and new stories of historical origins as a means to present the nation to itself and to the world in a new and positive way. 'Many people object to the idea of nations having a "brand". They claim that national identities are far too complex and many-voiced, and that, in any case, it would be wrong for anyone to manage them. Yet in practice all modern nations ... manage their identities in ways that are not dissimilar to the management of brands by companies.'[2]

National branding is often tied up with claims about maintaining supposedly ancient traditions. Although Britain is an invented nation, only sixty-nine years older than the United States of America, it is not unusual to hear British politicians make grand claims, usually in response to what they perceive as the interference of 'Europe', about 1,000 years of glorious British history being under threat. In a television interview in 1962 the Labour Party leader Hugh Gaitskell claimed that entry into the European Economic Union would mean 'the end of Britain as an independent nation state ... It means the end of a thousand years of history.'[3] At the Conservative Party Conference in 1992 Prime Minister John Major claimed, in an attempt to reassure party members worried about the possibility of Britain being forced into a federal Europe, 'And those who offer us gratuitous advice, I remind them of what a thousand years of history should have told them – you cannot bully Britain.' In similar fashion, this time in defence of what he called Britain's 'unnameable essentials', Major claimed in 1994 that 'this British nation has ... a Parliament and universities formed over seven hundred years ago, a language with its roots in the mist of time ... This [nation] is no recent historical invention: it is the cherished creation of generations.' In a speech to the Labour Party Conference in 1997 Prime Minister Tony Blair made the following claim: 'We are one of the great innovative peoples. From the Magna Carta to the first Parliament to the industrial revolution to an empire that covered the world; most of the great inventions of modern times came with Britain stamped on them.' Leaving to one side whether or not it is wise for a Labour Prime Minister to boast about the achievements of empire, his grasp of British history is a little shaky. The Magna Carta was written in 1215, while the first parliament, the so-called 'Mother of Parliaments', was established in 1295. Both of these events occurred a long time before the establishment of Britain as a nation.

Although all these accounts are clearly intended to produce a positive image of Britain, they may in fact produce the opposite effect, presenting Britain as a backward-looking nation with a rich past but not much of a future. Seeing Britain as an old country living off its historical capital may be particularly unhelpful when an institution wishes to present Britain as a vibrant and innovative country. David Mercer, Head of Design at BT, makes this very clear:

> nearly ten years ago [i.e. around 1987], British Telecom did research into the appropriateness of the name British Telecom in overseas markets. We found that we had problems with the name in certain parts of the world – Japan in particular – where the name 'British' was understood to stand for 'of the past', 'colonial', not about innovation, not about high technology, or the future or moving forward. Given the fact that we are in a fast-moving, highly innovative, creative area in telecommunications, the name British was a problem, and that is why we changed from British Telecom to BT.[4]

Nature and nationality

Nations often seem rooted in the very nature that provides them with their geographical space. Part of the sense of belonging is bound up in the way the territory itself is articulated symbolically, making the fit between nature and nation seem natural. This is often the result of the ways in which territorial space has been made to signify by artists and writers. In the opening episode of the BBC documentary series, *A*

Picture of Britain, David Dimbleby announces 'Our love of this country-side seems natural to us, yet it is only in the last three hundred years that we have learned to appreciate the beauty of our landscape.' The documentary then charts the way in which painters and writers have changed our perception of the British landscape, demonstrating and detailing the cultural construction of what now seems like a perfectly natural way of seeing and belonging.

Similarly, the 'discovery' of folk culture across the eighteenth, nineteenth and twentieth centuries was an integral part of emerging European nationalisms. From the middle of the eighteenth century to the beginning of the twentieth we find the same idea repeated over and over again: folk culture is the very embodiment of the nature of a nation; in it, the national and natural blur. Folk song, for example, is presented as almost an outgrowth of nature, a nature in which the culture of the nation can be grown. For this reason, if for no other, it should be collected and treasured.

National identity, as demonstrated by the symbolic articulation of landscape and the 'discovery' of folk culture, is a form of identification. What we are invited to identify with is what Benedict Anderson calls an 'imagined community'.[5] Anderson demonstrates how nationality, or nationness, is constructed using cultural artefacts. A nation 'is imagined because the members of even the smallest nation will never know most of their fellow-members, meet them, or even hear of them, yet in the minds of each lives the image of their communion'.[6] What distinguishes all nations is how they imagine themselves. A nation always consists of both horizontal and vertical relations. The former are relations of national belonging, the latter are relations of, for example, social class, ethnicity, gender and generation. Whereas belonging to the nation is a membership supposedly based on equality, vertical relations are rarely, if ever, other than relations of inequality. If a nation is to remain cohesive, horizontal relations must always work to control the potential disruptive effect of vertical relations. In a point that repeats Colley's claim about the role of war in the construction of Britain, Anderson observes that nation-building involves constructing an imagined community in which, in spite of the existence of obvious inequalities, horizontal relationships appear more important than vertical relations.

Anderson sees the emergence of the nation corresponding with the development of two particular nation-enabling cultural forms: the novel and the newspaper. The daily newspaper, for example, with its juxtaposition of news stories, presents its own imagined community, inviting the reader to make coherent sense of what might otherwise appear an arbitrary array of items. It mimics and reinforces the type of imagination necessary in order to figure oneself as belonging in the imagined community of the nation. The very act of reading a daily newspaper reinforces and reproduces a sense of communal belonging.

> We know that particular morning and evening editions will overwhelmingly be consumed between this hour and that, only on this day, not that. The … ceremony … is performed in silent privacy, in the lair of the skull. Yet each communicant is well aware that the ceremony he performs is being replicated simultaneously by thousands (or millions) of others of whose existence he is confident, yet of whose identity he has not the slightest notion. Furthermore, this ceremony is incessantly repeated at daily or half-daily intervals throughout the calendar. What more vivid figure for the secular, historically-clocked, imagined community can be envisioned? At the same time, the newspaper reader, observing exact replicas of his own paper being consumed by his subway, barbershop, or residential neighbours, is continually reassured that the imagined world is visibly rooted in everyday life.[7]

It is not difficult to add to Anderson's nation-enabling media. Radio and television and many other aspects of everyday life operate in ways that allow us to imagine ourselves as part of a nation.

Regulatory fictions and regimes of truth

We should not, however, assume that our nationality is freely imagined. On the contrary, nationality is something similar to what influential feminist theorist Judith Butler calls a 'regulatory fiction'.[8] Nationality is a fundamental part of the networks of signification we call culture. Raymond Williams, one of the founding figures of British cultural studies, writing in 1961, defined culture as 'a particular way of life, which expresses certain meanings and values not only in art and learning but also in institutions and ordinary behaviour … the characteristic forms through which members of the society communicate'.[9] What I find particularly interesting about his definition is the connection he makes between culture and signification. Williams is later even more explicit about this connection, defining culture as 'a realised signifying system'.[10] While there is more to a nation than signifying systems, it is nevertheless the case that 'it would ... be wrong to suppose that we can ever usefully discuss a social system without including, as a central part of its practice, its signifying systems, on which, as a system, it fundamentally depends'.[11] Signification is fundamental to our sense of national belonging. To share a national culture is to interpret the world, to make it meaningful and to experience it as meaningful in recognisably similar ways. Signification materially organises national practice. So-called 'culture shock' happens when we encounter radically different national networks of meaning; that is, when the 'natural' or 'common sense' of our national community is confronted by the 'natural' or 'common sense' of another national community.

However, national cultures are never simply shifting networks of shared meanings; on the contrary, they are always both shared and contested networks of meanings. National cultures are where we share and contest meanings of ourselves, of each other and of the social worlds in which we live. This way of thinking about national cultures is best understood using Italian Marxist Antonio Gramsci's concept of hegemony. Gramsci uses hegemony to describe processes of power in which a dominant group does not merely rule by force but leads by 'consent'. Hegemony involves a specific kind of consensus, one in which a social group presents its own particular interests as the general interests of the national formation as a whole; it turns the particular into the general. It works by the transformation of potential antagonism into simple difference, working to subsume vertical relations of inequality into horizontal relations of national belonging. This is operative in part through the circulation of meanings that reinforce dominance and subordination by seeking to fix the meaning of social relations and national belonging. As Williams explains,

> It [hegemony] is a lived system of meanings and values – constitutive and constituting – which as they are experienced as practices appear as reciprocally confirming. It thus constitutes a sense of reality for most people ... It is ... in the strongest sense a 'culture' [understood as a realised signifying system], but a culture which has also to be seen as the lived dominance and subordination of particular classes.[12]

Hegemony involves the attempt to saturate the social with m~~~~ that support the prevailing structures of power. In a hege~ ation, subordinate groups appear to actively support and s values, ideals and objectives, which incorporate them into the prevailing structures of power. However, hegemony, as Williams observes, 'does not just passively exist as a form of dominance. It has continually to be renewed, recreated, defended, and modified. It is also continually resisted, limited, altered, challenged'.[13] Although hegemony is characterised by high levels of consensus, it is never without conflict; that is, there is always resistance. For hegemony to remain successful, conflict and resistance must always be channelled and contained – rearticulated in the interests of the dominant.

There are two conclusions we can draw from the concept of culture as a realised signifying system when thinking about national belonging. First, although the nation exists in all its enabling and constraining materiality outside culture, it is only in culture that the nation can be made to mean. In other words, signification has a performative effect: it helps construct the realities it appears only to describe. Marxist theorists Ernesto Laclau and Chantal Mouffe use the word 'discourse' in much the same way as I am using the term 'culture'. According to Laclau and Mouffe,

> If I kick a spherical object in the street or if I kick a ball in a football match, the physical fact is the same, but its meaning is different. The object is a football only to the extent that it establishes a system of relations with other objects, and these relations are not given by the mere referential materiality of the objects, but are, rather, socially constructed. This systematic set of relations is what we call discourse.[14]

I would call these systematic relations culture. However, both positions share the view that to stress the discursive or the cultural is not to deny the materiality of the real. The discursive or cultural character of something does not mean that it does not really exist. The fact that a tennis ball is only tennis as long as it is part of a system of culturally constructed rules does not mean that outside these rules it is not a physical object. In other words, objects exist independently of their discursive or cultural articulation, but it is only within discourse or culture that they can exist as meaningful objects in meaningful relations. For example, earthquakes exist in the real world, but whether they are

> constructed in terms of 'natural phenomena' or 'expressions of the wrath of God', depends upon the structuring of a discursive field. What is denied is not that such objects exist externally to thought,

but the rather different assertion that they could constitute themselves as objects outside any discursive condition of emergence.[15]

To argue that culture is best understood as a realised signifying system is not a denial that the material world exists in all its constraining
and enabling reality outside signification. The material world will continue to exist whether anyone signifies it or not. But the material world,
including the nation, exists for us – and only ever exists for us – articulated in signification. A national culture like Britishness therefore consists of a network of shared and contested meanings organised around
relations of power.

The second conclusion we can draw from seeing a national culture
as a realised signifying system concerns the potential for struggle over
meaning in a social formation. Given that different meanings can be
ascribed to the same 'sign' (that is, anything that can be made to signify),
meaning-making (i.e. the making of culture) is therefore always a potential site of struggle. The making of meaning is always entangled in what
Russian theorist Valentin Volosinov identifies as the 'multi-accentuality'
of the sign.[16] Rather than being inscribed with a single meaning, a sign
can be articulated with different 'accents'; that is, it can be made to mean
different things in different contexts, with different effects of power.
Therefore, the sign is always a potential site of a conflict of social interests
and is often in practice an arena of struggle and negotiation. Those with
power seek to make the sign appear uni-accentual. That is, they seek to
make what is potentially multi-accentual appear as if it could only ever
be uni-accentual. This is important because, as Stuart Hall, perhaps
the leading cultural studies academic, points out, 'Meanings [i.e. cul-
tures] ... regulate and organise our conduct and practices – they help
to set the rules, norms and conventions by which social life is ordered
and governed. They are ... therefore, what those who wish to govern and
regulate the conduct and ideas of others seek to structure and shape.'[17]
Meanings have a 'material' existence in that they help organise practice,
they establish norms of national behaviour. As Hall also makes clear,
'The signification of events is part of what has to be struggled over, for it
is the means by which collective social understandings are created – and
thus the means by which consent for particular outcomes can be effectively mobilized.'[18] Signification is, therefore, fundamental to a sense of
national belonging. There is not anything natural about nationality.
One is not born British, one becomes British. National identities consist

of the accumulation of what is outside (i.e. in culture) in the belief that it is an expression of what is inside (i.e. in nature). As a result, national subjects only become recognisable as national subjects through conformity with recognisable standards of intelligibility. As Judith Butler puts it, in a discussion of sexual identity that is also applicable to national identity, '"naturalness" [is] constituted through discursively constrained performative acts ... that create the effect of the natural, the original, and the inevitable.'[19] The performance of nationality creates the illusion of a prior substantiality – a core national self – and suggests that the performative ritual of nationness is merely an expression of an already existing nationality. However, our nationality is not the expression of the location in which we are born, it is performatively constructed in processes of repetition and citation, which gradually produce and reinforce our sense of national belonging.

Butler's concept of performativity should not be confused with the idea of performance understood as a form of playacting, in which a more fundamental identity remains intact beneath the theatricality of the identity on display. National performativity is not a voluntary practice, it is a continual process of almost disciplinary reiteration. National identity is created through repeated and sustained social performances and involves citations of previous performances of nationality.

> Performativity cannot be understood outside of a process of iterability, a regularized and constrained repetition of norms. And this repetition is not performed by a subject; this repetition is what enables a subject and constitutes the temporal condition for the subject. This iterability implies that 'performance' is not a singular 'act' or event, but a ritualized production, a ritual reiterated under and through constraint, under and through the force of prohibition and taboo, with the threat of ostracism and even death controlling and compelling the shape of the production, but not ... determining it fully in advance.[20]

Our national identities depend upon the successful performance of our nationalities, and there is therefore a whole array of rituals, symbols and institutions that work to ensure that our sense of national belonging is mostly unconscious and successful. But whether unconscious or not, the array establishes what French post-structuralist Michel Foucault calls a regime of truth. As he explains, 'Each society has its own regime of truth, its "general polities" of truth – that is, the types of discourse it accepts and makes function as true.'[21]

National identities are made from a complex mix of rituals, symbols and stories. Every country has its dominant or official narratives of its distinctive nationhood. It is these narratives that seek to draw us into place as members of a particular national community. Institutions, rituals, ceremonies, symbols and other means of signification tell these dominant or official stories. We encounter them on coins, stamps, flags, anthems, festivals, parades, passports, war memorials, folk songs, museums, national heroes and heroines. British examples might include Trooping the Colour, Changing the Guard, the Grand National, the FA Cup Final, certain rivers and mountains, particular monuments, the Union Jack, the BBC, the Houses of Parliament, fish and chips, the Highland Games, the Notting Hill Carnival, the Edinburgh Festival, the Eisteddfod, drinking warm beer. These are just some of the many rituals and symbols that seem to articulate Britishness. Similarly, the stories a nation tells about itself are a fundamental aspect of its official identity. Britain has many such stories: the home of fair play, the stiff upper lip in times of danger, the Battle of Britain, the Blitz, doing the decent thing, an island people, the imperial nation, the birthplace of parliamentary democracy and constitutional monarchy, the first industrial nation, the cradle of scientific and technological innovation, the sporting pioneer (inventing badminton, cricket, football, golf, hockey, rugby, snooker and tennis), the birthplace of the English language and island of poets and playwrights. It is these shared meanings, embedded forms of signification, that construct and maintain a sense of Britishness. These are the stories we are told in various ways and at various times about 'our' history, 'our' customs, 'our' habits, 'our' values, etc. These stories, and many more like them, help construct a sense of what Britishness is for both people in Britain and for those looking at Britain from abroad. These are by no means the only stories the nation tells itself and others, but it is always in response to stories like these that other stories, perhaps oppositional narratives, have to negotiate and struggle. We may not simply accept these stories, but they do have the power of a certain common sense; they set the agenda in terms of what it is to be British.

The official stories of British identity are told by a number of institutions, the Foreign and Commonwealth Office, the British Tourist Authority, the British Council, the BBC. Each in its different way articulates a powerful sense of Britishness. National identity is not based on the critical detail of these stories but on their generalised performance and reiteration. National stories of identity are always selective and simplified, presenting generalisations that we are invited to accept without looking too deeply into their potential complexities and contradictions. When Blair told the Labour Party Conference that the British Empire is something of which we can all be proud, he was not expecting a detailed and critical engagement with this claim or with the empire but rather a general acceptance that the ability to construct such an empire is something to admire. In similar ways, Dunkirk, the Battle of Britain, the Blitz, the Somme, Trafalgar and Waterloo are rolled out as significant national moments in British history without any expectation that these national moments need be examined in any critical detail. The whole purpose of these stories is to bind people together, to encourage the situating of their individuality within the collectivity that is Britishness. It does not even matter if the stories are untrue. One common theme of these stories, as we have already noted, is the timelessness of Britishness. It is something that has always existed: we are an island people especially chosen by God to do wonderful things in the world. Even when the stories do not extend our greatness to the beginnings of time, they always seem to want to insist on at least a millennium of wondrous contributions to humanity. Tony Blair's speech (10 May 2007) to confirm his forthcoming resignation as Prime Minister is a wonderful example of this kind of rhetoric: 'This country is a blessed nation. The British are special, the world knows it, in our innermost thoughts, we know it. This is the greatest nation on earth.'

Our sense of national belonging may be drawn to our attention by the more spectacular national events, but it is in the mundane routines of everyday life, seemingly so natural and so rooted, that our sense of national belonging seems most grounded. Much of the repertoire of national belonging consists of the taken-for-granted, routine practices of everyday life. Although the state clearly limits and encourages patterns of national life, particularly evident in educational and media policy, much of our sense of national belonging takes place outside the official displays of nationalism. Michael Billig writes of what he calls 'banal nationalism', referring to the many ways in which our sense of national belonging is reproduced by the endless reiteration of 'we' and 'us' and 'our' in the discourses of everyday media.[22] It is a daily process of 'naturalisation' in which the socially constructed is made to seem natural. The naturalness of national belonging, however, can suddenly be exposed as culturally constructed by the arrival in our lives of people who bring to Britain a different sense of what is natural and obvious.

This is perhaps one of the reasons immigration often produces such heated and irrational debate.

Beyond fantasies of monoculture

In the new global economy, Britain has moved from the centre to the periphery. British identity has even become less important to the British population itself, with only about 50 per cent regarding it as an important part of their identity. Devolution, globalisation, new forms of cultural diversity resulting from recent patterns of immigration, the end of empire, closer integration with mainland Europe: all of these factors draw attention to complexity and change as key factors in understanding contemporary Britishness. However, such factors are not new to Britain. It has always been a hybrid nation, always mixing together different cultures and ethnicities. Like any nation, complexity and change are fundamental to its existence. Britishness has always been far less unified than it is imagined. It has always been a diverse and pluralistic culture of cultures, characterised by differences of many varieties, including those based on ethnicity, region, religion, social class, gender and generation.

Britain is a vibrant society with a rich ethnic diversity. We should not really speak of British culture at all but of British cultures. Multiculturalism is, therefore, a deeply misleading term in that it depends on a notion of cultural absolutism, which supposedly exists before the many varied aspects of the 'multi' are brought into contact. But this is not how cultures work. Cultures are always already multicultures in that they always consist of difference and sameness. It is only ever culture in the singular in discourses of power or in naive discourses of resistance. Moreover, what should be regarded as something positive, something to celebrate, is too often presented as a negative, something to constrain and control. Overt and organised racism is only one aspect of this negativity. It is nevertheless an irrational and damaging aspect, one that brings despair and destruction to the lives of many British people.

Britain still lives in the shadow of empire and its loss. Its legacy is everywhere, from patterns of migration from peoples of the former colonies to the honours system, in which it is still possible to be awarded the Order of the British Empire and the Medal of the British Empire. The most disfiguring and damaging legacy of empire is racism and xenophobia which often claim a natural relationship between Britishness and whiteness or Britishness as essentially Anglo-Saxon. The imperial narrative of Britain's greatness has often worked to make the relationship between nationality and colour appear absolutely natural. This assumed relationship makes no sense in contemporary Britain, but it also makes no sense in terms of the geographical space that Britain now occupies. In historical terms, for example, black people were here long before the English, who were preceded by various Celtic tribes and by the Romans, who brought with them people from Africa, the Middle East and Asia.

Against the disfiguring threat of racism and xenophobia and the ridiculous fantasies of racial purity, cultural-studies academic Paul Gilroy invites us all to embrace 'the simple ideals' of recognising that we are all fundamentally similar: 'human beings are ordinarily far more alike than they are unalike.'[23]

> We need to know what sorts of insight and reflection might actually help increasingly differentiated societies and anxious individuals to cope successfully with the challenges involved in dwelling comfortably in proximity to the unfamiliar without becoming fearful and hostile. We need to consider whether the scale upon which sameness and difference are calculated might be altered productively so that the strangeness of strangers goes out of focus and other dimensions of a basic sameness can be acknowledged and made significant.[24]

This would produce a Britain, a great Britain, that had truly managed to move out of the debilitating shadow of empire.

Notes

1   L. Colley, *Britons: Forging the Nation, 1707–1837* (New Haven, Conn.: Yale University Press, 1992), p. 5.
2   M. Leonard, *Britain ™: Renewing Our Identity* (London: Demos, 1997), p. 43.
3   H. Gaitskill, (1962) "Classic Podium: The End of 1000 Years of History', available online at www.independent.co.uk/arts-entertainment/classic-podium-the-end-of-1000-years-of-history-1190761.html (accessed 26 February 2010).
4   Quoted in Leonard, *Britain ™*, p. 39.
5   B. Anderson, *Imagined Communities* (London: Verso, 1991).
6   Anderson, *Imagined Communities*, p. 15.
7   Anderson, *Imagined Communities*, pp. 39–40.
8   J. Butler, *Gender Trouble: Feminism and the Subversion of Identity* (London and New York: Routledge, 1999), p. 180.
9   R. Williams, 'The Analysis of Culture', in J. Storey (ed.), *Cultural Theory and Popular Culture: A Reader* (Harlow: Pearson Education, 2006), pp. 32–40; p. 32.
10   R. Williams, *Culture* (London: Fontana, 1981), p. 207.

11 Williams, *Culture*, p. 207.

12 Williams, *Culture*, pp. 207, 108.

13 R. Williams, *Marxism and Literature* (Oxford: Oxford University Press, 1977), p. 112.

14 E. Laclau and C. Mouffe, *Hegemony and Socialist Strategy*, 2nd edn (London: Verso, 2001).

15 Laclau and Mouffe, *Hegemony*, p. 108.

16 V. N. Volosinov, *Marxism and the Philosophy of Language* (New York: Seminar Press, 1973).

17 S. Hall, 'Introduction', in S. Hall (ed.), *Representation* (London: Sage, 1997), p. 4.

18 S. Hall, 'The Rediscovery of Ideology: the Return of the Repressed in Media Studies', in J. Storey (ed.), *Cultural Theory and Popular Culture: A Reader* (Harlow: Pearson Education, 2006), p. 137.

19 Butler, *Gender Trouble*, pp. xxvii–xxix.

20 J. Butler, *Bodies That Matter: On the Discursive Limits of 'Sex'* (London and New York: Routledge, 1993), p. 95.

21 M. Foucault, 'Truth and Power', in J. D. Faubion (ed.), *Michel Foucault Essential Works: Power* (Harmondsworth: Penguin, 2002), p. 131.

22 M. Billig, *Banal Nationalism* (London: Sage, 1995).

23 P. Gilroy, *After Empire: Melancholia or Convivial Culture?* (London and New York: Routledge, 2004), p. 4.

24 Gilroy, *After Empire*, p. 3.

2
_____

Language developments in British English

Introduction

Languages do not change at a steady pace. They reflect the developments that take place in the culture of which they form a part. Some events in English history had immediate and dramatic linguistic consequences, such as the huge influence of French on English vocabulary and spelling after the Norman Conquest, or the even greater influx of loan words from European languages during the Renaissance, which virtually doubled the size of the English word stock. At other times, the pace of linguistic change was relatively slow, such as during the eighteenth century, where the desire for order and stability was reflected in the publication of the first major dictionaries, grammars and pronunciation manuals of the language. Today, we are experiencing a new period of rapid and widespread language change, but not for any one particular reason; rather, a range of social, economic and technological factors have combined to make the decades on either side of the millennium linguistically quite extraordinary.

Pronunciation

Of all aspects of spoken language, pronunciation is the most noticeable. Individual words and grammatical constructions are occasional in nature, whereas pronunciation is pervasive. We can say nothing without pronouncing it. As a result, we are particularly alert to changes that affect the way people articulate their vowels, consonants and syllables, or that alter the way they use stress, intonation, rhythm and tone of voice. In a word, we are sensitive to changes in *accent*.

The primary purpose of an accent is to identify where someone is from, geographically or socially. It is a badge of belonging – and its strength lies in the fact that it can be used in circumstances where other markers of identity fail. Badges are useless if the wearer is around the corner or in the dark. Accents transcend such limitations. There is also a naturalness about them that facilitates their function. People have to buy and display their badges and flags of identity. With accents, they only have to open their mouths.

Sensitivity about accents is everywhere, in all languages, but the situation in Britain has always attracted special interest. This is chiefly because there is more regional accent variation in Britain, relative to the size and population of the country, than in any other part of the English-speaking world – a natural result of 1,500 years of accent diversification in an environment which was both highly socially stratified and (through the Celtic languages) indigenously multilingual. George Bernard Shaw was exaggerating when he had phonetician Henry Higgins say (in *Pygmalion*) that he could 'place a man within six miles. I can place him within two miles in London. Sometimes within two streets' – but only a little.

Two major changes have affected English accents in Britain over the past few decades. The attitude of people towards accents has altered in ways that were unpredictable thirty years ago; and some accents have changed their phonetic character very significantly over the same period.

The main change in attitude has affected the prestige accent in England, known as 'Received Pronunciation' (RP). This is an accent that emerged at the beginning of the nineteenth century, associated with the way upper-class and well-educated people spoke, especially in the 'golden triangle' of London, Oxford and Cambridge. It came to be the norm in the English public schools, and when the products of those schools left the country to run the British Empire, they took the accent with them, thus making RP the 'official' voice of Britain around the world. When the BBC was formed in the 1920s, Lord Reith opted for this accent as the one most likely to be nationally understood, and during the twentieth century RP became the uncontested prestige accent of Britain. For many it was the public auditory image of the country, still valued today for its associations with the Second World War years, with the royal family and with leading classical actors such as Laurence Olivier. In 1980, when the BBC made its first attempt to use a regionally accented announcer on Radio 4, the decision aroused such virulent opposition that it was quickly reversed. Susan Rae, the Scots presenter in question, was withdrawn.

Twenty-five years on, and Susan Rae's voice was once again being heard on Radio 4. And in August 2005 the BBC devoted a whole week to a celebration of the accents and dialects of the British Isles. (*Accent* refers to pronunciation only; *dialect* to grammar and vocabulary as well.) The 'Voices' project, as it was called, was an attempt to take an auditory snapshot of the way Britain was sounding at the beginning of the new millennium. Every BBC regional radio station was invited to take part, and local presenters arranged recordings of the diversity within their area, as well as programmes that explored the history and nature of local accents and dialects. The impact of the project was considerable and can still be followed (through the website at www.bbc.co.uk/voices). It was institutional recognition of a fundamental change in attitudes to regional speech which had taken place in Britain. There is now a much greater readiness to value and celebrate linguistic diversity than there was a generation ago.

As far as broadcasting was concerned, it was the rapid growth of local commercial radio during the 1980s that fostered the new linguistic climate. Regional radio gained audience (and national radio lost it) by meeting the interests of local populations, and these new audiences liked their presenters to speak as they did. At the same time, national listening and viewing figures remained strong for such series as BBC Radio 4's *The Archers* and ITV's *Coronation Street*, where local accents were privileged. The trend grew in the 1990s and developed an international dimension: alongside the London accents of the BBC soap opera *EastEnders* were the Australian accents of *Neighbours*. Soon, non-RP accents began to be used as part of the 'official' voice of national radio and television, most noticeably at first in more popular contexts, such as on Radio 1 and in commercial television advertisements. Some regional accents from the time even became part of national consciousness, widely mimicked in the manner of catch phrases – such as a 1977 Campari ad in which Lorraine Chase responded to the come-on line 'Were you truly wafted here from paradise?' with the immortal response, 'No, Lu'on airport.' Before long, regional voices began to be heard presenting other channels and are now routine, illustrated by the Scottish accents of several weather forecasters on BBC television or the South Welsh accent of Huw Edwards reading the BBC News. Non-indigenous accents, especially from the West Indies and India, began to be heard. Old attitudes die hard, of course, and there will still be those who mourn the passing of the days when a single accent ruled the British airwaves. But they are a steadily shrinking minority.

RP continues to have a strong presence in public broadcasting, but its phonetic character has changed. Accents never stand still, and indeed radio is the chief medium where accent change can be traced. Anyone listening to radio programmes made in the 1920s and 1930s cannot fail to be struck by the 'plummy' or 'far back' sound of the RP accent then – when, for example, 'lord' sounded more like 'lahd' – but even the accents of the 1960s and 1970s sound dated now. And changes continue to affect RP. It is difficult to illustrate them without the help of phonetic transcription, but I can perhaps rely on our auditory memory to ask readers to compare the voice of the Queen, as classically heard in a speech for the opening of parliament or a Christmas message, with the voices of Prince Harry or Prince William, two generations on. There are many differences. The Queen would never, for example, replace the final consonant in such words as 'hot' with a glottal stop; the youngsters often do. Nor would she use the central vowel quality heard in 'the' in such words as 'cup'; her version is articulated much further forward in the mouth, more in the direction of 'cap'.

The BBC, or any other national broadcaster, does not introduce language change. Rather, it reflects it, and thereby fosters it by making it widely known. This has been the case with 'Estuary English', a variety which became noticed when it attracted media attention in the early 1990s, though the phenomenon had been evolving over many years. The estuary in question was that of the river Thames, and the people who were noticed as having an estuary accent lived on either side of it, chiefly to the north. The variety is characterised not only by accent but also by certain words and grammatical constructions, such as the use of 'right' as a tag question (*It starts at six, right?*) or 'innit' ('*isn't it?*'). Phonetically it can be roughly placed as an accent intermediate between RP and Cockney. Nationally known figures who use it include Jonathan Ross, and it is used by the two characters played by Pauline Quirke and Linda Robson in the BBC television comedy series of the 1990s, *Birds of a Feather*, as well as by some of the characters in *EastEnders*. The accents are not identical, and that is important. Estuary is a broad label, covering a number of closely related ways of speaking. (RP was never homogeneous either.)

One of the most noticeable pronunciation trends of the past twenty years has been to hear the way in which features of Estuary English have radiated from the London area to other parts of the country. They have travelled north towards Yorkshire and west towards Devon, and they are widespread in East Anglia, Kent and along the south coast. It is not that they have replaced the local accents of these areas (though this sometimes happens); rather, they have modified the phonetic character of those accents, pulling the vowels and consonants in different directions. Old-timers in a rural village now sound very different from the younger generations who live there. As part of the 'Voices' project, a television documentary was made (called *Word on the Street*) about four generations of a family living in Leicester. One could hear the changes from old to young: an East Midlands accent was present in all of them, but in several different forms.

It is this proliferation of accents which is the national pattern today. People sometimes claim that 'accents are dying out'. What they have noticed is the disappearance of old rural ways of speech as the people who used them pass away. But the people who now live in these localities still have accents, albeit very different in character. The Estuary English heard in Hampshire is very different from that heard in Leicestershire. Nor is Estuary English the only contemporary pronunciation trend. In the major population centres of the country we hear a new phenomenon: a remarkable increase in the range of accents within the community, brought about largely by the influx of people of diverse ethnic origin. In Liverpool, there used to be only 'Scouse'; today we can hear Chinese Scouse, Jamaican Scouse and an array of accent mixes reflecting the growing cosmopolitan character of that city. London, of course, is where this trend is most noticeable. There are well over 300 languages spoken in London now, and the English used by these ethnic communities inevitably reflects the linguistic background of the speakers. New combinations of sounds, words and grammatical constructions can be heard, such as the mix of Bengali and Cockney used by members of the Bangladeshi community in East London. Every British city today displays such accent and dialect mixes.

To understand why Estuary English has spread so widely and so rapidly we have to appreciate that it is the result of two complementary trends. First, an improved standard of living for many people formerly living in London's East End allowed them to move 'up-market' into the outer suburbs and the townships of the home counties of England's south-east. As they began to interact with their new neighbours, their accents naturally accommodated to them. 'Accommodation' is the term sociolinguists use when talking about the way in which accents influence each other. People from different accent backgrounds who are in good rapport will find features of their accents rubbing off on each other. In a case where people want to 'fit in' to a society that speaks in a different way, and where careers and success can depend on the incomers developing a good relationship with the incumbents, the direction of the accommodation is largely one-way. Thus, Eastenders began to adopt features of Essex or Kent or Hertfordshire speech, when they moved into those localities, rather than the other way round. At the same time, people from counties further afield were commuting to London in increasing numbers, their travel facilitated by the new motorway system and faster rail connections. With cities such as Hull, Leeds, Manchester and Bristol now only a couple of hours away, huge numbers of people arrived in London with regional accents and soon found themselves accommodating to the accents of the city. It was now the Midlands and West Country commuters who adopted some of the London ways of speaking. And when these commuters returned home, they brought those London features back with them. And thus the accent spread.

Cutting across the Estuary English influence is an unknown set of other trends, all prompted by the increased mobility of the working and playing population. The BBC programme about Leicester showed some members of the family attending a biking convention elsewhere in the country. Bikers were there from many counties and presented a huge range of accents. When they talked to each other it was possible to hear their accents accommodating – often in a conscious and jocular way, as when one speaker mimicked another. An individual short-term encounter of this kind is unlikely to have a long-term effect, of course, but in contexts where people routinely interact in this way, accent change is normal. And commuters, by definition, have routine.

It is not that one accent replaces another. Rather, features of two accents combine to make a third. When an RP speaker is influenced by a regional accent, or vice versa, the result has been called 'modified RP', and there is modified Scouse, modified Geordie (the accent associated with the city of Newcastle), modified everything these days. I myself am a heavily modified speaker, using an accent which is a mixture of my original North Welsh (where I now live), Liverpool (where I spent my secondary-school years), and the south of England (where I worked for twenty years). Apart from the overall auditory impression of my accent, which is difficult to 'place', it displays certain features characteristic of all modified accents, such as inconsistency – for instance, I sometimes say *example* and *bath* with a 'short *a*', and sometimes with a 'long *a*' (*exahmple, bahth*). And because I accommodate to my (now grown-up) children, who have been influenced by a more recent set of trends (such as American English), I sometimes say *schedule* with a *sh*- and sometimes with a *sk*-. There are hundreds of such variant forms in my speech.

As regional speech achieved a greater public presence – both privately, through increased social mobility, and publicly, through the new broadcasting scenario – attitudes towards individual accents began to change. Sociolinguistic research since the 1980s has identified two major trends: an increase in positive attitudes towards certain regional accents and an increase in negative attitudes towards RP. The methodology is to use reaction studies. People are invited to give their opinion of an accent using a wide range of questions, such as whether it sounds 'educated', 'sincere', 'honest', 'friendly', 'warm', 'intelligent' and so on. Traditionally, RP has been the accent that attracted all the positive values; regional speech would typically attract negative ones, with urban accents in particular being poorly rated.

The turnaround has been quite dramatic. Several regional accents now achieve strongly positive ratings such as 'warm' and 'customer-friendly'; whereas RP has begun to attract negative ratings such as 'insincere' and 'distant'. And organisations that rely for their income on voice presentation have noticed the change. Call centres in Britain, until recently, provided a convenient index of change. Formerly, the voice answering the phone at a national enquiry centre would have been RP, with local accents heard only in regional offices (and not always then). During the 1990s, there was a noticeable increase in the use of local accents at national level. The voice you would hear in enquiring about car insurance or a mortgage would very likely be Edinburgh Scots or Yorkshire (the two most preferred accents). Not all regional speech was favoured: in particular, some urban English accents, such as Birmingham's, still generated negative reactions.

The qualification 'until recently' should be noted. One of the trends in the 2000s has been the outsourcing of call centres to India, so that the voice we now hear at the other end of a phone is likely to display one of the range of educated Indian accents, some of which are not very different from RP, but with a more staccato ('syllable-timed') rhythm. The accents have been controversially received, with some listeners finding them difficult to understand, some finding them unpleasant, some finding them quite attractive and some not noticing anything at all. It remains to be seen whether the reactions to these accents will diminish as people become more familiar with them.

Increasing familiarity there has to be, because the call-centre phenomenon is but a tiny part of a global trend towards the internationalisation of English which has been in progress since the mid twentieth century. It is now a truism to talk of English as a 'global language'; but a less noticed consequence of this spread has been the growth of 'new Englishes' around the world, in countries which have adopted English as a local lingua franca and have adapted it to express their identity. Alongside British English and American English, we now find Nigerian English, Singaporean English ('Singlish'), Jamaican English and dozens of other varieties, distinguished primarily by vocabulary and pronunciation. Each country is developing its own norms, but one trend is widely heard: the development of syllable-timed speech, as opposed to the 'stress-timed' speech characteristic of traditional British accents. Stress-timed speech takes place when the rhythmical beats fall at roughly regular intervals in the stream of speech, resulting in a 'tum-te-tum' rhythm widely heard in English poetry ('The *curfew tolls the knell of parting day*'). By contrast, in syllable-timed speech, each syllable carries a beat, so that the result is more like a 'rat-a-tat-a-tat'. The voices of the Daleks in *Dr Who* ('ex-ter-mi-nate') were syllable-timed, as is a great deal of contemporary rapping. And as one listens to the speech of people from Jamaica or South Africa or the subcontinent of India – whether in their original country or in a British city suburb – we hear a kind of accent characterised by these new rhythms. There hasn't been anything like it in a thousand years of English pronunciation history.

Vocabulary

The second main index of language change is vocabulary – the loss of old words and senses and the arrival of new ones. It is difficult to arrive at any accurate contemporary quantification. Whether a period of a language has been a particularly significant one for lexical change only becomes apparent after it has happened. The reason is that we never know which of the new words we hear around us are going to be permanent features of English and which are transient – the slang and fashionable usage of the moment. Studies of the new words and phrases which were being used in English during the 1970s suggest that as many as 75 per cent of them ceased to be used after quite a short period of time.

Collections of 'new words' made by various publishers and dictionary-providers, based on words which have been seen in print, indicate that hundreds of new expressions appear each year. For example, the Oxford University Press publication, *Twentieth Century Words*, contains a selection of about 5,000 items such as:

- from the 1990s: applet, Blairism, Britpop, cool Britannia, Dianamania, docusoap;
- from the 1980s: AIDS, backslash, bog-standard, BSE, cellphone, designer drug;
- from the 1970s: action replay, Betamax, biotechnology, cashpoint, club class, detox.

The average is 500 items a decade – roughly one a week – and this is only a *selection* from everyday written language. *The Longman Guardian New Words* collected those words which had come to prominence in written English in 1986: it contained around 1,000. No one has yet devised a technique for capturing the neologisms that enter the spoken language and which are rarely (sometimes never) written down.

That there should be so many new words entering the language should come as no surprise when we consider the many walks of life that motivate them, such as the arts, business, computing, the environment, leisure, medicine, politics, popular culture, sports, science and technology. The range can be illustrated by this set of headwords, taken from letter F of *The Oxford Dictionary of New Words*, a selection of some 2,000 items in 1997 said to be 'in the news':

face, in your	feel-good
fajitas	feminazi
false memory syndrome	fen (plural of fan)
fantasy football	feng shui
FAQ	file transfer protocol
fattism	film-on-demand
fatwa	First Nations
fax-on-demand	flame (= abuse)
feeding frenzy	flatline
feel-bad	flesh-eating disease

FLOPS (in computing)
Floptical
fluoxetine
flying bishop
FOB (Friend of Bill,
        i.e. Clinton)
foodie
footballene
for-profit
Fourex, Four-X
foxcore
fox-watch
freeride
Friday Wear
from hell (as in 'neighbours
        from hell')
frozen embryo
FTP
fuck-me (as adjective)
full-blown AIDS
fullerene
full monty, the
full pindown
full-video-on-demand
fully abled
functional food
fundholder
fundie (= fundamentalist)

Two points should be noted. First, over half the expressions contain more than one word, and this is typical of the collection as a whole: when we talk about 'new words' entering the language, we mean multi-word expressions as well as single words. Second, several of these items represent a whole 'family' of derived forms. 'Flame', for example, referring to online abuse, gave rise to 'flamer', 'flamage', 'flaming', 'flame war', 'flame bait', 'flame mail', 'flame on' and 'flame off'.

Plainly, the array of new words reflects the trends, inventions and attitudes seen in contemporary society. But this raises an interesting question: how do we define 'contemporary society' from the viewpoint of language change? During the 1980s, it is safe to say that virtually all the new vocabulary people heard in Britain – whether generated within Britain or introduced from elsewhere (e.g., the USA) – would have come from British sources – newspapers, magazines, radio, television or the local worlds of occupational idiom and street slang. But since the arrival of the Internet in its various manifestations (such as email, chat rooms, the World Wide Web and blogs), it is now possible for anyone (who has the electronic means) to directly encounter English in its worldwide lexical variety. A decade ago, it would have been extremely difficult for me to have explored the extensive regional vocabulary of, say, South Africa, without actually going to the place. Now, at the click of a mouse, I can call up the *Cape Times* and find myself reading (in November 2006) such opaque headlines as the following:

- Floors to Lead Bok Sevens in Dubai. (Kabamba Floors is to be the captain of the Springbok Sevens – a seven-a-side rugby team.)

- No Fynbos Hater. (Fynbos is a South African evergreen shrub.)
- Redefining ANC Needs Debate, Not Toyi-Toying. (A toyi-toyi is a militant dance.)

The cumulative impact of global English vocabulary – in the broadest sense, to include the distinctive names of people and places in foreign localities – is already very noticeable on the Internet and must eventually make an impact on our British linguistic consciousness. First of all, our comprehension of the foreign vocabulary will grow, and in due course some items will enter our spoken or written production. It is not, after all, an entirely passive situation. The millions of (predominantly younger) Britons who now routinely enter chat rooms, write or respond to blogs, play virtual-reality games and actively participate in community domains such as MySpace are encountering an unprecedented range of varieties of English. In the one chat room there may be participants from South Africa, Hong Kong or any other part of the English-speaking world. Different dialects of English become neighbours on the same screen, as do different levels of competence in the use of English. As a result, accommodation will be widespread – and operate in any direction. British people may be influenced by South African English – and of course vice versa. Nor are educated regional standards always going to be respected. An incorrect use of a word by a participant is not necessarily going to be corrected by other chat-room members. Rather, it might be adopted as a 'cool' usage – as happened in one group when 'comptuer' was mistyped for the word 'computer' and everyone thereafter chose to use it. In the short term, none of these accommodations is likely to be very influential; but in the long term some usages are bound to become current.

The Internet

And the long term is becoming shorter. Lexicographers used to say that a new word might take anything up to a generation before it became a permanent part of a language. That is how long it could take for people to start hearing it, then using it, and then routinely putting it down on paper. Today, a new usage can be around the world in seconds, in written (online) form, and a search for it a few days later can yield thousands of results. The Internet is without any doubt the largest corpus of English vocabulary there has ever been and presents us in our homes with more variant forms of the language than has ever been seen before.

The impact of all this variation on the character of the language as a whole is as yet unclear. But the pressures we all feel when we encounter someone else's use of language which is different from our own are bound to increase.

It is not only vocabulary which is being affected. Spelling is affected too. Thanks to 800 years of diverse linguistic influences on English, the current spelling system contains a great deal of irregularity, and there have often been proposals for spelling reform. Apart from Noah Webster's shaping of American spelling in the early 1800s, none of them have ever succeeded – and it is easy to see why. Even if one could agree on an optimal new system – something that the different groups of spelling reformers have never managed to achieve – any such system, imposed from above by a committee or government, presents huge problems of practical implementation. But the Internet suggests that a 'top-down' simplification of spelling is not the only way. It could easily be that some of the more extreme irregular forms might gradually simplify as a result of repeated public encounter online – a 'bottom-up' movement, in which people vote for change with their fingers.

This could never have happened in recent centuries. Any incorrect spelling in a text presented for print would have been eliminated by the copy-editors and proof-readers employed by publishers. Only the occasional error would ever have slipped through their eagle eyes. But on the Internet, in such contexts as blogging and chat, there are no copy-editors or proof-readers, and people can spell however they want. Naturally, there is a system of checks and balances: if people spell too idiosyncratically, no one will understand them. But no one misunderstands if a word such as 'rhubarb' is spelled 'rubarb' (over 50,000 hits on Google in June 2007) or 'diarrhoea' is spelled 'diarrea' (over 2.5 million hits). The pressure to maintain correct spelling is so great, through the educational and publishing systems, that it will take a much greater force to change public perceptions of what counts as correct. The Internet may be that force.

Grammar and punctuation, the two other great shibboleths of English usage, are also implicated. Neither readily change. The number of grammatical changes which have taken place in English since Shakespeare's time is small indeed. When we read Jane Austen, writing around 1800, there are only a tiny number of places where her grammar feels different from ours. And we see the same minuscule process of change today. Despite all the linguistic variation that we see around the world in the use of English, only a tiny number of usages affect grammar. Examples include the use of the tag question 'or not' in Singapore ('They're coming, or not?') or the use of the present continuous in India ('I am remembering what you were saying') or the use of 'gotten' in American English. The same point applies to punctuation and capitalisation. The rules governing present-day practice in these areas were finally established in the nineteenth century and have been assiduously (though not always successfully) taught ever since. They change very little. One recent trend is the tendency to simplification, introduced by graphic designers in the second half of the twentieth century, so that full stops are dropped after abbreviations ('BBC' and 'Mr' instead of 'B.B.C'. and 'Mr.') and apostrophes dropped in such cases as '1960s'. A similar trend has affected the use of capitals in names, as seen in lower-case initialisms (such as 'vodafone') and midcap or bicap usages (such as 'eBay' and 'AltaVista'). But most of the orthographic conventions we use in Britain today are exactly the same as they were a century ago.

The exception is the Internet – not in the Web, where most English-language sites reflect conventional standard usage, but in the linguistically unmoderated domains, such as emails, chat rooms, instant messaging and blogs. Here some radically different practices are common, in extreme cases including the omission of all capital letters and the dropping of all but a few punctuation marks. To see why this could happen, we have to appreciate that several of the rules of punctuation and capitalisation are totally arbitrary – that is, they have no effect on meaning. The rule which says that the personal pronoun 'I' should always be a capital letter, for example, was introduced early on in English linguistic history, and everyone has learned to live with it – but if we were to use a lower-case 'i' instead, as people now often do in informal internet communication, no problem of meaning results. What is fascinating is to see the way people are discovering and exploiting the flexibility of English orthography in this way. How much punctuation can be dispensed with and still retain intelligibility? Once upon a time (in Old English), there was no punctuation, apart from a few marks to guide the inflection of the speaking voice. The Internet is renewing our connection with those early manuscripts and may eventually give us a clue as to how much punctuation is actually critical for the communication of meaning.

The same point applies to grammar. Not only does the Internet expose us to regional grammatical variation on a global scale, it is also exposing us to a wider range of stylistic variation than we have experienced in print before. The kind of language we would traditionally see in print would be typically formal. Informal English would be restricted to certain contexts, such as conversation in a novel or a play. And there are several grammatical features that identify formality in standard English, such as not ending a sentence with a preposition: 'That is the man I was talking to' is much more informal than 'That is the man to whom I was talking', and the latter would be the recommended form in traditional grammars, along with a couple of dozen other prescriptive rules, such as 'never split an infinitive', or 'never begin a sentence with *and*'. What the Internet has done is allow us to put up on a screen, in the same type of printed graphic presentation as we see in any piece of formal language, the whole spectrum of informal English, ranging from slightly to radically informal. It is now possible to see blogs in which utterances run on with little or no punctuation, in much the same way as James Joyce ends *Ulysses*, and displaying all the colloquialism and dynamic changes of direction that we would previously only have encountered in informal conversation and never seen in print. A fresh kind of abbreviated language ('texting') has emerged in response to the limited character displays of mobile-phone screens. As a result, the expressive stylistic range of the written language has been enormously increased by computer-mediated communication. And it has all happened so quickly (within a decade, for most people) that there is a great deal of uncertainty as to how best to manage the changes, especially in schools, to ensure that children appreciate the importance of acquiring the well-established conventions of standard English, in order to ensure mutual intelligibility between generations and across regions (both national and international).

A balanced perspective

The Internet has been a major factor in bringing language change to the attention of the general public, but it is by no means the only factor. The broadcasting media have played their part – and so too has literature. Indeed, long before the Internet achieved its impact, we were aware of emerging global varieties of English through the work of the poets, novelists and dramatists who wrote in their local dialects – writers such as Benjamin Zephaniah (Caribbean), Chinua Achebe (West Africa) and Kamala Das (India). Today, we continue to experience non-indigenous varieties of English in British writing as a new generation experiments with non-standard styles of expression. Novels such as Jonathan Safran Foer's *Everything is Illuminated* or Suhayl Saadi's *Psychoraag* illustrate fresh voices that rely for their effect on a blend of standard and non-standard usage, both within and across languages.

These books illustrate the increasingly multi-dialectal character of contemporary writing. Earlier novels such as Irvine Welsh's *Trainspotting* or Roddy Doyle's *Paddy Clarke Ha Ha Ha* tap into rich veins of indigenous Celtic expression – Scots and Irish respectively. But the notion of 'indigenous' is itself no longer clear-cut. Saadi's novel, for example, is written in a mixture of standard English, Glaswegian and Urdu. There is frequent code-mixing: 'Sheila C's music seems tae slip like silence fae wan silver disc tae another. *Khamoshi, khamoshi, khamoshi.* Ah've nivir been thur but Ah wish Ah hud.'[1] He himself was born in Yorkshire; and Glasgow has many British-born Asians, several born in Scotland. Plainly, the traditional divisions between Germanic and Celtic, native and foreign, and first language and second language are blurred when we consider the language and languages used today in multi-ethnic Britain. And we must not forget the scale of what is happening. London is now one of the most multilingual cities in the world.

The published literature is but the tip of an iceberg of ethnic expression which is increasingly being given a public presence on the Internet. The proliferation of accents which we have seen to be a feature of contemporary Britain has its counterpart in a proliferation of dialects, many of which are now being written down – often for the first time. In the absence of a literary tradition, there is a great deal of uncertainty about how exactly to write them down. Different spelling conventions are used by different authors, and there is often inconsistency within the same author. What Saadi writes as 'fae', another writer in the same dialect might represent as 'frae', 'nivir' as 'niver', and so on. What we are seeing repeatedly in contemporary writing is the struggle of regional and ethnic dialects to achieve a coherent literary identity within a writing system that has for over 200 years been tuned to the sounds and structures of RP and standard English.

It is crucially important to avoid confrontation. It is all too easy for pedants to condemn the non-standard English of young people on the Internet or the new literary voices and to interpret these processes of language change as language deterioration. Conversely, it is all too easy for the new generation to revel in the linguistic freedom which the Internet provides and to disregard the literary canon, much of it written in standard English, which is their heritage. One of the most urgent tasks facing us at present, accordingly, is to devise an appropriate philosophy and practice of language management in which the different forms and functions of standard and non-standard English are brought into a mutually enlightening relationship. If there are trends in usage which are genuinely damaging – such as the use of obfuscating or insulting vocabulary – these need to be identified and corrected. If there are trends which are artificially constraining – such as the imposition of unreal prescriptive rules – these need to be identified and avoided. Teachers of English are the cadre of professionals who are most involved in developing this relationship; but it is no easy task, given the speed and multidimensional complexity of contemporary language change. They will, however, be much helped if they find their work to be part of an informed cultural climate in which other institutions – such as broadcasting, literature and academia – share their sociolinguistic concerns, and it is towards the formation of this climate that I hope the present volume will make a contribution.

Note

1 Suhayl Saadi, *Psychoraag* (Edinburgh, Black and White Publishing, 2005), p. 50. *Khamoshi* = 'quiet'.

3

Schooling and culture

Introduction

The focus of this chapter is on what is currently the period of compulsory schooling – that is, on education from five to sixteen years and thus on the primary (five to eleven) and secondary (eleven to sixteen) stages. It is difficult, though, to maintain this focus with complete precision. Policy changes, implemented from 1997 by the Labour Government, mean that most children begin their schooling at three or four and that these years are as closely regulated in their content and procedures as any other. Conversely, for increasing numbers (currently, about 40,000) of fourteen-year-olds, school is no longer the institution in which most of their learning is organised – vocational education, based in colleges of further education, or in workplaces, takes over. To add to the complexity, English secondary education has been redesigned on a principle of institutional diversity. In place of the largely non-selective, local-authority-controlled comprehensive system of the period 1965–90, there has developed a multiplicity of school types, all subject to government regulation in terms of curriculum, pedagogy and assessment but widely different in status, in ethos, in the composition of the student population and in level of success. Post-sixteen, the principle of diversity retains its force. From 2015, participation in education or training up to the age of eighteen will become compulsory, but here, too, a wide gulf of status will separate academic provision, concentrated in school-based 'sixth forms' from the vocationally inflected courses provided in further-education colleges.

These English patterns need to be understood in a more global context. Until the late twentieth century, the history of schooling in Europe could plausibly be written in national terms. School systems were founded as part of a process of nation-building, were provided with common procedures and values by a national corps of functionaries and were instrumental in the promotion of national identities above local loyalties and cultures. The Belgian writer Nico Hirtt has commented sardonically that the graveyards of the First World War are testimony to the school's effectiveness in this latter respect. The school also provided a focus for intense conflicts over inclusiveness and democracy: the meaning of citizenship and social rights were contested in battles over the shape of national education systems.[1]

Over the past twenty years, however, another agenda has taken shape, whose drivers and reference points are more global than national and whose impact on the purposes ascribed by governments to schooling has become increasingly clear. The agenda has been shaped by international organisations – especially the Paris-based Organisation for Economic Co-operation and Development (OECD) – which have provided both a widely circulated discourse and a much-utilised set of policy tools.[2] In Europe, it has been translated into operational form by the European Union, whose council meeting in Lisbon in 2000 marked a new and more detailed stage of policy elaboration. Declaring that the EU, facing the challenges of globalisation and of a burgeoning knowledge economy, must by 2010 transform itself into a world-leading 'competitive and dynamic knowledge economy', the Council placed the education systems of Europe at the heart of a programme transforming the EU's economic and social strategy.[3] Education was now too significant to be left to the haphazard and variegated process of nationally determined change, and it was advisable to adopt 'a European framework' that defined 'fundamental new educational competences', redesigned the governance of education systems and introduced new partners to them – most notably from the private sector.[4]

This new orthodoxy exercises an increasing influence on education, across Europe. But it is not, as it were, inscribed on blank and receptive national surfaces. Its schema interact with national systems whose histories vary considerably. It combines in diverse ways with already-established interests – business, the churches, educational hierarchies, teachers and their organisations. It has at its disposal state apparatuses whose competence and effectiveness differ markedly from country to country. It confronts more or less organised opposition that draws from national traditions of educational reform and contestation. Thus, while it is possible to speak of a globalised policy agenda, this agenda – *pace* the influence of the EU and the OECD – takes different forms in different places. Even within the small space of Britain, this rule of difference applies. No country in Britain is unaffected by the policy orthodoxy: Wales, as much as Scotland and England, speaks of a knowledge economy, an upskilled workforce and global competitiveness.[5] But these principles have different local inflections. The relatively unified nature of the policy community in the Celtic countries, as well as the strength of national traditions of schooling in which ideas of inclusiveness play a prominent part, mean that global orthodoxies are assimilated with relatively little controversy into policy designs in which national distinctiveness and cohesion are claimed as competitive advantages. Antagonism between competing versions of educational futures is harder to detect.

Even within Britain, England is a separate case. At the 1970s highpoint of post-war educational reform, its educational culture was in many ways more radicalised than those of other home nations, and this experience has still a kind of shadow life that haunts the imagination of policy-makers with the threat of its revival. Conversely, in the 1980s and 1990s, schooling in England felt more deeply than other countries the impact of Conservatism. English exceptionalism characterises also the post-1997 period. Under New Labour, schooling has been subject both to centralised curricular control and to marketisation and privatisation to an extent that has taken it to what might be called the extremes of policy orthodoxy. Currently, England is experimenting with institutional and curricular reforms that promise a new kind of schooling – business-sensitive, institutionally autonomous, 'personalised' in its model of learning – and that entail a further set of transformations beyond those which, ever since the 1980s, have swept in successive waves over the school. These achievements and aspirations are evaluated in different ways. In 2002, the European Round Table of business interests (Vivendi, Nestlé and others) cited England as the country in which reform had made the strongest advances; for those with other perspectives, England is the educational spectre haunting Europe – the homeland of a 'neo-liberal' model in which schooling is subordinated to an economic agenda, opposing voices marginalised and egalitarian ambitions abandoned.[6]

Progressivism

Between 1960 and 1980, governments throughout Western Europe worked in the belief that 'more and better education [was] an end in itself and at the same time one of the most important factors in economic growth.'[7] Spending on education increased to unprecedented levels, and secondary schooling – at least in its lower years – was reshaped along comprehensive lines. Changes in institutional form were accompanied by a modification of school cultures. Quantitative expansion, policy-makers realised, was not enough: there needed also to be changes in curriculum and in pedagogy. As George Papadopoulos puts it, 'public authorities were forced to shift their attention to how, coping beyond numbers, their educational offerings could be made relevant to the diversified needs of their vastly expanded and variegated clientèle.'[8] What Papadopoulos called this 'quest for relevance and equality' was thus to some extent fostered by the institutions of the central state, which recognised that educational change had a cultural dimension.[9] In England, the official reports of the period – such as the Newsom Report *Half Our Future* in 1963 – were marked not just by a desire to upskill the workforce but also by a troubled sense of the cultural presence of working-class students and of the fact of cultural difference; Newsom's persistent theme was the reluctance of both the 'old' working-class cultures of the inner cities and the 'new' popular cultures of youth to engage with the kinds of education they were offered. At the same time, in the decentralised and spacious school system established by the 1944 Education Act, some groups of teachers pursued parallel concerns. The period from 1960 to 1980 was one in which dispersed professional influ-ence over educational processes increased: reform was filtered through layers of schoolteacher, local authority and teacher-educator influence in ways that furthered less the economic and social preoccupations that were voiced in government reports than a child-centred emphasis on 'progressive' pedagogy. Summarising the outcomes of this process, Peter Woods writes about a period of primary education in England that was 'heavily influenced by the theories of Piaget, Vygotsky, and Bruner [and] was dominated by a discourse of child-centredness, discovery learning, and care'.[10] Woods sketches various 'teaching strategies' avail-able to teachers in this period, which included:

> starting from the child (using prior and pupil knowledge); mak-ing home and school links ... This involves incorporating some of the child's home experiences and culture into that of the school; developing empathy [to] ... widen perspectives, provide comparative material for one's own self and situation, and aid the critical formu-lation of thought; [interest] in the uses and misuses of literacy, and indeed of a wide range of literacies.

In one sense, the stress of approaches such as these fell on sensitivity towards the individual child and respect for the complexity of learners' achievements. In another, it suggested something broader – a socio-cultural perspective on learning in which children's cultures were recognised and 'official' cultures of education extended. This latter emphasis derived not just from the classic progressivism of the early twentieth century but also from more contemporary thinking about the relationship between schooling and culture. Under the influence of a post-1956 New Political Left – for which questions of 'culture' were of central political importance – there occurred in some parts of a dispersed system of schooling a process of revaluation. Once regarded in terms of marginality or deficit, the cultures of subordinate groups were increasingly seen, from the late 1950s onwards, as a significant educational resource, about which teachers needed to know more. 'There exists', as one teacher put it in 1961, 'not merely this sort of élite culture … but some different kind of culture which it is necessary to seek out by going into other people's experience.'[11] Others spoke of their teaching as 'a long apprenticeship to the worlds, values and subcultures of youth'.[12] Part of this apprenticeship involved coming to terms with a conflict between the norms and expectations of formal education and 'the complexities of the real world which children and young people inhabit'.[13] In the process of seeking out such complexities, cultural achievements were revalued: working-class speech and story were claimed as evidence that there existed a '"common working-class culture", disconnected from the powerful institutions and high cultural traditions of society' but rooted instead in a community and possessing qualities of depth and resistance.[14] The development of new kinds of cultural understanding thus became a means of extending the range of educational possibility so as to include learners from subordinate social groups.

Later in the 1970s other dynamics came into play. Between 1969 and 1974, the relative social peace of what Hobsbawm called the 'golden age' came to an end: a series of working-class protests and emerging social movements challenged inequalities, claimed rights of participation and recognition and asserted militant identities.[15] In some urban centres, curricular practice reflected these developments: the questions raised by social movements found their way onto the everyday agenda of classrooms; what happened in schools was linked to challenges to the established forms of identity, knowledge and power that were developing outside it. Around questions of 'race' and anti-racism, these shifts were particularly striking.[16] In the late 1960s, black and Asian parents protested against the channelling of their children towards schools for the 'maladjusted' and against policies that sought to disperse them, through bussing, across a range of schools. From the early 1970s, teachers began to develop curricula that were explicitly anti-racist and anti-imperialist. By the 1980s, the London Association for the Teaching of English had developed the argument about cultural politics and classroom practice to a new stage: curriculum change was brought about, 'first by the voice of black pupils and the black community, and second by overt racism on the streets'.[17]

Thus there developed – not universally, but in pockets of the state system – a radical educational culture that questioned the values, traditions, purposes and allegiances of the school and worked on alternative practices, which were to some extent sympathetic to the experiences and cultural meanings of subordinate social groups and therefore committed to the understanding of the school as a place where cultural meanings were brought into relationship with each other and, in the process, remade. Like Raymond Williams, whose writings both reflected and motivated educational rethinking, this movement imagined a 'common culture' in which the meanings and agency of subordinate groups could be recognised. Its ideas and practices were those of a minority of teachers, but they gained nonetheless a wider significance, not least because of the way in which they affronted the basic principles of a resurgent force, Conservatism, and in doing so stepped into the front line of political conflict.

Conservatism

At no point in English educational history, even at its most radical moments, have Conservative cultural themes – tradition, nation, authority and allegiance – been extinguished, and from the passionate vantage point they provide, the effects of educational reform have continually been criticised, often as part of a more general response to modernity. T. S. Eliot in 1949 claimed that the 'headlong rush to educate everybody' entailed 'lowering our standards' and 'abandoning the study of those subjects by which the essentials of our culture are transmitted; destroying our ancient edifices'; in the more succinct phrase of another literary conservative Kingsley Amis, two decades later, 'more will mean worse.'[18]

As Eliot's cadences suggest, these positions were habitually defensive. From the 1940s onwards, traditionalist conservatism was challenged and, to an extent, displaced: elitist cultures could not thrive in mass-education systems; commercial popular culture further eroded their base; attacks on selectivity and the knowledge traditions associated with it were often effective. Yet, weakened though it was by an educational politics of egalitarianism and cultural diversity, Conservatism made from the 1970s onwards a spectacular comeback, through Thatcherism. It did so, first of all, as a critique of the new. In the 1970s, primary education was struggling through a difficult process of transformation; so were the secondary and tertiary systems, which had become 'massified' without a coherent programme for curricular, pedagogic and institutional change. This prolonged and in the event uncompleted period of transition allowed Conservatism its second wind. Invoking a golden age of education, in which academic values had everywhere prospered, the right supplied many of the resources for a resonant critique of educational reform. In the process, especially in England – though less so in Scotland and Wales – this transition played a crucial destructive role: it became, as it were, a solvent of the post-war settlement, only to be itself subsumed, later, within a larger and more compelling programme of neo-liberalism.

Neo-conservative themes – traditionalist, xenophobic – were central to Thatcherism. They provided it with a populist discourse in which disenchantment with educational reform could be persuasively expressed. They offered a critique of an English school system allegedly dominated by libertarian, relativist, multiculturalist forces; they supplied the elements of an alternative, in the form of a programme of intervention by an authoritative state, in which social cohesion would be organised around a racialised Englishness and a freezing of gender roles in the mould of the 1950s. The critique, widely diffused by sympathetic media, did much to discredit the more radical curricular experiments which had developed within the general process of reform and succeeded in associating such reform with a supposed decline in educational standards.

In a series of executive decisions and Acts of Parliament from 1981 to 1993, Conservatism destroyed the ways in which the relationship between education and culture had been configured in the post-1944 period, eclipsing alternative programmes for change, along with their institutional bases. The Conservative programme, however, was one of construction as well as critique, of creation as well as destruction. It established a highly specified national curriculum, as well as an associated system of testing, and in doing so effectively terminated the possibility of non-governmental reform, insulating the curriculum from local-level pressure. It set up a system of regular and combative school inspection. By devolving financial powers to school level, and by making the funding of schools partly dependent upon their success in attracting students and in competitive bidding for government money, it laid a basis for the emergence of powerful new management cultures, in which questions of performance – of outcomes measured against centrally determined and non-negotiable criteria – became dominant.

Nevertheless, despite these achievements, the alternative offered by the right – measured in terms of its own cultural commitments – was a failure. The Conservative strategy was an ambivalent, regressive type of modernisation, the driving force of which was a section of the party more concerned with the defence of traditional versions of the national culture than with the development of a programme attuned to social and cultural change. Under the increasing influence of this traditionalist right, Conservative policy in the early 1990s sought to unify the curriculum around nationalist and socially authoritarian themes. It asserted the centrality of national history, of European art and music, of the standard form of English. At the same time, it prioritised a version of 'basic skills' and disparaged new kinds of knowledge – most notoriously media studies: 'it is hard for parents to have much confidence in the exam boards', said the Secretary of State for Education in 1992, 'when some of them include television programmes such as *Neighbours* and even *'Allo, 'Allo* in their English syllabuses.'[19] Policy was hostile to the recognition of cultural difference and sought to efface from the curriculum most traces of a response (literary, historical, musical) to the presence of new migrant populations.

Conservatism thus developed an archaic programme that responded to profound processes of cultural and social change – inward migration, hybridity, loss of empire – with a reassertion of historically superseded models of community. The image of schooling to which it looked was that of the self-governing elite institution that transmitted an undisputed version of the national culture to a homogeneous population. It tended to see mass secondary and tertiary education, like the diversity of contemporary culture, less as products of social and economic change than of political influence – especially that exerted by public-sector professionals and left-wing politicians. In doing so, Conservatism tended to overlook the solvent effects of the hectic, market-driven process of transformation that its own economic policies had done much to promote, and its attempt to develop a directed and explicitly retrogressive programme of curriculum transformation was defeated in 1993–4 by teachers' refusal to implement a testing system in which such values were embodied. Subsequently, as Thatcherism began to decompose, the cultural right ceased to play a significant educational role. Later policies would build on the market-focused managerialism that Conservatism's institutional reforms had created, and could always find a niche position for 'traditional education', as a marker of educational distinction in a marketised and differentiated system. But as a programme, cultural conservatism could not provide the basis for the relentless 'economising' of the school at which its New Labour successor aimed.

New Labour readings

New Labour's educational reference points are provided by the reading of social and economic change offered by global policy orthodoxy. The OECD insider, George Papadopoulos, summarised the organisation's understanding of the watershed of the 1980s in these terms:

> The combination of resource constraints, high unemployment and demographic downturn had a direct input on the demand for education as well as on the perception of its role and its contribution to social and economic development. Coinciding with the advent of conservative governments in a large number of [OECD] member countries, it brought a dramatic change in the political context of education. Continued growth could no longer be taken for granted either as a feasible or even a desirable objective. Constraints on public spending were particularly telling. As one of the major components of public budgets, education had to share the burden of restraint … Resource limitations raised new questions about the setting of priority objectives, in contrast to the earlier situation where a multiplicity of educational objectives could be pursued more or less simultaneously. This scramble for priorities among different interest groups sharpened the political conflicts around education.[20]

The implications of even this guarded analysis are clear enough: with the economic restructuring that had begun in the mid 1970s, education began a long and still unfinished process of remaking. In this process, the forms taken by the school system in the post-war decades were subjected to hostile scrutiny, and the rationales that had sustained their development were called into question. Educational expansion was no longer thought to contribute as such to economic growth. Notions of education as an investment in human capital continued to be influential but now 'in the more refined form of micro-economic analyses of the economic significance of individual segments of potential labour power in terms of profitability', with a view to guiding investment towards sectors 'with a favourable cost benefit factor'.[21] In short, government policies were increasingly dedicated to servicing the requirements of a new stage of economic development, at a low cost, and with maximum effectiveness; in Tony Blair's words, 'for years education was a social cause; today it is an economic imperative.'[22]

In pursuit of this imperative, New Labour repudiated the past. Neither traditional conservatism nor social-democratic egalitarianism were spared; rather than celebrating the achievements of its social democratic predecessors, the Blair Government offered unrelenting criticism. The story is told that between 2001 and 2007, recruits to the then Department for Education and Skills (DfES) were instructed to assume that history began with the 'year zero' of 1988, when the Conservatives' Education Reform Act was passed. Before that point, educational history was a record of failure. The Labour Governments of Clement Attlee (1945–51) and Harold Wilson and James Callaghan (intermittently from 1964 to 1979) had presided over a largely 'unskilled' working population that had possessed 'jobs for life' in local industries. A stagnant economy produced a school system in its own image. In the supposedly static society of the long boom, there was 'a general acceptance that only a minority would reach the age of 16 with formal skills and qualifications'.[23] Comprehensive reform had not done enough to challenge this acceptance, and by setting 'social' as opposed to 'economic' goals it had contributed to stasis. Overreacting to the failings of the selective system, and dominated by the 'ideology of unstreamed teaching', it had failed to differentiate among students and to design different provision according to aptitude and ability.[24] Hence mass illiteracy; hence slow rates of economic growth.[25]

These verdicts on the educational politics of a previous era – perceived as an entirely different country from that of Britain post-1997 – were connected to a sense of social and economic discontinuity that was not without foundation. The collapse of manufacturing industry and the financialisation of the economy which were initiated by Conservatism had profound effects, not least on the culture of schooling. The sociologist Mike Savage depicted a national landscape of deindustrialisation from which 'the working class has been largely eviscerated as a visible social presence', no longer a 'central reference point in British culture'.[26] In this emptied space, rather than there being socially recognised tensions between class-specific practices, the practices of the middle class, focusing on the pursuit of positional advantage through the exercise of 'choice', 'have increasingly come to define the social itself'.[27] Paul Willis, likewise, noted the collapse of the youth labour markets into which the school once transferred its largely unqualified products and suggested something of its impact: the 'probabilities of a reliable and decent wage through manual work have been radically decreased for substantial parts of the working class ... [and] the threat of its removal has become a permanent condition for all workers.'[28] Thus, Willis continues, 'the pride, depth and independence of a collective industrial tradition' had given way to 'the indignities of flexible and obedient labour'.[29] From the perspective sketched by Savage and by Willis, the cultural reference points which were visible to educationalists in the years before the deluge had disappeared. Partly in consequence, the connections between educational practice and a complex of social movements which were deemed to embody a principle of hope became hard to assume. In the new situation, Labour's indifference to cultural difference, and its stress on achievement, in terms of criteria which were both conventional and accepted as beyond question, seemed persuasive.

Labour was working with the grain of educational change. In the mid 1980s, over 40 per cent of students failed to gain any examination passes by age sixteen, and over half left education at the first opportunity, aged sixteen. From 1985 on, with the introduction of the examination for sixteen-year-olds, the GCSE, and the drying up of employment opportunities for school-leavers, participation in examinations increased. By the end of the 1990s, the proportion of school-leavers registering no success in examinations was halved, and over half of the cohort attained more than five GCSE passes in the top A–C grades; the proportion of students who left school at the earliest opportunity had fallen to less than a third. Student attitudes to education also changed. Longitudinal surveys of attitudes found rising levels of satisfaction among students about their school experience, while the emergence of 'new traditions' and rituals of schooling, focusing on the annual release to students of their examination results, resymbolised schooling around the experience of certification – something that could not have occurred when only a minority of students were entered for examinations.[30] Thus, while the educational programmes developed by New Labour were certainly 'economised', in the sense of servicing a market economy, and strongly differentiated along lines of social class, they also expanded the possibilities of access and attainment for social groups which had previously been excluded from them.

Cultural landscapes

The counterpart of New Labour's repudiation of educational pasts is the presentation of its own policies under the heading of 'modernisation' – a term which is ubiquitous across the EU. 'Modernisation' is a loose and flexible concept that condenses an evaluation of the past, as a zone of exhausted tradition, with an assertion that curricula, pedagogy, purpose and governance must all be transformed in line with contemporary realities. It is justified by a system of interrelated maxims, constantly repeated at every level of education, from the classroom to the ministerial meeting. The societies of the EU are knowledge societies, in which competitiveness and wealth depend on innovation and flexibility. Information and the capacity to use it are essential. Education and training systems must provide the 'intangible capital' that is central to knowledge economies, but they cannot effectively do so because institutionally and pedagogically they are outdated.[31] They must operate in a new way, to develop 'autonomous individuals', capable of constant 'reconversion' – the transmission of 'consolidated knowledge, traditions and habits' is no longer useful. The school cannot develop this new type of human subject without itself being transformed: as the German enthusiast for reform, Jürgen Kluge, puts it, 'independent pupils' require 'independent schools', in which responsiveness to market conditions and enthusiasm for working with new 'partners', mostly from the private sector, should become the norm.[32]

In terms of its national management, the modernised system has two main features. First, there is an immensely powerful system of data collection, data evaluation and target setting, a technology that provides for the instant enforcement of norms and for high levels of conformity on the part of schools. It depends upon the standardisation of provision – the national curriculum of 1988 was the first step in this process. On the basis of standardisation, government has developed a set of performance indicators in the form of measurable and comparable data, generated primarily by pupil scores in national tests and examinations. Performance results are fed back to schools so that their achievements can be compared to those of other schools and underperformance can be identified and acted upon. (English data systems are now sophisticated enough to allow comparisons between schools with similar socio-economic populations, as well as tracking of the performance of individual students.) Finally, data collection provides a basis for a system of rewards (for instance, the granting of 'specialist' status and extra funding) and sanctions, up to and including closure.

Accompanying these elements of centralisation is a second element: a 'reagenting' of the school whose effect is that the social actors characteristic of an earlier period – local authorities, teacher trade unions – play a greatly diminished role, while other social actors – managers, private partners – are centrally placed. In contrast with the period of social-democratic reform, the development of policy through a process of encounter between different social interests has become less important than its elaboration through networks of operationally powerful but not strongly autonomous agencies, local and national, whose origins and points of reference lie in the priorities of national government and which serve to link the micro-world of classroom interactions to macro-level objectives of standards and achievement.[33] New Labour retained the agencies of Conservative centralisation and added others of its own making. Permanent agencies such as the school-inspection organisation Ofsted, the Training and Development Agency (for teachers and other school staff) and the Qualifications and Curriculum Authority (QCA) were complemented by major conjunctural initiatives – notably the literacy and numeracy strategies – which were nationally directed and locally pervasive. Woven through all these activities was a continuous thread of private-sector involvement. In relation to curriculum standardisation, management training, performance management of teachers, inspection of schools, assessment systems, target-setting and monitoring of student performance, the Government has turned as a matter of course to the private sector, arguing in the process that the sector is both cost-effective and dynamic and is uniquely capable of bringing about change. 'For most of the twentieth century', wrote Blair's education adviser in 2001, 'the drive for educational progress came from the public sector.' Now, though, it is the 'growing and vibrant private sector that possesses ... the energy, knowledge, imagination, skill and investment ... to meet the immense challenge of educational reform'.[34]

Leaders and their teachers

Labour's has been a directive, top-down conception of policy that has reshaped schooling at every level. Its limitations, however, have become clear to policy-makers: lasting educational change requires the element of consent, as well as that of force, and policy's more recent turns have acknowledged that this is so. But what is envisaged is less the democratisation of reform than its capacity to mobilise human resources of the school behind policy agenda. For this task – as the number of knighthoods awarded to English headteachers suggests – local leadership is vital. In the words of a European Commission document, decentralisation offers a means of 'taking the political debate on quality down to lower levels of the education system'.[35] At these lower levels, 'stakeholders' can be 'empowered' by 'making them more responsible for defining what they understand by quality in education and giving them "ownership" of their part in the education system'.[36] Here 'leadership', as opposed to mere 'management' becomes important.

Leadership, of course, has a strong cultural dimension. The theories of business organisation favoured by reformers make much of issues of 'culture' – of the norms, values, procedures and rituals that are unique to individual organisations. In such accounts, culture is highly plastic and amenable to direction from above; issues of cultural conflict are downplayed. To 'turn around' a school from failure to academic success is, in these narratives, a work of cultural transformation. Managers must become cultural leaders, working on emotions and relationships as much as systems and regulations. They must identify and then transform the culture of their organisation so that it is based on a commitment to 'quality', as that term is defined by the policy agenda. This mission, conceived as one of personal vocation, is everywhere celebrated in the discourse of school reform. The job of an educational leader, said Tony Blair's chief policy adviser, is – Moses-like – to take teachers to a promised land from which they will not want to return.[37] Or, as the French sociologist van Zanten more analytically puts it, 'the legitimacy of bureaucratic hierarchies is dismissed in favour of the personal vision and capacity to mobilise individuals and to organise group work by an educational leader.'[38]

In this context, the work of teachers is also reordered. The directive element is certainly present in this process, evidenced by the post-1987 powers of management to direct teachers' work, to bring about their dismissal, and – from 2000 onwards – to link salary levels to 'performance'.

But policy would also like to develop a more persuasive strand that offers teachers a place in an educational design of a different kind, where innovation, collectivity, complexity and professional sophistication are important. A contrast is drawn here between a future which will integrate strategic clarity with professional satisfaction and a past in which teachers' claims to professionalism rested upon tacit knowledge and, in as much as they had a strategic element, were linked to strategies for maintaining an autonomy which was individual in character. It is these claims which are now seen as problematic. In Susan Robertson's summary of policy orthodoxy, the 'dominant model of the teacher working alone' – of the teacher as artisan, we could say – is no longer viable in a knowledge society that demands that they should work collaboratively, to produce authoritative, generalisable, evidence-based knowledge about how learners learn, and about 'effective' teaching works.[39]

'Creativity' and regulation

It is one thing to identify an archaic model but quite another to replace it. The problems here run deep: New Labour has brought into being a strongly managed teaching force, yet what it desires is one which is autonomous (within limits), risk-taking and creative. Similar tensions traverse its policies in other areas, most notably in relation to the curriculum and to the kinds of student and parent identities that education, from the perspective of policy, might contribute to forming.

'Creativity' has emerged since 2001 as an important, if still minor, element in the policy repertoire; once the watchword of a romantic critique of industrialism and of the miseries of mass education, it has been revalued as a quality vital to business innovation and to the communicative demands of informational capitalism.[40] Thus, accepting to some extent that a highly regulated and punitively inspected curriculum has unwanted effects on the morale of teachers and the satisfaction levels of students, the DfES attempted to underwrite 'enjoyment', alongside 'excellence' as a principle of schooling.[41] Along with the Department of Culture, Media and Sport (DCMS), the DfES also funded 'Creative Partnerships', a project designed to promote creativity in schools through linking them to 'creative practitioners' in other fields. The programme is justified in terms of the qualities of initiative, innovativeness and team-working that are supposedly required by post-Fordist economies. This repositioning of 'creativity' entails its migration from the cultural-political to the economic domain and relates less to a process of dialogue between teacher experiment and culturally located learners than to one of resource exploitation: 'creativity: find it, promote it' exhorted a document issued by the QCA.[42]

More generally, the tensions between regulation and innovation are managed through strategies in which the requirements of the new social order are translated into the language of personal development. Salient here is a strategy of responsibilisation – what Sharon Gewirtz calls 'the process of inculcating a culture of self-discipline or self-surveillance among welfare subjects', through techniques which include portfolio assessment, homework policies, learning contracts and home–school agreements.[43] The responsibilisation of individuals requires another innovation: the personalisation of the curriculum, a process in which traditional subject boundaries will dissolve. Personalisation has nothing in common, ministers insist, with the child-centredness of an earlier era. Whereas the ideal of progressive education was a notion of individual development and self-realisation combined to a greater or lesser extent with an idea of collective emancipation, personalisation operates with different and more explicit norms; it is an attempt to identify the individual learning strategies that are most effective in reaching an externally given and predefined outcome. It does not involve a curriculum claiming to respond primarily to students' interests, nor a pedagogy that encourages children to 'be themselves' but is rather based on offering support to individual students in order that they may reach defined targets. The support includes the use of information and communication technologies and of 'learning mentors', not necessarily qualified teachers, to work with students in small groups. Above all, it means 'curriculum choice', particularly during the fourteen-to-nineteen stage, when academic and vocational pathways become available.[44] At this point it becomes difficult to distinguish personalised learning from a form of selection, and the appeal to individual need folds into the reproduction of social divisions.

Such a slippage is characteristic of the general ensemble of what could be called late-phase New Labour policy, which has combined themes of autonomy, creativity and inclusion with those of regulation – to the point of authoritarianism – and differentiation. The fault lines of this combination are evident at several points. Parents, for instance, are awarded by policy a role of partnership, as active collaborators in the production of educated children; yet unsuccessful parents, whose children regularly play truant, can be sent to jail, while the inclusive rhetoric of partnership is belied by a simultaneous focus on parents as educational consumers, in ways that lead through the encouragement of parental choice to increasing social segregation between schools and pupils.[45] There are similar tensions in the identities ascribed to students. One strand of policy champions alongside creativity and personalisation, the ideas of children's rights and the necessity for governors and inspectors to listen to the 'student voice'. But from another direction, rights are called into question, as evidenced by the rising numbers of students expelled from school, at the behest of tribunals in which 'the headteacher has total authority, occupying ... the role of legislator, senior police officer, prosecutor, judge, jury and character witness.'[46] More generally, because current orthodoxy is emphatically uninterested in the cultural experiences of students, particularly those from marginal groups, attempts to incentivise and responsibilise sections of the student population are always likely to be problematic. As Louise Archer and Hiromi Yamashita point out in the relation to 'inner city masculinities', 'rational and individualistic government education policies and strategies may have little impact on increasing the boys' identification with, or engagement with, formal learning, since they do not address the boys' strong emotional attachment to ideas grounded outside of the educational context.'[47]

Thus, while ethnographers continue to point to a disjuncture between official education and local cultures – precisely the ground on which education radicals worked in an earlier period – policy tends to overlook it. Yet, at the same time, in the shadow of the 'war on terror', New Labour has been much concerned with issues of cultural and community cohesion, with the development of what ministers have called a sense of 'Britishness', and with the centring of citizenship education on what are seen as shared and characteristically British values such as 'tolerance, respect and freedom of speech'.[48] In this way, the governments of Blair and Brown found themselves turning back towards some of the themes of Conservatism, albeit with a greater sense of the differences that must be recognised and negotiated if a shared sense of national identity is to be achieved. But whether the type of school created by the reforms of the post-1988 period is capable of such a cultural dialogue is open to doubt.

Recuperations

We can thus speak of policy tensions that make conflicting cultural demands of the school. But we should also note by way of conclusion that these demands are also subject to a complex historical patterning. New, economically focused education programmes assimilate, utilise and recuperate positions and practices from diverse points of origin. Elements of traditional conservatism coexist with neo-liberalism; and progressivism, lifted from the realm of culture-criticism and given a business-orientated inflection, rubs shoulders with them both. In these senses, we can speak less of a cancellation of the discourses of social democratic and progressive reform than of their recombination, and of their insertion into a new economised ensemble of discourses, whose main point of reference is the need to ensure education's close compatibility with rapid, market-driven change. The new creativity can usefully be understood in this way, as an attempted re-enchantment of the school that draws on educational traditions whose original impulse was to relate formal learning to the life-world of the learner, and whose original 'bearers' saw themselves as working towards a democracy of knowledge that recognised the creativity of subordinate cultures. But in England, as across Britain and Europe, schools experience these traditions under a new, economised sign.

Notes

1 K. Jones, C. Cunchillos, R. Hatcher and N. Hirtt, *Schooling in Western Europe: The New Order and its Adversaries* (Basingstoke: Palgrave, 2008).

2 M. Henry, B. Lingard, F. Rizvi and S. Taylor, *The OECD, Globalisation and Education Policy* (Amsterdam: Pergamon, 2001); C. Laval and L. Weber, *Le Nouvel Ordre éducatif mondial* (Paris: Nouveaux Regards, 2002).

3 Quoted in M. van der Wende, 'Europe's Agenda on Global Competition', *International Higher Education* 49 (autumn) (2007), p. 11.

4 European Parliament, *Lisbon European Council 23–24 March 2000, Presidency Conclusions*, (Lisbon: European Parliament, 2000), available at www.europarl. europa.eu/summits/lis1_en.htm (accessed 3 March 2010).

5 K. Jones, *Education in Britain: 1944 to the Present* (Cambridge: Polity Press, 2003).

6 R. Hatcher, 'Getting Down to Business: Schooling in the Globalised Economy', *Education and Social Justice*, 3 (2) (2001): 45–9.

7 G. Papadopoulos, *Education 1960–1990: The OECD Perspective* (Paris: OECD, 1994), p. 59.

8 Papadopoulos, *Education*, p. 59.

9 Papadopoulos, *Education*, p. 59.

10 P. Woods, 'Creative Teaching and Learning: Historical, Political and Institutional Perspectives'; paper given at ESRC Creative Teaching and Learning Seminar, University of Exeter, March 2004.

11 J. Dixon, 'Contribution to NUT [National Union of Teachers] Conference' (verbatim minute), *Popular Culture and Personal Responsibility* (London: National Union of Teachers, 1961), p. 315.

12 A. Dewdney and M. Lister, *Youth, Culture and Photography* (Basingstoke: Macmillan, 1988).

13 S. Hall and P. Whannel, *The Popular Arts* (London: Hutchinson, 1964), p. 13.

14 R. Hewitt, 'The New Oracy: Another Critical Glance', paper to the Conference of the British Association of Applied Linguistics, 1989.

15 E. W. Hobsbawm, *Age of Extremes: The Short Twentieth Century, 1941–1991* (London: Michael Joseph, 1994).

16 T. Carter, with J. Coussins, *Shattering Illusions: West Indians in British Politics* (London: Lawrence & Wishart, 1986); I. Grosvenor, *Assimilating Identities: Racism and Educational Policy in Post-1945 Britain* (London: Lawrence & Wishart, 1997).

17 Quoted in Jones, *Education in Britain*, p. 127.

18 T. S. Eliot, *Notes Towards a Definition of Culture* (London: Faber & Faber, 1949), p. 11; K. Amis, *Whatever Became of Jane Austen and Other Essays* (Harmondsworth: Penguin, 1981), p. 181.

19 J. Patten, 'Speech to Conservative Party Conference', 1992.

20 Papadopoulos, *Education*, p. 141.

21 Papadopoulos, *Education*, p. 142.

22 T. Blair, Speech to National Association of Head Teachers, 1 May 2004.

23 DfEE, *Schools Building on Success* p. 4

24 T. Blair, *New Britain: My Vision of a Young Country* (London: Fourth Estate, 1996), p. 175.

25 DfEE, *Schools Building on Success*, p. 4.

26 M. Savage, 'A New Class Paradigm?', *British Journal of Sociology of Education*, 24 (4) (2003): 535–41.

27 Savage, 'A New Class Paradigm?', p. 536.

28 P. Willis, 'Foot Soldiers of Modernity: the Dialectics of Cultural Consumption and the 21st Century School', *Harvard Educational Review*, 73 (3) (2003): 390–415; p. 397.

29 Willis, 'Foot Soldiers of Modernity', p. 3.

30 Centre for Educational Sociology, Social-Class Inequalities in Education in England and Scotland, Special CES Briefing Number 40 (Edinburgh: CES, 2006).

31 Quoted in A. Novoa, 'The Restructuring of the European Educational Space: Changing Relationships Among States, Citizens, and Educational Communities', in J. Fink, G. Lewis and J. Clarke (eds.), *Rethinking European Welfare: Transformations of Europe and Social Policy* (London: Sage, 2001), pp. 249–276; p. 258.

32 J. Kluge, *Schluss mit der Bildungsmisere* (*The End of Education Misery*) (Frankfurt: Campus Verlag, 2003), p. 15.

33 K. Jones, 'An Old Future; a New Past: Labour Remakes the English School', in R. Johnson and D. Steinberg (eds.), *Blairism and the War of Persuasion: Labour's Passive Revolution* (London: Lawrence & Wishart, 2004).

34 M. Barber, 'High Expectations and Standards for All, No Matter What: Creating a World Class Education Service in England', in M. Fielding (ed.), *Taking Education Really Seriously: Four Years' Hard Labour* (London: Routledge, 2001), pp. 17–43; p. 17.

35 European Commission, DG for Education and Culture, *European Report on Quality of School Education: Sixteen Quality Indicators* (Luxembourg: EC, 2001), p. 10.

36 European Commission, *European Report on the Quality of School Education* (Brussels, European Commission, 2001), p. 10.

37 M. Barber, quoted in Jones *et al., Schooling in Western Europe*, p. 140.

38 A. van Zanten, 'Educational Change and New Cleavages Between Head Teachers, Teachers and Parents: Global and Local Perspectives on the French Case', *Journal of Education Policy*, 17 (3) (2002): 289–304; p. 291.

39 S. Robertson, 'Re-Imagining and Rescripting the Future of Education: Global Knowledge Economy Discourses and the Challenge to Education Systems', *Comparative Education*, 41 (2) (2005): 151–70; p. 159.

40 D. Buckingham and K. Jones, 'New Labour's Cultural Turn: Some Tensions in Contemporary Educational and Cultural Policy', *Journal of Education Policy*, 16 (1) (2001): 1–14.

41 DfES, *Excellence and Enjoyment* (London: DfES, 2003).

42 QCA, *Creativity: Find It, Promote It* (London: QCA, 2003).

43 S. Gewirtz, *The Managerial School* (London: Routledge, 2002), p. 161.

44 D. Miliband (Minister of State for Education), 'Personalised Learning: Building a New Relationship with Schools', Speech at North of England Education Conference, Belfast, 8 January 2004.

45 D. Reay, 'Education and Cultural Capital: The Implications of Changing Trends in Education Policies', *Cultural Trends*, 13 (2) (2004): 1–14.

46 D. Monk, '(Re)constructing the Head Teacher: Legal Narratives and the Politics of School Exclusions', *Journal of Law and Society*, 32 (3) (2005): 399–423; p. 400.

47 L. Archer and H. Yamashita, 'Theorising Inner City Masculinities: "Race", Class, Gender and Education', *Gender and Education*, 15 (2) (2003): 115–32; p. 129.

48 J. Meikle, 'Lessons on Slave Trade and Empire to Teach Pupils "British Identity"', *The Guardian*, 26 January 2007.

4
———

The changing character of political communications

Introduction

It is late on a Friday night in 2006. On BBC 1, the British broadcasting personality Jonathan Ross is hosting his chat show. His first guest is the Hollywood actor Bruce Willis; his next is the tennis player Martina Navratilova; and his third guest is the newly elected leader of the Conservative party, the official parliamentary opposition to the Labour Government, David Cameron. Following a brief film, chronicling Cameron's rapid rise through the party, he banters with Ross about politics, and then the host begins to explore his guest's adolescence. Did he have pictures of Margaret Thatcher on his wall, did he have – it is broadly hinted – sexual fantasies about her? Cameron is momentarily nonplussed, unsure of how to deal with the question, but he negotiates his way out of his embarrassment and the interview continues.

This moment captures much that is now commonplace about modern British political communication. A leading politician makes himself available for an exchange, not with a heavyweight political interviewer but rather with a talk-show host. The rationale is obvious: this is the way to reach the largest possible audience and to convey a side of the political leader that might otherwise not get communicated, and to convince his audience that 'he is one of us'. Cameron was doing what other politicians have done before. He was communicating his politics, but using means and platforms that were not typically part of traditional political practice.

Early in the same year that Cameron was to be found squirming on Ross's couch, many of the same viewers will have seen a Member of Parliament dressed in a leotard pretending to be a cat. George Galloway, of the vocal but small political party Respect was a housemate on the UK television programme *Celebrity Big Brother* on Channel 4. He too justified his appearance on the show on the grounds that this was a good way to get his message across to those who would otherwise not hear what he had to say. Both experiences and both justifications are symptomatic of how political communication in Britain has developed over the past few decades. What has happened and why is the subject of this chapter.

A brief history

Mass media's presence in politics is now so widespread and familiar that it is sometimes hard to recall that it was not always like this, that there was a time when elections were not covered by television, when there were no microphones, let alone cameras, in the Houses of Parliament, when some politicians disdained the idea of advertising or of appearing on 'the box'. In an attempt to recover these memories, it is worth looking at how the various traditional sites of politics have found themselves 'colonised', as Thomas Meyer puts it, by mass media.[1]

Elections

There are many stories to be told about the history of political communications in Britain, and many, if not most, of them are about elections, and about the ways in which parties and politicians have sought to win over the voters. Pippa Norris identifies three key phases in this history.[2] The first – the premodern period – sees election campaigning as largely ad hoc and focused on a series of public meetings, typically involving the party leader. This phase gives way, in the late 1950s and early 1960s, to the modern period, during which the media became the object of party attention. The first general election to be covered on television was that held in 1959. As the focus shifted away from draughty halls to television studios, and to the emerging technology of broadcasting, so the degree of coordination and funding of election campaigns increased. Campaigning was more and more the responsibility of professional communicators and their associated industries (opinion polling, advertising, focus groups, etc). This trend was to create the conditions for the postmodern era – the one we now inhabit – in which the campaign is permanent and the professionalisation of political communication is complete, in which voters are targeted and messages honed to the constituencies being addressed. Bob Franklin bemoans this state of affairs, in which sound bites and photo opportunities have become more important than 'the informed advocacy of policy' and where the suit a politician wears 'is at least as important in the battle for the hearts and minds of voters as the policies of the politician who wears it'.[3]

Norris's history is essentially one that marks the increasing presence of the mass media. Campaigns are organised around, on the one hand, the working routines of journalists. Press conferences are timed to meet news deadlines. On the other hand, the content and character of the campaign are designed to generate images (the photo opportunity) and slogans (the sound bite) that 'play well' to the party's agenda on the screen. Politicians become increasingly aware of, and trained in, the skills needed to communicate through television and radio. Parties produce guidebooks for candidates in which they are advised on what to wear and how to pose for photographs. They learn what questions to ask before giving an interview and what answers to give during it.

Political parties advertise more and more frequently for personnel who can work on the presentation side of politics. They hire Hollywood film directors for their election broadcasts; they agonise over the music to accompany their campaign. They recruit advertising and PR experts to help them 're-brand' and even to help them decide on policy. All of this is directed towards producing 'good coverage'. And to a large extent, it works. Election coverage increasingly reflects the images and messages that parties want to project.

These changes are, of course, not only to be found among the political contestants. The media industry changes too. Rules are devised for the coverage of elections. More and more airtime is devoted to election coverage (even as the media's attention to politics generally declines). The attitudes and behaviour of journalists change too. Steven Barnett identifies a shift from deference to cynicism in the way in which politics and politicians are treated.[4] Where once interviewers would hardly dare interrupt their political guests, now they treat them with scarcely veiled contempt. The figure of Jeremy Paxman, the main presenter of BBC's *Newsnight*, best fits this new era, most famously cross-examining the then Home Secretary, Michael Howard, in May 1997, about his role in prison-service politics. Paxman made twelve attempts to ask the same question, while Howard gave the same, stonewalling answer.

> PAXMAN: Did you threaten to overrule him [Derek Lewis, director general of the prison service]?
> HOWARD: I did not overrule Derek Lewis.
> PAXMAN: Did you threaten to overrule him?
> HOWARD: I took advice on what I could and could not do.
> PAXMAN: Did you threaten to overrule him?
> HOWARD: ... and I acted scrupulously in accordance with that advice. I did not overrule Derek Lewis.
> PAXMAN: Did you threaten to overrule him?

And so on.

Paxman's disdainful attitude was revealed in his ever more raised, sceptical eyebrows and his slow and ever lower slump into his seat. It was clear that Paxman regarded his task – and politics more generally – as a joke, as beneath contempt.

Government communications

The changes in political communication, though typically focused on the election and on the party, are not confined to them. Government communications have also been transformed. This has been most often captured in the emergence of the proactive Downing Street press office, in which figures such as Bernard Ingham and Alastair Campbell, press secretaries to Prime Ministers Margaret Thatcher and Tony Blair respectively, have sought to manage and manipulate the coverage given to the Government, and especially to the Prime Minister. The proliferation of media advisers, and the increasing management of media relations that has characterised the transformation of the political party, can also be witnessed in the conduct of modern government.

Secrecy and suspicion have long defined the pervasive attitude of those who run British government, such that civil servants talked of the 'dangers' of publicity, and hence the need to avoid it. The bulwark of this was the Official Secrets Act and the various codes of conduct that it enshrined. Its more human face was 'the Lobby', the exclusive club of journalists given privileged access to government information on an anonymous and unattributable basis.

Now, it might be contended, there is a sense that what is involved is careful manipulation rather than the stonewall of secrecy. The Official

Secrets Act has been reformed, and it has been joined by the Freedom of Information Act, and the Lobby too is no longer the secret club it once was, but the Government still retains considerable power over what is published about its activities. It does so partly because of the legal framework that surrounds it but also because of the professionalisation of its communications responsibilities.

In the British context, the Government's task has been made easier by the apparent decline in investigative journalism. Newspapers have devoted less resources to investigative journalism, partly as a result of the changing strategy of owners and partly in response to the competitive pressures with rival outlets. In the drive for ratings and advertising revenue, broadcasters have also cut the outlets for investigative journalism (the programmes *World in Action* and *This Week* being the obvious victims). These changes in the media skyline have also served to change the form and content of political communications.

Government advertising

Less commonly noted, but in many ways as important, has been the increasing use of advertising by government. British governments have, of course, long used forms of advertising to convey public information – from wartime warnings that 'walls have ears' to reminders in the 1960s to use safety belts in cars and to 'clunk click every trip'. What is new, according to Margaret Scammell, is that neutral public information has become a form of propaganda.[5] The full panoply of advertising techniques, together with a large budget, have been deployed to make adverts that do not simply inform the public of their rights and of the risks they run but rather speak of the care and compassion of their government. (So, for example, we have the campaign to encourage recruits to the teaching profession or that to enable women to re-enter the job market.)

The British Government became in the late 1990s the largest spender on advertising in the UK. According to critics such as Bob Franklin, this spending was devoted less and less to communicating public information and more and more to promoting the interests of the party in government.[6] To the extent that this was the case, this was a further example of the transformation of political communication. Arguably, though, government advertising has always had a propaganda dimension, from the above-mentioned wartime posters to posters encouraging people to drink more milk in the 1950s.

Government online

Early in 2007, news reports claimed that a government website had collapsed after a million protesters had emailed their opposition to a proposal to introduce road pricing. This was an example of a new aspect of political communication, the e-petition. In its struggle to control the way it is represented in the media, the Government had developed forms of communication that attempted to bypass journalists. The Internet provided a weapon in this contest since in principle it allowed direct communication between the public and the Government.

One of the more recent examples of this trend was New Labour's use of the YouTube site to communicate with the public. A number of government ministers recorded interviews which could be viewed on the site. (Journalists gleefully recorded how few hits each received.) Elsewhere, the Number 10 Downing Street site provided opportunities – it was claimed – to engage with government, opportunities which were also made available at the local level. The ostensible purpose of these initiatives was, on the one hand, to make government more transparent and, on the other, to give access to ordinary citizens. The reality has proved rather more complex. Scott Wright argues that many of these official sites function – if they work at all – to convey messages from the centre to the citizen, rather than vice versa.[7]

The new-media technology has played into quite traditional uses and strategies. On the one hand, it has acted as a mouthpiece for officialdom rather than as a forum for consultation and dialogue. On the other, it has provided an opportunity for parties and politicians to speak 'directly' to the public and to avoid the mediating effects of journalists.

Political movements and non-governmental organisations

Although political movements and non-governmental organisations (NGOs) often represent themselves as giving direct voice to public concerns or causes, they too are in the business of political communication. And because such movements have tended to find themselves on the edges of the political mainstream, and as such have been denied access to traditional platforms for political communication, they have been drawn to less conventional ways of conveying their message. They have resorted, in particular, to the use of popular culture, and especially popular music. As Seth Hague and his colleagues have shown, political and social movements have long used musicians and others to represent their cause.[8] Folk music and traditional jazz accompanied the rise of the Campaign for Nuclear Disarmament (CND) in the 1950s, just as punk and reggae became the soundtrack of Rock against Racism in the 1970s.

What we have witnessed more recently are the ways in which NGOs have followed this pattern. Visit the website of almost any 'big name' NGO – Oxfam, Amnesty, etc. – and it is likely that you will find a reference to a celebrity endorsee. These stars do not just endorse the cause; they actively promote it. NGOs can now be found sponsoring rock tours of bands such as Coldplay or events such as the Glastonbury Festival. 'Live8', the campaign to reduce developing countries' debt led by Bob Geldof, is an example of this process. In the jargon of the PR business, this is known as 'experiential marketing'. The message of the movement or the cause is conveyed not so much in the slogans and the stage announcements but in the way the event as a whole is experienced. These same NGOs are also in the business of supplying music downloads, which help to raise money as well as awareness. War Child (www.warchild.org.uk) is the most developed illustration of this trend.

All of these examples represent emerging forms of political communication in which new modes of communication are tied to new technological possibilities. They have given rise to greatly expanded press departments and to the appointment of celebrity liaison officers in NGOs and other such organisations.

Popular communication

The most dramatic example of the new forms of political communication made possible by new-media technologies is, of course, the blog (the web log in which people make their personal reflections, ruminations and confessions available to all on the Internet). Here, if some of the rhetoric is to be believed, we are witnessing the emergence of new forms of popular, political communication. It is new not just because of the format or because of the speed of response it allows, but rather its newness or distinctiveness is alleged to lie in the way it usurps the traditional role of journalists as mediator and interpreter. News and political commentary, it has been suggested, is being wrested from the hands of the profession traditionally entrusted with such things.

There is a contrast to be drawn between the proliferation of individual blogs and the collectivist efforts of campaigning organisations or networks such as Undercurrents (www.beyondtv.org/undercurrents) or Indymedia (www.indymedia.org.uk). The latter forms part of a movement to establish a distinct, alternative perspective on mainstream news organisations and the mainstream news they disseminate. Their aim is to get the news out about particular groups of people who would otherwise be ignored, and to represent political values and opinions that, they believe, are systematically ignored. They are committed to a self-conscious and deliberate rival politics. By contrast, it is impossible to generalise in the same way about blogging and the so-called 'blogosphere', to the extent that these both replicate and diverge from the mainstream in their political content. And where the alternative media appeal to a collective identity, bloggers, at least as media actors, represent themselves as individuals, one voice among many. The point is that, whatever the distinctions to be made between alternative media and blogging, there are many forms of popular, political communication, and the differences between them are not to be captured only in the political ideas or values they espouse. The forms of their organisation and the genres of their communication differ too.

By way of summary, it is apparent that in recent decades we have seen many changes in the form and character of political communication. We have seen new technologies emerge and new opportunities for communication accompanying them. One such example is that of the Conservative leader David Cameron's webpage (www.webcameron.org.uk), in which videos show his days as a classroom assistant or shadowing the police, and other pages reveal his policy positions and much else besides. We have also seen transformations that have to do with regulatory activity and with journalistic practice. The question that hangs over these various changes is what drives them and how they are they to be explained or understood.

Explaining changes in political communication

Many factors can be adduced to account for this history. At one level, and in particular reference to election campaigning, it can be attributed to copying the example of others. The most obvious role model is the USA, where the techniques of the postmodern campaign were developed and exported via the exchange of personnel between, for instance, former

US President Ronald Reagan's campaign team and that of the former UK Prime Minister Margaret Thatcher, or between Tony Blair's New Labour and Bill Clinton. Underlying this cultural exchange were more profound shifts. These involved the breakdown of traditional party and class allegiances, the process of electoral dealignment, which created citizens whose loyalty could not be counted upon, and who could not be courted by the traditional methods. Instead, parties now had to persuade voters that the policies they offered were the ones that people wanted, policies that themselves were carefully tested via market research. Voters were now to be seen as consumers in the political marketplace, and political communications had to change to reflect this.

Changes in the basis of electoral behaviour could be seen as part of larger social trends. David Swanson and Paolo Mancini characterise this as a process of modernisation in which traditional social ties – the church, the trade union, the political party – break down and with them the systems of political allegiance and social order that they supported.[9] The media become the key political intermediaries between the people and those who govern them. As a result, the nature of political communication changes too. It is no longer about the traditional bonds of locality and class, no longer about confirming a social disposition. Instead, it is 'personalised'. Relations with politics are built around the perceived and projected 'personalities' of political leaders. The political leader – and especially their personal characteristics – becomes the focus of political communication. Political leaders compete through the images they convey – David Cameron cycling to work, or Labour's Gordon Brown in earnest conversation with schoolchildren.

For other commentators, this same process is not to be explained by major structural changes but rather by the ways in which certain forms of communication have colonised others. This is the argument advanced by Meyer who contends that the conventions of mass-media communication have come to dictate all forms of communication. The slow, deliberative processes of politics have been replaced by the instantaneous response of the news agenda. The slogan of commercial advertising has become the sound bite of politics. Although such a thesis carries with it an element of technological determination, of politicians, parties and movements adapting to the new technology, whether of broadcasting or later of the Internet, the key lies in the particular form of communication rather than in the hardware that carries the signal.

It might – glibly – be contended that there are as many accounts of the transformation of political communications as there are writers on the topic. In actuality, the range is less varied than this might suggest. There are those who attribute the change to *political* processes and those who blame them on the *media*. There are those who attribute it to the inexorable logic of the *technology*, and those who attribute it to the *political economy* of media. It is not within the scope of this chapter – or the capacity of this author – to judge between these competing accounts. Save to say that how you make sense of these changes will have vital importance to any strategy of reform, if you deem the direction of change to be undesirable for whatever reason. And this is the topic to which we now turn.

The commodification of the public sphere

I will now highlight some of the issues and debates that are emerging in discussions of contemporary political communication. Political communication is not just a matter of standing up and speaking about politics. There is also the matter of attracting the attention of an audience, of getting them to listen to what you have to say. This latter is a question of style and performance. Attention has to be grabbed; it cannot be assumed. Indeed, the audience – the 'public' – is constituted in the act of communication, partly by the mode of address and partly by the technological form in which it exists. Political communication is contained by its medium and by the conventions and principles that organise that medium.

All discussion of political communication incorporates within it, whether explicitly or not, some notion of the public sphere, that sense of space evoked by Jürgen Habermas in which public discourse about politics is able to take place.[10] Recalling the *agora* of Ancient Athens, the public sphere represents an ideal of relatively unconstrained deliberation. Its existence depends, however, on a particular set of conditions, on a particular political economy of media. In eighteenth-century England, this was created by a proliferation of small magazines and a café society. The development of electronic mass media and a press dependent on advertising and on mass circulation created a new economic order and a new set of priorities. News became a product to be valued in the marketplace; and communication more generally changed in a similar fashion. The space available to political deliberation is eroded. Put simply, the documentary on political corruption and injustice, the staple fare of the current-affairs and investigative-journalism series *World in Action*, has been replaced on British television by documentaries on rogue builders and dodgy customer service.

Civic or cynical journalism

The journalist John Lloyd, in a polemical book called *What the Media Are Doing to Our Politics*, has contended that journalists and their employers are threatening the quality of political communication.[11] His attack emerged in the aftermath of the Hutton Inquiry into the question of whether the Blair Government had 'sexed up' intelligence on the threats posed by Iraq. Lloyd was one of the few journalists not to side with the BBC. He – like Lord Hutton himself – believed that the BBC had failed in its journalistic duty.

His wider point was that the default position of British journalism was to regard politics as riddled by deception and corruption. Its most extreme incarnation is to be found in the fortnightly satirical magazine *Private Eye*, where politics is regarded as an entirely worthless, even futile, pursuit, and where all politicians are vain, ignorant, untrustworthy or incompetent – or all four. Where many in the media blamed the increase in political apathy on the failure of politicians to keep their promises, Lloyd took the view that public apathy and disillusionment owed more to the media's treatment of politicians than to their actual behaviour. In his history of political journalism, Steven Barnett supports Lloyd's view, to the extent that he argues that journalism has moved from a position of deference to politicians in the 1950s to disdain and now to cynicism.[12]

Addressing this erosion of trust, the philosopher Onora O'Neill has drawn attention to the lack of accountability in journalism.[13] Unlike the politicians they attack, journalists are not publicly answerable for what they do. As a profession, journalism is almost entirely unregulated, save for the laws of libel and secrecy that apply to all public pronouncements. Some might say that this was a condition of freedom of speech, but this would be to misunderstand the role of journalists. They are not there to speak for themselves – if they were it might not be appropriate to regulate their activities; but they are there for the public, to provide reliable information, to pursue the public interest. Such a duty requires that they can be relied upon to fulfil their duty, and the guarantee of this lies in some system of regulation and accountability.

There are two issues here. The first concerns the question of whether the quality of political communication is determined by the practice of journalists (and the media more generally). The second is whether, if the media are to blame, a system of accountability would make any material difference.

The future of political journalism

The issue of the regulation of journalism swiftly shades into one about the future of it. A whole spate of issues are, of course, raised by the advent of new media, but the one that has attracted much attention concerns its implications for the practice and profession of journalism. As the number of bloggers grows daily, as camera phones and the like record news events, so it seems that the business of reporting, or commenting on, the world is no longer confined to the professional journalist. Indeed, those very professional journalists are themselves increasingly drawing upon the contributions of their audiences for their content. The blogger, it might be suggested, threatens all hierarchically organised forms of political communication, whether the newspaper or the official webpage.

Regulating the new public sphere

Just as there are debates about the state of the traditional public sphere, so questions are being raised about the 'new public sphere' of the World Wide Web. For some writers, the Internet makes possible a recreation of the near ideal of the public sphere to which Jürgen Habermas alludes in *The Structural Transformation of the Public Sphere*.[14] The costs of entry to the new public sphere are minimal; many voices can flourish amidst the virtual café society of the World Wide Web. It is unregulated and free. Although, of course, it is not quite like this. The Internet is being commercialised and commodified; the once-independent websites MySpace and YouTube have been taken over by News Corporation and Google respectively. Meanwhile, governments in China, Singapore and elsewhere continue (with the cooperation of Google, etc.) to regulate the virtual space occupied by their citizens. But independent of these features of the political economy of the Internet, there are normative questions about the need for (and form of) regulation of it in any case.

Celebrity politics and the dumbing-down debate

The trends in political communication that we described earlier have issued in one particular trend: the emergence of the celebrity politician. David Cameron's appearance on Jonathan Ross's show is one example – as was then Prime Minister Tony Blair's on Des O'Connor's light-entertainment show or former Conservative Party leader William Hague on Jeremy Clarkson's chat show; as was George Galloway's appearance in the celebrity version of the reality TV programme *Big Brother* or Charles Kennedy hosting the satirical quiz *Have I Got News for You?* In each case, the elected politician seeks to reach a new and larger public and in doing so to cultivate a persona that will secure votes. In a similar way, political parties have sought lists of celebrities to endorse their campaigns, so Bono of the group U2 addresses the Labour Party conference and actor Arnold Schwarzenegger the Conservative conference. The parties and politicians have learnt to communicate in new ways in new settings.

Elsewhere, there is celebrity politics of a different kind. Here social movements increasingly deploy celebrities, particularly from the world of popular music, to lead or at least to represent their causes. Bob Geldof, mentioned above, is probably the best-known such celebrity politician, and his Live8 in June 2005 was a classic example of a celebrity-led political campaign. Geldof and his fellow musicians deployed the familiar, traditional arts of political communication. They made speeches; they lobbied politicians. But they also communicated by other means, most notably through music. What is intriguing about such examples is how musicians, actors and sports stars acquire the ability and the right to speak out about politics.

The emergence of these different types of celebrity politician has provoked a debate about the consequences for democracy. For their critics, they are symptoms of the declining quality of political communication, a decline that is also to be witnessed in the fall in the quality of news media – the tabloidisation of broadcasting and broadsheets. For their supporters, they represent a recognition of the need to remain relevant and to learn to adapt to new forms of communication.

One particular example of this trend, and of the debates provoked by it, was the ITV television game show, *Vote for Me*.[15] Broadcast in 2005, it was structured like *Pop Idol* and other such talent competitions, but rather than the winner securing a recording contract, they obtained the opportunity to contest a seat in the forthcoming general election. The competitors were set tasks; there was a panel of judges; and there were regular public votes to eliminate contestants. The ostensible (public-service) purpose of the show was to re-engage disillusioned voters with politics. For the programme's critics, it was another example of the 'banalisation' of politics under commercial pressure, disguised in the rhetoric of public-service broadcasting.

Style and performance as political communication

Underlying debates about dumbing down are larger ones about the very nature of communication itself. What is apparent now – and what has always, you might argue, been true – is that communication is not simple about a communicator, a message and a receiver. It is not a simple matter of an object (the message) being moved from one place to another. The process is much more complicated, and indeed rarely follows this straightforward path. As writers such as John Corner, Stuart Hall and John B. Thompson, among many others, have noted, the issue is rarely the message; it is the meaning, and this is dependent on many things, of which the written or spoken words are only one element.[16] Meaning is conveyed through, or inferred from, tones of voice and facial gestures. It depends on the resources and skills of both the speaker and the hearer. What happens is as much a matter of performance as mere utterance. We need only to think of the complex meanings, and the disputes about those meanings, that have taken place around political posters.

During the campaign in the run-up to the 2005 UK general election, the Labour Party produced a series of advertisements in which Michael Howard, the leader of the Conservative opposition, was held up to ridicule – there was a play, for example, on the idea that 'pigs might fly'. This idea, and others used by Labour, became the centre of a fierce dispute. The advertisements, it was claimed, were anti-Semitic and, as such, constituted a vicious attack upon Howard, who is Jewish. Whether or not this was the intention, the point is that this dispute brought home the complex character of political communication and the meanings generated by it. A similar row was generated when the Conservatives used advertisements in which Tony Blair was given red staring eyes ('devil eyes' as they were dubbed). The British Advertising Standards Authority banned the ads, reinforcing the thought that images can 'wound'.

A further implication of this is that political communication is not confined to the formally defined arena of politics. Political communication can be seen to be taking place when musicians strum guitars and when audiences laugh at comedians. Ideas about politics, and political values, may be invoked during soap operas such as *EastEnders* and current-affairs programmes such as *Newsnight*. Although UK soap operas typically avoid all references to conventional politics of any kind, it is certainly arguable that, in seeking to represent the 'real world' (as a self-contained community), they evoke an account of 'common sense' in which viewers are led to see that world operating in a particular way, driven by particular attitudes and actions, some of which are 'good' and some 'bad'. To this extent, soaps might be said to represent a view of what is normal and acceptable in our understanding of power and its operation.

And the headlines again …

In the short period covered by this chapter, we have seen a radical transformation in the nature of political communication. For some writers, this change is symptomatic of a new order, one captured in what Colin Crouch labels as 'post-democracy'.[17] This is a world in which the vestiges of democracy remain – the formal institutions and processes – but the reality is marked by elite control, a control engineered through the use of the media to give the *appearance* of populist democracy, while the exercise of real power is confined to the elite. The media presents the rituals of democracy, inviting us to share in the semblance of political participation, while we are denied its actuality.

There is a danger, however, of being swept up in such dystopian visions. It is certainly true that new technologies have transformed the opportunities for political communications, but the uses to which such technologies have been put have been affected by the regulatory structure that has accompanied their introduction. Both the USA and the UK have essentially the same technologies of mass communication, but their uses still vary considerably. The UK continues to ban political advertising on television; it is hard to imagine the US system managing without it. And while the advent of the Internet, as with television decades earlier, is transforming political communication, it is doing so within a regulatory framework that qualifies talk of inevitable changes of one kind or another.

At the same time, we have also seen a radical transformation in the way in which political communication is analysed and studied. We may now all note that 'politics exists only on television', but political science (and many other areas of the social sciences) was relatively slow to notice this. Textbooks on British politics only very gradually began to introduce chapters on 'the media'. There were few academic articles on the subject and very little funded research. In recent years, this situation has changed dramatically. Now every textbook has its statutory chapter on the media. There are now journals and research centres dedicated to the subject. We now know much more about how political communications are organised, what they involve and what influence they have. More and more students leave university having studied the mass media, and many aspire to careers within them. If anything, the forms of political communication have changed very little compared to the attention devoted to them. Indeed, you might contend that contemporary British culture is marked less by what it contains and how it is disseminated and more by how it is read and experienced by a people sensitised by the plethora of signs and symbols that mark their day, trained in the business of deconstruction and actively engaged in judging the performances of would-be performers and would-be celebrities.

Notes

1 T. Meyer with L. Hinchman, *Media Democracy: How the Media Colonize Politics* (Cambridge: Polity, 2002).
2 P. Norris, *Electoral Change since 1945* (Oxford: Blackwell, 1996).
3 B. Franklin, *Packaging Politics*, 2nd edn (London: Arnold, 2004), pp. 120, 139.
4 S. Barnett (2002) 'Will a Crisis in Journalism Provoke a Crisis in Democracy?' *Political Quarterly*, 73 (4) (2002): 400–8.
5 M. Scammell, *Designer Politics: How Elections Are Won* (London: Macmillan, 1995).
6 Franklin, *Packaging Politics*.
7 S. Wright, 'Electrifying Democracy: Ten Years of Policy and Practice', *Parliamentary Affairs*, 59 (2) (2006): 236–49.
8 S. Hague, J. Street and H. Savigny, 'The Voice of the People? Musicians as Political Actors', *Cultural Politics*, 4 (1) (2008): 5–23.
9 D. Swanson and P. Mancini (eds.), *Politics, Media and Modern Democracy* (New York: Praeger, 1996).
10 J. Habermas, *The Structural Transformation of the Public Sphere* (Cambridge: Polity, 1992).
11 J. Lloyd, *What the Media Are Doing to Our Politics* (London: Constable, 2004).
12 Barnett, 'Will a Crisis in Journalism Provoke a Crisis in Democracy?'
13 O. O'Neill, *The Philosophy of Trust* (London: BBC Books, 2002).
14 Habermas, *The Structural Transformation of the Public Sphere*.

15 V. Cardo and J. Street, '*Vote for Me*: Playing at Politics', in K. Riegert (ed.), *Politicotainment: Television's Take on the Real* (New York: Peter Lang, 2007), pp. 109–28.

16 J. Corner, *Television Form and Public Address* (London: Edward Arnold, 1995); S. Hall, 'Encoding/Decoding', in S. Hall, D. Hobson, A. Lowe and P. Willis (eds.), *Culture, Society and the Media* (London: Routledge, 1980), pp. 56–90; J. Thompson, 'Mass Communication and Modern Culture: Contribution to a Critical Theory of Ideology', *Sociology*, 22 (3) (1988): 359–83.

17 C. Crouch, *Post-Democracy* (Cambridge: Polity, 2004).

5

Contemporary Britain and its regions

Modernity, postmodernity and regions

The notion of regional culture has been disparaged in the contemporary period. Modernisation – and its bedfellows, standard-isation and homogenisation – were assumed to erode the importance of 'local attachments'.[1] The creation of welfare states and national education and media systems typically meant that, for social scientists at least, the 'local' or 'regional' was a residual category of diminishing significance. Similarly, postmodernity – and its bedfellow, globalisation – is seen, typically, as attenuating further the 'local' dimension of life. In this view, in the contemporary era, cultures are formed by global flows of people, commodities and images and not in 'closed' localities.[2] Quite often, especially in cultural and academic commentary, the very idea of regional culture is viewed as normatively problematic, hinting at backwardness and reaction.[3] At the very least, throughout most of the modern period, the term 'regional' has been used to denote something culturally 'inferior' or 'subordinate'.[4]

This chapter is concerned with whether we can identify particular-ities in social practice and cultural products that might mark a discern-ibly regional culture in the UK. There has been a strongly normative dimension to this debate since the publication of Richard Hoggart's *The Uses of Literacy* was published in 1957.[5] This book was both a foun-dational text for British cultural studies and one that identified the impacts of mass culture on distinctive local forms of working-class life, which were negative in Hoggart's view. Ian Jack's recent contribution to the debate compares Arnold Bennett's depiction of life at the beginning of the twentieth century in the Potteries – an industrial district in the

English Midlands – with life there today and questions whether it is 'so fundamentally different from life in London that it has nourished a new, refreshing kind of literary sensibility, which the metropolis ... has been too slow to recognise'.[6] Writing in *The Guardian* (formerly *The Manchester Guardian*), Jack maintains that the transformation of England since the beginning of the twentieth century has destroyed local particularities:

> England was many different places then. With the end (or at least drastic shrinking) of pot-making, mining, smelting, weaving, spinning, farming, fishing, engineering, church-going, and the settling over all of the great *pax consumia*, it is hard now to see it. Like the 'Manchester' that used to precede this newspaper's title, differences and distinctions have vanished.[7]

More emphatically, as early as 1974, the then Director of the Northern Arts Association, responding to the poet Basil Bunting's call for a programme to promote 'Northumbrian art', described it as 'a bit fatuous'. He continued, 'I'm not from these parts. I'm from the Home Counties. I regard my mission as bringing the arts to the North. Northumberland is dead, and so is its so-called folk culture. So are the pits.'[8] Yet, despite these assumptions and those of modernisation theory, the rise of the region as a terrain of political action is visible across the globe. Political science has devoted much attention to the resurgence of 'territorial politics', especially in Europe, in recent times.[9] More generally, 'despite the apparent post-modern fragmentation of identity, discourses of belonging constructed around place remain important.'[10] In its cultural, rather than obviously political form, 'regionalism may mean the spiritual and intellectual activity by which a region tries to oppose the standardizing effects of the capital.'[11] This chapter is concerned with contemporary regional culture and the processes of its production and reproduction in the UK, focusing particularly on the periphery for reasons that will be explained below.

The emergence of the 'new regionalism' in Europe, including the reassertion of 'small nationalisms', while typically associated with the promotion of particular economic and welfare demands, has frequently contained a cultural dimension. Regions are contained within a physical landscape but are social and cultural constructs that embody historically contingent practices and discourses in which actors produce and give meaning to bounded material and symbolic worlds in order to create intersubjective meanings.[12] Memories shared by their constituents give regions (and societies in general) their (moral) particularity.[13] Thus: 'the revalorization of regional culture is an important part of the creation of a modern regional identity.'[14] Regionalism can be understood as a '*performative discourse* which aims to impose as legitimate a new definition of the frontiers and to get people to know and recognize the *region* that is thus delimited in opposition to the dominant definition'.[15] This is evident, for instance, in the rise of Scottish and Welsh nationalism in the UK, where the revival of cultural distinction in art and literature has been an important contributor to contemporary politics suggesting the persistence of territorial ontologies, which draw upon a shared sense of historical belonging.[16]

Whether Scotland and Wales should be viewed through the prism of debates about regionalism, however, is a moot question. There is a large literature about nationalism and national identity which can be brought to bear on this subject. Moreover, Scotland and Wales contain their own regional and local identities: divisions between North and South Wales and between Edinburgh and Glasgow, for instance, represent important cultural axes worthy of attention in their own right in relation to debates about regional culture. In order to explore the idea of regional culture, this chapter pays special attention to representations of the English North. There are other perspectives, but a Northern English angle is particularly useful for illuminating the nature of regionality in Britain.

Roads into London

Defining a regional culture is a difficult task. Raymond Williams described 'culture' as 'one of the two or three most complicated words in the English Language'.[17] The adjective 'regional' further complicates the matter. Williams notes that 'regional' has a complex cultural history. For instance, traditionally in England, defining a work of literature as a 'regional novel' may be a 'simple acknowledgement of a distinct place and way of life, though probably more often this is also a limiting judgement' – novels written in London, no matter how parochial, are never 'regional'.[18] Thus, within the sociology of taste and discernment, we can highlight the important 'metropolitan-provincial cultural distinction'.[19]

Following Williams's injunction, in the British context, it is necessary to begin by acknowledging the long-standing and entrenched cultural, as well as economic and administrative dominance of London over the rest of the country. Devolution to Scotland and Wales in the long run may lead to the creation of stronger counterweights to London's dominance over British life, but the tide of history here is powerful. As Ford Madox Ford noted in *The Soul of London* published in 1905:

> In England administration has remained with fair constancy at Westminster, near enough to the centre of the country. Wealth has always come into England by the Thames at London. At any rate in later centuries, the tendency has been for the Administration to settle near the centres of wealth, and the combined attractions have made the tract of marsh and flat ground in the lower basin of the river the centre of the Arts, of the Industries, of the Recreations and the moral 'tone', not for England alone, but for wider regions of the earth.[20]

In England all roads lead to London. The centripetal and 'standardizing effects' of London are exceptionally strong. Prior to devolution Britain was frequently described as the most centralised country in the Organisation for Economic Co-operation and Development in terms of its system of government. Within England, the autonomy of local government remains severely circumscribed, raising a comparatively small proportion of its own income. Regional economic inequalities are wide and widened significantly during the 1980s and 1990s. The traditional (heavy) industries, including coalmining, steel-making and engineering, which had dominated the populous parts of the North, declined rapidly in the last quarter of the twentieth century. Moreover, newer industries, including high technology and financial and other producer services grew disproportionately in and around London during the same period, in the context of policies of financial liberalisation pursued by successive governments after the Conservative election victory of 1979.

It was during this period that the term 'North–South Divide' was introduced, notably in the media, to describe not just a widening economic gap but also a sense of diverging political and cultural outlooks. By the early 2000s, the term 'North–South Divide' had fallen out of fashion, and the media tended to focus on the 'regeneration' of the larger Northern cities, such as Manchester, Leeds and Newcastle upon Tyne. This new script tends to emphasise the transformation of city centres, the provision of new cultural infrastructure and visitor attractions, more or less explicitly, suggesting that an 'old-fashioned' Northern culture has been left behind, along with the industries and communities that spawned it. This account – which is offered by some in the North as well as the national media – overlooks the fact that while the northern regions shared to some degree in a sustained period of national economic growth around the turn of the twenty-first century, the evidence that relative inequalities have been closed, at best, is sparse.[21]

'Structures of feeling'

According to Raymond Williams,

> We need to distinguish between three levels of culture, even in its most general definition. There is the lived culture of a particular time and place, only fully accessible to those living in that time and place. There is the recorded culture, of every kind, from art to the most everyday facts: the culture of a period. There is also, as the factor connecting lived culture and period cultures, the culture of selective tradition.[22]

The combination of these factors determines the 'structure of feeling' of a time and place that characterises 'approaches in tones and argument' and which is 'deeply and widely possessed' in a society.[23] Although Williams' original use of the term 'structure of feeling' in *The Long Revolution* was in relation to generational shifts in cultural sensibility, the term appeared throughout his writing, and we can adapt this hermeneutic device to the understanding of particular places.[24] In the epilogue to his excavation of the roots of the English imagination, Peter Ackroyd, in searching for 'many striking continuities in English culture', identifies

> the territorial imperative, by means of which a local area can influence or guide all those who inhabit it. The example of London has often been adduced ... English writers and artists, English composers and folk-singers, have been haunted by this sense of place, in which the echoic simplicities of past use and past tradition sanctify a certain spot of ground.[25]

Williams has drawn attention also to the contested nature of cultural understandings. He argues that in any particular period, 'there is a central system of practices, meanings and values, which we can properly call dominant and effective.'[26] At the same time, though, there are 'alternative' and 'oppositional' forms of culture, which are not part of the dominant effective culture and which can be distinguished between 'emergent' forms (of new meanings and values) and 'residual' forms, that is, 'meanings and values which cannot be verified or cannot be expressed in the terms of the dominant culture, are nevertheless lived and practised on the basis of the residue – cultural as well as social – of some previous social formation.'[27] These cultural tendencies might be usefully analysed within the context of the ebbs and flows of the 'metropolitan-provincial cultural distinction' and the extent to which 'residual' and 'oppositional' cultures are associated with particular places.[28]

'Northernness' as a 'structure of feeling'

Ian Taylor *et al.* have operationalised some of these concepts to understand the culture of local feeling and everyday life in the North of England, identifying a distinctive 'Northernness' through interviews with groups of people in Sheffield and Manchester.[29] The 'Northernness' expressed by their respondents is rooted in the region's overall industrial history and refers to 'a set of values (e.g. collectivism and a sense of community, but also, perhaps, of hard physical labour – "graft" – masculinism and insularity) which distinguish it from the South of England, from the Midlands and from other parts of the country'.[30] Far from seeing this old culture obliterated by the forces of contemporary social and economic change, Taylor *et al.* are concerned with charting the renegotiation of local difference in the light of these changes.

The accounts of the cities offered by Taylor *et al.* are concerned with the interaction of their topography, their 'structures of feeling' (linked to their particular industrial histories from the nineteenth century) and the exercise of memory and myth that are used to represent the facts of local identity. In the case of Sheffield, its geographical location and its historic dependence on the cutlery and steel industries, together with its strongly Labour political traditions, helped to define its identity as a 'city apart', albeit one with 'a marked sense of personal and civic autonomy' derived from the attitudes of the skilled cutlery workers, known locally as the 'Little Mesters'.[31] By contrast, Manchester's historic role as 'Cottonopolis' and city of free trade dominated by 'Manchester Men' – among the richest in the British Empire – means that as well as containing working-class and socialist traditions it is also characterised by 'a self-confident and even brash form of classless populism, orientated to the pursuit of wealth and personal success through commercial enterprise'.[32] This Mancunian structure of feeling 'sees itself connected up to a larger world and larger set of possibilities, rather than simply an industrial Northern city caught within a narrow labour metaphysic'.[33]

'Madchester': 'Northernness' and mass culture

An important question concerns the interactions of this 'structure of feeling' with the larger forces of mass culture. In this context, Dave Haslam has explored the history of popular music in Manchester: 'You can't write about pop music without writing about Manchester and you can't write about Manchester without writing about pop music.'[34] Haslam, who was the principal DJ at the legendary Hacienda club in its heyday in the late 1980s and early 1990s, charts the musical tradition in the North-West from the music halls that produced Gracie Fields and George Formby through Northern soul and *The Smiths* to the 'Madchester' years of the late 1980s and early 1990s (which were chronicled in the film *24 Hour Party People*) and on to the contemporary club scene. Despite these changing forms, Haslam sees a substantive continuity in so far as the popular culture of the North-West remains underpinned by a 'sense of loss' that results from 'the waves of change' that have continually crashed over the city. These themes have been recounted by Bernard Sumner of *Joy Division*: 'By the age of twenty-two, I'd had quite a lot of loss in my life. The place where I used to live, where I had my happiest memories, all that had gone. All that was left was a chemical factory. I realised then I could never go back to that happiness. So there's this void. For me *Joy Division* was about the death of my community and my childhood.'[35] Haslam sees the musical tradition as characterised by an essential open-mindedness, an oppositional quality and a self-assertion that produces 'discontented visionaries' marked by independence and non-conformity as well as an underlying melancholy. He identifies these traits in the broader culture of the region, which, in turn, is a product of a particular history:

> Perhaps Lancashire's cotton trade – renowned for importing cotton, then colouring and reworking it, and then selling it on – is the pattern for this kind of non-precious, non-purist attitude and perhaps [Manchester's] non-parochial attitudes were also born years ago, in the mix thrown up by the industrial revolution: Irish immigrants, German and Jewish businessman, Scottish engineers and Lancashire mill girls. The more recent links with Jamaica,

West Africa, Pakistan and India have built on this, opened the city's eyes to new experience, and increased the hybrid nature of modern Manchester.[36]

Reflecting on the nature of Northern soul – the dance-hall scene centred on the Wigan Casino, a celebrated nightclub, which promoted US soul music, especially Motown – Joanne Hollows and Katie Milestone see it as imbued with 'Northernness' and representing 'a refusal of the South's claims to legitimacy and distinction'.[37]

> Because the scene was organized around old American records, it didn't need London's economic and cultural power in order to survive. In this way, as both a provincial and basically a working-class form, northern soul rejects the legitimacy of more powerful taste formations within the United Kingdom (while also being unable to displace them).[38]

Instead, they claim, Northern soul was inspired by a set of interregional affiliations between Northern England and the US 'Rustbelt', notably Detroit. These distinctive forms of music suggest that although continually threatened by the North's significant other, London, and by the forces of globalisation, Northernness is able to reproduce itself, albeit within the context of enduring inequalities in cultural and material capital.

Our friends in the North: 'Northernness' and literary representation

Taylor *et al.* maintain that local and regional media in the form of local newspapers and regional-television news broadcasts help to reproduce local and regional culture.[39] In reality, though, this is one field where consolidation and centralisation are eroding local distinctiveness and quality.[40] Nevertheless, the notion of a distinctive Northern culture, embodying the themes identified by Halsam, continues to be reproduced in television dramas destined for a national audience. Acclaimed films and television programmes such as Alan Bleasdale's *Boys from the Blackstuff*, set in Liverpool; Paul Bucknor and Simon Beaufoy's *The Full Monty* set in Sheffield; Lee Hall's *Billy Elliot*; Ian La Frenais and Dick Clements' oeuvre, including *The Likely Lads* and *Whatever Happened to the Likely Lads?* and *Auf Wiedersehen Pet* and Peter Flannery's *Our Friends in the North* (originally a play for the Royal Shakespeare Company) – all set in the north-east of England and exploring aspects of its 'Geordie' identity – take the region as both subject and setting, and each suggest the culture has a distinctive quality at odds with that of the South but formed in relation to it, although some of these writers are no longer permanent residents of the region.

An important regional cultural difference might be viewed in the contrasting ethos of the two major British soap operas *Coronation Street* (set in 'Weatherfield', a fictional working-class district of Manchester) and *EastEnders* (set in Albert Square, in the fictional 'London Borough of Walford'):

> Indeed, *Coronation Street* and *EastEnders* offer politically-opposed
> ways of imagining the British working class. *Coronation Street*
> presents a socialistic community where people basically want to
> help each other out, and suffering is greeted with compassion …
> *EastEnders* offers a blackly Tebbit-flavoured vision where everybody
> is perennially poised to rip off their neighbours, and anybody who
> does show even a flicker of compassion – like Dot Branning – is
> invariably exposed as a dupe. As one Corrie scriptwriter put it: 'If
> you are run over on *Coronation Street*, somebody will take you in and
> give you a cup of tea. If you are run over on Albert Square, they'll
> steal your wallet and shag your wife while you bleed to death.'[41]

Most viewers of these soaps will see some truth in Johann Hari's carica-
ture. But the different imaginaries of British working-class culture are regionally rooted. In the case of North-East England, by end of the nineteenth century, despite the presence of a powerful bourgeoisie, accord-
ing to Colls, 'the working class presence was pre-eminent.'[42] Historically, regionality and class have been entwined and conflated: the working class was Northern and the North was working class. Regions were marked by the localised character of their class practices.[43] So the competing soap operas present contrasting regional imaginaries, as well as class ones. 'Ducking and diving' and 'wheeling and dealing' represent the self-perceptions of the East End of London according to one socio-
anthropological study, which identifies a distinctive tradition based on the blurring of notions of entrepreneurship and criminality, which, for instance, can be seen embodied in some of the principal characters in *EastEnders*.[44] This can be contrasted with solidaristic self-perception embodied in the art of the North.

One confluence of class, region and literature is found at the Live Theatre in Newcastle upon Tyne, the seat of 'Geordie High Culture'.[45] Notably, the theatre has been the proving ground for a set of performers typically associated with the presentation of the North-East in film, television and theatre. But it has also been the focus for a group of writers – including novelists, playwrights and poets – for whom the North-East is both setting and subject, albeit not necessarily the only one. The contemporary writers associated with the theatre include Lee Hall, Peter Flannery, Tom Hadaway, Alan Plater, Sean O'Brien and Julia Darling. But this contemporary literature draws upon a longer tradition that can be traced back to the 1930s. Harold Heslop in the 1930s and Jack Common in the 1950s contributed major novels about working-class life in the region. Sid Chaplin, from the 1940s onwards, wrote novels and short stories first about mining life in County Durham (*The Leaping Lad and Other Stories* [1947]; *The Thin Seam* [1950]) and then about the changes wrought by modernisation on Tyneside in the 1960s (*The Day of the Sardine* [1961] and *The Watchers and the Watched* [1962]), which amount to what D. J. Taylor calls a 'case history of a disappearing world'.[46] During the 1970s, Alex Glasgow and James Mitchell, among other things, wrote screenplays for the seminal *When the Boat Comes In*, which depicted life in the North-East in the inter-war period. A key figure was C. P. Taylor, a prolific playwright not only for the Live Theatre but also for the West End and Royal Shakespeare Company, and his themes were broad: in *Good* (1981) according to Alan Plater, he produced 'arguably the definitive piece written about the Holocaust in the English-speaking theatre'.[47] Glasgow, Plater and Chaplin collaborated on *Close the Coalhouse Door* (1969), a play produced at the end of the 1960s which foretold the end of mining and the particular masculinities it had produced and shaped the literature and art of the following decades. Lee Hall has described the artistic ethos of the Live Theatre as combining 'the irreverent, the pathetic, the wryness towards political cant while being thoroughly informed by a socialist perspective'.[48]

This ethos is exemplified in *Billy Elliot: The Musical* (2006), the libretto of which was written by Lee Hall, with music by Elton John and direction by Stephen Daldry, which opened in London's West End in 2006. *Billy Elliot: The Musical* presents a subtle and ultimately sympathetic account of life in the County Durham village of Easington during the 1984/5 miners' strike – perhaps more so than the film *Billy Elliot* (2000), which had a somewhat different sensibility, although the screenplay was also by Hall. The performance is preceded by newsreel footage of the Durham Miner's Gala – then Europe's largest annual working-class demonstration – at the time of the nationalisation of the coal industry in

1947, while the opening and closing scenes have the Easington Miner's Lodge banner as their backdrop. The musical reaches its crescendo with what can only be described as a hymn to socialism, which represents a rare addition to the canon of West End musicals.

The recent literary representations of the North-East have been concerned with life after the death of coalmining and shipbuilding. These changes were anticipated in the later work of Chaplin and that of Plater. They include the transformation of gender and ethnic relations and the built environment that was produced by nineteenth-century industrialisation. Yet much of the contemporary literature being produced about the North demonstrates a concern and awareness of how the past continues to shape the present. In Gordon Burn's novel *The North of England Home Service* (2003), set mainly on Tyneside, one of the characters, an incomer, notes of the former mining village in which he lives, 'The interpenetratedness of the life that had been lived under ground for generations and the modern lives currently being lived above ground was something that was constantly making itself felt.'[49] Among other things, the novel captures in detail the dislocating effects of social and economic change for Ray Cruddas, a once-famous Geordie comic and his minder, a former boxer. Especially through its depiction of Ray's retro working-man's club, which offers a kind of ersatz historical 'Northernness' to contemporary audiences, Burn's novel offers not just an elegy about the place, and its place in the English past, but a reflection on how we think about that past.

Landscape and history: 'Northernness' as poetic muse

The theme of the past and what we make of it recurs in contemporary literature from and about the North. In *Another World*, her novel about war and memory set on Tyneside, Pat Barker says, 'you should go to the past, looking not for messages or warnings, but simply to be humbled by the weight of human experience that has preceded the brief flicker of your own days.'[50] Historical understanding in narratives of regional identity is frequently interwoven with an emphasis on the role of landscape as a reference point, for, in the modern era, as Seamus Heaney notes, 'it is to the stable element, the land itself, that we must look for continuity.'[51] As Sue Clifford and Angela King stress, landscape is largely a cultural artefact, a social product, a cultural projection on a specific place.[52] It is replete with cultural and ideological connotations, while history, as

Catherine Brace has shown, is appropriated in order to 'set apart' a landscape as distinctive.[53] Such 'topophilia' speaks of the 'affective bond between people and place or setting'.[54] Landscape and dialect are intimately related because of the relationship of the latter to topographical nomenclature. Thus, Sarah Greaves observes, 'a dialect belongs to a landscape, that is to say a geography and biology, a history and a body of myth and legend'.[55] The cultural construction of regions is facilitated by the 'baptism of essential landmarks'; indeed, 'space cannot be known, shared and memorized except by language', while regions are associated with a 'music of place names'.[56] And, through 'the stimulus of names, our sense of place is enhanced'.[57] In England, class, region and dialect are intertwined, for, as Raymond Williams notes, 'the only class speech in England is that of the upper and middle classes; the speech of working class people is not socially but regionally varied.'[58]

These concerns can be identified in a clutch of poems from the British Isles that were published from the 1960s onward.[59] These poems 'respond to devolutionary and internationalizing pressures by crossing localized memoir with historical excavation'.[60] Such poems include Basil Bunting's *Briggflatts* (1966), Geoffrey Hill's *Mercian Hymns* (1971), Ted Hughes' *Remains of Elmet* (1979) and Gillian Clarke's *The King of Britain's Daughter*, all of which reassess the historical geography of the Atlantic archipelago. More recently, Katrina Porteous's *Dunstanburgh* (2004) similarly melds concerns with landscape and natural and human history. They represent, in Seamus Heaney's words, a search for 'Englands of the mind', in which 'a kind of piety toward their local origins, has made them look in, rather than up, to England'.[61] According to John Kerrigan, 'aware that history remakes places, and acutely sensitive to the dislocating effect of modernization, these sequences are hungry for vestiges of situated particularity.'[62] Moreover, they signal 'a resistance to bureaucratic centralism and the homogenizing power of globalization'.[63]

The local epics that have emerged from British and Irish poetry, while eschewing provincialism and nostalgia and frequently transgressing modern borders, demonstrate a profound historical sensibility: 'all poets steer by the light of vanished stars, their chosen precursors or admired quasi-ancestral voices.'[64] In such epics, modern nations are fragmented and contingent and embody a complex historical geography, as in Geoffrey Hill's Mercia:

> King of the perennial holly-groves, the riven sandstone: overlord
> of the M5: architect of the historic rampart and ditch, the citadel at

Tamworth, the summer hermitage in Holy Cross: guardian of the
Welsh Bridge and the Iron Bridge: contractor to the desirable new
estates: saltmaster: money-changer: commissioner for oaths: mar-
tyrologist: the friend of Charlemagne.
'I liked that', said Offa, 'sing it again'.[65]

The place of the region

This chapter has outlined the dimensions of a distinctively Northern
'structure of feeling' in England, as a means of shedding light on the
nature of regional culture in contemporary Britain. 'The North' is by
no means the only regional category by which we can explore this idea,
but it is a very useful one. A concern with regional culture in Britain
can be found in the tension between 'dominant' and 'residual' cultural
forms, which are found along the metropolitan–provincial cultural
axis. These might be seen as examples of what Sigmund Freud termed
'the narcissism of small differences', which he described as 'a convenient and relatively innocuous way of satisfying the tendency to aggres-
sion and facilitating solidarity within the community'.[66] The most
impressive products of contemporary regional culture, however, are not
those that express a simple concern with the region but that situate the
region in its historical geography, including its relationships with other
places, notably London and the South, but also with the places which
have been the sources of flows of people and ideas, which have produced
a 'hybridised' contemporary culture, but nevertheless one contained
within a particular cultural landscape.[67] Into this category would fall,
among other things, Peter Flannery's *Our Friends in the North*, Gordon
Burn's *North of England Home Service, Billy Elliot: The Musical* and, perhaps
above all, Basil Bunting's *Briggflatts*, which, according to Sarah Greaves,
is concerned with the 'poetics of dwelling'.[68]

Normatively, the idea of regional culture – or 'provincialism' –
remains important because in a period of quickening human, cultural and material flows, 'it signifies rootedness, belonging and a
local distinctiveness not yet inflected by the universalizing claims of
globalism.'[69] As Jeremy Seabrook observes in relation to regional change
in Britain: 'If the pain of passing of provincial life has been denied, it is
because everything that succeeded it has been tendentiously and insist-
ently portrayed not as a mixture of the gains and losses that accompany
all social change, but as irresistible progress towards a beckoning future
over which dispute is not possible.'[70] The elegiac character of much

writing about the contemporary North can be located in the interstices of the attachments and longings in which the problematic of community is located and which has a particular character in marginalised communities. As Michael Sandel argues:

> The global media and markets that shape our lives beckon us to a world beyond boundaries and belonging. But the civic resources we need to master these forces, or at least to contend with them, are still to be found in the places and stories, memories and meaning, incidents and identities, that situate us in the world and give our lives their moral particularity.[71]

Regional life in Britain continues to exhibit a particular 'structure of feeling' which is both reflected in – and the result of – forms of cultural production that continue to explore its moral particularity.

Acknowledgement

This chapter draws on work funded by the Leverhulme Trust. I am grateful to Paul Rubinstein, Richard Foster and Leanne Bunn and the editors of this volume for comments on an earlier draft.

Notes

1 F. W. Morgan, 'Three Aspects of Regional Consciousness', *Sociological Review*, 31 (1) (1939): 68–88.
2 S. Hall, 'Culture, Community, Nation', *Cultural Studies*, 7 (3) (1993): 349–63.
3 A. Amin, 'Regions Unbound: Towards a New Politics of Space', *Geografiska Annaler*, 86B (1) (2004): 33–44.
4 R. Williams, *Keywords* (London: Fontana, 1983), p. 253.
5 Richard Hoggart (1957) *The Uses of Literacy*, London, Chatto & Windus.
6 I. Jack, 'Blurring the Line', *The Guardian Review*, 25 October 2003), p. xx.
7 Jack, 'Blurring the Line'.
8 Quoted in P. Quartermain, *Basil Bunting: Poet of the North* (Durham: Basil Bunting Poetry Centre), p. 10.
9 M. Keating, *The New Regionalism in Western Europe* (Cheltenham: Edward Elgar, 2000).
10 B. Graham, 'The Past in Place: Historical Geographies of Identity', in B. Graham and C. Nash (eds.), *Modern Historical Geographies* (Harlow: Pearson, 2000), pp. 70–99; p. 95.
11 E. W. Gilbert, 'Geography and Regionalism', in G. Taylor (ed.), *Geography in the Twentieth Century* (London: Methuen, 1957), pp. 345–71; p. 349.

12 A. Paasi, 'Region and Place: Regional Worlds and Words', *Progress in Human Geography*, 26 (6) (2002): 802–11.
13 N. Entrikin, 'Political Community, Identity and Cosmopolitan Place', *International Sociology*, 14 (3) (1999): 269–82; A. Macintyre, *After Virtue* (London: Duckworth, 1982).
14 Keating, *The New Regionalism*, pp. 84–5.
15 P. Bourdieu, *Language and Symbolic Power* (Cambridge: Polity, 1991), p. 223.
16 Keating, The *New Regionalism*; D. McCrone, *Understanding Scotland: The Sociology of a Nation* (London: Routledge, 2001); J. Tomaney, 'End of the Empire State? New Labour and Devolution in the United Kingdom', *International Journal of Urban and Regional Research*, 24 (3) (2003): 677–90.
17 Williams, *Keywords*, p. 87.
18 Williams, *Keywords*, p. 265.
19 P. Bourdieu, *Distinction: A Social Critique of the Judgement of Taste* (London: Routledge, 1986); Williams, *Keywords*, p. 265.
20 F. M. Ford, *The Soul of London* (London: Dent, 1905), pp. 34–5.
21 A. Pike, A. Rodriguez-Rose and J. Tomaney, *Local and Regional Development* (London: Routledge, 2006).
22 R. Williams, *The Long Revolution* (London: Chatto & Windus, 1961), p. 61.
23 Williams, *The Long Revolution*, p. 22.
24 Williams, *The Long Revolution*, pp. 48–71; for an extended treatment of the concept see R. Williams, *Marxism and Literature* (Oxford: Oxford University Press, 1977).
25 P. Ackroyd, *Albion: The Origins of the English Imagination* (London: Vintage, 2004), p. 449.
26 R. Williams, 'Base and Superstructure in Marxist Cultural Theory', *New Left Review*, 1 (82) (1973): 3–16; p. 9.
27 Williams, 'Base and Superstructure', p. 10.
28 Williams, *Keywords*, p. 265.
29 I. Taylor, K. Evan and E. Fraser, *A Tale of Two Cities: Global Change, Local Feeling and Everyday Life in the North of England* (London: Routledge, 1996).
30 Taylor *et al.*, *A Tale of Two Cities*, p. 23.
31 Taylor *et al.*, *A Tale of Two Cities*, p. 42.
32 Taylor *et al.*, *A Tale of Two Cities*, p. 53.
33 Taylor *et al.*, *A Tale of Two Cities*, p. 59.
34 D. Haslam, *Manchester, England: The Story of a Pop Cult City* (London: Fourth Estate, 2000), p. xxiv.
35 Quoted in Haslam, *Manchester, England*, p. xxiv.
36 Haslam, *Manchester, England*, p. 258.
37 J. Hollows and K. Milestone, 'Welcome to Dreamsville: A History and Geography of Northern Soul', in A. Layshon, D. Matless and G. Revill (eds.), *The Place of Music* (New York: Guilford, 1998), pp. 83–103; p. 88.
38 Hollows and Milestone, 'Welcome to Dreamsville', p. 88.
39 Taylor *et al.*, *A Tale of Two Cities*.
40 B. Franklin and D. Murphy (eds.), *Making the Local News: Local Journalism in Context* (London: Routledge, 1998).
41 J. Hari, 'Why *Coronation Street* Fills Me with Pride', *The Independent*, 3 April 2006.

42 R. Colls, 'Born Again Geordies', in R. Colls and W. Lancaster (eds.), *Geordies: The Roots of Regionalism* (Edinburgh: Edinburgh University Press, 1992), pp. 1–34; p. 23.

43 P. Cooke, 'Class Practices as Regional Markers: A Contribution to Labour Geography', in D. Gregory and J. Urry (eds.), *Social Relations and Spatial Structures* (New York: St Martin's Press, 1985), pp. 213–41.

44 D. Hobbs, *Doing the Business: Entrepreneurship Detectives and the Working Class in the East End of London* (Oxford: Oxford University Press, 1988).

45 D. Lancaster, 'Newcastle: Capital of What?', in R. Colls and W. Lancaster (eds.), *Geordies: The Roots of Regionalism* (Edinburgh: Edinburgh University Press, 1992), pp. 53–70; p. 64; M. Roberts (ed.), *Live Theatre: Six Plays from the North East* (London: Methuen, 2003).

46 D. J. Taylor (2005) 'Key to the Sardine Can: Sid Chaplin', *The Guardian*, 30 April 2005, available online at www.n-spaces.net/blog/2008/11/key-to-sardine-can-sid-chaplin.html (accessed 26 February 2010).

47 A. Plater, 'No Frills', *The Guardian*, 6 November 2004, available online at www.guardian.co.uk/stage/2004/nov/06/theatre.stage (accessed 26 November 2010).

48 L. Hall, 'Introduction', in M. Roberts (ed.), *Live Theatre: Six Plays from the North East* (London: Methuen, 2003), p. xiv.

49 G. Burn, *The North of England Home Service* (London: Faber, 2003), pp. 46–7.

50 P. Barker, *Another World* (Harmondsworth: Penguin, 1999), p. 43.

51 S. Heaney, *Preoccupations: Selected Prose, 1968–78* (New York: Farrar Straus and Giroux, 1980), p. 149.

52 S. Clifford and A. King (eds.), *Local Distinctiveness: Place, Particularity and Identity* (London: Common Ground, 1993).

53 C. Brace, 'Finding England Everywhere: Regional Identity and the Construction of National Identity, 1890–1940, *Cultural Geographies*, 6 (1) (1999): 90–109.

54 Y. F. Tuan, *Cosmos and Heart* (Minneapolis, Minn.: Minnesota University Press, 1991), p. 4.

55 S. R. Greaves, 'A Poetics of Dwelling in Basil Bunting's *Briggflats*', *Cercles*, 12 (2005): 64–78; 74.

56 P. Claval, *An Introduction to Regional Geography* (Oxford: Blackwell, 1998), p. 142.

57 Heaney, *Preoccupations*, p. 132; Tuan, *Cosmos and Hearth*.

58 R. Williams, 'Fiction and the Writing Public', *Essays in Criticism*, 7 (4) (1957): 422–8; p. 425.

59 J. Tomaney, 'Keeping a Beat in the Dark: Narratives of Regional Identity in Basil Bunting's *Briggflatts*', *Environment & Planning D: Society & Space*, 25 (2) (2007): 355–75.

60 J. Kerrigan, 'Divided Kingdoms and Local Epic: *Mercian Hymns* to *The King of Britain's Daughter*', *Yale Journal of Criticism*, 13 (1) (2000): 3–21; p. 3.

61 Heaney, *Preoccupations*, p. 169.

62 Kerrigan, 'Divided Kingdoms and Local Epic', p. 5.

63 Kerrigan, 'Divided Kingdoms and Local Epic', p. 5.

64 J. McGonigal and R. Price, 'An Introduction', in J. McGonigal and R. Price (eds.), *The Star You Steer By: Basil Bunting and British Modernism* (Amsterdam: Rodopi, 2000), p. 6.

65 G. Hill, *Mercian Hymns* (London: Deutsch, 1971).

66 S. Freud, *Civilization and Its Discontents* (Harmondsworth: Penguin, 2002),
    p. 50.
67 Hall, 'Culture, Community, Nation'.
68 Greaves, 'Poetics of Dwelling'; Tomaney, 'Keeping a Beat in the Dark'.
69 J. Seabrook, 'The End of the Provinces', *Granta*, 90 (summer) (2005): 227–41; 228.
70 Seabrook 'End of the Provinces', pp. 237–8.
71 M. J. Sandel, *Democracy's Discontent: America in Search of a Public Philosophy* (Cambridge,
    Mass.: Harvard University Press, 1996), p. 349.

6
_____

Contemporary British cinema

Introduction

The UK Film Council, the government-sponsored body responsible
for allocating public funds to film-making, declares that 'Cinema is an
immensely powerful medium at the heart of the UK's creative industries and the global economy. Cinema entertains, inspires, challenges
and informs audiences. It helps shape the way we see and understand
ourselves and the world'.[1] Yet the task of examining the extent to which
British cinema encourages us to 'see and understand ourselves and
the world' is not entirely straightforward, since British cinema is, and
always has been, a complex site of representation. Additionally, the cinema audience for British films is relatively small since US films dominate the box office and DVD sales; many British films do not get released
or only reach art-house audiences, while some are broadcast on television. There is also the complicating issue of classification. Indeed, most
analyses tend to begin with a preamble about how difficult it is to define
a British film, especially since much of current production is funded by
a variety of sources originating from several countries. The debate generally considers the amount of British 'cultural content' which may or
may not be reflected in its personnel, locations and subject matter. Yet
it is clear that many films engage with the multifarious aspects of living in Britain and that, as John Hill has observed, 'while British cinema
may depend upon international finance and audiences for its viability
this may actually strengthen its ability to probe national questions.'[2]
Indeed, the need to differentiate products in the global market provides
an economic rationale for displaying 'British' themes and identities on
screen in an attempt to carve a niche in territories such as the USA, a

market that is particularly difficult for foreign films to access. In addition, as the films discussed in this chapter demonstrate, the increasingly transnational production context for British films sharpens their critical perspective on many aspects of British life and culture.

The sentiment behind Hill's comment is therefore far from being concerned purely with economics. A long-standing imperative to reflect contemporary issues is revived with the desire for British films to probe 'national questions'. The critical acclaim of the social-realist 'New Wave' dramas produced by the 'Angry Young Men' in 1958–64, including *Room at the Top* (dir. Jack Clayton, 1959), *Saturday Night and Sunday Morning* (dir. Karel Reisz, 1960) and *A Kind of Loving* (dir. John Schlesinger, 1962), provides an example of how British films have been appreciated primarily for their ability to comment on issues of their time, here class and gender. More recently, the success of Mike Leigh's *Vera Drake* (a UK-French co-production, 2004) at international film festivals and at the box office attests to the continuing interest in British films that seek to probe social issues, even if these are represented via narratives set in the past. The persistence of the realist imperative might also take other forms, for example, the national and international success of *The Full Monty* (dir. Peter Cattaneo, 1997), a film about six unemployed steel workers in Sheffield who form a successful male striptease act that ironically gives them back their self-respect and revives a sense of local community, was based on its ability to address a social issue in a comedic fashion. Even so, in this case it is not so much the *fact* of a film representing an 'issue' but *how* this has been done that has attracted critical comment. It has been argued that *The Full Monty*'s sentimental populism does in fact mask a Blairite fantasy whereby self-help can alleviate social deprivation and conceal the persistence of deeper-seated ethnic and class divisions.[3] In this way, contemporary British cinema comments on (or ignores) a range of complex themes that are relevant to 'national questions', even if their ostensible intention is to suggest otherwise. This chapter will explore the range of representations that typify British cinema according to key themes that provide contexts for examining contemporary cinema. The first is films that present nostalgic images and themes, commonly referred to as 'heritage' cinema, and that comment on both the past and present in complex ways. The second is films that deal with issues of contemporary youth culture (a dominant strand in recent British films), while the third theme concentrates on how cinema reflects and comments upon pressing social issues such as experiences of ethnicity and asylum. The final section demonstrates how, in the context of an increasingly regional and hybrid conception of Britishness, space and identity have become central preoccupations in many contemporary films.

Nostalgia: 'heritage' past and present

From many perspectives, British culture is steeped in nostalgia. The 'heritage' industry's ability to evoke nostalgic responses for times not directly experienced by its consumers is similarly reflected in films that mobilise affective regimes set in both the past and the present. While it is not my intention here to summarise in detail the well-known academic debates that have focused on 'heritage' cinema since the 1980s, there is no doubt that the style or genre has had a profound impact on the ways in which British films are seen to offer cultural commentary about the contemporary mobilisation of the past. I would agree with Claire Monk, however, that in analysing the broad impact of heritage cinema it is necessary to consider films set in both the past and the present, since the latter in particular offer an exclusive, reactionary version of Englishness, represented by films such as *Four Weddings and a Funeral* (1994) and *Bridget Jones's Diary* (2001), which is arguably more marked than in heritage films set in the past.[4]

The heritage film has diversified considerably since being identified primarily with adaptations of the novels of E. M. Forster, such as *A Room with a View* (dir. James Ivory, 1985), *Howards End* (dir. James Ivory, 1992) and *Maurice* (dir. James Ivory, 1987), which can be described as 'intimate epics of national identity played out in a historical context … melodramas of everyday bourgeois life in a period setting' created by a non-British, Merchant–Ivory production team but featuring British themes and actors.[5] The 'museum aesthetic' of these films has attracted critical attention in so far as their *mise en scène* is considered to be either too distracting and seductive to foreground any social or ironic critique that the films' narratives might otherwise offer or, conversely, a key site of pleasure for a diverse range of audiences and an example of how a melodramatic *mise en scène* – that is, all 'those elements placed in front of the camera to be photographed' – can offer a complex, often contradictory commentary on the mores of class society.[6] One might argue, for example, that in films such as *The Remains of the Day* (dir. James Ivory, 1993) *mise en scène* actually *becomes* the focus of critical commentary about the bizarre operations of domestic service in a large country house. In one scene, an elderly servant has become ill on a staircase and has uncharacteristically left his dustpan and brush in full view. This lapse causes anxiety because it becomes the focus of suspense when the objects need to be removed out of sight of the master, a ridiculous situation in view of the gravity of the servant's illness. The timely removal of the offending items demonstrates another servant's professionalism while at the same time contributing to the *mise en scène* as an active element and means of demonstrating the human cost of a social system based on inequality and privilege.

The heritage film can, therefore, be seen as a typical example of the ways in which many British films have become hybridised as generic forms, capable of conveying a range of complexities that centre on narrative, setting and *mise en scène* that defy reductive or generalised categorisation. In this way, films such as *Elizabeth* (dir. Shekhar Kapur, 1998) mobilise a heritage theme of royalty while at the same time incorporating an eclectic, postmodern style that resonates with other British films that revive older generic forms such as the gangster film in *Sexy Beast* (dir. Jonathan Glazer, 2000) and *I'll Sleep When I'm Dead* (dir. Mike Hodges, 2003). These films pay homage to *Get Carter* (dir. Mike Hodges, 1971) and *The Long Good Friday* (dir. John Mackenzie, 1980), demonstrating that 'heritage' can in fact be loosely used as a means of describing generic homage with reference to particular regimes of visual representation that have been developed more in relation to cinema than to history. Heritage functions as a palimpsest upon which narratives about aspects of British life – past and present – can be inscribed.

Thus, while Mike Leigh claimed he was not influenced by films of the 1950s for *Vera Drake*, it is clear that the film draws on a cinephilic sensibility that demonstrates an awareness of the heritage aesthetic described above.[7] Set in 1950, about Vera (Imelda Staunton), a working-class woman whose family is unaware that she performs backstreet abortions 'to help out young girls', the film displays the past with sets that are evocative of a 'heightened realism', establishing a verisimilitudinous address that encourages us to recognise the period even if we have not experienced it directly. The minutiae of detail, from domestic crockery and wallpaper to clothes, is convincing, acquiring narrative weight as the film progresses from its opening shots, which capture Vera in the kitchen, photographed from outside the door as her family walk in and out of the frame while she busily attends to the cooking, humming a cheery tune. This technique – of holding a shot while allowing the actors to move in and out and for a clear view of the decor and props – is repeated on different occasions, acquiring a pictorial resonance that demonstrates the dynamic elements of the film's *mise en scène*. Later, when Vera is cleaning a rich woman's house, we see her again from outside the doorway, but this time the items on display are similar to the contents of the affluent properties in heritage films. Yet the nostalgia, the cosiness, is reserved for Vera's house, since it is there that we experience a sense of belonging, of a small, interdependent community whose unity is threatened when Vera is arrested. The film contains a class critique, as social inequalities form its major theme. Again, *mise en scène* is a key visual register when, for example, Vera crouches on the floor to clean Mrs Fowler's fender, a small figure dwarfed by the magisterial marble fireplace as her employer nearly steps on Vera when reaching for a card on the mantelpiece. When Vera visits a young West Indian woman to perform an abortion, the room is dark, bare and minimally furnished. The harshness of the surroundings accentuate our perception of the woman's evident fear and ignorance about what to expect once Vera has gone. By contrast, a rich young woman who has become pregnant can pay to go to a clinic after being referred by a psychiatrist because she has been told what to say to convince him to make the recommendation. She is housed in a comfortable room, the deed is done, and she returns home afterwards with her problem neatly solved. Each set has a pristine quality that illuminates the set designer's achievement while displaying items that ironically have acquired a heightened commercial value in a contemporary culture interested in vernacular china and antique kitchen appliances. Indeed, these items are invested with economic and symbolic status in visual, virtual and print culture that similarly promote commodities from the past, or designs which are imitative of the past, to constitute significant indicators of taste and identity. In *Vera Drake* this sensibility acquires an additional generic function that produces an ironic comment on this changed, contemporaneous value of the *mise en scène*. When we see the kitchen of Frank (Adrian Scarborough), Vera's brother-in-law, and his wife Joyce (Heather Craney), who have recently moved to a house, the same camera positioning is used to contrast the more modern, brighter, sparser setting with the few cramped rooms Vera shares with her family. Although the film does not relate to the majority of British films of the 1950s, it does share resonances with the 'new wave' films' critique of materialism and its association with female characters, whereby Vera's complete lack of interest in making money is contrasted with Joyce's incessant desire for the latest domestic appliances and a television, a caricature that is exaggerated to the extent of her appearing to use becoming pregnant to get her husband Frank to buy her what she desires. As soon as Vera is disgraced, Joyce, with her socially mobile aspirations, takes the opportunity to persuade Frank to distance himself from his brother's family with whom she would rather not identify.

Other films are similarly influenced by an aesthetic awareness of heritage sensibilities, but from a different perspective, as with Pawel Pawlikowski's *My Summer of Love* (2004). This film is not set in the past and draws on a broad range of influences that evoke a sense of the 'Northern pastoral' rather than the more usual industrial settings associated with the British 'new wave' films of 1958–64, or the post-industrial North of *The Full Monty* or *Brassed Off* (1996). It nevertheless shares some of the themes and stylistic traits of 'the new wave' including 'that long shot of our town from that hill', a term used by Andrew Higson to describe characters viewing the industrial landscape from a hill that can be seen as an expression of the director's authorial, outsider commentary.[8] While this observation is generally taken to indicate a middle-class perspective on working-class culture, its use in *My Summer of Love* is rather generic shorthand to beckon to a locale that this particular narrative assumes is familiar to the audience. *My Summer of Love* features a cross-class romance that takes place between two young women in rural Yorkshire. The masculine angst of the 'new wave' has been reversed with these characters who inhabit an uneasy relationship with their class background. Tamsin (Emily Blunt) lives in a mansion while Mona (Natalie Press), an orphan, lives in a pub with her brother, a born-again Christian who is converting the pub into a religious centre. Our first view of Tamsin is in an ironic shot that frames her with her white horse, a statuesque figure seen from above as Mona lies on the grass beneath her. She is subsequently identified with an iconography of class including classical music, which she plays badly on the cello, or a stylised bohemianism that pervades her parents' mansion. Similarly, Mona is depicted at odds with her surroundings, without a home, in a somewhat liminal state as the two young women appear to be most free when riding on an old motorbike over the hills, accompanied by non-diegetic music (Edith Piaf singing 'La Foule') that recalls a *nouvelle vague* sensibility. The film's theme of rebellious, careless youth is reminiscent of French films in that tradition such as Godard's *À bout de souffle* (1960).

While very different from *Vera Drake*, the film similarly adopts some visual strategies more usually associated with the stylistics of 'classic' heritage films. These pictorial compositions are ravishingly beautiful shots of the countryside, of blue and pink skies, of Tamsin's family mansion and of the exotic, idyllic summer she spends with Mona, who is seduced by the hedonistic, bohemian life she discovers with Tamsin. As in *Maurice*, or even television's *Brideshead Revisited* (1981), the pleasures of homoerotic attraction are explored through visual sumptuousness. Combined with elements of quirkiness that are reminiscent of Terrence Malick's *Badlands* (1973), Tamsin and Mona enjoy a brief time of intimacy, acting out a fantasy life listening to Edith Piaf records in the rambling mansion, dressing up and defying convention in public. The film has a dreamy quality that reflects this experience while at the same time introducing the themes of pretence and betrayal that bring the summer and the relationship to an end. Mona's trust in Tamsin is shattered when she discovers that she has been used for idle amusement, as erotic distraction for a rich girl who has lied about having a sister who died and who will return to boarding school rather than run off with Mona. The film's visual and thematic intensity is accentuated by the temporal notion of 'summer', of an idyllic time that will inevitably pass. Similarly, Tamsin and Mona's young age marks them as being open to new experiences, another theme of many contemporary British films that also deal with aspects of youth culture.

Youth culture: matters of life and death

Trainspotting was undoubtedly the film that ensured that the most frequent cinemagoers, aged between fifteen and thirty-four, became increasingly the major focus of representations on screen. Its strident critique of bourgeois living and depiction of drug abuse amongst the Scottish 'underclass' established a trend of films which were similarly innovative in terms of style and theme.[9] For while *Trainspotting*'s content was bleak, its style was visually and aurally energetic, incorporating surrealist elements and a Britpop soundtrack and featuring a striking, ironic voice-over narration by the lead character Renton (Ewan McGregor). The '*Trainspotting* effect' reverberated in films such as *Twin Town* (dir. Kevin Allen, 1997) and *Human Traffic* (dir. Justin Kerrigan, 1999), that sought to reflect the Welsh experience by being set respectively in Swansea and Cardiff. While these films are aimed at a younger audience than *Vera Drake* they nevertheless present a similar preoccupation with notions of community, in this case young people drawn together by drugs, a shared lifestyle and self-consciously occupying an outsider status in relation to the older generation. *Human Traffic* explores this by focusing on club culture in a formal attempt to duplicate the 'rave' experience that some critics found unsuccessful.[10] The film borrows from *Trainspotting* the frenetic aesthetic that moves in and out of characters' consciousness as thoughts are immediately reproduced as surreal events on screen. In terms of relevance to the traditions of British cinema, this technique pre-dates *Trainspotting*, since it was used distinctively in *Billy Liar* (dir. John Schlesinger, 1963), another example of a British 'new wave' precedent informing a contemporary film. Also, *Human Traffic* takes place over a weekend, as its leading character Jip (John Simm) declares: 'Forget work, forget your family, forget your latest insecurity – the weekend has landed!', a premise that resonates with Arthur Seaton (Albert Finney) being 'out for a good time' in *Saturday Night and Sunday Morning* as well as with Renton's 'Choose Life' speech in *Trainspotting*. The forty-eight-hour escape from dead-end jobs for the characters in *Human Traffic* provides an interlude of freedom, a similarly structured temporal technique as in *My Summer of Love*.

Friendship between five people is the major theme of *Human Traffic*, with each character being introduced via voice-over, as in *Trainspotting*. The love of verbal dexterity is a trait these films borrow from Tarantino but in a starkly different context. *Human Traffic* does not seek to pronounce on the drug issue, but its style allows it to articulate different opinions, contrasting the friends' enthusiasm with intercut shots giving dire warnings, often in a caricatured fashion. The dead-end job is tolerated so the weekend's highs can be paid for, the film providing in one of its ironic intercuts an account of how drugs are circulated in clubs, their managers aware of what is happening and profiting from the transactions. The contrast between the intense excitement and build-up to going to the club with Sunday's 'low', when the friends are dispersed and have awkward conversations with their parents, communicates a sense of the fragility of their experience of friendship, based as it is on a mutual desire to have a good time for a brief period in their lives when they need not make other plans; the concept of a life on hold is one that reverberates in many youth-culture films. *Human Traffic* is a sensitive exploration of 'the chemical generation' in scenes such as Jip's desperate attempt to talk his way into a club so one of their group without a ticket can join them for the long-anticipated night out. As noted earlier, this trope of contrasting the working environment as mundane and endured for enabling the weekend 'event' to happen harks back to the theme of *Saturday Night and Sunday Morning*. In this and other respects there are clear continuities between older and contemporary cinema culture.

Even darker issues are addressed by *28 Days Later*, another film aimed primarily at the younger, core cinema-going audience. Produced by the same team as *Trainspotting*, *28 Days Later* is a hybrid genre film (including horror, thriller and science fiction) that explores the theme of total devastation caused by a deadly virus known as 'the rage', which is spread after animal-rights activists release an infected monkey from a research facility in Cambridge. In twenty-eight days, the virus spreads, killing all but a few survivors including Jim (Cillian Murphy) who awakes in hospital from a coma to discover that the virus has claimed thousands of lives, with news of it reaching Paris and New York. The unfamiliar sight of London devoid of cars and people is conveyed by digital technology, one of the first major British feature films to use the format. This grainy aesthetic adds to the film's 'grunge' effect, which is also evident in the costuming and serves the additional function of heightened realism. Jim explores the post-apocalyptic world, which is spectacular for its strange emptiness, familiar London landmarks such as the London Eye and Big Ben acquiring a sinister appearance as he wanders through the empty streets. Eventually Jim meets other survivors, Selena (Naomie Harris), and then Frank (Brendan Gleeson) and Hannah (Megan Burns), a father and daughter. Together they form a sort of family and leave London in an abandoned taxi to locate a military encampment of other survivors outside Manchester. The sequences of their journey north have many of the normal conventions of a road movie as they drive through beautiful countryside and survive further attacks from 'the infected'. At the end of their journey Frank is however contaminated by the virus and shot by one of the soldiers. The encampment is a large country house which is an ironic usage of a location more usually reserved for heritage films. Rather than finding temporary security, Jim, Selena and Hannah find that the soldiers are ruthless in their terror of becoming infected, their own worst enemies as the film develops a devastating exploration of human nature in crisis. Jim, Selena and Hannah eventually escape and try to attract the attention of a plane that gives them hope that they will be rescued. Yet we do not know at the end of the film whether the rest of the world is in a similar state of devastation or, indeed, whether they will be saved.

The sense of community that is confined to older teenagers and 'twenty-somethings' evident in the previous films discussed is not demonstrated in *28 Days Later* as the catastrophe brings disparate people together and communicates respect for the older generation who are not caricatured as in *Trainspotting* and *Human Traffic*. Indeed, the characters who are most threatening and 'uncool' in *28 Days Later* are the young army officers who have become brutalised by the crisis. By contrast, the tender feelings Jim has for his dead parents when he finds that they have committed suicide rather than be infected by the 'rage' is another example of how this film's different generic mix and dark theme works against creating 'youth' as an autonomous and idealised grouping.

A nightmare scenario that is rooted in realism is the result of genre hybridity combined with location shooting. An eerily empty supermarket provides a momentary sensation of security, as familiar habits of pushing shopping trolleys and picking favourite foods creates a nostalgic sense of the past for the survivors, a memory of 'normal' life. The film tapped into contemporary fears about techno-science, genetic engineering and AIDS with its critique of experiments on animals in the opening sequence when we see monkeys as victims of the 'rage' tests. The virus is carried in the blood which has connotations of fears about AIDS, as well as the appearance of new infections, which in this case are the result of human intervention.

Despite the terrifying scenario, the stylistic energy evident in *Trainspotting* was repeated, and the cast included Christopher Eccleston as the military commander. Eccleston had also starred in director Danny Boyle's successful thriller *Shallow Grave* (1994), and was associated with other 'revival' British films such as *Elizabeth*. These aspects contributed to the film's box-office success in Europe and the USA, representing the transnational appeal of much recent British cinema. In addition, it shares with *Human Traffic* and *My Summer of Love* a stylistic foregrounding of place with its shots of the city and the rural landscape which have the effect of combining a local address with a more global sensibility. While each film has its particular locale, which may or may not be familiar to audiences, their basic topographies could also be identified with other cities and landscapes, evoking a kind of shorthand familiarity that opens up these films to international audiences.

Ethnicity and asylum

As the previous films discussed have challenged any homogeneous notion of British film culture, those that reflect the experience of different ethnic groupings similarly work to broaden a sense of how cinema is capable of engaging with changing social and economic realities. Comedy, as Nigel Mather points out, has been a particularly significant genre in this respect since

> the comic mode, when effectively mixed with dramatic and compelling explorations of ethnicity in 'everyday' British society, is ... particularly well suited to depictions of 'hybrid' groups and communities, who may be involved in the process of formulating new identities and priorities, but do not necessarily wish to forget or deny the emotional, spiritual and cultural journey which they have undertaken, en route towards a new future, spiritual home or 'promised' land.[11]

Since the decline of the independent film workshops of the 1980s that produced some innovative, experimental films detailing Black British experience, including *The Passion of Remembrance* (dir. Maureen Blackwood and Isaac Julien, 1986), *Handsworth Songs* (dir. John Akomfrah, 1986) and *The People's Account* (dir. Milton Bryan, 1988), more populist forms have been successful at the box office, produced by filmmakers from the Asian, African and Caribbean diaspora. While operating in different generic contexts, comedy has tended to dominate the output of directors such as Gurinder Chadha whose most notable films have been *Bhaji on the Beach* (1993) and *Bend It Like Beckham* (2002) which examine the experience of multiculturalism in Britain and the intergenerational conflicts that can result from the tension between tradition and hybrid identities which can be described as 'British-Asianness'.[12] *East Is East* (dir. Damien O'Donnell, 1999), adapted from a stage play by Ayub Khan-Din, explores the clash between first and second generation Pakistani immigrants in Salford in the 1970s. George Kahn (Om Puri) is married to Ella (Linda Bassett), a white English woman, but is determined to bring up his children as traditional Muslims. They rebel and refuse to accept the wedding plans Kahn hatches with other Asian families, which are a source of comedy as well as acute observation about the strains on family life wrought by cross-cultural identities and allegiances. As Sarita Malik has commented, *East Is East* is predicated on the deployment of a classic 'culture clash' discourse in which 'the struggle to acquire "Black Britishness" or "British-Asianness" … is typically attributed to the supposedly irreconcilable differences between an antiquated tradition of religious or cultural fundamentalism and a modern, enfranchised, secular lifestyle'.[13]

In this respect the film can be compared to *My Son the Fanatic*, scripted by Hanif Kureishi, which presents the opposite scenario in which the father, rather than the son, is at odds with tradition. It is a darker comedy in which Parvez (Om Pari), a Pakistani-born man who works as a taxi driver in Bradford, sees his son reject Western values in favour of religious fundamentalism and is shocked to see him participate in violent Muslin action against prostitutes who Parvez knows through the taxi service. The only solace he finds is with Bettina (Rachel Griffiths), one of the prostitutes with whom he develops a relationship, which is presented as loving and outside of the stressful conflicts that dominate the rest of his life. As Dave has commented, in both films 'the desire for pure, unitary, cultural identities based on traditional certainties is pitted … against the wishes of those for whom identity is irretrievably caught up in the "cultures of hybridity" that have arisen as a result of diasporas created through post-war, post-colonial migration.'[14] Unlike his son, Parvez cannot extricate himself from the life and tastes he has acquired in Britain, and he can see through the hypocrisy of a Muslim teacher from Pakistan, who stays in his house at the request of his son to give religious instruction but whose real agenda is to immigrate to Britain. On the other hand, the world of prostitution and nightclubs that Parvez comes to know through his job is depicted as violent, racist and exploitative, lightened only by his friendship with many of the women and their culture of mutual support. No easy solutions are given in a film that explores the fractured relationships experienced by men such as Parvez whose job places him in the position of contemplative observer, a situation that the film depicts by containing many shots of him looking out of his car, much as Travis Bickle does on the streets of New York in Martin Scorsese's *Taxi Driver* (1976).

Last Resort (2000) and *Dirty Pretty Things* (dir. Stephen Frears, 2002) focus on more recent experiences of immigration from Eastern Europe. Pawel Pawlikowski's *Last Resort* is about Tanya (Dina Korzun), a Russian woman who comes to Britain with her son in search of her English fiancé who never appears. She decides to apply for political asylum, beginning a process that leaves her in bureaucratic limbo, detained in a holding area in 'Stonehaven', filmed in the seaside town of Margate.

This jaded environment of amusement arcades and bleak housing is the background for exploitation by men out to profit from immigrants by involving them in the internet porn business. Wanting to return to Russia but desperate for cash, Tanya becomes friendly with Alfie (Paddy Considine), an arcade manager, who eventually helps Tanya and her son escape from Stonehaven. Much of the film focuses on the degradation experienced by asylum-seekers who are virtual prisoners while they are caught up in the bureaucratic mire of detention. The film exploits the irony that this takes place in an environment designed for pleasure, and many shots capture the resort's faded glory in heritage fashion as pic-torially constructed shots of the bay, seafront and iconic 'Dreamland' amusement arcade (featured in Lindsay Anderson's short film of 1953) contrast with a grim tower block that is Tanya's temporary home. Familiar or comforting notions of place are challenged as the setting exaggerates her loneliness and isolation, shot in a desaturated palette of greys and other muted colours. The bleak apartment she shares with her son has paper peeling off one wall, which ironically is patterned with palm trees. Alfie paints it blue, provides them with furniture and a television and offers kindness which develops into love for Tanya, who nevertheless still wants to return to Russia.

The uprooting of Tanya and her son is conveyed visually through shots that are resonant of a bleak iconography of the Eastern Bloc with its grey concrete tower blocks. At the same time, the place is recognis-able as Margate, producing a sort of visual shorthand for environments of displacement and alienation that are not necessarily confined to a sin-gle location. Massey's observations about the negative impact of 'time-space compression', in which people on the move such as Tanya have little control over a process that generally exaggerates unequal power relationships, are pertinent to this film.[15] In this case, the new technolo-gies are used to exploit the refugees in Stonehaven for the internet porn business. Ironically, more basic technology such as the telephone is dif-ficult to access as we see queues of immigrants outside one seafront box, frustrated by the process and language. On the other hand, as pointed out by Roberts, the telephone box

> provides a focal point around which the asylum seekers and refugees gather. The exilic and diasporic spaces of London or other possible transnational connections permeate the experiental and geo-political borders of Stonehaven ... The phone box becomes a

transnational space by which a metonymic 'last resort' of parochial, historically contingent England is steadily undone.[16]

From another screen perspective, *Last Orders* (dir. Fred Schepisi, 2001), adapted from Graham Swift's novel, uses Margate jetty as the final destination for spreading the ashes of Jack (Michael Caine), whose friends journey there by car from London. Their memories of Jack are recalled in flashbacks along the way, with Margate functioning in this instance as a seedy but nevertheless fondly remembered holiday destination, representing in this case 'parochial, historically contingent England' rather than the more desolate representations offered in *Last Resort*.

Yet seaside resorts are not only traumatic for immigrants, as shown in artist Tracey Emin's loosely autobiographical film *Top Spot* (2004), which documents the home-grown sexual exploitation of teenage girls born and brought up in Margate. Even this film, with its poignant and harrowing accounts of teenage experience, contains shots of great symbolic beauty, using a combination of formats and techniques such as Super 8 footage and slow-motion cinematography. Emin intended the film to be a 'universal story' rather than its imagery and narrative relating solely to Margate.[17] The film's focus on six adolescents, their fantasies and traumatic experiences, including rape and suicide, uses Margate as a place which is seductive but also the background from which they wish to escape. One of the characters, for example, dreams of going to Egypt: we see shots of Margate intercut with Cairo, which has its own version of 'Dreamland'; on another occasion we see Cleopatra's Needle in Ramsgate (near Margate) as the background to one of the girls eating chips. This suggestion of a local-global imagination is consistent with other films' use of location as a graphic and symbolic means of visualising the impact of globalisation.

Place, space and identity

Homi K. Bhabha has written about some of the key differences between 'diversity' and 'difference', which can be usefully applied to British cinema. He states that while celebrating cultural diversity involves a desire to return to fixed, 'pre-given cultural contents and customs ... that live unsullied by the intertextuality of their historical locations, safe in the Utopianism of a mythic memory of a unique collective identity', cultural difference, on the other hand, is more of a dynamic process that recognises cultural exchange and interaction.[18] I would argue that the films I have discussed in this chapter attempt to represent the latter as explorations of the places, spaces, specificities of and interactions between many coexisting identities that relate to the global/local realities of modern society. There are other films, however, for which this is more problematic. The successful cycle of romantic comedies tends to present a more hermetically sealed world in which difference is largely ignored in favour of using London as a site of a 'fairy-tale' existence for the mostly affluent characters in films such as *Notting Hill* (dir. Roger Michell, 1999) *Bridget Jones's Diary* (dir. Sharon Maguire, 2001) and *Love Actually* (dir. Richard Curtis, 2003).[19] In these films the characters' quest is towards the attainment of romantic fulfilment, and the environments in which they live display a *mise en scène* of contemporary privilege that in particular is represented through property, for example, the large period houses of *Notting Hill*. American actors often feature as major characters, emphasising a cross-cultural dimension that can be seen to relate to their production companies' aspirations for overseas distribution as well as to the funding structures behind the films which frequently involve American financial participation.[20] In this case, 'national questions' are hardly probed but perhaps in their exclusion of 'difference' the films nevertheless reveal, as Paul Dave has argued, 'the insecurities of the middle class'.[21]

The London featured in the romantic comedies is indeed a world away from its depiction in Gary Oldman's *Nil by Mouth* (1997) or in Michael Winterbottom's *Wonderland* (1999). The latter depicts one working-class family's experiences over four days within a cityscape that is marked by a fractured and uncertain sense of time and space. The postmodern city is represented by time-lapse shots, slow-motion and speeded-up images that suggest the transnational experience of travelling in tube trains, of crowded city streets, of people entering and leaving pubs and, from the view of one character's high-rise flat, of iconic London landmarks such as St Paul's Cathedral. The four days in the life of the family are thus inserted within a much larger canvas that conveys the pace, fluidity and alienating space of contemporary city life. In an approach that is similar to some of the strategies deployed in the social-realist British film, *Wonderland* includes shots of the landscape which are not necessarily related to the advancement of the narrative. This 'realistic surplus' of shots of the characters walking along the street which are interspersed with speeded-up or slowed-down shots of the cityscape, allows bodies and *mise en scène* to become part of Winterbottom's expression of the complex 'reality' of urban living.[22]

A range of other disparate images of London can be observed in films including *Lock, Stock and Two Smoking Barrels* (dir. Guy Ritchie, 1998), *Croupier* (dir. Mike Hodges, 1998) and *Bullet Boy* (dir. Saul Dibb, 2004). In these films the criminal underworld engulfs the characters, as perpetrators or victims. For Dave, the notion of the 'urban pastoral' developed by Stallabrass is instructive in understanding *Lock, Stock and Two Smoking Barrels* for its nostalgic preoccupation with images of a glamorous, criminal, masculine 'underclass' which is evocative of the 'retro' culture of contemporary 'New Lad' magazines.[23] The representation of violence and guns is reminiscent of Tarantino's style, which parodies and celebrates older films, in this case *Get Carter*, and displays a similar, cartoon-like disregard of squeamishness or political correctness.[24] *Croupier* presents London as part of the worldwide casino network. The central character, Jack (Clive Owen), an aspiring writer, is lured back into the croupier job he learned in South Africa. The London setting is hardly obtrusive, except for a prominent Underground sign in one of the exterior shots and dark streets that are reminiscent of a *film noir* aesthetic. The majority of the other sets are literally underground, in the basement flat Jack shares with his partner and in the casino, an environment that reacquaints him with a gambling world he despises. In spite of his professionalism, frequent insistence that he is not a gambler and the distancing effect of his voice-over narration, which is the novel he is writing about the casino, he too becomes corrupted. The easy money, global language of gambling and proximity to criminal activity is depicted as compulsive but ultimately destructive of personal relationships and integrity.

Bullet Boy, set in Hackney, is about Ricky (Ashley Walters), a young black man who has just left prison, and the difficulties he has trying to extricate himself from gangland crime and a local culture of violence. His younger brother Curtis (Luke Fraser) seems destined to follow the same pattern, particularly after he takes a gun that has been given to Ricky and accidentally shoots a friend. Ricky's involvement in revenge crimes ultimately leads to his own murder, an event that resolves Curtis to reject the world of violence with a symbolic act at the end of the film of hurling the gun into the canal. In this film guns are not glamorised, except within the videogames we see Curtis watching in the high-rise flat he shares with his brother and mother, who despairs of the cycle of inevitable violence that has claimed her older son. A different, more hybridised sense of the 'urban pastoral' is suggested by the proximity of the flats to wasteland where Curtis plays and which invest the landscape with an ominous, borderland sensibility. The interior settings are also marked by this tension when on some occasions we see the flat decorated for a party or the site of a family meal, as a safe haven with a spectacular view, while on others this domesticity is disrupted by a rough police search and by the knowledge that the gun given to Ricky has been hidden there. As with *My Son the Fanatic*, the differences explored in this film are not so much between communities but rather differences within them. Curtis's rejection of the culture that has doomed his brother is the film's utopian theme while at the same time it has drawn attention to the social deprivation and dead-end jobs that determine its persistence.

Contemporary British cinema therefore displays a wealth of images that explore a dynamic, if depressing, culture of difference on many levels, as these examples have shown. Perceptions of the many varied experiences of living in Britain have produced a cinema that fails to deliver comforting images of national cohesion with which British cinema has been associated in the past. These often sit uncomfortably with how other countries, particularly the USA, tend to represent Britain and Britishness in their own movies. Yet, as we have seen, British films that shy away from producing stereotypical representations often find a niche market when distributed abroad, and they have been assisted by the increasing plurality of exhibition sites and trends towards transnational production. Many British films have been able to take advantage of the increasingly diverse market which includes release on DVD and television transmission including, as soon as Film Four became a freely available digital channel in 2006, a season of British films, as well as notoriety through the European film-festival circuit. Funding packages that consist of a range of European and American financing and distribution can also have the effect of films gaining access to markets that have proved notoriously difficult for British films to penetrate. While it is far from the case that British cinema is a rival to Hollywood, it nevertheless occupies an important space in transnational cultural production, a space that in recent years has demonstrated considerable richness and diversity.

Notes

1   See www.ukfilmcouncil.org.uk (accessed 18 Aug 2006).

2   J. Hill, 'British Cinema as National Cinema', in Valentina Vitali and Paul
    Willemen (eds.), *Theorising National Cinema* (London: British Film Institute, 2006),
    pp. 110–11.

3   P. Dave, *Visions of England: Class and Culture in Contemporary Cinema* (Oxford: Berg,
    2006), pp. 70–1.

4   For a summary of the 'heritage film' debate see A. Higson, *English Heritage,
    English Cinema: Costume Drama since 1980* (Oxford: Oxford University Press,
    2003); C. Monk, 'The British Heritage-Film Debate Revisited', in C. Monk
    and A. Sargeant (eds.), *British Historical Cinema* (London: Routledge, 2002),
    pp. 177–91.

5   A. Higson, 'The Heritage Film and British Cinema', in A. Higson (ed.), *Dissolving
    Views: Key Writings on British Cinema* (London: Cassell, 1996), pp. 232–48;
    p. 233.

6   On *mise en scène* see D. Bordwell and K. Thompson, *Film Art: An Introduction*, 2nd edn
    (New York: Alfred A. Knopf, 1986), p. 387.

7   M. Leigh interviewed by E. Lawrenson in *Sight and Sound*, 15 (1) (2006): 12–15;
    p. 12.

8   Terry Lovell, 'Landscapes and Stories in 1960s British Realism', in A. Higson (ed.),
    Dissolving Views: Key Writings on British Cinema (London: Cassell, 1996),
    pp. 157–77; p. 171.

9   For a discussion of representations of the 'underclass', in British film see
    C. Monk, 'Underbelly UK: The 1990s Underclass Film, Masculinity and the
    Ideologies of "New" Britain', in J. Ashby and A. Higson (eds.), *British Cinema, Past
    and Present* (London: Routledge, 2000), pp. 274–87; Dave, *Visions of England*,
    pp. 83–99.

10 X. Brooks, review in *Sight and Sound*, 9 (6) (1999): 46–47; p. 47.

11 N. Mather, *Tears of Laughter: Comedy-Drama in 1990s British Cinema*
    (Manchester: Manchester University Press, 2006), p. 112.

12 A term used by S. Malik, 'Beyond "The Cinema of Duty"?' in A. Higson (ed.),
    Dissolving Views: Key Writings on British Cinema (London: Cassell, 1996),
    pp. 202–15; p. 213.

13 S. Malik, 'Money, Macpherson and Mind-Set', *Journal of Popular British Cinema*, 5
    (2002): 90–103; p. 97.

14 Dave, *Visions of England*, p. 13.

15 D. Massey, 'A Global Sense of Place', in A. Gray and J. McGuigan (eds.), *Studying
    Culture* (London: Arnold, 1993), pp. 232–46; p. 239.

16 L. Roberts, '"Welcome to Dreamland": From Place to Non-Place and Back Again
    in Pawel Pawlikowski's *Last Resort*', *New Cinemas: Journal of Contemporary Film*, 1 (2)
    (2002): 78–90; p. 83.

17 T. Emin, commentary on DVD of *Top Spot* (Tartan DVD, 2004).

18 H. K. Bhabha, *The Location of Culture* (London: Routledge, 1994), p. 34.

19 See R. Murphy, 'Citylife: Urban Fairy-Tales in Late 90s British Cinema', in
    R. Murphy (ed.), *The British Cinema Book*, 2nd edn (London: British Film Institute,
    2001).

20 S. Street, *Transatlantic Crossings: British Feature Films in the USA* (New
    York: Continuum, 2002), pp. 204–6, 212–14.

21 Dave, *Visions of England*, p. 46.

22 On 'realistic surplus' see J. Hill, *Sex, Class and Realism: British Cinema and Society,
    1956–63* (London: British Film Institute, 1986), p. 132; On costume in *Wonderland*, see

S. Street, *Costume and Cinema: Dress Codes in Popular Film* (London: Wallflower, 2001), pp. 73–84.

23 Dave, *Visions of England*, p. 84. On 'urban pastoral' see J. Stallabrass, *High Art Lite: British Art in the 1990s* (London: Verso, 1999).

24 See also A. Sargeant, *British Cinema: A Critical History* (London: British Film Institute, 2005), p. 331.

7
_____

Contemporary British fiction

Introduction

At the end of the twentieth century it has for the first time become
possible to see what a world may be like in which the past, including
the past in the present, has lost its role, in which the old maps and
charts which guided human beings singly and collectively through
life, no longer represent the landscape through which we move, the
sea on which we sail. In which we do not know where the journey is
taking us.[1]

Ours is not the first age to think of the 'contemporary' in terms of a loss
of the representative power of existing historical maps, but the metaphor has become almost tiresomely familiar to us. Recognising that the
map has now come to function primarily as a placeholder term for all
those complex and mysterious _cognitive_ frameworks through which we
orient ourselves in space and time, Fredric Jameson suggests that maps
'enable a situational representation on the part of the individual subject to that vaster and properly unrepresentable totality which is the
ensemble of society's structures as a whole'.[2] Jameson's idea of 'cognitive
mapping' is a useful way of beginning to think about the contemporary
'space' of fiction and evolutions in fictional forms which provide peculiarly appropriate vehicles for the articulation of the complex 'structure
of feeling' of our own historical moment.

Assuming a date of 1980 as the beginning of the 'contemporary' (for
reasons that will soon become apparent), it was at this moment that
Salman Rushdie, one of its great practitioners, argued for the elevation
of the novel over other cultural forms precisely for its unique ability to
take 'the privileged arena of conflicting discourses _right inside our heads_'.[3]

Even a paid-up postmodernist such as Rushdie still defends the novel in terms of the primacy and privacy of the liberal imagination: 'the interior space of our imagination is a theatre that can never be closed down; the images created there make up a movie that can never be destroyed.'⁴ But the images and the techniques for their projection must change. And, accordingly, his 1982 essay 'Imaginary Homelands' famously called for innovatory forms of fiction and fictional languages which would allow newness to enter the world. Concluding with a quotation from Saul Bellow's *The Dean's December* where the Dean takes the wild barking of a dog to be its protest against the limits of the dog world (also implying Wittgenstein's melancholic recognition that even if a lion could talk, we could never know for certain what he was saying), 'For God's sake', the dog is saying, 'open the universe a little more!' Rushdie goes on to observe: 'I have the feeling that the dog's rage, and its desire, is also mine, ours, everyone's. "For God's sake, open the universe a little more!"'⁵ This chapter will explore some of the ways in which the contemporary British novel, as well as our cognitive maps of the world (if not the universe) have been opened up and expanded since 1980.

New maps: the novel after 1980

The appearance of his second novel, *Midnight's Children*, in 1981, was the single most significant moment in the history of contemporary British novel publishing and instrumental in opening up the universe of British fiction and novels about Britain. Ironically, it coincided with a symbolically resonant political act of closure: the British Nationality Act, which deprived Black and Asian British people of citizenship rights by power of birth (*ias solis*). Like the novel, the Act also served to provoke questions about the problematic nature of belonging and the emotional and existential meanings of homelands, real and imaginary. Initially located in the fiercely disputed border territories of Kashmir, *Midnight's Children* is a marvellously decentred allegory of the history of India from the first moment of Independence. The new state is immediately torn apart by Partition, political factions and the incompatibility between Nehru's technologically driven programme of centralisation and Mahatma Gandhi's advocacy of local and decentred traditional village networks. In a few weeks in 1947, over a million lives were lost in the ensuing conflicts, and the brave new post-colonial world brought into existence at the stroke of midnight began almost immediately to splinter, crack and fall apart.

Drawing on a hybrid mix of techniques from the European novel, South American magic realism, Indian myth, European fairytales, Bollywood cinema and the tales of the Arabian Nights, the pivotal conceit of the novel is that the body of Saleem, its narrator, and one of the children born on the midnight hour of Independence, begin to somatise the splits and schisms of the new independent state. Opening comically with Aziz, Saleem's father-to-be, medically inspecting his future bride's body through a succession of holes in a sheet, the conceit of the hole and the partitioned body soon dissolves into the aching cavern that has opened up at the heart of India. As partition turns to violence, those now bereft of history and place are left with an emotional vacuum to be filled only with the promises of new nationalisms or theocratic fervour. The fragile and disintegrating body is conflated with the emerging 'unrepresentable totality' of the new post-colonial and globalised worlds of the late twentieth century.[6]

The integrity of Saleem's personal identity is further jeopardised by telepathic powers connecting him to the thoughts of the other children born on the stroke of midnight, 15 August 1947. Effectively a transistor radio, his head is also a fictional device that fantastically reconciles Nehru's vision of a modernised and technologised nation fully imbricated in global economic networks and Gandhi's belief in the importance of preserving local traditions and belief systems and resisting the lure of universalising discourses. He gradually becomes aware that 'consumed multitudes are jostling and shoving inside' him.[7] For his head is also Rushdie's vision of the new transnational novel, with its melange of voices resisting the fanatical purisms that are the destroyer of worlds. Sitting 'like an empty pickle jar in a pool of Anglepoise light', Saleem is the post-colonial writer, situated in a new and globalised world and opening himself to the possibility of mixing and mingling and preserving different versions of history.[8] To be 'right inside the head' of this consciousness is to be 'anything but whole, anything but homogeneous'.[9]

Fredric Jameson provided one of the most resonant images of the cultural postmodern in his description of the architect and developer John Portman's Westin Bonaventure Hotel in Las Vegas. He describes a typical saunter though this building: the gardens in the back first of all admit you to the sixth floor and then you walk down a flight of stairs to find the elevator that takes you to the lobby. However, if you enter by the front of the building, you are immediately admitted to the second storey, which is a shopping mall. To get to the registration desk, you would then need to take another escalator (or 'people mover' to use Portman's own terminology). Not surprisingly, and despite its iconic fame as a temple of capitalist exchange, the shopkeepers complain that customers never return, for they are unable to retrace their steps. But, for Jameson, the point of the building is that once inside we cannot find our way out. The building has become a simulacrum of and substitute for the city itself. The building is an icon of and testimony to the 'incapacity of our minds, at least at present, to map the great global multinational and decentred communicational network in which we find ourselves caught as individual subjects'.[10] To walk through the Bonaventure Hotel is to become acutely self-conscious of the disjunctive relations between body, space and time in the contemporary world. And throughout the 1980s, as the stable maps of the world shifted, fiction too became self-reflexively preoccupied with the problematic nature of representation: the Bonaventure became *the* icon for postmodernity and for postmodern activities and productions across the arts, including the fiction of the decade. Numerous writers explored the connections between the temporally and spatially disorientating experience of the fabricated worlds of postmodernity and the ontology of the novel as a textual world axiomatically constructed out of other textual worlds. Julian Barnes's *Flaubert's Parrot* (1984) presented its country doctor-narrator in maniacal pursuit of the real Flaubert, in a quest propelled by his wife's sexual betrayal and his paranoid identification with the husband of the fictional Emma Bovary. Jeanette Winterson's *Sexing the Cherry* (1989) narrated its seventeenth-century events through a post-Einsteinian lens where event and narration, model and reality, are no longer distinguishable and where the great dualisms established in the seventeenth century (symbolised in the beheading of Charles I) begin to break down, promising release from the binaries of gender, sexuality and race: male and female, heterosexual and homosexual, white and black.

For as well as the acceleration of communications and the compression of space and time, the history of the period is one of break-up of empires, migrations of peoples, civil wars, generational conflicts, the economic and political decline of Europe and the emergence of new identity politics around gender, race, sexuality and ethnicity. In 1977, Tom Nairn warned that Britain itself was breaking up.[11] The rise of Welsh and Scottish nationalism, the immigration into the UK of overseas people from its former dominions, new ethnic cultures and the influence of American popular culture were all eroding formerly stable concepts of

British identity and national belonging. Yet, for much of the 1970s, critics had complained loudly about the 'exhaustion of the English novel', its inwardness and timidity and its failure to respond to the changing world order. David Lodge talked of the 'novelist at the crossroads': an image suggesting the potential for movement forward and resolution of crisis but sounding a note of caution, hesitancy, limited options on a map already drawn.[12] George Orwell's stereotypical image of the quintessentially 'English' writer, quietly tending his back garden whilst the guns rumble in the distance, however, disappeared in the 1980s as the novel and the nation-state began to 'explode' and a new generation of novelists began to write from the margins, moving away from the preoccupations of the English domestic novel to develop new kinds of migrant fiction. The process began to accelerate after 1980 as writers began to unite in response to the 'Thatcher effect'. For, whether regarded as a force for radical change or a lamentable reinvigoration of Little Englandism, it was evident that the entry into office of Mrs Thatcher coincided with a burgeoning era of trans- and multinationalism, globalisation, neo-liberalism, post-colonialism, the proclaimed End of History and the move away from party and towards identity politics.

Thatcherism and the novel

Martin Amis's *Money* (1984) was the first and most ferocious fictional critique of 1980s' greed and the new entrepreneurialism associated with the deregulation of world money markets. In this Pandemonium, late capitalism has emphatically invaded every corner of existence: 'You can't drop out any more. Money has seen to that. There's nowhere to go. You cannot hide from money.'[13] John Self, media entrepreneur, is a victim of money (the novel is subtitled 'A Suicide Note'); he wakes every morning in an addictive haze, feeling 'invaded, duped, fucked around … violated'; he senses an England 'scalded by tumult and mutiny, by social crack-up in the torched slums'.[14] Self inhabits a modern inferno produced by the unpredictable global flows of money – 'I am a thing made up of time lag, culture shock, zone stuff' – and, even before his final descent into destitution, he feels chillingly excluded from the sidewalking middle management of Manhattan with their 'faces as thin as credit cards' and their fascinating world of thought and culture.[15] Like Saleem, his 'head is a city', but only 'hoboes hang out' there; he knows that, despised and hated by the established bourgeoisie, he is also their product: 'you might have thought to let us in, but you never did. You just gave us some money.'[16] This same sense of the pervasive reach of money surfaced fictionally in unlikely places.

In Anita Brookner's *Hotel du Lac* (1984), for example, Edith Hope's retreat to a discreet Swiss hotel and her defensive adherence to myths of romantic love, are crudely shattered by the entry of the predatory and sadistic Mr Neville, a microchip millionaire who forces on her a marriage 'partnership' as a business deal that rescues her from loneliness and supplies him with a compliant company hostess who will politely ignore his continued sexual shenanigans. In Alasdair Gray's *Lanark* (1981), a bleak vision of Glasgow in the 1950s is projected onto the fantastic realm of Unthank, a purgatorial extension of Duncan Thaw's miserable artist-manqué existence in a city whose creativity has been stifled and destroyed. Like the Uglino episode in Dante's *Inferno*, here is an underworld where humans feed off each other and where the inability to relate to or feel for others, which brings on Thaw's skin inflammations, is magnified into the condition of dragonhide where humans metamorphose into reptilian shapes.

Towards the end of Thatcher's period of office, however, writers began to signal the emergence of a 'new world order'. Malcolm Bradbury's novel *Doctor Criminale* (1992) captured the mood of transition with its reflection of pervasive tribal tension and its mix of journalists vying with streetwise historians and spin-doctored politicians to sum up the times, announcing the End of History, the Close of the Cold War, the New World Order. Retrospective accounts began to appear, dissecting Thatcher's attempted revival of Britain's imperial identity (especially during the Falklands War of 1982) and her proclaimed return to Victorian values. The title of Kazuo Ishiguro's *The Remains of the Day* (1989) picked up Rushdie's use of 'remains', describing the way that, for the migrant, fragments of the past, memories, domestic objects, take on a kind of numinous quality, come to carry a weight of symbolic investment.[17] Ishiguro's tale of the English butler looking back on his professional and personal losses, with musings on the tasteful beauty of the English landscape, the Englishness of butlers and the quintessential ingredient of the truly 'great' butler, makes for poignant comedy and astute political anatomy. The way in which self-aggrandisement hides behind a self-deprecatory disavowal of personal responsibility, its compatibility with emotional repression and denial and training in loyalty and obedience: this behavioural constellation had been identified by Hannah Arendt as the 'banality of evil' at the heart of

Nazism. Narrated at the time of Suez, as Britain began to acknowledge the end of its imperial power, the novel was published near the end of Thatcher's ludicrous attempt to revive the myth of imperial greatness. The butler's tale of loyalty to his proto-fascist master, during the events leading up to the Munich Crisis of 1936, not only laid bare the potential for evil of such nostalgic attachments to notions of nation, family, empire and class status but also intimated their appropriation and transformation in the coming of the new professional and globalised world that had arisen out of the ashes of empire. Described by Martin Amis as a dry mother, Thatcher had nevertheless seemed to inspire, through the manipulation of complex emotions such as shame and nostalgia, a cultural unity reminiscent of wartime Britain.

Ishiguro's novel captured a complex history without a single explicit reference to the 1980s. Many novelists combined realism with more fantastic or overtly self-consciously literary modes. David Lodge drew on the campus novel genre explicitly to revive Disraeli's two nations of rich and poor in *Nice Work* (1988). Ian McEwan's dystopian *The Child in Time* (1987) pictured a nation retreating into infantilism and time-warp and swarming with beggars. Hanif Kureishi's *The Buddha of Suburbia* (1990) breathed new life into the portrayal of class, enquiring into the suburban life of the lower middle classes in his tale of Karim, the actor-son of a first-generation Indian immigrant father. Craving acceptance and assimilation, Karim's entire existence is performance, one minute adapting the mantle of Mowgli (whose story was first told in 1895 in the second volume of Kipling's *The Jungle Book*) in an unreconstructed depiction of the imperial stereotype of the native (for a supposedly avant-garde white theatre director) and the next strutting and posing in hip hangouts, listening to The Clash and the birth of punk. But his father, who has abandoned Karim's English mother to take up with a middle-aged, New Age would-be interior designer, is also anxiously performing the role of suburban Buddha, supplying a dash of exoticism for the new culturally expressive and feminised lifestyle of the British lower middle classes in the 1980s. Like Karim, he too consciously conforms to and performs an English stereotype of the Oriental in order to escape the fear of shame at unconsciously displaying behaviours that might be regarded as foreign or inappropriate. Indeed, most of these 'condition of England' novels in the 1980s combined postmodern pastiche or double-voicing with an adherence to what Martin Amis, in *The War Against Cliché* (2001), referred to as the strength of the Victorian novel.

But the 1980s was also the high period of academic 'theory' (wonderfully satirised in 1990 in A. S. Byatt's historical romance and satire of academic blindness and greed, *Possession*), and, for a while, the realistic novel became the bête noire of literary theorists. Realism, understood as the generic expression of liberal humanism, was seen to produce an illusory consensus by suppressing and disguising the contradictions or *aporias* opened up by the metaphoric and differential nature of language. In this view, realism claims to 'reflect' a world which is, in fact, always already constructed. Moreover, if there is no realm independent of language, then each world is incommensurable with others and is a construction only comprehensible within its own terms. Novelists, however, were rather less inclined to see forms and ideologies quite so neatly categorised and conveniently paired; perhaps because the novelist, at least since Henry Fielding, has become used to inhabiting self-evidently constructed worlds. With hindsight it is apparent that academic critics were too ready to interpret British novelists' indifference towards or muted interest in their own post-structuralist preoccupations as a sign of the insularity and decline of the British novel, and to privilege and laud those writers who showed a more florid postmodern symptomology.

But the problematisation of representation was already at the heart of fictions such as Iris Murdoch's first novel *Under the Net* (1954), which played with the later ideas of the philosopher Ludwig Wittgenstein and his belief that we can never get 'under the net' of language to make direct contact with a reality unproblematically 'named' by words; and even Derrida admitted his inability to write on Beckett's already deconstructionist fiction: 'how could I ever avoid the platitude of a supposed metalanguage?'[18] In any case, prominent novelists such as Doris Lessing, Muriel Spark, William Golding and John Fowles had also played out textualist anxieties throughout the 1970s, using a plethora of metafictional devices and motifs: labyrinths, mirrors, mise-en-abyme effects, characters reading texts in which they appear, authors stepping into their fictions. All that changed between the 1970s and the 1980s was that, increasingly, the perception of the fabricated, constructed and provisional nature of the world became normalised and domesticated and was no longer simply the property of the intellectual.

The break-up of the British novel?

What *was* new, however, and not unrelated to this linguistic self-reflexivity, was a more widespread impulse to discover new stylistic combinations and to forge new fictional languages: the grotesque meta-fictional slapstick of Amis; the exuberant and corporeal language of Angela Carter; Rushdie's unique mixing and mingling of Hindi, Urdu and English intonation and phonology to create a hybrid language (Angrezi) and with it a new mythology of the mongrel. These writers hugely influenced the next generation of novelists such as Will Self, Hanif Kureishi, Zadie Smith, Hari Kunzru, Nicola Barker and Ian Sinclair. After 1981, the field of British fiction certainly began to look different, though this is arguably as much the consequence of voices from outside moving to the centre and reinvigorating the language than it is a reflection of postmodernism per se. It is this shift of emphasis that has most defined British fiction of the contemporary period. The impulse came not only from writers from outside the British Isles but from those who felt internally colonised within it. Writers such as James Kelman and Irving Welsh began to experiment with the Scottish vernacular and, like Rushdie, to globalise the local. In the early 1980s, Kelman began experimenting with free indirect discourse, mixing standard and vernacular languages without implying the usual hierarchisation. By the time of *How Late It Was, How Late*, which won the Booker Prize in 1994, he had developed a unique modernist vernacular that bestowed on the disinherited and the underclass an inner life as real as that of James Joyce's Bloom or Samuel Beckett's tramps and loners.

Writing his editorial (in 1993) to the second Granta's *Best of Young British Novelists*, its (American) editor Bill Buford recalled the period leading up to the first (1983) volume: before 1980, he wrote, there would have been nothing to promote; the older generation (Iris Murdoch, Kingsley Amis, Angus Wilson, Muriel Spark, William Golding) were still going strong, and, of younger novelists, the scene was entirely dominated by Martin Amis and Ian McEwan. But he describes how, in January 1980, it all began to change: he read a short story that seemed to offer something tantalisingly new and eventually tracked its author, Kazuo Ishiguro, to a bedsit in Cardiff; a few months later, Adam Mars-Jones published his first story and would soon help to launch a new generation of 'queer' fiction; in 1981, Salman Rushdie's *Midnight's Children* and Alasdair Gray's *Lanark* appeared, along with Timothy Mo's first novel, *Sour Sweet*, about the experiences of a first-generation Chinese immigrant family in London, and Ishiguro's own *A Pale View of Hills* was published in 1982, a haunting tale of an immigrant Japanese woman coming to terms with the traumas of her memories of Nagasaki and the suicide of her younger daughter.[19]

As he read the novels submitted for the 1993 list, Buford felt himself

> growing increasingly irritated with the notion of a British novel,
> which was really an irritation with the word British, a grey,
> unsatisfactory, bad-weather kind of word, a piece of linguistic
> compromise. I still don't know anyone who is British. I know people
> who are English or Scottish or Northern Irish (not to mention born
> in Nigeria but living here or born-in-London of Pakistani parents
> and living here … or the born-in-Nigeria-but-living here-Nigerian-
> English.[20]

By 1991, Lodge too was referring to an 'aesthetic supermarket' with a bewilderingly diverse array of styles and globalised cultural capital, and Bradbury, with prescient recognition of the domestication of post-modernism, took the commercial metaphor even further, describing the field as a 'great shopping-mall world of pluri-culture' where 'genres leak freely into each other' and 'various layers and categories of culture, from the avant-garde to the populist, constantly interpenetrate'; he would not have been surprised by the news that David Mitchell's avant-garde *Cloud Atlas* was at the top of the list on Richard and Judy's TV show *The Big Read* in 2004.[21]

But it was Rushdie's trope of migrancy that became the most powerful and definitive fictional metaphor for contemporary experience. English is now a world language, he argued in 1983, and so it possesses a world literature. The day of the narrowly conceived tradition of the 'British' novel is over. Just as the migrant writer is not tied to any such national tradition or 'legend-haunted' civilisation and may live in several places, so the migrant can choose his or her literary parentage from any number of traditions and mix them at will, and so the novel, like the nation (in Homi K. Bhabha's account), must also become *disseminated*, can no longer remain parochial or stranded in this or that ghetto of nation, race or single tradition. Fiction will now mix realism and fantasy in an ever-open sea of stories where 'we are inescapably international writers at a time when the novel has never been a more international form'.[22] According to Bhabha, 'the "locality" of national culture is neither unified nor unitary in any relation to itself, nor must it be seen as simply "other" in relation to what is outside or beyond it. The boundary is Janus-faced and the problem of outside/inside must itself be a process of hybridity.'[23] And if the migrant is demonised for representing just such a threat to boundaries, then even more reason why the author must give up the role of monotheistic deity to become as devilish and as metamorphosing as this world without maps: like Gibreel, the protagonist of his novel, *The Satanic Verses* (1988), who declares gleefully, as he shape-shiftingly hurtles from the exploding aircraft and falls through the London skies: 'I am going to tropicalise you.'[24]

Although Britain was actually already 'tropicalised', it required outside and inside perspectives to throw back more authentically hybridised pictures of itself. Writers such as Kazuo Ishiguro, Timothy Mo and Salman Rushdie brought a heightened awareness of 'writing from a kind of double perspective because they, we, are at one and the same time insiders and outsiders in this society. This stereoscopic vision is perhaps what we can offer in place of "whole sight".'[25] 'Whole sight', a phrase from John Fowles's *Daniel Martin* (1977), was also the Hungarian Marxist critic György Lukács's vision of the novel from the 1920s through the 1950s as a panorama of the relations between individual lives and historic pressures achieved through the integration of diverse but representative focalisations into a totality presided over by an authoritative omniscience.[26] Doris Lessing (another migrant writer) had expressed fears in the early 1970s that the novel could no longer represent history in this way, through the integration of the small personal voice into the larger collective, because the individual voice was increasingly unable to carry this kind of representative power in a fragmenting and divided world.[27] (Indeed, in the contemporary period, novelists such as Monica Ali, Zadie Smith and Hanif Kureishi, writing out of specific ethnic communities, have vociferously and controversially refused the role of 'representative' or spokesperson even for a particular group.) Lessing's *The Golden Notebook* (1962) expressed the fear that this classic realist kind of writing in an age of information would devolve into an extended sociological report, utterly failing to capture or embody the 'structure of feeling' of its age.[28] Lukacsian realism could not be produced in good faith in a fragmented and perspectival world, but neither could the committed writer retreat into the kind of solipsistic exploration of the individual consciousness which had seemed to become the trajectory of literary high modernism after the 1950s. Rushdie's substitution of the idea of 'double vision' for Lukacsian 'whole sight', and his sense of building worlds at a tangent to the material worlds of history, were offered as mutually interdependent ways out of Lessing's dilemma.

Through such representation, the exotic might eventually become ordinary, hybrid mingling simply everyday conviviality. The narrator of Zadie Smith's *White Teeth* (2000), suggests that perhaps this is happening at the start of the millennium, but slowly and unevenly. For Smith, the twentieth century has been 'the century of strangers, brown, yellow and white … the century of the great immigrant experiment'.[29] Yet 'it is only this late in the day that you can walk into a playground and find Isaac Leung by the fish pond, Danny Rahman in the football cage, Quang O'Rourke bouncing a basketball, and Irie Jones humming a tune.'[30] But a minor chord sounds in the note of optimism, expressing what is still buried: the still unpronounceable names of children that 'secrete within them mass exodus, cramped boats and planes, cold arrivals, medical checks'.[31] For migrancy is always also about loss, disinheritance, nostalgia, trauma and the complex transformations of memory. If for Rushdie, 'It is the great possibility that mass migration has given the world, and I have tried to embrace it', others have been more circumspect.[32] Migrancy might be a provocative catch-all image for a generalised postmodern condition, but there is risk here of losing important distinctions between different kinds of migrant experience. That of the new and second-generation Black and Asian British, of refugees from Eastern Europe and of those fleeing war-torn and oppressive regimes: they are hardly the same nor is their experience at all like the global tourists, the jet-setting affluent and the transnational communities of the media and managerial classes of the new global economies.

For not all migrants become cosmopolitan citizens of nowhere. Rushdie has certainly received his fair share of criticism (even before the publication of *The Satanic Verses*) from those who have viewed his extrovert and flamboyant postmodernist aesthetic as a reflection of his English public-school and Cambridge education and his metropolitan intellectual lifestyle in New York. For to be migrant, whether across nations, regions, classes or systems of belief, might mean to feel, painfully, that one no longer has a home, and to yearn to return to something that no longer exists except in the sepia tints of memory (reflected in the etymology of the word 'nostalgia').

Monica Ali, Zadie Smith and Andrea Levy, for example, have all written eloquently about the way in which the most familiar experience of the migrant is not so much celebratory hybridity as the feeling of having become altogether invisible: déclassé or downtrodden in the new culture. Their preferred mode is closer to the traditional *Bildungsroman*, and Ali's *Brick Lane* (2003), for example, transposes Virginia Woolf's literary modernism, preserving its poetic precision and impressionism, even borrowing specific motifs from *Mrs Dalloway* (1925): Nazneen's sense of being invisible as she walks the streets, the haunting memories of suicide and falling, her fascination with the solitary tattooed lady who stares out of the window in the opposite block of flats. But the techniques that Woolf developed to 'tunnel' into the consciousness of women characters such as Clarissa Dalloway are transformed as they are redeployed to capture the experience of London immigrants: an experience of poverty and environmental ugliness, plastic furniture, concrete tower blocks, puddles, excrement, overcrowding and cultural isolation. Nazneen is closer to Rezia (Septimus Smith's Italian wife, who feels estranged and dislocated, struggling with an alien culture and a mad husband) than to Clarissa: Ali's novel moves the marginal and migrant character to the centre.

Empathy and experience: entering fictional worlds

The critical debate over the value and significance of the kind of fiction that might most authentically represent migrant experience has been fierce, but the allegedly stark opposition of realism and postmodernism has largely dissolved, especially in the work of later writers such as Monica Ali, Zadie Smith and Andrea Levy. Stuart Hall's essay 'New Ethnicities' (1988) identified two 'moments' of media representation of ethnic minorities in the 1980s, the first an attempt to counter negative stereotypes with positive identities and the second a more postmodern, performative recognition of the constructedness of all identities.[33] In fiction, however, the double voicing of outside-in and inside-out perspectivism tended consistently to produce representations somewhere between the two, though Rushdie's more extrovert performances tended to overshadow the work of less exuberant stylists such as Anita Desai, whose more understated, but poetically beautiful, representation of the effects of Partition on an Indian Muslim family in *Clear Light of Day* (1980) was published just before Rushdie's *Midnight's Children*.

Writing shortly after the terrorist bombing of the World Trade Center, Ian McEwan insisted that the novel is an important instrument of ethical understanding in a world that seems ever more uncontrollable and threatening. Almost all novels depict imaginary, embodied but self-reflexive, consciousnesses engaging a world that never presents itself simply as neutral 'facts' but is always already imbued with values.

The novel is an extension of that human capacity to manufacture coun-
terfactuals, which is the fundamental requisite for compassion and
allows us to put ourselves in the place of the other:

> This is the nature of empathy, to think oneself into the minds of
> others. These are the mechanisms of compassion … It is hard to be
> cruel once you permit yourself to enter the mind of your victim.
> Imagining what it is like to be someone other than yourself is at the
> core of our humanity … The hijackers used fanatical certainty to
> purge themselves of the human instinct for empathy.[34]

McEwan's defence of the novel is surprisingly similar to Rushdie's;
both are compatible with a broadly liberal defence of the imagination,
despite their evident stylistic differences. His recent novel, *Saturday*
(2005), records a day in the life of a neurosurgeon Perowne who wakes
early one morning in the belief that a terrorist bomb is about to fall over
his area of London. During the course of the novel, Perowne's profes-
sionalised materialist understanding of consciousness as the workings
of neuronal circuits, dendrites, shuttles and looms of mental operation,
is challenged: first by his own aesthetic response to the wondrous beauty
of the brain as an organ of the body (one of the truly brilliant descriptions in the novel) and second by the compassion and forgiveness which
he extends in operating on the brain to save the life of the already-
damaged Baxter who has menaced his family. For the scientifically
materialist Perowne is led to recognise his own responsibility as a moral
agent because he sees that it is Baxter's genetic disease that has led to his
violent attack. Because Baxter is biologically incapable of such agency,
Perowne makes the ethical demand of himself to exercise his own moral
free will in the act of heroic compassion that saves his assailant's life.

Many novels of the 1990s began to explore new techniques for representing the pain and trauma arising out of the transitions, transformations and historical disjunctions of the post-war period. Pathology,
disordered affect and disassociation were common themes, dealing with
subjects as various as the Holocaust, sexual abuse, stalking and compulsive erotic behaviours, death, terrorists and other kinds of disaster.
McEwan's technique in novels such as *The Child in Time* and *Enduring Love*
(1997) was to introduce a cataclysmic disaster into a mildly complacent
English bourgeois domestic situation. More daring was Martin Amis's
Time's Arrow (1991), which took an idea from the psychologist Robert Jay
Lifton's interviews of the 1980s with former Nazi doctors, where Lifton

had commented that the common thread running through them was that 'the narrator, morally speaking, was not quite present'.[35] Disavowal of guilt operated through 'doubling' behaviours that had allowed these doctors to dissociate themselves morally from their own participation in killing and destruction. The concentration camp 'selections' (note the evolutionary nomenclature) were carried out with all the fervour of a messianic belief in their healing powers, as they saw themselves helping to forge a new Aryan race. Amis took the idea and brilliantly embedded it in a fiction where the Nazi reversal of killing and healing is mediated through the device of time running backwards in an imagined anti-entropic retelling of the Holocaust, and through the device of a split narrator where the 'feeling tone' of Tod, the former Nazi who narrates the novel, resides in Tod's body but cannot connect with his thoughts, just as Tod knows his thoughts but has no access to his 'feeling-tone'.

Lifton himself became a leading figure in the identification of post-traumatic stress disorder as manifesting largely through modes of dissociation. His work was influential in subsequent discussions of and attempts to define False Memory Syndrome. Pat Barker used this model of dissociation in her *Regeneration* trilogy of the 1990s, exploring the first attempts to recognise the psychological underpinnings of shell-shock as a mode of trauma, during the First World War (when Freud began to define the syndrome as a form of hysterical displacement with classic symptoms of blindness, mutism, deafness and varieties of tics and bodily distortions or paralysis). Barker's trilogy introduced fascinating nuances of class and sexuality (stammering, for example, is depicted as a class-blind affliction, but mutism is exclusively a symptom of non-commissioned officers).

Interestingly, the commitment to the novel as an ethical vehicle came more and more to be affirmed through fictional interrogation of the seduction and consolation of varieties of *false* consciousness, including what had become popularly known as False Memory Syndrome. The novel has always narrated history and explored the workings of memory, modes of evasion and denial, from Walter Scott to Marcel Proust and James Joyce. But in the 1990s, novelists began to engage with the scientific work on evolution and consciousness which was challenging the prevailing philosophical tradition from Plato through Kant that regarded emotion as a hindrance to and distraction from reason. The new science revealed that, conversely, human beings act irrationally and often with disastrous moral consequences when their emotions are disconnected from their thoughts: ethical behaviour requires recognition of our capacity for disavowal, denial and disconnection. In McEwan's (recently filmed) *Atonement*, Briony, the protagonist and still-aspiring novelist, has been rereading Woolf's great modernist novel of consciousness *The Waves* (1931). She thinks how 'a great transformation was being worked in human nature itself, and that only fiction, a new kind of fiction, could capture the essence of the change. To enter a mind and to show it at work, or being worked on, and to do this within a symmetrical design – this would be an artistic triumph.'[36] This novel of 2002, however, is about Briony's abuse of the aesthetic imagination for, as in Conrad's *Lord Jim*, empathy is hijacked to buttress an escapist fantasy used to avoid the pain and suffering that real reparation would require.

Salman Rushdie's *Shame* (1983) is one of many novels of the period that engaged the political implications of this ethical insight, distinguishing between the political abuse of the imagination to build oppressive regimes and the ethical fiction that, in drawing attention to its own fictionality, represents a proper use of the imagination: 'It is the true desire of every artist to impose his or her vision on the world, and Pakistan, the peeling, fragmenting palimpsest, increasingly at war with itself, may be described as a failure of the dreaming mind.'[37] By the 1990s, many writers had turned to reflect on the place and power of stories in human life and often in the evolutionary terms of their survivalist value as part of our species nature. A number of novelists who had flirted with the postmodern suggestiveness of uncertainty principles and the new physics in the 1980s (particularly Ian McEwan, Jeanette Winterson and Martin Amis) later began to engage significantly with the new evolutionary biology. Writers became increasingly fascinated by the sense that stories exist precisely because they allow us to empathise with, understand and come to recognise what the neuroscientist Antonio Damasio calls, the 'feeling of a feeling', the emotional beginning of the growth of conscious awareness and therefore of the understanding of self, world and other.[38] Just as trauma, memory and the retelling of history enter the fictional landscape in this decade, so too does a return to storytelling and the storyteller, as in Jim Crace's *The Gift of Stones* (1988), A. S. Byatt's *The Djinn in the Nightingale's Eye* (1994) and Salman Rushdie's *Haroun and the Sea of Stories* (1990) with its leading question 'What good are stories that aren't even true?'

Whether experimental, poetic or closer to traditional realism, engaging with the death of the author or the rebirth of the storyteller, what runs as a common thread through the enormous diversity of contemporary novels from 1980 to the present is a preoccupation with the crossing of boundaries or borders, of space, time, histories, ontologies, races, genders, class, species, persons. Common motifs include revenants (Ali Smith's *The Accidental*, 2004), cyborgs (Fay Weldon's *Life and Loves of a She-Devil*, 1983), spirits (Ben Okri's *The Famished Road*, 1991), ghosts (Pat Barker's *Regeneration Trilogy*, 1991–5), clones (Kazuo Ishiguro's *Never Let Me Go*, 2005), tramps and down-and-outs (James Kelman's *How Late It Was, How Late*, 1994), transsexuals (Angela Carter's *The Passion of New Eve*, 1977), monsters (Jeanette Winterson's *Sexing the Cherry*, 1989), throwbacks (Doris Lessing's *Ben in the World*, 2000), hybrids (Angela Carter's *Nights at the Circus*, 1984), mimics (Hari Kunzru's *The Impressionist*, 2002), metamorphosis (Alasdair Gray's *Lanark*, 1981), shape-shifting (Salman Rushdie's *The Satanic Verses*, 1988), vampires (Rushdie's *Shame*, 1983), nomads (Bruce Chatwin's *The Songlines*, 1987), borderline personalities (Pat Barker's *Border Crossing*, 2001), celebrity self-dispossession (Andrew O'Hagan's *Personality*, 2003); the mixing of fantasy and realism, the grotesque and surrealism (J. G. Ballard); the mixing of genres (Ian McEwan); the mixing of art and life (fictional confessions which retain the author's name such as Winterson's *Oranges Are Not the Only Fruit* (1985)); life-writing and pathography (especially child-abuse themes as in David Eggars's work).

Rather than the terms 'postmodernist' or 'realist', it might be more productive to see contemporary writers as engaging a distinctive mode of displaced and perspectival semi-allegorisation. In many of these novels, although the reader is teased into pre-emptive allegorical definition and closure, closer reading reveals that our desire for the crystalline map confiscates a more meditative opening onto unfamiliar resonances of the vocabularies of these new and strange worlds. Ballard's fiction, for example, draws extensively on surrealism in his construction of bizarre and claustrophobic worlds – high rises, concrete islands, closed cars, electronically circuited residential estates of the super-rich – which serve as complex poetic metaphors for contemporary culture. Novels such as A. S. Byatt's *Angels and Insects* (1992) set up apparently clear-cut analogies (here between the ant colony and the incestuousness of the Victorian patriarchal family) which then seem to resolve into apparent allegories (here colonial abuse) but end as complex 'laminations' (Byatt's own term), seams of experience running as parallel worlds that never quite meet and that refuse containment in neat interpretive templates. Deliberately calling up impulses of hermeneutic mastery in readers, the desire to make everything add up in neat explanations, these novels finally and self-consciously frustrate the quest for interpretive closure.

It is not always the case, however, that critics can live in such doubts, ambiguities and hesitations. Many of the reviews of Ishiguro's recent *Never Let Me Go*, for example, presented it as a story about human clones farmed for their organs and then criticised it on the literal-minded grounds of their improbable passivity. But the ease with which we adapt to atrocious ideological regimes is precisely what fascinates Ishiguro: in this sense we are all clones, just as we are butlers. And living also in the knowledge of our mortality, we are very like these particular clones: we are human and mortal, and one day, our donations over, we will also need 'carers', as our bodies expire. The novel stages a debate about the place of art in a capitalist and scientifically materialist culture that views the human body in entirely utilitarian terms. The children's lives at the school are in some sense redeemed by the inculcation of the belief in self-expression, and the novel portrays as human, all too human, their ensuing jealousies, factions, territorial tussles, petty vindictiveness, spiritual and romantic yearnings, fear of loss, preoccupation with status. The crazy rage of Tommy, his grotesque 'becoming animal' dances and gesticulations, are an occasional but very real protest against his profound but buried sense that the children are a threatening reminder to their guardians that all humans are zipped-up bags of organs. Looking into the face of Madame, Kathy H sees a disgust and fear of the alien that humans feel for insects or for what is projected as abject or waste: the human body reduced to material function. The last image of the novel, as Kathy moves across the flat horizon of the Norfolk field after Tommy has died from his final 'donation', is of a barbed-wire fence where rubbish has blown and caught: flapping plastic and bits of debris stand out against the bleak chill light of the dying afternoon. The image is simply left to resonate: rubbish, waste, consumer culture, materialist philosophy, the Angel of History. 'Look in the toilet', Ruth shouts as the children search for their originals, their parents: inspect the gutters, trawl the underclass, interrogate the dropouts and druggies and prostitutes who sell their bodies to survive. A comment on the laboratory routines of genetic engineering is precisely what the novel is not.[39]

The 'international novel'

Kazuo Ishiguro, like Salman Rushdie, seems to be a novelist who has slipped comfortably into the role of 'international writer', taking on themes of global significance in double-voiced fictions that resist simple or particularised allegorical reduction. Yet a less sanguine view of the internationalisation of the British novel is that the new globalised fiction market and the celebration of the 'hybrid' are simply evidence of a continuing Orientalism: a capitalist exoticisation and appropriation of post-colonial experience. The 'internationalisation' of prizes such as the Booker is seen as further evidence of the commodification of writers from former colonies and the commercial control still exerted through neo-imperialism. Ishiguro has brilliantly fictionalised this controversial debate from the perspective of the writer in *The Unconsoled* (1995), set almost entirely in a hotel in an unidentified middle European town: a place of nowhere, in a continent whose borders keep changing and whose place in the world has become uncertain. It is the fictional (inner space) equivalent of Jameson's (hyperspace) Bonaventure Hotel, a kind of map of the contemporary 'international' writer's mind, the inner sources of his creativity and the external and global appropriations of his local performances. The novel opens in the hotel lobby in a thin shaft of sunlight with the muffled sound of a piano rising just audibly against the hum of traffic from outside. Mr Ryder, the great pianist, arrives to prepare for the performance that is intended to restore to the damaged town the glories of its former high-cultural community and repair the bruised self-esteem of its burghers. From this comically kitsch beginning, with its atmosphere of Bergman meets Coen Brothers meets Kafka with Austro-Hungarian decor circa 1930, a dash of German high Romanticism and some French decadence (with the sinister puppet-master Hoffmann presiding over the entire *mise en scène*), there ensues a surreal psychodrama.

Ryder's experience begins with an elevator ride in which he hears a lengthy plaint from Gustav, the porter, about the dying role of porters and from which he steps out into his boyhood bedroom, noticing the same tear in the rug and listening to the voices of his parents raging below as he did as a ten-year-old child. He seems to be reliving the moment when he realised the tear could be incorporated into the terrain for his play soldiers and that 'the blemish that had always threatened to undermine my imaginary world could in fact be incorporated into it.'[40]

For the rest of the novel, he travels endless corridors of this hotel laby-rinth, which has echoes of earlier representations of entrapment in mys-terious labyrinths, as in Richard Strauss's opera *Ariadne on Naxos* (1912) as well as Franz Kafka's novel *The Castle* (1922). Time is projected onto the dimension of space. Like all hotels, a place of professional reserve where strangers stumble into the intimacies of each others' lives, here, Ryder walks through walls, encounters dissociated or split-off versions of himself and is granted a kind of uncanny omniscience as he seems tele-pathically to enter the minds of others who might also be projections of himself: like the elderly, dissolute but once famous, one-legged con-ductor Brodsky, who careers onto the stage, propped up by an ironing board, a kind of travesty of Herman Melville's late Romantic and larger-than-life one-legged character, Ahab, the tortured and driven questor of *Moby-Dick* (1851). The concert never takes place; Ryder moves on, aban-doning a woman who claims to be his wife, and a boy, Boris, who may or may not be his son and is both uncannily familiar and a stranger to his largely absent, could-be father. For over 500 pages, Ryder endeavours to find a space and time to rehearse and perform his art. But he has lost his 'schedule' and is for ever hurried and harried and besieged by the numerous and varied demands made on him as redeemer of the lost triumphs of *Kultur* and community. The novel ends as he moves on to another European city.

Most reviewers were entirely baffled. Few realised that Ishiguro began the novel after an exhausting world-promotional tour, part of the process where the contemporary writer, like the book, has now become a packaged commodity, the possession of publisher, marketing agents, booksellers and international audiences, critics and reviewers. For the novel is a meditation on the tension between historical ideas about the creative arts and their place in a culture and the varieties of new exter-nal pressures on the contemporary writer in an internationalised cul-ture market: the conflicting demands of political representation and ethical obligation and the commercial implications of producing cre-ative work within a global economy. Historical images of authorship are embodied in the varied cast of characters: Freudian neurotics, Romantic geniuses, traditional bards. Brodsky, like a maimed rock star returned from rehab, babbles continuously about his damaged genius and hys-terically flaunts the wound that he believes places him beyond every-day moral obligation. It is a not unfamiliar image. But Ryder, the lauded and serious contemporary international artist, is expected to be part of a cosmopolitan world of 'caring professionals', an international ethicist who must exercise a kind of impossible telescopic philanthropy as he is compelled to respond to local demands without knowledge or time to acquire customs and histories. Commercial forces control his schedule, and global demands confiscate rehearsal and performance time; he has become a stranger to his family and loved ones and barely knows who he is.

'One's own self-worth is tied to the worth of the community to which one belongs, which is intimately connected to humanity as a whole', wrote the great African writer Wole Soyinka in 2007.[41] But what of the many writers mentioned in this essay who do not 'belong' in this sense or who are trying to escape from oppressive modes of belonging: to nations, genders, races and classes, who exist between communities or in imaginative spaces of nowhere, who begin again and again each time they write to rebuild the very ground beneath their feet? They too are the writers in Britain, in the contemporary period, whose fictions have provided many of the new maps for our uncharted realities.

Notes

1 E. W. Hobsbawm, *The Age of Extremes: The Short Twentieth Century* (Harmondsworth: Penguin, 1994), p. 160.
2 F. Jameson, *Postmodernism; or, The Cultural Logic of Late Capitalism* (London: Verso, 1991), p. 51.
3 S. Rushdie, *Is Nothing Sacred?* (London, Granta Books, 1990), p. 13.
4 S. Rushdie, *Imaginary Homelands* (London: Granta, 1992), p. 426.
5 Rushdie, *Imaginary Homelands*, p. 21.
6 Jameson, *Postmodernism*, p. 51.
7 S. Rushdie, *Midnight's Children* (London: Picador, 1991), p. 4.
8 Rushdie, *Midnight's Children*, p. 14.
9 Rushdie, *Midnight's Children*, p. 237.
10 Jameson, *Postmodernism*, p. 44.
11 Tom Nairn, *The Break-Up of Britain* (London: New Left Books: 1977).
12 D. Lodge, 'The Novelist at the Crossroads', in M. Bradbury (ed.), *The Novel Today: Contemporary Writers on Modern Fiction* (London: Edward Arnold, 1977), p. 100.
13 M. Amis, *Money* (Harmondsworth: Penguin, 1985), p. 145.
14 Amis, *Money*, p. 67.
15 Amis, *Money*, p. 245, 35.
16 Amis, *Money*, p. 30, 247, 59.
17 Rushdie, *Imaginary Homelands*, p. 12.
18 J. Derrida, *Acts of Literature*, ed. Derek Attridge (London: Routledge, 1992), p. 60.

19 B. Buford, in *Granta: Best of Young British Novelists*, 43 (Harmondsworth: Penguin, 1993), p. 11.

20 Buford, in *Granta: Best of Young British Novelists*.

21 Both Lodge and Bradbury are quoted in J. Wood, 'The Slightest Sardine', *London Review of Books*, 26 (10), May 2004, pp. 11–12; p. 11. S. Windisch Brown (ed.), *Contemporary Novelists* (New York: St James's Press, 1996), p. viii.

22 Rushdie, *Imaginary Homelands*, p. 20.

23 H. K. Bhabha, *The Location of Culture* (London: Routledge, 1993), p. 4.

24 S. Rushdie, *The Satanic Verses* (London: Viking, 1988), p. 354.

25 Rushdie, *Imaginary Homelands*, p. 19.

26 G. Lukács, *The Meaning of Contemporary Realism* (London, Merlin, 1979).

27 D. Lessing, *A Small Personal Voice* (London: Flamingo, 1994).

28 R. Williams, *The Long Revolution* (London: Chatto & Windus, 1961), p. 48.

29 Z. Smith, *White Teeth* (Harmondsworth: Penguin, 2001), p. 271.

30 Smith, *White Teeth*, p. 281.

31 Smith, *White Teeth*, p. 326.

32 Rushdie, *Imaginary Homelands*, p. 394.

33 S. Hall, 'New Ethnicities', in D. Morley and K. H. Chen (eds.), *Stuart Hall: Critical Dialogues in Cultural Studies* (London: Routledge, 1996), pp. 441–9.

34 I. McEwan, *The Guardian*, 15 September 2001.

35 R. J. Lifton, *The Nazi Doctors: Medical Killing and the Psychology of Genocide* (New York: Basic Books, 1986), p. 8.

36 I. McEwan, *Atonement* (London: Vintage, 2002), p. 282.

37 S. Rushdie, *Shame* (London: Picador, 1984), p. 87.

38 A. Damasio, *The Feeling of What Happens* (London: Vintage, 2000), p. 30.

39 K. Ishiguro, *Never Let Me Go* (London: Faber, 2005), p. 153.

40 K. Ishiguro, *The Unconsoled* (London: Faber, 1996), p. 16.

41 W. Soyinka, interview in *The Guardian*, 28 May 2007.

8

Contemporary British poetry

Introduction

In June 2004, the Poetry Society heralded the 'next generation' of British poets, listing in their roll-call the likes of Patience Agbabi, Nick Drake, Tobias Hill and Gwyneth Lewis, all poets first published in the previous decade.[1] This next generation followed ten years after the new generation of poets had been announced. The 1994 new-generation list – twenty poets from Simon Armitage to Carol Ann Duffy – was part of the media buzz of the moment in which poetry was, however briefly, cited as 'the new rock 'n' roll'.[2] The resulting media attention did not lead to a huge increase in the sales of poetry collections, but Neil Astley's Bloodaxe anthology *Staying Alive* had already demonstrated that there might be a wide and popular audience for the right kind of poetry package.[3] At present, the awareness and dissemination of contemporary poetry has been expanded to an international scope particularly through internet technology such as the online *Contemporary Poetry Review*. With innovative presses entering the field (notably Salt Publishing in 2002), undeterred by the low sales rates for individual slim volumes, the contemporary British poetry scene appears quite vibrant and dynamic.

Amidst this dynamic poetry scene and its expanding audience, the idea of a next generation serves to interrogate the issue of poetry's direction from this contemporary moment; it poses the question of whether contemporaneity, so acute a concern of the postmodern condition, is equally relevant for current poets. The ongoing animosities between 'mainstream' and 'experimental' poetry in Britain and the triumph of the democratic voice, what some critics would see as dominant trends in

British poetry since 1945, may now be being eclipsed by a need to confront the requirements of a world for which 'postmodern' no longer seems an accurate description. In a recent study, Marjorie Perloff, herself a staunch supporter of the experimental in American poetry, has written that 'at the beginning of the twenty-first century, the ... term [postmodernism] seems to have largely lost its momentum.'[4] But where Perloff unearths the 'seeds of the materialist poetic which is increasingly our own' in 'the aesthetic of early modernism', the account of contemporary poetry offered in the following pages is one that faces forwards, resisting a retroactive urge.[5] This chapter explores the current and emergent generation of writers and the established poets they publish alongside and inherit from without getting too caught up in the idea of succession that the term 'next' implies: its intention is to consider the concerns of contemporary poets and to explore what comes after the relativism of postmodern aesthetics, whether there is a place in contemporary poetry where the lyrical is not rejected in favour of irony (or vice versa) but instead the two are combined in poetic attempts to confront the possibility of a future after (post)modernism.

Place, space and language

In writing about the contemporary British poetry scene one cannot ignore the place of Irish poetry in any canon (revisionary, mainstream or alternative) of 'British' writing. Blake Morrison and Andrew Motion, in their *Penguin Book of Contemporary British Poetry*, subsumed Irish and Scots writers into their notion of British, an error I intend to avoid here.[6] Poetry from the island of Ireland is a vigorous force in contemporary writing, with figures such as Paul Muldoon, Eavan Boland, Medbh McGuckian and Ciaran Carson (and of course Seamus Heaney). Yet, while Northern Irish poetry extends beyond the simplistic label of 'contemporary British', the parameters of this volume would require a somewhat arbitrary distinction between Irish and Northern Irish poets. Thus, to avoid that awkward division, Northern Irish poetry is not included within this chapter. In looking at British poetry, I will, however, be centrally considering Scottish and Welsh poetry as energetic parts of a heterogeneous field of poetry in which the writing of Black British poets is also crucial: engagement with the work of Scottish, Welsh, Black British and other poetries reveals the extent to which the very boundaries of 'Britishness' have been reconfigured in contemporary poetry. As Robert Crawford points out "'Where do you come from?" is one of the most important questions in contemporary poetry – where's home?'[7]

The last few decades have seen a fundamental shift towards what might be idealised as a greater inclusivity of disparate voices. Part of this is a movement away from a metropolitan centre (in London) and a central store of idiom and myth that privileges the (Queen's) English and a mythic English landscape. The previous generation of laureate poets, Philip Larkin and Ted Hughes (who accepted the position of Poet Laureate in 1984 after Larkin refused it), presented contrasting accounts of England. For Sean O'Brien there is, in Larkin's work, a 'melancholy delight ... [which] could almost make the reader patriotic', while Hughes's poetry is fundamentally 'uninterested by the developing social and political reality of the British Isles in his adult lifetime' concerned as he is with 'the natural world and its mythic function'.[8] Nonetheless, these two writers share in their absorption with this place (England) as one that is, or is being, lost and can only be partially glimpsed in decay through the form of poetry (Larkin) or must be forcefully recreated in poetry to resist the inevitable decay (Hughes). For both, it is Heritage that is being lost, a heritage that becomes a point of postmodern play and irony, or an exclusionary ideology to be resisted, in the poetry of subsequent generations. The redrawing of contemporary poetry along class, regional and vernacular lines in Britain was initiated by writers such as Tony Harrison and Douglas Dunn in the 1970s. Dunn, a Scottish poet living in Hull, emerged from under the influence of Larkin to articulate a point of view that is essentially vernacular, presenting an alienation from the traditions of high culture. The Leeds-based poet Harrison, particularly in the volumes *The Loiners* (1970) and *From 'The School of Eloquence' and Other Poems* (1978), explores the relationship between language, literature and power and between his own Northern working-class roots and voice and the culture of the intelligentsia. Both Harrison (in 'The Rubarbarians', *The School of Eloquence*, 1978) and Dunn (in *Barbarians*, 1979) offer a self-representation of their poetic art as 'barbarian' – rude eruptions into the stolidity of class-bound British literature. But this does not mean that either poet is somehow fixed in an archaic notion of class consciousness, and Harrison's range of intermedia work, with television and theatre, signals a transgression of boundaries and a desire to reach out to an audience located in a contemporary, media-saturated world.

The legacy of Harrison is most obviously taken up by Simon Armitage whose distinctive voice (Northern, youthful, stylishly composed of puns, jaunty rhythms and half-rhyme) presents sub-cultural material and refuses to defer to the high cultural establishment: he hybridises voice, culture and tone to great effect, as in the comic mixing of a Northern English accent with American idioms in 'The Stuff' (*Zoom*, 1989). Armitage emerges in the 1980s and shares with his contemporaries of that time (such as Glyn Maxwell) an acoustic virtuosity and a type of classless cultural savvy that does not make them apolitical (far from it in many cases) but that marks them as products of the Thatcher era in British politics and the 'cool' of the 1990s. The challenge to the politics of class, and the power structures of language and literature, continue in contemporary poetry with writers such as Liverpool-born Paul Farley demonstrating that although 'class' may be an out-of-date term in contemporary politics, the under-class, sub-class and subcultures of Britain provide much of the energy for contemporary British poetry.

British poetry since the 1970s has most obviously been invigorated by the increasing presence of Black British voices, voices that question many of the formal and cultural assumptions of this poetry. Linton Kwesi Johnson, Benjamin Zephaniah and Grace Nichols, with their emphasis on and explorations of oral rhythms and dub energies have brought new cadences into British poetry and opened the way for subsequent poets, such as Patience Agbabi, who fuse the performative aspect of their work with powerful presentations of racial identity in Britain. The challenges of such work are formal as much as thematic, requiring a reader or listener to respond with their body to a physical appeal, an apostrophe from a body or bodies that have a less than privileged place in British society. In the poetry of Johnson, Zephaniah, Nichols and others such as Fred D'Aguiar, what is being given expression is the ambivalence of Black Britishness itself and the questions such an appellation would open up about nationality, origin, language and authority. Challenges to linguistic authority, which might find a parallel in Tony Harrison's poetry, are made by Johnson (in 'If I Waz a Tap-Natch Poet', *Mi Revalueshanary Fren*, 2002) and John Agard (in 'Listen Mr Oxford Don', *Mangoes and Bullets*, 1990) as well as in many other pieces. Here what is at issue is the insertion of a hybrid voice, coming neither from here (imperial centre) nor there (colonies) but located in the body and experience of the poem and the poet. Patience Agbabi draws on the black street rhythms of rap and dance music in her work, and this recent poetry does signal a shift in poetic and performance techniques. Some of Agbabi's poems – 'E (Manic Dance Mix A)' and 'My Mother' from *RAW* (1995) and '1996', part of 'Weights and Measures and Finding a Rhyme for Orange' from *Transformatrix* (2000) – use the visual aspects of the page and thus upset the hierarchy of presence over written trace, while her use of dramatic monologue inserts an uncertain relationship between 'speaker' and poet/performer. Nonetheless, throughout her work and performances, Agbabi evokes an energetic, powerful and personal connection between poet and audience.

A range of Black British writers explore their location and their language, but the negotiation of belongingness through the lenses of language and origin is not just their concern. Tom Leonard, Don Paterson, Kathleen Jamie, and other Scottish poets and Oliver Reynolds, Owen Sheers and Gwyneth Lewis amongst Welsh poets, explore the relationship between place, race and language. Leonard's work challenges commonplaces and conventions, including, like Tony Harrison, the cultural authority of the elite and the repression of difference. His poetry, prose poems, poster poems and other modes of writing make use of a phonetically transcribed dialect of Glasgow to express a diverse and often disavowed community who are not the literary Scots of a 'traditional' culture and history. Leonard's example influenced subsequent poets, paving the way for Don Paterson to move between diverse idioms that include urban Scots and Scots-inflected English. In her poetry, notably in *The Queen of Sheba* (1994) and *Jizzen* (1999), Kathleen Jamie explores gender, nationality and language. Gwyneth Lewis writes in both Welsh and English, and in her 2003 English collection *Keeping Mum* the detective and psychiatric cases that unfold are also an investigation/discovery of a relationship to languages (a murdered mother tongue and the language of cities and the Internet) and to a motherland. Another contemporary poet, Owen Sheers, also explores the disjunctive linguistic and geographical identity of the Welsh – Sheers himself was born in Fiji. His second collection *Skirrid Hill* (2005) describes the landscape (rural, post-industrial and archaeological) of Wales but evokes in its very title a division or divorce that this land and its language seem necessarily to produce: 'Skirrid: from the Welsh *Ysgyrid*, a derivation of *Ysgariad* meaning divorce or separation.'[9]

White English poets too have re-engineered 'England', moving far away from the traditions of John Betjeman or Larkin and the myths of Hughes towards new ways of describing landscape, place and belonging. Alice Oswald in *Dart* (2002) creates a pioneering mode of historical-landscape poetry in which the river Dart tells its own story through the polyphony of voices from the human, natural and metaphysical worlds, while Tobias Hill's *Zoo* (1998) presents a defamiliarising urban-pastoral. Leonard's Scotland, Lewis's Wales, Agbabi's Black Britain and Oswald's English landscape are all places within the borders of Britishness but places that have redrawn the contours of what this Britishness is. As Moniza Alvi combines an Indian and Pakistani heritage with a British one in her poetry, so other poets insert the voices and spaces of their own disparate heritages into the poetry of Britain. What results is a redrawing of the map of 'Britain', one that makes its boundaries permeable and fluid, that positions a whole host of centres; on the Indian subcontinent, in America or in the Caribbean. This multiplying of British poetry, which relocates it both here and 'there' (outside the geographical boundaries of the British Isles) is not just the result of colonial encounters and diasporas but emerges from the myriad of passages out of and into Britain; the movement of some poets, such as Nick Drake, towards Eastern Europe, the complex positioning of Jackie Kay (a Scottish-Nigerian poet in Northern England) or Sujata Bhatt (an Indian-born poet writing in Germany and publishing in English in Britain) illustrates such passages. The blurring of national boundaries can also be seen in the work of Pascale Petit (a British poet born in Paris, brought up in Wales) who turns to the Americas (Amazonian cultures and the work of Frida Kahlo) for her sources and images. The nation space is thus multiplied and expanded to include hybrid identities which are empowered by their multiplicity. What emerges is not so much a fragmented sense of belonging and national identity but a plurality of possible positions from which legitimate visions of the contemporary moment can be articulated.

Fragmented bodies, gender and technology

The issue of fragmentation does not pertain only to questionings and new definitions of Britishness; the body has also come under question in the poetry of the past few decades. The process of fragmentation of physical being and the reconstitution of a bodily authenticity that is wary of assuming the status of an essential reality can be traced in the work of a number of poets and is particularly apparent when gender identity and sexed bodies are being considered. Andrew Duncan, describing the poetry of the 1970s, identifies a Gothic haunting in the somatic traces of dismembered social and individual bodies, seeing a 'Gothic violation of body image' in the 'massive availability of representations' that leads, for example, to the 'fantastic, hyperbolic body' of both the pin-up and the poetry of Jeremy Reed.[10] The culture of the 1970s and after reimagines the body and, through the appropriation and fetishisation of bodies both masculine and feminine, undermines the stability of personal identity and foregrounds questions of gender and sexuality. As Duncan suggests, the resonances of these concerns can be located in contemporary British poetry, where Gothic, fragmented bodies signal a haunted lack of somatic continuity and integrity. In a range of women poets, such as Penelope Shuttle, Carol Rumens, Liz Lochhead, Carol Ann Duffy, Helen Dunmore and Denise Riley, the female body appears, failing, suffering, controlled, examined and deconstructed. But it is certainly not just women who consider the fugitive, riven body. In his 1993 collection *British Subjects*, Fred D'Aguiar's investigation of a racial belonging also includes an investigation of the body in pieces, such as the resonant fragments explored in 'The Body in Question', while his 'Thirteen Views of a Penis' speculates on the 'decline of the Penis Age'.[11]

When bodily cohesion is dismembered, what are often also broken apart are boundaries and dualities that have been used to define the nature of humanity such as those between the human and animal. Selima Hill's often highly surreal poetry is concerned mostly with a menagerie of animals and relationships (relationships within families and between men and women). She concerns herself with the wide array of women's identities (as mother, wife, daughter, lover, goddess, patient, girl), writing poems that meld a psychological intensity with an imaginative whimsy. The titles of her collections indicate the extent to which her work blurs the physical and psychic distance between humans and animals – *My Darling Camel* (1988), *Trembling Hearts in the Bodies of Dogs* (1994, a selection from previous collections), *Bunny* (2001) and *Portrait of my Lover as a Horse* (2002). Pascale Petit's *The Zoo Father* (2001) and *The Huntress* (2005) concern a daughter, a dying father and a manic-depressive mother, but their world opens out into a fabulous realm of Amazonian and other creatures. These animal-mythical hybrids take over or merge with the protagonists, offering ways to imagine or embody painful familial secrets; they are "becomings-animal" that articulate pain and passion and, in the case of 'At the Gate of Secrets' (*The Huntress*), in which the daughter becomes a cosmic stag, a flight out of the limits of identity.

As the work of Hill and Petit exemplifies, the fragmented and metamorphosed body often figures an image or set of images that interrogate the cultural construction of gender and the power hierarchies of gender relations: both Hill (*Bunny*) and Petit (*The Zoo Father*) explore the disturbing manifestations of patriarchal power embodied in a masculine figure who abuses and manipulates a daughter, dehumanising and disturbing her bodily integrity and subjectivity. Across a whole range of contemporary British poetries, the configurations, discourses and prerogatives of sex and gender identity are explored and reworked. Carol Ann Duffy's poetry offers a thorough investigation and reconstitution of female identity, from earlier poems, such as 'Standing Female Nude' (*Selected Poems*, 1994), that challenge the traditional silencing and fetishisation of women, to her later *The World's Wife* (1999) collection of poems, which speak back to a masculinist tradition and history, endowing a range of historical, mythical and fictional women with a point of view and a bodily experience that ruptures the hegemony of the male perspective. In exploring women's sexuality, including a lesbian sexuality in which women's bodies speak to each other ('Warming Her Pearls' and 'Girlfriends'), Duffy also challenges the ocularcentrism and phallocentrism of male-orientated desire.[12] Jackie Kay gives voice to a range of experiences, not only of a black girl adopted into a white Scottish family in the collection *The Adoption Papers* but also to working-class male homosexuality (in 'Close Shave', *Other Lovers*, 1993), which speaks of a bodily yearning at odds with its prohibited status.

In male poets' examinations of gender and sex identity, David Dabydeen stands out, demonstrating an abiding interest in sexual politics in his poetry. Dabydeen explores what he terms 'the erotic energies of the colonial experience', considering the effect of colonialism on masculinity and the male body in poems in *Slave Song* (1984) and 'Caliban' from *Coolie Odyssey* (1988).[13] Simon Armitage's work considers the construction of masculinity and the performative aspects of male identity particularly in *Zoom!* (1989), and there is a self conscious and ironic handling of masculinity in Neil Rollinson's and Glyn Maxwell's poetry. In his collection *The Man in the White Suit* (1999), Nick Drake, while resolutely resisting the label of 'gay' poet, explores with tender intimacy the male bodies of lovers ('Eureka', 'Static') and the loss of friends to early death ('Heaven', 'The Very Rich Hours', 'Art and Mystery').

The blurring of human and animal that Hill and Petit present in their poetry and which resonates with the work of other poets is one way of identifying how transgressed boundaries can initiate an examination of the construction of gendered identity and the social norms and power networks of gender behaviour. But there is a different boundary that is transgressed in contemporary writing, one that also undermines traditional gendered hierarchies and that points towards the cyborg hybridity evoked by Donna Haraway in 'A Cyborg Manifesto'. For Haraway, the figuration of the cyborg, in which the distinctions between animal, human and machine are fundamentally undermined, can function to 'suggest a way out of the maze of dualisms in which we have explained our bodies and our tools to ourselves'.[14] '[R]esolutely committed to partiality, irony, intimacy and perversity', the cyborg is not a celebration of a streamlined techno-sphere or transcendence of the body, but an acknowledgment of the grotesque and amorphous configurations of bodies, spaces and machines that constitute the personal and economic realms of the contemporary world.[15] The implications of Haraway's cyborg can be seen in contemporary poetry that faces the liminal space between science and art and the new understandings of identity and writing that emerge from a human–technology interstice. The publication of the volume *Contemporary Poetry and Contemporary Science*, in which scientists, poets (including Paul Muldoon, Sarah Maguire, Simon Armitage and Don Paterson) and critics collaborate, demonstrates the current interconnections being drawn between poetry and science.[16] Poetry, though, has never been completely antipathetic to science and technology (consider the interest of many modernist poets in science), and many poets over recent years have taken scientific discourses or adopted figures or ideas from science to explore the contemporary world.

As Jane Dowson and Alice Entwistle point out, it is out of the intersection of scientific and mythic narratives that many contemporary women poets interrogate the status of science and the place of women and women's bodies in the contemporary world.[17] Notably, in a range of poems ('Electroplating the Baby', 'Love in the Lab', 'Pavlova's Physics', 'Leonardo and the Vortex', 'Quark' and 'The Alchemist', all in *Her Book*, 2000), Jo Shapcott deploys the vocabulary and perspective of science and technology to critique a reductive scientism and also to uncover the aesthetic and mystical possibilities of a world of molecules, symbols and transmutations. She posits the 'Mad Cow' as a figure of feminine subversion, drawing on the BSE scare in Britain in the 1990s where the epidemic of the neurodegenerative disease BSE (bovine spongiform encephalopathy) in cattle led to widespread culling and fears about human infection. With this 'Mad Cow' persona, first featured in her volume *Phrase Book* (1992), Shapcott imagines a perspective that undermines the authority of a patriarchally inscribed science and society. For Dowson and Entwistle, 'it is in this joyously post-scientific, unquestionably female creature that Shapcott reveals the undecidable, and politically and aesthetically productive, interrelation of the transforming discourses of science and myth.'[18]

Lavinia Greenlaw is the contemporary poet who most consistently considers the articulation of poetry with science. Poems such as 'The Innocence of Radium', 'Galileo's Wife', 'The Man Whose Smile Made Medical History' and 'Suspension', in *Night Photograph* (1993), explore the (gendered) authority of scientific discourse and its power to order and control the world. But Greenlaw's poems are not simply about the impact of science and technology on the world; her poems inhabit a landscape that is necessarily technological, which has the space travel, roads, pylons, cinema and radio waves of an unavoidable present in which human beings interact with the mechanical: in *A World Where News Travelled Slowly* (1997), Greenlaw explores a glass eye ('Millefiori'), an 'Iron Lung' and the mechanical imagination of childhood ('Invention'), while 'Bright Earth', in *Minsk* (2003), plays with scientistic objectivity in its listing of substances, objects and emotions. Technology is also, as in the work of Shapcott, a transformative and potentially beautiful configuration of the world such as the 'revolution' and 'fireworks' of transatlantic communication ('A World Where News Travelled Slowly'), and the harmony and unity of 'Electricity' and city sunset of 'From Scattered Blue' (both in *Night Photograph*). This is not to claim that male poets ignore the productivity of the interspace of science and poetry. David Morley in his *Scientific Papers* (2002), for example, draws on his experience in both creative and scientific writing (he teaches both at Warwick University) in poems that reveal that 'the practices of writing science and poetry are ... a single discussion of perception ... in the same laboratory of language.'[19] The poems in Morley's collection are presented as a 'series of findings', and they fundamentally engage with Darwin, Newton, Einstein, with zoology, oceanography, mathematics, physics and botany.

But beyond a thematic exploration of the power and perspective of technology and science, in formal terms an engagement with technology has been particularly productive for contemporary poetry. The use of digital mediums to create hypertext or cybertext poetry has lead to exciting innovations in active and interactive poetic forms. John Cayley, the foremost exponent of such innovations in British poetry, has produced dynamic and 'ergodic' pieces that make full use of the digital medium.[20] In pieces such as 'Book Unbound' (1995) and 'windsound' (2001) algorithmic programmes mean that the texts morph and alter differently for each reader/user. This digital poetry clearly foregrounds the role of the medium in the production of meaning, an inextricable relation between media and message that is usually only implicit in a codex (printed) text. It also introduces temporal and spatial dimensions to a text. Questions about the compression of space in the contemporary technological age are considered by Greenlaw in 'A World Where News Travelled Slowly', but in his pieces 'The Speaking Clock' (1995) and the work-in-progress 'wotclock', Cayley actually embeds the temporal embodiment of the text (as the words on the clock pass the time passes), requiring from the reader an acknowledgement of the text's instantiation in time in the act of reading.

History and ethics

Beyond questions about the temporal presence of poetry and its survival in an increasingly digital and multimedia age, contemporary poetry is more generally concerned with time, and with the ethical weight of history and memory. Postmodernism has broken up the oppressive grand narrative of History into the local histories that enable the articulation of other voices and experiences, but what is also evident is the elision of ethics in the historical play of postmodernism. Recent British poetry, in comparison, displays a real involvement with history and ethics. It is Geoffrey Hill, a poet impossible to assimilate easily into the schools and movements of twentieth-century British poetry, who leads by example in this area. Hill's work demonstrates an awareness of the poet's ties to his community and a belief in a poet's need to address issues of ethical and political moment. But what Hill also evinces is a self-consciousness of the burden of this contractual obligation to the community and to ethics: history is necessarily experienced and voiced by an individual, but what is undergone and spoken is the tradition, duty and inheritance of a community. From the poems in For the Unfallen (1959) onwards, Hill offers a poetry that bears witness and, in so doing, carries the weight of history as a personal but also necessarily communal vision of the relationship of the past to the present. Hill poses 'History as Poetry' in the title of an early poem (*King Log*, 1968), and, engaging with a Christian and Western history, often ancient or medieval, as well as with events of the recent past or contemporary moment, his work searches for the balance between authority and the renunciation of the authoritative. Recently this seeking of balance also comes, for Hill, to describe a reconciliation of the opposites of sensual and logical knowledge or 'reason and desire on the same loop' as he puts it in 'That Man as a Rational Animal Desires the Knowledge Which is His Perfection' (*Canaan*, 1996).

Hill is not a postmodernist, nor is he an anachronistic modernist, but his continuous engagements with Pound (in the essays in *The Lords of Limit*, 1984, and *The Enemy's Country*, 1991, and elsewhere) do suggest some common ground in terms of the language, ethics and historical perpetuity of poetry. Ezra Pound's *Cantos* as a 'poem including history' or T. S. Eliot's fragments in *The Waste Land* are not the immediate forebears of a contemporary poetic engagement with history, but their valorising of history and their insistence on the historical as a possible source of meaning and orientation in the modern world gesture towards the concerns of contemporary writers.

Craig Raine is often identified with the 1970s 'Martian School' of poetry, which originated with his poem 'A Martian Sends a Postcard Home' (*A Martian Sends a Postcard Home*, 1979). His poetry seems to fully inhabit a wry, postmodern attitude to the world, one in which the innocent perspective signals an estrangement from the realist, everyday world of the movement poets; the quotidian and reliable becomes bewildering and disorientating. But Raine is not simply a postmodern poet of ontological instability; he is concerned explicitly with history and its relation to the present. In his verse drama *1953* (based on Racine's *Andromaque*), the aftermath of the Second World War is radically altered by Hitler and Mussolini's victory, and the drama considers how it is only through the perspective of the past that the present, and its possible variations, can be understood. That the recall of history has an ethical import is central to what Raine attempts, and this becomes, in his 1994 *History: The Home Movie*, a remembering and memorialising of the domestic and mundane over the 'great' events of history. *History: The Home Movie* offers a survey of the twentieth century from the perspective of events in Raine's and his wife's family and includes local and domestic narratives: there is no overarching political account to hold it together. For John Kerrigan, this 'makes the sequence more largely disconnected', but Raine's text is concerned with exploring and vividly displaying the effects of politics and history, not with sub-suming them into a single narrative.[21] The lack of continuity and the local histories do not make *History: The Home Movie* a postmodern play with the past though. What this text signals is a shift in contemporary poetry towards an interest in history as it is experienced, in the ethics and effects of historical choices, and in the moral obligations we have to the history that shapes our contemporaneity.

Thus one can unearth the historical as an ethical force and a way of creating an authentic present in a range of contemporary poetry. In Jo Shapcott's work, the ethical weight of cultural memory and political events are explored in the piece 'Phrase Book', and history figures prominently in the writing of the 'next generation'. Alice Oswald's *Dart* is not just a nature poem but a text committed to voicing the past of a place, a place inhabited and inscribed, a place that carries human memory and human experience and which can be witnessed by the poet in her role of channelling the disparate voices, histories and memories of the river and the people who live and work on and by it. Gwyneth Lewis's historical impetus is also clearly inspired by place, in this case Wales, its colonial past and linguistic and physical heritage, and the poet's duty to and inheritance of the past. Paul Farley's *Tramp in Flames* (2006) forges poetry out of the archives of cultural memory, while Nick Drake writes of recent Eastern European upheavals in *The Man in the White Suit*, a text in which the political history of a place that marks its inhabitants becomes something that must be witnessed in poetry.

Raine's *History: The Home Movie* is a novel in verse, a form that is per-haps necessitated by the weight of history the text attempts to articu-late, but he is not the only contemporary writer to explore this form and its relationship to history. In all her novels, Bernardine Evaristo com-bines poetry and prose: *Lara* (1997) and *The Emperor's Babe* (2001) are nov-els in verse while the narrative of *Soul Tourists* (2005) is written in both poetry and prose. In all these texts, Evaristo works with not a desire for historical veracity but a search for an ethical truth to which different histories can bear witness. This ethical veracity, a giving life to a voice that can communicate its own past experience in the present day, is perhaps most prominent in *The Emperor's Babe*, which writes the experi-ence of Zuleika, a black slave girl in Roman London. Zuleika speaks in the vibrant hybrid tones of contemporary metropolitan youth culture rather than in an 'authentic' ancient voice.

From experimentation to lyric truth

The innovative forms of Evaristo's writing, combining the forces of prose narrative and poetic lyricism, point towards one of the central divisions in British poetry, the opposition between 'experimental' and 'mainstream' poetry, what Sarah Broom terms the different 'Tribes of Poetry'.[22] Broom goes on to demonstrate how tensions between experimental poetry – 'disjunctive in its procedures and draw[ing] attention to the materiality of language' – and the work supported by prominent and influential publishers and institutions persists to the present day despite recent attempts by *Poetry Review* to bridge the divide.[23] Though there is no absolute distinction between these different modes of poetry, with much 'mainstream' work of the past decade demonstrating a level of self-reflexive irony, it is the case that the more radically disjunctive modes of poetry fail to find institutional support. The avant-garde element of British poetry has been hugely overshadowed by particular big names – Betjeman, Hughes, Heaney – and the mid-century movement poets, most prominently Larkin, that, despite the British poetry revival of the 1960s and 1970s, continue to colour conceptions of the British poetry scene as realist, insular and formally conservative. This is the substance of Keith Tuma's claim that 'British poetry is dead' in America.[24] But one only needs to look at the poetry published by the small presses of Britain in the past decades to find the work of Maggie O'Sullivan, Cris Cheek, Adrian Clarke, Caroline Bergvall and Geraldine Monk who formally experiment with poetry, employing visual forms, typography and disjunctive syntax to open out the boundaries of poetry and to interrogate the significatory power of language, voice and text. Current outposts of experimentation in poetry in Britain can be found at Dartington College (which has run a performance-writing course since 1994), at the Contemporary Poetics Research Centre at Royal Holloway College, University of London, and, of course, at Cambridge, where the work of new writers continues to be inspired by J. H. Prynne.

Ian Gregson wishes to valorise the experimental in contemporary poetry, identifying a stream of avant-garde poetry that demonstrates an 'insistence on using poetry as a medium in which to say the most philosophically difficult things that can be said in expressive writing' in contrast to which 'much mainstream poetry seems … philistine.'[25] Gregson's dismissal of the mainstream seems to imply that any writer who has not wholly embraced post-structuralist challenges to the stabilities of meaning and the real are somehow uncultured and is a sorry indication of how value can accrue to the division of contemporary poetry into different tribes. 'Experimental' poetry is neither arcane intellectualism that poses a 'threat' to other poetries, as Don Paterson would claim, nor the only valid poetry of the moment.[26] I would want to support Andrew Roberts's point that 'Both the critique of essentialism in contemporary theory and the evident multiplicity of contemporary poetic practice militate against the belief in a single form of poetic value.'[27] In the current British poetry scene, a range of poetries coexist, ones that show an interest in mixed-media, sound and visual poetry, or links to the avant-garde American 'language poetry' tradition emphasising the materiality of the signifier and ones that embrace postmodern ideas of performativity and heterogeneity.

As this account of contemporary British poetry has shown, the wave of postmodernism and post-structuralist theories of language are no longer the driving force of current writing. What comes in their wake is not a reactionary return to a simpler version of reality, with stable conceptions of truth, history and meaning; instead, many contemporary poets search for ways to locate and articulate a veracity and an ethics that acknowledges postmodern irony and ambiguity but does not relinquish the possibility of expressing a lyrical truth. Carol Ann Duffy is exemplary in this. Her poetry has been characterised by an exploration of the way in which language constructs and speaks an individual with her use of dramatic monologue, a form that also enables the investigation of the social and linguistic construction of gender identity. But in her recent work Duffy has moved away from the postmodern ironies enabled by the dramatic monologue: in *Rapture* (2005), the voice of personal testimony predominates in a collection that, whilst acknowledging the instability of text and self and the power of language to construct or deform the world, celebrates the power of the love lyric to speak an emotional truth and to demonstrate the ethical imperative of human empathy. The interest in history, place, subjectivity and location in poetry being written now demonstrates a similar interest in ethical import. As with Duffy's work, contemporary British poetry is more concerned with presenting an empathetic truth than with asserting the novelty of its contemporaneity.

Notes

1 The full list of 'next generation' poets are Patience Agbabi, Amanda Dalton, Nick Drake, Jane Draycott, Paul Farley, Leontia Flynn, Matthew Francis,

Sophie Hannah, Tobias Hill, Gwyneth Lewis, Alice Oswald, Pascale Petit, Jacob Polley, Deryn Rees-Jones, Maurice Riordan, Robin Robertson, Owen Sheers, Henry Shukman, Catherine Smith and Jean Sprackland. See S. Armitage, *The Guardian*, 5 June 2004.

2 The 'new generation' poets were Moniza Alvi, Simon Armitage, John Burnside, Robert Crawford, David Dabydeen, Michael Donaghy, Carol Ann Duffy, Ian Duhig, Elizabeth Garrett, Lavinia Greenlaw, W. N. Herbert, Michael Hoffman, Mick Imlah, Kathleen Jamie, Jamie McKendrick, Sarah Maguire, Glyn Maxwell, Don Paterson, Pauline Stainer and Susan Wicks.
See *Poetry Review*, 'New Generation Poets' special issue, 84 (spring 1994).

3 N. Astley, *Staying Alive: Real Poems for Unreal Times* (Newcastle upon Tyne: Bloodaxe, 2002).

4 M. Perloff, *21st Century Modernism: The 'New' Poetics* (London: Blackwell, 2002), p. 2.

5 Perloff, *21st Century Modernism*, p. 3.

6 B. Morrison and A. Motion (eds.), *Penguin Book of Contemporary British Poetry* (Harmondsworth: Penguin, 1982).

7 R. Crawford, *Identifying Poets: Self and Territory in Twentieth-Century Poetry* (Edinburgh: Edinburgh University Press, 1993).

8 S. O'Brien, *The Deregulated Muse: Essays on Contemporary British and Irish Poetry* (Newcastle upon Tyne: Bloodaxe, 1998), pp. 30, 37.

9 O. Sheers, *Skirrid Hill* (Bridgend: Seren, 2005), p. v.

10 A. Duncan, *The Failure of Conservatism in Modern British Poetry* (Cambridge: Salt, 2003), p. 210.

11 F. D'Aguiar, *British Subjects* (Newcastle upon Tyne: Bloodaxe Books, 1994).

12 C. A. Duffy, *Selected Poems* (Harmondsworth: Penguin in association with Anvil Press Poetry, 1994).

13 D. Dabydeen, *Slave Song* (Aarhus, Dangaroo Press, 1985), p. 10.

14 D. Haraway, 'A Cyborg Manifesto: Science, Technology and Socialist-Feminism in the Late Twentieth Century', in *Simians, Cyborgs and Women: The Reinvention of Nature* (London and New York: Routledge, 1991), pp. 149–81; p. 181.

15 Haraway, 'A Cyborg Manifesto', p. 151.

16 R. Crawford (ed.), *Contemporary Poetry and Contemporary Science* (Oxford: Oxford University Press, 2006).

17 J. Dowson and A. Entwistle, *A History of Twentieth-Century British Women's Poetry* (Cambridge: Cambridge University Press, 2005).

18 Dowson and Entwistle, *Twentieth-Century British Women's Poetry*, p. 239.

19 D. Morley, *Scientific Papers* (Manchester: Carcanet, 2002), p. 85.

20 See E. Aarseth, *Cybertext: Perspectives on Ergodic Literature* (Baltimore, Md.: Johns Hopkins University Press, 1997); L. Pequenno Glazier, *Digital Poetics* (Tuscaloosa, Ala.: University of Alabama Press, 2001).

21 J. Kerrigan, 'Notes from the Home Front: Contemporary British Poetry', *Essays in Criticism*, 54 (2) (2004): 103–127; p. 118.

22 S. Broom, *Contemporary British and Irish Poetry* (Houndmills: Palgrave Macmillan, 2006), p. 222.

23 Broom, *Contemporary British and Irish Poetry*, p. 223.

24 K. Tuma, *Fishing by Obstinate Isles: Modern and Postmodern British Poetry and American Readers* (Evanston, Ill.: Northwestern University Press, 1999), p. 1.

25 I. Gregson, *Contemporary Poetry and Postmodernism: Dialogue and Estrangement* (Houndmills, Macmillan, 1996), p. 11.

26 D. Paterson and C. Simic (eds.), *New British Poetry* (Saint Paul, Minn.: Graywolf Press, 2004), p. xxiii.

27 A. M. Roberts and J. Allison (eds.), *Poetry and Contemporary Culture: The Question of Value* (Edinburgh: Edinburgh University Press, 2002).

9

Theatre in modern British culture

A dramatised society: diversity and participation

'We have never as a society acted so much or watched so many others acting', said Raymond Williams in his inaugural lecture as Professor of Drama at Cambridge University.[1] This was true enough in 1974, and now, in the early twenty-first century, Williams' concept of a 'dramatised' society is even more apparent. In making his generalisation, Williams was including all forms of drama, not only those that take place in theatres but also performances in film and television studios. He was also concerned, however, in attempting to define the place of live performance in an age of mechanical (and now, we should add, digital) reproduction. Throughout the twentieth century, developments in film, television, video recording and digital imagery have uttered repeated challenges to live theatre to justify its once-unique position in society as a site of performance, and there is certainly a sense in which the technological and digital media are the commercial and cultural rivals of live theatre rather than colleagues.[2] Any attempt to create a clear binary opposition between live and recorded or digital performance is further complicated by the fact that from the point of view of the practising professional there is actually a great deal of overlap and continuity between the two: the careers of most successful British actors and directors (and, to a lesser extent, designers and technicians) traverse the live and recorded media. Contemporary British theatre does not simply stand in opposition to other forms but is part of a network of performance practices that include the mediatised, the digitised, the recorded and the broadcast.

Digital technologies, too, have had a profound effect on live performance. The theatre has not been slow in exploiting the advantages offered

by, for example, computerised lighting and sound systems. The application of digital technology to live theatre to create multimedia performances combining live and recorded action has been a more contentious
route, but the scenographic and compositional possibilities offered by
this combination have been employed by specialist companies and also
integrated into the aesthetic of mainstream theatre. Just as the increasing sophistication of computer-generated graphics has revitalised film
animation, so it has increased the number and effectiveness of the ways
in which mixed-media performances can be generated in the theatre.
More radically, digital technology has enabled theatre to be created in
the digital environment itself – so that 'live' performances, spectator-
oriented or interactive, involving various combinations of live participants, virtual presences, avatars, robots or other humanoids, take place
wholly or partly online, on the computer screen, in the IT laboratory
and by way of the mobile phone.

The recent phenomenon of 'flash-mobbing', for example, has created
a form of public theatre facilitated by the digital communication possibilities of the Internet and mobile-phone technology. The flash-mob
event has a clear structure: following a set of instructions (usually on a
website), a group of people – typically hundreds – assemble in public,
carry out in unison a set of clearly scripted actions for a limited amount
of time, then disperse. The theatrics of the flash mobs have a clear affin-
ity with the 'happenings' of the 1960s, and like their hippy predecessors
the flash mobs have an ironic relationship to mainstream performance culture, reclaiming the performative in terms of an amorphously
democratic event whose first aim is fun. It is a performance without any
point, the creation of an ephemeral piece of art in a public place, and
flash mobbers disavow any political agenda or intent beyond that of
simply creating something for themselves – and, presumably, baffling
the onlookers who are not in on the joke. But the apparent spontan-
eity and egalitarianism of the performance belies the extent to which
flash-mobbing is a directed event, and one relying on the quasi-military
precision of the instructions, which the crowd must follow to the letter.
Like the internet technology that generated it, the democratic claims of
flash-mobbing are inherently paradoxical.

The flash mob may bear little resemblance to the conventional image
of theatre – plays, play-scripts, stages (with or without proscenium
arches), lighting, costumes, make-up and actors learning and recit-
ing lines, watched by audiences seated in rows. But this is the point. In

modern British society, theatre *is* all that, but it is also more than that. It is important to recognise the sheer diversity of ways in which theatrical practices and activities are braided within the culture of the UK. As a generic term, the word 'theatre' means far more than the performance of dramas in purpose-built playhouses. It also encompasses established forms of arts and entertainment such as mime, puppetry, stand-up comedy and variety acts ranging from conjurors to burlesque dancers. Many of these, such as opera, ballet and contemporary dance, can also be regarded as art forms in their own right, but they also share techniques, themes, buildings, audiences, funding council budgets and personnel with productions of classic and contemporary plays. And, like the flash mob, new forms have emerged to challenge established definitions of what theatre is. Many of these new theatre practices take place outside traditional theatre buildings: they happen in community centres, clubs, libraries, hospitals, churches and church halls, schools, arts centres, public squares, rock festivals, canal boats, motorway service stations, art galleries, living rooms, pubs, found spaces and site-specific venues. In some cases the relocation happens out of necessity; in many others it is part of a deliberate aesthetic, an exploration of performance, landscape and environment. The pioneering Welsh company Brith Gof, for example, staged their devised play *Haearn* (1992) in a derelict South Wales iron foundry, whose abandoned architecture was an intrinsic part of the production's juxtaposition of the Greek myth of Hephaestos with the contemporary reality of Wales's industrial decline. That site-specific theatre (once identified with 'alternative' theatres) has become an increasingly accepted part of mainstream theatre production is evidenced by the recent collaboration between Punchdrunk Theatre and the National Theatre in a production of *Faust* (2006) at a 'secret location' (a large warehouse) in Wapping.

Moreover, a large percentage of British theatre takes place outside not only traditional theatre buildings but also the more nebulous structures of theatrical professionalism. The once-absolute barrier between the professional and non-professional theatre worlds has become more permeable since the Employment Acts of the early 1980s weakened the position of the trade union Equity – which once controlled entry into the theatre professions with a rod of iron. The distinction still exists, however, and the importance of theatre-making in the non-professional sector should not be underestimated. Theatre in the UK is not only a creative industry, it is also a participatory activity. 'We have never as a society acted so much', said Williams, and throughout the UK there is an immense involvement in the making and performing of theatre in its various manifestations, radical and traditional. Much of this is focused on young people. Nearly every town and city – and many a small village – will have its own youth-theatre group, sometimes run by the regional repertory theatre as part of a larger outreach programme, sometimes run by enthusiastic amateurs or youth workers. Stagecoach Theatre Arts Company runs leisure-time performing-arts courses for children and teenagers in nearly 600 venues around the UK. In schools, too, drama is flourishing. The school play is often chosen so as to involve large numbers rather than an elite few, and modern musicals, especially those with an ironic twist, are now the most popular genre: *Return to the Forbidden Planet* outshines *The Tempest* in the school repertoire. Practical work within and related to curricular GCSE and A-level Drama and Theatre Studies provides opportunities for more focused and experimental and devised work, a tendency that continues into the university sector.

Amateur drama is also flourishing among adults, although the term 'amateur' itself remains a source of some embarrassment. The word retains little of its original meaning of 'lover' or 'enthusiast' and has taken on connotations of ineptness or poor quality. In the context of theatre, the very phrase 'am-dram' has become a synonym for what Peter Brook called 'Deadly Theatre'.[3] To many people it denotes the kind of theatrical ineptitude that Peter Quince and his rude mechanicals display in *A Midsummer Night's Dream* – stumbling and incoherent drama in which outdated plays are staged in outdated theatrical styles by untrained part-timers with little or no theatrical skill. It is true that amateur theatre is seldom the home of the most cutting-edge or experimental theatre and that it tends to follow behind the professional theatre in its programmes, its styles and its technical capacities. Nonetheless, as Greg Giesekam notes in his study of amateur drama in Scotland,

> If the truth is told, over the past nine months [the research team] did endure a few tedious evenings watching poorly presented theatre: but only half of them were at amateur or community events, while the rest were in the subsidized professional theatre. Neither type has a monopoly over either good or bad theatre (whatever they are). We are also probably not alone in thinking this, since the total audience for amateur, youth and community theatre in Scotland last year, at well over a million people, easily exceeded the audience for

> professional theatre – and they can't have all been shanghaied into
> going by the 40,000 or so people who are regularly involved in such
> activity.[4]

What is sometimes seen as a weakness of am-dram is also its strength: the intimate social relation between the actor and spectator. Amateur actors rarely play to audiences made up entirely of people that they do not know. Professionals play most of the time to strangers – the large mixed audiences of the national subsidised theatres such as the National Theatre, the Royal Shakespeare Company or the West End, with their large 'cultural tourist' audiences; or on tour to unfamiliar towns, playing there for anything from a day to a week but rarely longer; or even when performing at a regional rep – again very often in a town they do not know, in lodgings provided through their theatrical employers. However strong the sense of community between a professional theatre and its regular clientele, the actor is most often a stranger. Amateurs, on the other hand, play to their friends, or to friends of friends – an audience that already has knowledge of them (and many of whom may themselves have acted in other productions). For this audience, part of the pleasure is the double consciousness provided by the experience of watching people whom they know in everyday life play fictional parts. Such an audience may or may not be less critical or more forgiving of what it sees (and the jealousies and infighting of the amateur acting group are by no means merely a myth). But a different kind of community exists between the amateur audience and the stage and the professional audience and the stage.

The broader social function of amateur theatre tends to vary according to locality; there are regular differences, for example, between urban and rural groups. A rural group may see its prime function as being to provide access to theatre for relatively isolated communities, or those whose access is otherwise limited, but it may also have a very important function in terms of community formation – especially as villages themselves undergo crises of identity. In BBC Radio 4's *The Archers*, Linda Snell's annual village panto – with all the village politics it involves – gives an accurately comic sense of the way in which village incomers and established families interact in such a setting. Thus, in a large or complex village setting, the rural am-dram society may well sit alongside a rich variety of other village community activities – such as historical societies and football clubs. In other cases, the theatre group may be the only cultural activity in a village – the single point at which diverse members from a cross-section of social groups meet. Either way, rural amateur-dramatic activity is often intensely identified with locale – and indeed with competition. Inter-village rivalry may well spill over from the football field to the village panto.

Overlapping with the amateur theatre is 'community theatre'. This term has generally had a slightly different meaning in the UK from its meaning in the USA, where it covers most kinds of non-professional theatre-making, including amateur dramatics. This generalised meaning is now beginning to seep into British parlance, but, strictly speaking, community theatre has an identity separate from that of am-dram: it is usually theatre with some kind of social agenda, often involving the celebration of a place or social group. The blueprint for what most people think of as contemporary British community theatre was drawn up in the late 1970s by Ann Jellicoe and the Colway Theatre Trust. This provided an umbrella structure in which professional theatre workers such as writers and directors would work with local-interest groups, such as local-history societies, as well as amateur-dramatic clubs – to research, create and perform a play specifically about that community and its history. The performances are usually confined to the locale in which they were devised, although there are instances of crossover into mainstream venues such as David Edgar's *Entertaining Strangers*, which was originally written for Colway's Dorchester community play and restaged at the National Theatre's Cottesloe Theatre in 1987. If am-dram groups tend to be long-term affairs, sustained by the organisation of the club or society (or building) itself, community theatre has tended to be more project-based, and a community-theatre group may well form for the duration of a single production.

The distinction between professional and non-professional is blurred in the annual round of arts festivals, of which the Edinburgh festivals (several of them coincide and overlap) are the most famous. This, at least, is true from an audience's point of view. From the point of view of a performer, the Fringe continues to be a place of potential transition, where amateurs may be 'discovered' and so become professionals, and where fledgling professional careers of writers and performers may receive a much-needed boost from the award of a Fringe First or the prestigious Comedy Award. And, while the mainstay of the Fringe remains the play or, increasingly, the comedy act, Edinburgh is also one of the many festivals and carnivals that has become a showcase for street performers such as conjurors, buskers, escapologists, mime artists, musicians and acrobats. Estimates vary as to the exact economic value of Edinburgh's August festivals to the town's economy, but Scotland's

Minister for Tourism, Culture and Sport, Patricia Ferguson, quoted a 2005 report putting the annual figure at £127 million.[5] There are, it is true, continuing and increasing complaints that commercial success is stifling creativity, that the Fringe has become more commodified, more globalised and 'Disneyfied' and correspondingly less exciting, diverse and experimental; and that it has lost its identity as a truly alternative event. Paradoxically, though, these criticisms frequently emanate from Fringe participants themselves, many of whom are working against what they see as this dominant trend and are challenging, resisting and subverting the homogenising tendencies of a hegemony of the marketplace by offering (like Peter Buckley Hill and the Free Festival) alternatives to the alternative in the form of free events and non-commercial performances that continue to buck the mainstream. The tension between the commercial success of the Fringe and this continuing sense of resistance and reinvention ensures that the Festival retains its position of importance on the nations' artistic calendar.[6]

On a level that has nothing at all to do with cutting-edge experimental performance, theatre in Britain also features in a different kind of calendrical festival – and one in which the participants are by definition non-professional. The folk plays, festive performances and traditional dramas that continue to be staged at particular times and in particular places throughout the year range from the ceremonial performances of Guy Fawkes Night's effigy-burnings to the scripted dramas of mumming plays such as the East Midlands Plough Plays, peopled by casts of ploughboys and ladies, sergeants and doctors, devils and fools. In plays such as these, a time of year is marked and celebrated, and a community identity, both historical and geographical, is affirmed. The politics of folkloric practices is a complex issue, and the English in particular tend to be rather embarrassed by their own folklore. It is true, too, that performances such as these may be put to the service of an idealised and nostalgic vision of the past. Yet the local and traditional can also – as communities in the developing world have frequently demonstrated – be utilised as a site of resistance to the globalisation and commodification of culture. It may be time to re-evaluate, and to revalue, the function of traditional dramas in Britain.

While traditional dramas offer one kind of imaginative community with the past, another is offered by the kind of theatrical performance to be found in historical role-playing and living-history societies, whose members re-enact or recreate battles, tournaments, ceremonies or just everyday lives from past historical periods ranging from Roman times to the Second World War. These societies offer participants a double kind of pleasure: on the one hand there is the historian's pleasure in recreating the conditions of the past, which these societies often do in loving and scholarly detail. Traditional crafts and skills, such as basket-weaving or blacksmithing, are thoroughly researched and often revived. On the other hand, for many historical role-players, a more primitive attraction is that of play-fighting: much historical reconstruction revolves around combat of one sort or another, and many societies will offer regular training in stage-fighting and weapons use, as well as the opportunity to live out the fantasy of being an Elizabethan fencing master or a medieval knight. Living history is increasingly also used by museums, who employ performance in order to attempt to immerse and involve the visitor in a sense of the past. The Living History Village of Little Woodham, for example, recreates English rural life in the south of England at the outbreak of the English Civil War. Visitors encounter 'villagers', dressed in period costume, who both perform and interpret activities and events of everyday seventeenth-century rural life. At their worst, living-history performances repeat the clichés of a sanitised heritage industry; at best they offer an imaginative engagement that challenges received notions of the past.

A less scholarly, though more startling and purposive, kind of living history performance was staged at Murrayfield in Edinburgh in February 2006. In the minutes before the kick-off of the Calcutta Cup (the Scotland versus England Six Nations rugby match) the bemused England players were faced with a *Braveheart* re-enactment, as a horde of fourteenth-century Scots charged yelling at them in a terrifying welter of kilts, sporrans, claymores and face paint. It was an effective piece of psychological warfare, although the subsequent Scottish victory (18–12) probably owed more to poor English ball-handling than to the conjured spirit of Mel Gibson's William Wallace. But it is worth including here as one more example of the way in which theatrical performance has become woven into the fabric of British life. It permeates our culture, from the high-profile production at the National Theatre to the intimacy of the therapy session, from the church service to the schoolroom, from the amateur dramatic society to the sports arena. The social impact of this rich participatory culture is difficult to quantify, but it is hard to disagree with the conclusions of Stella Barnes, quoted in the most recent Arts Council report:

> All those kinds of things, playing, making stories, telling
> stories: they're essential, an essential part of our personal
> development and our cultural development and who we are and

what makes us human. And enabling ... people to find the ability to play is amazing regardless of any social outcome. I think theatre helps us know who we are by being someone else, and on that very essential personal level exploring who you are with people playing together is really extraordinarily powerful.[7]

Diversity and conflict

But while participation in theatre-making is popular, theatre-going is even more so, and for many people the imaginative play of theatre is most frequently experienced by proxy as a member of an audience. And if the first part of this chapter has stressed the variety of theatrical activity in the UK, this second part will focus on what might be considered the professional mainstream of the creative industry. This, of course, is a contentious term in itself: what, after all, constitutes the mainstream? The National Theatre? The Royal Shakespeare Company? London's West End theatres? All of these have their claim, but for most people in the UK their main point of contact with the professional theatre is probably in the form of the local subsidised theatre. I shall be looking, in this part of the chapter, at the Birmingham Repertory Theatre as an example of this kind of theatre.

A city-centre producing house, the Birmingham Repertory Theatre is one of the UK's best known subsidised regional professional theatres. Originally opened in 1913, it moved to its present premises in Broad Street in 1971 as part of the mid-century theatre-building boom. It has both a main auditorium with an audience capacity of 824 and a studio space ('The Door'), which holds about 140 and is used for smaller or more 'experimental' shows. It has a long-standing reputation for putting on new, experimental and sometimes controversial work as well as more mainstream, family-oriented entertainment. Its name is usually affectionately and proprietorially shortened to the Birmingham Rep, or just the Rep. In fact, the name is actually rather misleading. Birmingham's civic theatre has long outgrown the repertory movement from which it takes its name, in which a permanent resident company produced a wide variety of plays. Few of Britain's regional theatres now work on such a system; more usually they operate on a mixed economy of home-grown productions (in which each show hires its own separate cast) and imported productions by established medium-scale touring companies.

The Rep is probably one of the more ambitious and successful theatres of its kind, and its programme is fairly representative of regional theatres in cities around the country. Typically, the main house season might include a Christmas show aimed at a family audience, a Shakespeare play (either in traditional or experimental mode), other classic dramas, one or two modern comedies, usually proven on the London stage and aimed at a broadly mainstream audience and, if possible, starring a well-known celebrity, a musical, contemporary dramas with an established pedigree and inflected towards the local audience demographics and one or two examples of non-dramatic theatrical forms such as a contemporary dance piece or an Italian opera.[8] The studio programme is almost entirely devoted to new writing, some home-generated and some touring, some aimed at specific audiences (young people, minority or ethnic groups), some at a more general audience. This programme, which is more ambitious than that of most regional theatres, is characterised by, on the one hand, a striving for diversity and, on the other, a careful sense of balance: between the new and the old, the innovative and the safe, the home-produced and the imported, the familiar and the alien. This is the dilemma in which regional theatre programmers repeatedly find themselves: needing continually to redefine their audience without losing that sense of common interest on which they have traditionally depended. Nor is this 'core' audience itself homogeneous: theatre has traditionally been a site of cultural struggle between (for example) radical and reactionary and liberal and conservative tendencies among spectators as well as practitioners.

This cultural struggle often takes the form of tension between the theatre and its local authority funders, for, if a regional theatre like the Rep is a source of local and civic pride, it is also frequently a source of civic frustration. Relationships between regional theatres and local or municipal authorities are rarely calm for long. Since a large part of a regional theatre's funding comes from local-authority grants, it is often competing for meagre resources with other services such as housing, sanitation and social care. Even when well funded from local sources, a theatre might find that its own artistic vision may not be in harmony with local government expectations about the arts' contribution to social programmes and urban regeneration schemes. Regional theatres such as the Rep continually have to negotiate a complex set of often-conflicting demands.

Not least among these is the issue of regional identity. In Wales and Scotland, regional identity (in its broadest sense) may be sustained by a sense of difference from England and the English; in the English regions it is likely to take the form of a sense of difference from and competition with London, the metropolis. In the theatre world, this relationship between the regions and the capital is especially complicated, since London has traditionally been the centre of theatre-making. A regional theatre such as the Rep presents an experience which is both an alternative to the London theatre scene (West End, national or 'fringe') and yet also depends on it: as a source of comparatively new works and styles and also, to some extent, as a guarantor of quality.

This paradoxical combination of opposition and dependence between the regions and the metropolis becomes particularly acute when it comes to questions of funding and economic impact. There are 541 building-based professional theatres in the UK, forty-nine of which are in London's West End.[9] In 1998, the Society of London Theatre commissioned a major report into the state of West End theatre.[10] The Wyndham Report calculated that West End theatre was worth £1.1 billion annually to the UK economy at the time. A follow-up study by the Society of London Theatre for 2002/3 puts the figure at £1.5 billion.[11]

The contribution made by the other 492 UK theatres is estimated at £1.1 billion: rather less than the London theatres together. On the one hand, this total contribution of £2.6 billion is itself impressive, especially when one considers that '[T]his huge impact is generated by a minimal amount of public subsidy: £100 million in England, £12.8 million in Scotland, £6.4 million in Wales and £2.1 million in Northern Ireland.'[12] On the other hand, the disparity between the economic impact of London theatres and that of regional theatres reflects a long-standing dichotomy. The opposition between regionalism and metropolitanism, with the concomitant ideological debates about the nature of democracy and the arts, underlies many of the funding decisions of the Arts Council since its establishment after the Second World War. The 1940s and the 1950s saw an overt emphasis on London theatre as a centre of excellence; Jennie Lee, appointed as Britain's first Minister for the Arts in 1964, attempted to remedy this metrocentric bias. She increased Arts Council funding in order to invest in Scotland, Wales and the regions, leading to an unprecedented spate of new theatre building in the 1960s and 1970s, during which time 'no less than thirty-four … new theatres were situated in the English regions, in Scotland, and in Wales' – including the new home of the Rep in Broad Street.[13] As a result, '[r]egional theatre flourished in this period on an unprecedented scale.'[14] But while subsequent reviews of theatre funding (including 1984's disastrous 'Glory of the Garden' initiative, an ineffectual attempt to democratise the arts by devolving funding responsibility to the regions themselves) frequently stated their intention to support regional theatres, the day-to-day reality of most of these theatres – even ones as successful as the Rep – continued to involve a daily struggle for financial survival and an attempt to balance artistic excellence, support for emerging or experimental artists and companies, and appeal to sponsors, funding bodies such as the Arts Council and local authorities.

Ironically, then, against an impressive narrative of economic benefit both on a national and a regional level, there must be set the daily struggle for financial survival which most theatres face. When, in March 2001, the theatre sector received an additional allocation of £25 million Arts Council funding, it provided many theatres with some much-needed relief from the hand-to-mouth existence to which they had become accustomed. In particular, the funding review was aimed at revitalising the regional theatres of the UK and compensating in some way for the metropolitan bias that had developed over the last few decades of the twentieth century. The responses of these regional directors is not untypical:

> The recognition was that the theatre was on its knees – sometimes not even that, the theatre was dying pretty quickly. We were delighted that finally the Arts Council and the government listened to what we'd all been saying.
>
> Without it (theatre review money) I think we would have closed after two years. You can't run a theatre on the subsidy we had. We survived because of a very high level of earned income and also because we ran on a very small staff.[15]

The injection of funding did not, of course, come without conditions. Arts Council England's national policy for theatre in England, which accompanied the review, announced eight key priorities:

1. A better range of high quality work.
2. Attract more people.
3. Develop new ways of working.
4. Education.
5. Address diversity and inclusion.
6. Develop the artists and creative managers of the future.
7. An international reputation.
8. Regional distinctiveness.[16]

Stated baldly, such priorities, balancing as they do aesthetic value and social utility, appear unexceptionable. Few theatre managements saw them as anything but positive, since, for the most part, they tended to make explicit aims to which theatres were already committed. Yet, despite their apparent blandness, there are potential contradictions within these stated priorities which were brought to the fore by a production the Rep mounted in 2003.

The theatre's production of *Behzti* (*Dishonour*) by the young Sikh woman writer Gurpreet Kaur Bhatti was staged in December 2004 but was withdrawn from production early in the run following angry protests by Sikh community leaders and activists. The play, set predominantly in a *gurdwara*, a British Sikh temple, tells a story of sexual abuse; the corrupt Mr Sandhu who runs the temple has for many years repeatedly abused and raped the young women – and young men – of the community, with the collusion of the adult women within the community. Birmingham Rep's production of *Behzti* sparked off a week of protests from sections of the Sikh community, who were angered not only by the depiction of institutionalised abuse but also by the play's temple location. The protests ended in violence on 18 December 2004, when a 400-strong demonstration turned violent, with protesters entering and damaging the theatre building, culminating in three arrests. The Rep's management closed the show, not as an acknowledgement of the case of the play's opponents but on the grounds that it felt unable to guarantee the safety of the audience and cast.

British theatre has an honourable tradition of resisting censorship in the name of free speech. Two of the most famous cases of the late twentieth century, Edward Bond's *Saved* (1965) and Howard Brenton's *Romans in Britain* (1980) involved successful fights against censorship. The first led to the abolition of the Lord Chamberlain's authority over the licensing of playscripts, the other to the rout of activist Mary Whitehouse's Christian moral pressure group, the National Viewers' and Listeners' Association. In more recent times, another right-wing minority pressure group, Christian Voice, has failed to suppress the 'blasphemous' *Jerry Springer: The Opera* (2003) – although the campaign was effective in other ways, not least in the emotional toll it took on one of the authors, Stewart Lee. The case of *Behzti* was more complex, and the controversy put the Rep in a genuine double-bind. In previous cases, such as *The Romans in Britain*, the moral diagram could be clearly drawn from a white liberal perspective: it was a case of the heroic voice of the individual artist standing up against the forces of oppression. Even with *Jerry Springer: The Opera* (where the forces of oppression turned out to be a tiny, if vitriolic, group of protesters), the battle lines seemed clear. Here, however, the voices demanding the play's suppression belonged to an ethnic group who had certainly known racist oppression in the past and whose sensitivity about the image of their community was understandable. Their spokesmen were supported by leaders of the Birmingham Sikh community and by religious leaders from other faiths. The Roman Catholic Archbishop of Birmingham, Vincent Nichols, joined the demand for the play's closure, claiming that a play that violates the sacred place of one religion demeans, by implication, the sacred places of all. The protesters could not easily be written off as an extremist minority.

On the other hand, for the theatre not to support their own playwright – a young woman who was a member of the same minority community, and who had worked with young people and local community groups – was unthinkable. 'I wrote *Behzti*', Bhatti said, 'because I passionately oppose injustice and hypocrisy.'[17] In this she allies herself with British political playwrights, from Bond and Brenton to Caryl Churchill and Sarah Kane, who have taken it as an act of faith that the job of the serious theatre writer was to address urgent social and political issues. The problem for the Rep was that in *Behzti* the injustice and hypocrisy which were revealed were those existing within the immigrant Sikh community itself, and the Rep found itself increasingly alienated from the very minority that it was trying to attract. On the cover of the published text of *Behzti* the question is asked: 'In a community where public honour is paramount, is there any room for the truth?'[18] The theatre-makers found themselves in the middle of the real-life ramifications of just this question, and not only during the protests themselves: in the aftermath of the production, Gurpreet Bhatti and members of the cast were subjected to hate mail and threats of physical assault, so much so that the author herself was forced into hiding.

If the Rep found itself caught between conflicting social forces, it was also caught between conflicting sets of demands within the Arts Council's priorities document. *Bezhti*, after all, certainly addressed diversity and inclusion and was a genuine attempt to attract more people by dealing with topics of relevance to a particular ethnic group within the city. It was also attempting to meet the demand for high quality work: one of the criteria by which quality is judged in the field of realist drama from Ibsen onwards has been its willingness to take on difficult social issues. And, in profiling the work of the young Sikh playwright, the Rep was certainly meeting the target of developing new artists. Ironically, the very elements of the production that ensured it ticked so many Arts Council boxes also meant that it became a cause célèbre.

Conclusion

Since its origins in the *demos* of Ancient Athens, one of the functions that theatre has claimed for itself has been that of making a statement about the identity of the society or community that produced it: celebrating that society, articulating its concerns, defining it. Such wide-reaching claims have local and specific implications, and these are often thrown into sharp relief at moments of conflict and of actual or attempted censorship. Cases such as *Bezhti* remind us that live theatre retains the ability to act as a focus for larger current social and cultural concerns. On a more pragmatic level, it reminds us, too, of the actual complexity of such apparently simple criteria as the Arts Council's eight key priorities. And in Britain, where ethnic tensions are a part of everyday social reality, it is not surprising to find the theatre functioning as a site in which they are played out – not only on the stage itself but in the theatre event in its totality.

Notions of community have always played an important part in theatre. Many of the values of the participatory theatre that we looked at in the first part of this chapter depend upon an element of community-building. *Communitas*, too, is one of the words that theatre theoreticians frequently use to denote the sense of communication and complicity between stage and audience that live performance is able to create. But communities are complex things, and they can be oppressive as well as nurturing, while a 'range of high quality work' will throw up plays that are provocative and divisive as well as some that are celebratory and cohesive. If a successful theatre looks to sustain something of this *communitas* over a period of time, it is clear that in seeking to do this it will have to take on board all the contradictions of the concept of community in a postmodern, multicultural and increasingly digital Britain.

It is not clear that the conditions under which it will be doing this will be propitious. The material and psychological benefits of the 2001 theatre funding review were palpable, and reinvigorated regional theatres responded with renewed artistic and creative energy. Nonetheless,

concerns that the increased subsidy following the theatre review
would prove to be only a temporary respite, and that Arts Council
England would feel that it has 'done its bit for regional theatre' have
proved well founded. At the time of writing (the Winter of 2006-7), a
new review of British arts funding is in the offing, and all the signs
are that it will involve significant cuts. A New Labour government
whose 'Cool Britannia' initiative once championed Britain's cultural
industries – 'heralding the best of the new and celebrating the creativity that gives rise to it' – now appears (as *The Guardian* theatre critic
Lynn Gardner has argued) to regard the creative arts with suspicion.[19]
As local authorities prepare to cut spending, as the Department of
Culture, Media and Sport looks set to face a 5 per cent budget cut, and
as the plans for the 2012 Olympics divert funding towards sport rather
than the creative arts, things once again look bleak for the sector.[20]

Notes

1 R. Williams, 'Drama in a Dramatized Society', in *Writing in Society* (London: Verso,
   1984), pp. 11–21; p. 11.
2 See P. Auslander, *Liveness: Performance in a Mediatized Culture* (London and New York,
   Routledge, 2003).
3 P. Brook, *The Empty Space* (Harmondsworth: Penguin, 1972), pp. 11–46.
4 G. Giesekam, *Luvvies and Rude Mechanicals? Amateur and Community Theatre in Scotland*
   (Edinburgh: Scottish Arts Council, 2000), p. 8.
5 Scottish Executive News, government press release, archived online at www.scot-
   land.gov.uk/News/Releases/2005/01/20143302 (accessed 29 January 2007).
6 J. Harvie, *Staging the UK* (Manchester: Manchester University Press, 2005),
   pp. 74–111.
7 B. McDonnell and D. Shellard, *Social Impact Study of UK Theatre* (London: Arts Council
   England, 2006), p. 3.
8 See www.birmingham-rep.co.uk/core_asp/whatson.asp (accessed 30
   January 2007).
9 D. Shellard, *Economic Impact Study of UK Theatre* (London: Arts Council England,
   2004), p. 4.
10 T. Travers, *The Wyndham Report: The Economic Impact of London's West End Theatre*
   (London: Society of London Theatre, 1998).
11 Shellard, *Economic Impact Study*, p. 5.
12 Shellard, *Economic Impact Study*, p. 7.
13 P. Hollis, *Jennie Lee: A Life* (Oxford: Oxford University Press, 1997), p. 250;
   G. Rowell and A. Jackson, *The British Repertory Movement: A History of Regional Theatre
   in Britain* (Cambridge: Cambridge University Press, 1984), p. 89.
14 Harvie, *Staging the UK*, p. 21.
15 A. Martin and H. Bartlett, *Implementing the National Policy for Theatre in
   England: Baseline Findings* (London: Arts Council England, 2003), p. 9.

16 Arts Council of England, *The National Policy for Theatre in England* (London: Arts Council England, 2000), pp. 5–7.

17 G. K. Bhatti, *Behzti (Dishonour)* (London: Oberon Books, 2004), p. 18.

18 Bhatti, *Behzti*, back cover.

19 C. Smith, *Creative Britain* (London: Faber, 1998), p. 5.

20 L. Gardner, 'Make a Scene about Theatre Funding', *Guardian Unlimited* (18 December 2006).

10

Contemporary British television

Introduction

British television was often referred to in the past as 'the best in the world', but now the very idea of thinking of television as intimately bound to a sense of national pride seems almost quaint in a period where, especially for many young people, television is losing its special role as a focal point for a shared national culture. But the contribution of television to a unified British culture was of the utmost concern when the British Broadcasting Corporation (BBC) first started a television service in 1936, building on the approach it had established as the only radio broadcaster. While the BBC was always expected to be loyal to the nation-state in times of crisis or war, it was also structured to be at one remove from direct government control so that it could not be used simply as a propaganda tool for whoever was in political power. This ideal of political impartiality and unbiased information contributed to an ethos of television as a public service that was also free from commercial pressures, financed not by advertising but through a directly paid licence fee, offering improving education as well as entertainment for the masses. When Independent Television (ITV) was introduced in 1954, its reliance on advertising for finance was also offset by stringent public-service regulations to ensure it also fulfilled these broad aims.

This first era of television was based on a very small number of networks addressing a relatively undifferentiated, mass audience within national boundaries. The second was an era of expanded choice with multi-channel systems gradually being added which offered more minority-interest programmes. This happened gradually in the UK: the mainstream BBC and ITV terrestrial channels were supplemented by BBC 2 in 1964, Channel 4 and the Welsh language channel S4C in 1982 and Channel 5 in 1997, while the cable companies NTL and Telewest (now merged into Virgin Media) and Sky satellite television also increased capacity from the mid 1980s. There is a widespread agreement that we have now entered into a third era in television. British television is at the forefront of changes that are affecting broadcasting systems throughout the world as a result of a huge expansion in the number of channels, many of them originating from outside the UK, and its convergence with the Internet. Programmes can now be accessed via a range of interactive computer devices and watched on multipurpose screens, which vary from very small mobiles to large, flat, high-definition screens hanging on the wall, rather than the 'box in the corner' that has been the norm until now. The speed of change affecting the industry has sparked a period of intense corporate and political debate over how to adapt British television to these new economic and technological imperatives. Contested ideas about how the mixed system of public service and commercial provision should change to remain economically viable are accompanied by concerns about maintaining the quality of distinctively British programming in the face of globalising pressures.

Culturally powerful interests in the UK have over the past seventy years established and maintained television as a democratic 'public sphere' as well as a conduit for popular entertainment. Debates over the relative claims of 'public service' or 'the market' to be able to deliver 'quality' television that provides for minority as well as majority tastes and interests have recurred at regular intervals. The audience, in whose name this political wrangling is conducted, has been defined by two key rhetorical figures: the 'citizen' of a nation-state and the 'consumer' in a global market. These are not static categories but are open to redefinition as, for instance, new claims for citizenship emerge or new markets are exploited for profit. Neither are they entirely separate, as increasingly citizenship has become redefined in consumerist terms with the government merely providing the conditions within which private enterprise can deliver the services for which consumers pay.

The regulatory framework for this approach was established in the 2003 Communications Act, which is the most comprehensive legislation of its kind in British history. It is now being implemented by Ofcom, an organisation set up by the Government to regulate the converging communications industries, whose close relationship to government is

maintained by their appointing six of its nine board members, including the chair. But whereas regulation in the past has maintained a tight
control over the content of broadcasting, Ofcom's primary task has been
redefined by the Government as economic regulation to promote competition. As part of this remit, they have been charged with overseeing
the successful transition to a fully digital service and reviewing the provision of public-service broadcasting within the overall ecology of the
British market. This chapter will explore these contemporary developments in British television and assess some of the effects it is having on
content as producers and audiences adapt to these transformations.

The impact of technological change

> 2006 was the year when convergence stopped being a concept and
> became instead a corporate priority.[1]

Digital technology towards the end of the 1990s brought a new era of
abundance in which the number of channels has multiplied and their
global reach extended while new interactive and storage capabilities are
now being added. The complete replacement of analogue television is
planned to roll out in the UK region by region between 2008 and 2012.
By 2008, nine in ten UK households already had digital television while
over half of secondary televisions in bedrooms and kitchens were also
now digital. This has been boosted by the high take-up of Freeview, a
free-to-air digital service of around thirty-five channels, while only just
under half of UK households pay extra for cable and satellite subscription services with their 350 or so channels. Previous objections to a two-
tier system of access based on ability to pay are to some extent answered
by this development and by the announcement of a £600 million programme of support financed out of the licence fee to help the over-
seventy-fives, the disabled and other people on low incomes to convert
their television sets to digital.

   Whether via niche channels or assumptions about what genres will
appeal to audiences at different times of day on the mainstream channels, viewers within Britain are addressed not simply as citizens of a
nation-state but according to their age, class and gender, as well as
more varied cultural tastes. Premium content for which subscribers
are willing to pay is the foundation of Sky television's success in the
UK with sport marketed to men and movies to women, in addition to
the six channel 'mixes' from which subscribers can select. Free-to-air

Table 10.1. *Annual percentage shares of viewers (individuals) in 2006.*

	BBC 1	BBC 2	ITV 1	Channel 4	Five	Digital
2000	27.2	10.8	29.3	10.5	5.7	16.6
2001	26.9	11.1	26.7	10.0	5.8	19.6
2002	26.2	11.4	24.1	10.0	6.3	22.1
2003	25.6	11.0	23.7	9.6	6.5	23.6
2004	24.7	10.0	22.8	9.7	6.6	26.2
2005	23.3	9.4	21.5	9.7	6.4	29.6
2006	22.7	8.8	19.7	9.8	5.7	33.3

Source: Broadcasters Audience Research Board Ltd.

broadcasters are following suit as they split their programming across a steadily increasing number of digital channels. For example, the BBC now offers the youth oriented BBC 3 and the more high-brow BBC 4, News 24, BBC Parliament, as well as the children's channels CBBC and CBeebies and the interactive service BBCi. Table 10.1 shows the upward trend for digital viewing and the impact on audiences for the more established channels, with the BBC and ITV seeing the greatest losses.

The expansion of digital channels has had various effects on the kinds of programmes produced and their scheduling. High-budget peak-time programmes on the BBC still get made, such as the popular 'family' sci-fi drama *Dr Who* (recently revived by well-known TV-drama writer Russell T. Davies's update of its quirky appeal), period costume dramas based on nineteenth-century novels such as Charles Dickens's *Bleak House*, light-entertainment shows such as the celebrity dancing contest *Strictly Come Dancing*, or the natural-history series *Planet Earth*, but they are potentially much less visible amongst the increased volume of low budget 'ordinary television' that is required to fill this expanded air time. More intensive marketing of 'event television' seeks to maximise the visibility of these programmes using the cross-promotional potential of multiple channels, web-based and mobile media. For example, the new *Dr Who* series, which returned after a gap of fifteen years, was preceded by a documentary on BBC 3 and a fake fan website 'Have You Seen This Man?', which then continued as a metatextual blog, as well as the usual trailers. Niche programmes form the 'long tail' that characterises the pattern of viewing in an era of expanded choice. In comedy, for example, contemporary performers such as black female comedian Jocelyn Jee Esien in *Little Miss Jocelyn* or *The Thick of It*, a risky political satire of New Labour's inner circle written by Armando Iannucci, can be tried out and only moved to the main channels if they are a success. More upmarket programmes that once would have found a place in the mixed schedules of the main channels are now to be found on the digital channel BBC 4 instead, often as part of themed short seasons of programmes on topics of current concern such as terrorism or climate change. Digital channels with very low viewing figures and budgets to match at the other end of the 'quality' spectrum rely on cheap imports and repeats, often airing the same programmes several times across a day or week, or on extended live shows based on one talking head, as in, for example the expanding range of phone-in quiz or shopping channels, such as Quizmania and QVC, which, along with the newly legitimate corporate-sponsored channels represent commercial television in its 'purest' form.

The potential for 'on-demand' downloading of programmes in the UK has been enabled by the increased availability of high-speed broadband connections to the Internet, available by 2008 to over half of all households, although a wide gap remains between those on high and low incomes. The impact of this development is in its early stages but will soon transform television into something more like an online retailer, alongside the scheduled service we know today. First into the market, Sky+ at its launch invited consumers to use its download and playback technology to 'Create Your Own TV Channel', while Channel 4's 4OD, the BBC's iPlayer and Virgin's cable service now also give access to a free seven-day catch-up download option for selected programmes. Ofcom has identified the need for a new level of 'media literacy' enabling the population to find and access content amongst a continually expanding range of possibilities and to ensure the success of these new developments. New business models are also emerging, such as copyright systems enabling payment of producers on the basis of serial usage, whereas rights were previously forfeited to the broadcasters. The financing provided by spot advertising may also be replaced in the future by adverts downloaded as personalised content based on viewer preferences.

Future trends in media consumption are signalled by the data from Ofcom on sixteen to twenty-four-year-olds who are not only spending more time accessing content online but who are also developing 'communities' that construct and share material rather than simply downloading pre-packaged programmes. Broadcasters are catching up with these so-called 'Web 2.0' developments by buying in the expertise of successful internet operators, as in ITV's purchase of the social networking site Friends Reunited. The BBC piloted the Creative Archive, along with partners Channel 4, the Open University and the British Film Institute, amongst others, which opened selected content for free non-commercial uses based on a 'creative commons' licence. Its website masthead, 'Find It, Rip It, Mix It, Share It' invited us to imagine playful uses for archive material enabling a more expansive understanding of media literacy than in Ofcom's more functional approach.[2] But commercial objections to free access will have had to be negotiated for this public-service initiative to survive, and much of the archive will be retained to be exploited for profitable uses, just as DVDs of programmes have been sold in the past. The attempt to attract youth audiences has led the BBC to team up with Google's YouTube website to carry promotional clips that allow UK users to click through to the full programme free of charge, although it also carries two commercial BBC Worldwide channels for global audiences offering entertainment and news. This encroachment onto YouTube of the mainstream broadcasters may, however, simply reduce its appeal to young people who were previously attracted by its anarchic, unregulated content.

Technological developments have also changed the processes of production. The BBC, for example, has moved to fully integrated cross-platform commissioning and production, supported by a unit dedicated to developing technological innovations for new-media uses. This means that new television programmes are now being commissioned along with 'brand extensions' on other platforms such as the Internet or mobile phones. Or ideas may flow in the other direction, with interactive content designed for the BBC website influencing programmes for broadcast. The natural-history programme *Springwatch* presented by Bill Oddie is a highly successful example of this trend with its 'brand' connecting content across radio, television, mobiles, print media and the Internet. The BBC's digital policy seeks to offer opportunities to outside people and organisations. A higher percentage of content, up to 50 per cent, is now commissioned in partnership with independent producers, and so-called 'user-generated' material will be drawn from multiple sources, with the BBC acting as a host and aggregator for a wide range of amateur content. Meanwhile, the miniaturisation of digital cameras, which during the 1990s made possible the intimate portrayals of everyday life in the generic innovations of reality programming, has now moved to the 'personal digital production' of news. This includes use of camera-phone footage from 'citizen journalists', whose on-the-scene 'scoops' at the scene of the 7 July terrorist bombings in 2005 are seen as a turning point. Regional news segments at the BBC are now produced from start to finish by a single 'video journalist' whatever their previous production expertise. The cost saving allows more time for development, moving the news away from its previous reliance on press releases for pre-planned media events and towards more intimate projects, while the reduction in coverage of on-the-day stories has some journalists complaining that it's no longer recognisable as news. These developments are perceived in some quarters as a threat to the quality guaranteed by professional expertise, but it is too early to say what impact they will have in the long term.

British television in a global market

[T]elevision is simultaneously global and national, shaped by the globalization of media economics and the pull of local and national cultures.[3]

Global television addresses diverse cultures of taste that cut across national boundaries. In describing this 'post-national television', Timothy Havens notes the way in which assumptions about taste cultures are exchanged internationally via buyers and distributors at trade fairs so that programming strategies for attracting audience segments are quickly copied across the world and become part of the common-sense assumptions about audiences that structure the schedules.[4] But despite globalising tendencies, markets remain primarily national in orientation where the costs of making local content can be afforded. A medium-sized market such as Britain can support a viable industry but regulation and public-service financing maintains the current high levels of domestic production. Investment per capita is more than in any other country in the world, with three-quarters of terrestrial television still made in Britain (though there are wide differences between channels) compared to only one fifth of domestic cinema.[5] Audiences generally prefer local content, but it is expensive to provide, and the majority of 'ordinary' television – soaps, sitcom, national news and current affairs – is not suitable for export. The continuing ability of drama serials, such as *Coronation Street* (ITV, 1960–) and *EastEnders* (BBC1, 1981–), to top the ratings ensures their place in the early evening schedules across the week despite being rooted in the working-class cultures of a regional locale and their consequent lack of global appeal.

Relaxed rules for foreign ownership of the commercial broadcasters Five and ITV enabled by the 2003 Communication Act were intended to help boost the global impact of domestic production, but the Act may mean instead that imported programmes will fill up the schedules once their remaining public-service obligations are removed. Many transnational channel headquarters are already located in the UK because of the liberal laws governing satellite transmission and the renewal of satellite licences. Both terrestrial broadcasters are in need of a renewed programming strategy at the time of writing, as a result of declining audiences, advertising and share values. ITV was substantially weakened by the failure in 2002 of its subscription digital venture and is struggling to find a role in the changed television marketplace. The sex and sensationalism of Five's launch strategy has been replaced by a greater reliance on drama series from the USA in an attempt to take it upmarket prior to its takeover by RTL in 2005.

Although the USA and Britain dominate the export market, together creating a global culture in television, Britain's 10 per cent share comes a very long way behind America's estimated 75 per cent and in monetary terms, at £430 million, is a fraction of the £7.7 billion total revenues earned by the domestic industry.[6] 'The idea that TV exports might function as a showcase for Britishness and British life is contradicted by the realities of the marketplace where Britishness is not a major selling point'; instead, it is seen as 'stuffy, class conscious, parochial'.[7] In the past, Britain was seen as a provider of 'quality' programmes as an alternative to US fictional entertainment, with high-budget period drama, factual programmes and innovative 'oddball' comedy finding niche markets on the margins, such as PBS or HBO in America. The USA dominates the global market in fiction (90 per cent), while one-off dramas made in the UK rely on co-production money, and topics with global relevance, such as the award-winning *Sex Traffic* (Channel 4, 2004), whose drama about trafficked women spanned Eastern and Western Europe, Canada and the USA. Its multi-strand narrative was able to address the political and ethical complexities of the global trade in women while also offering a gripping drama of suspense whose threads were drawn together in a climax centred in the city of London and its migrant communities. It offered a realist version of a modern cosmopolitan Britain sharing many of the same concerns as other regions of the world.

More generally, it is those programmes that are not recognisably British and that can be 'indigenised and adapted to the receiving culture' that are more successful in the global market.[8] Success often depends on the ease with which programmes can be re-voiced into other languages, such as the children's animation series *Bob the Builder* and *Teletubbies*, or natural-history programmes such as *Blue Planet* and *Planet Earth*, but here again the trend is towards co-production and co-financing deals with US companies such as the Discovery Channel. Some high-risk attempts have been made to remake sitcoms and series drama for the US market with, for example, the more 'alternative' *Queer as Folk* drama series and 'reality sitcom' *The Office* finding niche success, but many others have failed to survive the process of translation.

These two shows exemplify the tradition of the short-run, single-writer series in the UK, which is seen to foster innovation but which limits their commercial potential in the US market. *Queer as Folk's* innovative portrayal of a diverse group of gay men set in the club scene of Manchester city's 'queer quarter' challenged television's previously cautious approach to minority sexual cultures and was a cult success with gay audiences. The concept transferred to the USA to enable it to be exploited further through a spin-off serial that was team-written and stretched over several seasons. But the most significant commercial success in recent times has been in sales of formats for hybridised lifestyle, reality and quiz shows such as *Changing Rooms, Who Wants to Be a Millionaire* and *The Weakest Link*. In these cases, it is their acquired production expertise that is sold rather than the programme itself, thereby reducing the risk of failure; these are then produced locally and fully adapted to the domestic culture.

One exception is the global value placed on the BBC's long-established reputation for impartial news, which has been maintained in the face of competition from the rise of other worldwide news channels such as CNN. BBC World is the only British overseas channel. 'Seen in 270 million homes in more than 200 countries', it carries international news and 'the best of the BBC's lifestyle and factual programming'.[9] Unlike the globalising strategies pursued by transnational corporations such as MTV, BBC World broadcasts a single feed rather than being customised for different national and regional markets. It targets an elite, cosmopolitan audience who can understand English. It forms part of the commercially funded BBC Worldwide, which accounts for half of all UK television's export revenues.[10]

The future of public service television

> Television is important. But not as important as the people who work in it think it is.[11]

The product of a cultural attitude as much as spectrum scarcity, public-service broadcasting is now under severe pressure from proponents of the 'customer service' model, who argue that regulating for quality, plurality, balance and impartiality will be irrelevant when the interactive capability of broadband services enables entertainment for every taste and political discussion from every perspective. In view of the digital transition, Ofcom's conviction is that broadcasting is becoming analogous to any other customer service which 'needs to deliver content according to the retail imperatives of convenience, price, range and quality'.[12] Ofcom predict only the most minimal of public-service obligations by digital switchover as broadcasting ceases to be a special case and becomes instead merely part of the larger communications landscape. Only where there is 'market failure' is there any need to 'bridge the gap between what a well-funded broadcasting market would provide and what UK citizens want'.[13] As Gillian Doyle and Douglas Vick point out, this redefines public-service broadcasting in consumerist terms – giving people what they want – rather than the high principles that informed the system in the twentieth century, that is to say, to act as a force for cultural improvement and a public sphere for political debate for citizens of a nation-state, which aimed, in the words attributed to the BBC's first Director General, Lord Reith, to give people what they need.

One of the areas of political wrangling as television merges with the Internet is how to handle the regulation of content to avoid 'harm and offence'. Ofcom envisages a system in the future that relies far more on self-regulation by producers and consumers, backed up by laws that offer protection against risks such as incitement to racial hatred, invasions of privacy, libel or obscenity, as is now the case for the print media and the Internet. Media organisations, they argue, have the incentive to maintain consumer trust in their 'brand'. 'Media literate' consumers, meanwhile, will be encouraged to become self-regulating, helped by information that allows them to avoid content they might find offensive for themselves or harmful for their children. In the short term, however, scheduled broadcasts will retain most of the existing controls, such as the 9.00 p.m. 'watershed' for adult material, whereas video-on-demand services will rely more on advance content guides and PIN protection.[14]

The continuing relevance of a publicly funded BBC in the digital era is another key issue. The BBC remains the only broadcaster partially outside Ofcom's regulatory control and has a weighty role to play in sustaining the public-service purposes of television. It has been fighting for its survival ever since the 1986 Peacock Report recommended getting rid of the licence fee paid by every household with a television. More recently, its relations with Government were severely dented by a row over its reporting of the events leading up to the invasion of Iraq and the Hutton Report's controversial subsequent critique of the BBC's governance, which precipitated the forced resignations of its Director General and Chair of the Board of Governors. A new trust, holding the Executive Board to account, has been put in place to oversee the BBC's activities.

Renewal of its Royal Charter up to 2016 and a new licence fee settlement up to 2012 are two victories in the medium term over the forces ranged against the BBC. The Charter sets out, for the first time, a definition of the public purposes of the BBC as sustaining citizenship and civil society; promoting education and learning; stimulating creativity and cultural excellence; representing the UK, its nations, regions and communities; bringing the world to the UK and the UK to the world; and building digital Britain.[15] It identifies audience evaluation of quality, impact and value for money as the central arbiter and 'audience reach' as the primary measure indicating universality of their provision rather than the competitive drive of the 'ratings'. The requirement to schedule a high proportion of well-funded, innovative and challenging UK-made programmes is a central priority. The BBC's contribution to regional economic and cultural development is to be strengthened by shifting some production activities from London to the north of England. Further expansion of online services at the expense of its commercial competitors has been curtailed.

In the longer term, Ofcom wants to break the BBC's monopoly on state funding. It has recommended distributing money from the licence fee to a wider range of content providers, as was first suggested by the Peacock Committee in 1986. One beneficiary could be Channel 4 who after twenty-five years of broadcasting has asked for a public subsidy to protect its public-service role in the face of a projected long-term decline in audiences and advertising revenues. The final section offers a more extended discussion of Channel 4's address to the 'citizen consumer' and its current strategy for commercial survival in a global market while remaining true to its public-service purposes.

Programming for the citizen consumer

Channel 4 continues to be a unique national asset of which Britain can be proud.[16]

Reality TV has rapidly come to occupy a place at the forefront of contemporary television – a position from which it seems to 'speak' particularly clearly to the ways in which broadcasters are seeking to attract audiences in the multichannel landscape.[17]

Channel 4's remit is to cater for audiences not served by ITV, to encourage innovation and experimentation and to encourage wider access to programme-making for under-represented groups. Under the control of a board of trustees rather than shareholders, its unique public–private status and system of commissioning from independent producers has enabled it to adapt quickly to the changing environment. Channel 4 has built up a successful stable of digital channels although, since it began to sell its own advertising in the 1990s, its main channel has been criticised as being indistinguishable from commercial rivals with an early evening sequence of a quiz show (*Countdown*), game show (*Deal or No Deal*), chat show (*Richard and Judy, Paul O'Grady*), cartoon (*The Simpsons*) and soap (*Hollyoaks*). Despite retaining the hour-long news at 7.00 p.m., the channel's first chief executive laments that the 'quiet seriousness' of discussion and documentaries in peak time has been substituted by 'reality, lifestyle, US acquisitions and shock docs' and by an obsession with 'adolescent transgression and sex'.[18] The reality game show *Big Brother* and its *Celebrity Big Brother* spin-off deliver its highest ratings for several months of each year, helped by the tabloids and celebrity magazines that circulate the scandalous events precipitated by the twenty-four-hour surveillance on which this genre depends.

Although these critics may be right about a shift in genres, provenance and subject matter, these kinds of sweeping criticisms invariably arise from the specificities of the writer's own tastes and expectations, which are formed in a particular era and social milieu. Channel 4's youth audience of sixteen to thirty-four-olds, which it needs in order to attract advertisers, have grown up in a changed media environment and have different cultural tastes and ideas about what counts as quality programming; nor do they care whether programmes are made in this country as long as they can relate to the content. Minority-appeal arts, current affairs and documentary programmes whose absence is noted have moved to the digital channel More 4. In terms of quality, the really important question is whether the programmes are good of their type. US-originated drama series such as *Lost, Sex and the City, The Sopranos, Six Feet Under*, and *The West Wing* for example, have been aesthetically innovative and, in some cases, politically progressive additions to the schedules. The many documentaries about sexual topics, which have played a significant role in Channel 4's late-night schedules from the mid 1990s, vary widely in quality from the tawdry to the enlightening; but at their best they can be seen as enabling a welcome shift towards more open and less puritanical attitudes towards sex in British culture.[19] *Big Brother* was innovative when it first aired in 2000, offering amongst other things a solution to the financing of multi-channel television through the additional revenues generated by phone-in voting, which has been widely copied since. But the format has always been controversial. Indeed, *Celebrity Big Brother 5* (2007) became the centre of an international media and political furore when one participant, Bollywood star Shilpa Shetty, was the subject of alleged 'racist bullying'. It provoked calls for Channel 4's licence to be revoked for inciting racial hatred, while her eventual win of the vote was used by the Government as evidence of the nation's credibility as a tolerant multicultural society.

We can also see how the belief in British television's role as a force for education and improvement of its populace has survived both the generic transformations of factual television and the commercial priorities that dominate the rhetoric of Ofcom's cultural policy. The generic innovations of popular factual entertainment, a global as well as British phenomenon, which has been accelerating since the early 1990s and which comes under such umbrella titles as 'lifestyle', 'makeover' or 'reality' programming, is generally acknowledged to be an ingenious solution to the problem of filling the exponential rise in broadcasting hours. These formats constitute a growing component of what has been termed 'ordinary television', and are very hard to classify given the dynamic processes of hybridisation that occurs as producers search for the next big hit.[20] They have multiple generic precursors, both factual and fictional: chat shows, fly-on-the-wall documentaries, talent contests, game shows, celebrity sitcoms and soap operas, which get mixed and matched in different ways. Castigated as 'trash TV' for elevating the trivial and manipulating both participants and viewers, or alternatively praised for democratising television, their engagement with the every-day lives of ordinary people and their private experience, both pleasant and traumatic, offers emotional knowledge about events, about what it's like from 'the inside'.[21]

Just as the BBC has had to balance popular appeal with its claims for 'public value' in order to justify the universal licence fee, so Channel 4, in making a case for public funding, draws attention to those of its factual entertainment shows that also prioritise education and a ver-sion of British culture that foregrounds diversity and social inclusion. Channel 4's annual report in 2006, for example, cites the celebrity chef Jamie Oliver's award-winning *School Dinners* as an example in a context where television's influence on the growing problem of child obesity has become an increasingly high-profile political issue in Britain, with Ofcom announcing restrictions on the exposure of under-sixteens to advertising on television for foods that are high in fat, salt and sugar despite an estimated loss of £39 million in revenues.[22]

Jamie's progress from 'Jack the Lad' to 'Food Campaigner' sums up his trajectory from when he was first discovered by a television pro-ducer as a young chef, while also demonstrating both the commercial and public-service potential of reality genres. He became a power-ful commercial brand following the success of his three series of *The Naked Chef* (1999–2001), including being credited with the revival of Sainsbury's supermarket through his promotion of this British chain. His central presence as a celebrity presenter was also the foundation of the show's global appeal, despite differences in national culinary trad-itions.[23] This kind of lifestyle show harks back to the 'hobbyist strand' of close-up demonstrations of cookery, gardening and DIY techniques that were part of the 'improving' impetus of British television culture but which are now more focused on celebrity presenters and the melo-drama of participants' emotional reaction to 'an instantaneous dis-play of transformation'.[24] A sense of intimacy is accentuated through a shared experience of time as participants and viewers count down to this moment and by the colloquial tone of the address: 'The voice of life-style media is "chatty" – utilising a diversity of regional accents, uses of slang, ways of talking and writing that de-emphasise authority and play on chattiness and matiness', and which works to make expertise ordin-ary, accessible and inclusive.[25] Both Rachel Moseley and Joanne Hollows show how the programme's complex presentation of his lifestyle, using a realist docusoap narrative style, constructs a hybrid 'youthful' national identity for Jamie, whose style of cooking is based in a British provincial culture of pub food learned, as a child, from his publican father but inflected by his subsequent training in a top-end Italian restaurant in London, mirroring the more general shift towards a cosmopolitan food culture in urban middle-class Britain.[26] He combines the familiar media figures of the 'new lad' and the 'new man' in his self-conscious use of Cockney slang, the urban 'mod' cool of his Vespa scooter as he travels round London to buy the ingredients, his 'Italian' attention to cooking at home for his friends and his 'missus' while presenting 'the domestic as a site of play' to distance it from women's work.[27]

The more serious 'professional' approach of the 'chef-turned-socially-conscious-food-campaigner' comes more to the fore in his subsequent programmes. *Jamie's Kitchen* (2002) is in the popular format of the 'teenage makeover' in which fifteen disaffected and low-achieving young people are trained to become kitchen workers in a top-class London restaurant specifically set up for the project, a scheme that has been successfully reproduced in several other countries. And while *Jamie's School Dinners* (2005) has an element of 'lifestyle in collision' in which a situation is contrived to foreground clashes in lifestyle, especially those based in class differences here, as in the globally successful format of *Wife Swap*, this dramatic element is strongly combined with a transformative discourse in which each of the parties are changed by the encounter.[28] 'In the drab kitchens of a South London secondary school, passion and high drama raged as Jamie Oliver and his sometimes sceptical team of dinner ladies struggled to re-invent school dinners, not only creating radically new menus on impossibly tight budgets but, at the same time, winning the hearts and minds of the children they served', claims Channel 4.[29] Its policy impact was swift with the Department for Education and Skills announcing new nutritional standards for school meals and hundreds of millions of pounds to achieve them, but the clash of class and regional cultures was revealed in subsequent news stories showing resistant mothers passing fast food over school fences to their children.

Conclusion

The 'era of abundance' in the digital age has changed television's ideological role, reducing its power to delineate the centre and the margins, to influence the shared assumptions of a national culture. Instead, it is suggested we should now think in terms of 'diversity' and a questioning of the 'myth of the centre' that television claims for itself.[30] Commercially, the battle of the ratings for peak-time programmes, which has dominated the industry for fifty years, is becoming less central, as economic survival depends less on sheer numbers as on the intensity of engagement with a wider range of more tightly defined user communities. Rather than mourning this loss of national cohesiveness in a narrative of cultural decline, I would rather tell a more optimistic story about television that helps us to imagine a future that is not necessarily better or worse but just different and that can be harnessed for both good and bad purposes, just as it was in the past.

The policy debates reveal a continuing commitment in the digital environment to the British tradition of public-service values in order to promote the formation of an informed and cosmopolitan 'citizen-consumer' and now 'citizen-producer'. But there is greater emphasis on the market as a means to regulate and deliver this, and on the audience's capacity to choose and to participate. 'In a world of so many choices, the audience cares about trust, taste, relevance, usefulness', argues one new-media commentator.[31] 'Trust' in a market-led system depends on protecting the commercial value of the 'brand' and, as Ofcom has suggested, leaving the industry to decide on and police self-regulating codes of practice. The worry is that this leaves out of account the broader interests that make up a democratic public sphere and may encourage a 'tabloid' cultural agenda as companies seek to manipulate the risks and benefits of scandalous publicity. The creation of content for a diversity of 'tastes' can also be left to the market, but this ignores the processes of taste formation that informed the original conception of public-service television. One answer is to supplement Ofcom's more narrowly conceived promotion of media literacy with a national strategy for media education and a public culture of critical debate to inform shared values and to challenge existing cultural hierarchies and exclusions. 'Relevance' and 'usefulness' may be discovered through 'the wisdom of crowds' harnessed by 'friend of a friend' network technologies to make visible what is available but will also require forms of specialist expertise to anticipate and mould content for those uses in imaginative ways. An expanded conception of media literacy needs to encompass the creative and technical skills for producing media which can now be distributed more widely. We still need a range of public-service institutions, such as the BBC and

Channel 4, to make this possible, but working in partnership with other cultural and educational organisations. The metamorphosis of British television into the digital media of the future requires widespread public engagement with accompanying debates about ethics, quality and taste, embedded in a broader culture of creativity, if we are to sustain and enhance its full potential to enrich the lives of its citizens.

Notes

1 C. Sinclair, 'Foreword', in M. Magor (ed.), *Transforming Television: Strategies for Convergence* (Glasgow: The Research Centre, 2006).
2 See http://creativearchive.bbc.co.uk (accessed 25 November 2006).
3 S. Waisbord, 'McTV: Understanding the Global Popularity of Television Formats', *Television and New Media*, 5 (4) (2004): 359–83; p. 359.
4 T. Havens, *Global Television Marketplace* (London: BFI, 2006), p. 159.
5 S. Harvey, 'Ofcom's First Year and Neo-Liberalism's Blind Spot: Attacking the Culture of Production', *Screen*, 47 (1) (2006): 91–105.
6 J. Steemers, *Selling Television: British Television in the Global Marketplace* (London: BFI, 2004), p. 41.
7 Steemers, *Selling Television*, p. 212.
8 Steemers, *Selling Television*, p. 14.
9 BBC, Annual Report and Accounts for 2006, available online at www.bbc.co.uk/bbctrust/assets/files/pdf/review_report_research/bbcannualreport.pdf (accessed 1 March 2007).
10 Steemers, *Selling Television*, p. 213.
11 Stephen Carter, Ofcom Chief Executive, quoted in D. Currie, Speech to the Royal Television Society, 2006, available online at www.ofcom.org.uk/media/speeches/2006/09/rts180906 (accessed 20 November 2006).
12 D. Currie, 'Ofcom Annual Lecture', 1 November 2006, available online at www.ofcom.org.uk/media/speeches/2006/11/annual_lecture (accessed 20 November 2006).
13 G. Doyle and D. W. Vick, 'The Communications Act 2003: A New Regulatory Framework in the UK', *Convergence: The International Journal of Research into New Media Technologies*, 11 (3) (2005): 75–94.
14 S. Carter, 'Broadcasting, Convergence and the Public Interest', speech to the Royal Television Society, 18 September 2006, available online at www.ofcom.org.uk/media/speeches/2006/01/rst (accessed 20 November 2006).
15 BBC, Annual Report, 2006.
16 Andy Duncan, Chief Executive of Channel 4, *Review 2005*, available online at www.channel4.com/about4/pdf/2005_final_review.pdf (accessed 26 February 2010).
17 S. Holmes and D. Jermyn (eds.), *Understanding Reality Television* (London: Routledge, 2004), p. 1.
18 J. Isaacs, 'Too Much Reality', *Prospect Magazine*, 16 December 2006, available online at www.prospect-magazine.co.uk/artcile_details.php?id=7950 (accessed 14 July 2009).

19 J. Arthurs, *Television and Sexuality: Regulation and the Politics of Taste* (Maidenhead: Open University Press, 2004).

20 F. Bonner, *Ordinary Television* (London: Sage, 2003).

21 J. Corner, 'Afterword: Framing the New', in S. Holmes and D. Jermyn (eds.), *Understanding Reality Television* (London: Routledge, 2004), pp. 290–9.

22 A. Duncan, 'Maximising Public Value in the "Now" Media World', in M. Magor (ed.), *Transforming Television: Strategies for Convergence* (Glasgow TRC, 2006), pp. 18–29; p. 27.

23 F. Bonner, 'Whose Lifestyle Is It Anyway?', in D. Bell and J. Hollows (eds.), *Ordinary Lifestyle: Popular Media, Consumption and Taste* (Maidenhead: Open University Press, 2005), pp. 35–46.

24 C. Brunsdon, 'Lifestyling Britain: The 8–9 Slot on British Television', *International Journal of Cultural Studies*, 6 (1) (2003): 5–23.

25 D. Bell and J. Hollows (eds.), *Ordinary Lifestyle: Popular Media, Consumption and Taste* (Maidenhead: Open University Press, 2005), p. 15; R. Moseley, 'Real Lads Do Cook ... But Some Things Are Still Hard to Talk About: The Gendering of 8–9', *European Journal of Cultural Studies*, 4 (1) (2001): 32–9.

26 Mosley, 'Real Lads Do Cook'; J. Hollows, 'Oliver's Twist: Leisure, Labour and Domestic Masculinity in the *Naked Chef*', *International Journal of Cultural Studies*, 6 (2) (2003): 229–48.

27 Hollows, 'Oliver's Twist', p. 239.

28 T. O'Sullivan, 'From Television Lifestyle to Lifestyle Television', in D. Bell and J. Hollows (eds.), *Ordinary Lifestyle: Popular Media, Consumption and Taste* (Maidenhead: Open University Press, 2005), pp. 21–34.

29 Channel 4, *Review* (London: Channel Four Television Corporation, 2006).

30 N. Couldry, *Media Rituals: A Critical Approach* (London: Routledge, 2003).

31 J. Jarvis, *Media Guardian*, 15 January 2007, p. 6.

11
_____

British art in the twenty-first century

Introduction

In September 2008, as the financial markets in London and New York went into freefall, the British auction house Sotheby's held a two-day sale of 263 works by the British artist Damien Hirst. Despite an economy that was by all accounts heading into recession, the Hirst sale realised £111 million, far exceeding the £63 million which was estimated. Many cultural critics, art historians and academics find Damien Hirst's financial success baffling. But there is little doubt that as the highest-paid living artist to date, an examination of the Damien Hirst phenomenon can tell us much about the current state of British art. Rather than regarding Hirst's spectacular success as the product of individual genius, this chapter will examine the social, political and economic conditions that made that success possible. By doing so, it will also cast light on the fundamental changes that have occurred in the relationship between art and society in contemporary Britain and will consider how those changes have affected the kind of art that is produced.

Although Britain has produced a number of significant artists over the centuries, it has never managed to achieve the status of either Paris or New York as a wellspring of modern art. This is largely due to a modernist tendency to understand art history as a linear evolution of recognisable styles such as cubism or abstract expressionism. Despite the fact that Britain sends a higher proportion of its population to art school than any other European country, British art has proved difficult to categorise. The fact that the art colleges are located all over the country, rather than centred in London, has fostered a certain regionalism and, concomitantly, a broad range of styles and interests such as narrative and landscape, whether urban or rural. While individual artists such as Henry Moore, Francis Bacon and Lucien Freud among others have achieved international recognition, they tend to be considered exceptions to the perceived insularity of British art rather than as part of a recognisable school, movement or style.

Beginning in the late 1980s, however, the perception of British art as eclectic, eccentric and essentially inward-looking began to change. During the following decade a group of young London-based artists, including Damien Hirst, Sarah Lucas and Abigail Lane, and collectively known as the 'Young British Artists' or 'YBAs', achieved an international reputation that put London on the map as a key site of contemporary cultural production. Which individual artists belonged under the YBA banner is a complex issue, since a number of the artists associated with the movement, including Tracey Emin for example, would now deny allegiance to the label, while many others have faded into relative obscurity. However, some, such as Damien Hirst, the artist regarded as the founder of the group, have subsequently flourished. Hirst and the 'movement' he helped to create were central to the reinvention of London as a significant economic capital. This reflects the contemporary recognition that in order to attract the kind of people who manage global capital, it is necessary to create the kind of culturally vibrant city they would want to live in.

Until the impact of the Nazi occupation during the Second World War, Paris was considered to be the centre of modern art. But, as Serge Guilbaut points out, after the war, New York 'stole' that title by systematically promoting the New York-based abstract expressionist painters as the new avant-garde.[1] Government promotion and sponsorship of avant-garde art is not unique. The calendar of the global art world is marked with important international biannual exhibitions such as Venice, Istanbul and São Paulo. Individual countries are represented by carefully selected artists testifying to the fact that the export of culture is important ideological business. Eva Cockcroft excavated this terrain when she mapped the relationship between the CIA and the state-sponsored shows of abstract-expressionist painting that toured Latin America and Europe during the post-war period.[2] Cockcroft's essay exposes the way in which the work of artists such as Jackson Pollock was used by the American Government as a symbol of freedom and individuality at a time when such rhetoric was a crucial tactic in America's Cold War against the Soviet Union.

In the last two decades of the twentieth century, Britain had no such enemy. Nevertheless, there was a concerted investment in projecting the image of a reinvented Britain spearheaded by a cultural renaissance of art, music and fashion. Alongside the importance of selling the idea of 'Creative Britain' abroad was the secondary domestic imperative to democratise the arts and to increase audiences, thus making galleries and museums less reliant on government funding. Art is always produced within a social context, and the ascent of the 'Young British Artists' movement was determined by a very particular set of social and economic circumstances. Despite their image as youthful, provocative outsiders, the YBAs had grown up with the Thatcherite ethos of entrepreneurialism, and, as such, they were more than willing participants in a fabrication that served a number of political agendas.

The YBAs emanated from London and began to be visible in 1988 with the show *Freeze*, which included works by, amongst others, Hirst and Lucas. Ten years later, they were, as an identifiable group, a spent force. The time frame is interesting because it spans the 'high' Thatcherism of the late 1980s to the birth of 'New Labour' in 1997, and it is the only time in recent history that a contemporary British art movement successfully captured the attention of both the national and international mainstream media. An examination of the conditions that made this possible is revealing not least because the radical changes in government arts policy under both these political regimes demonstrates the collapse of any significant difference between the Conservative and New Labour attitudes to the arts. As a cultural brand, Young British Art heralded in a new order in which the visual arts in Britain were no longer the province of a cultural elite. Art was the new rock and roll, its consumption part of a hip urban lifestyle. In 'Creative Britain', contemporary visual art became another facet of the entertainment and tourism industries.

Young British Art was also one of the more successful publicity campaigns of the 1990s. Coined by Charles Saatchi – the advertising guru behind Margaret Thatcher's Tory government – the term, even now, would be recognised by many. Within five years of their somewhat lacklustre beginning, YBAs were exhibiting at the Venice Aperto (1993) and the Istanbul Biennale (1999). In 1994, the National Lottery came into being and, with it, the Millennium Fund, intended to revitalise the cultural infrastructure of the country. It was also in 1994 that Nicholas Serota, Director of the Tate Gallery, began to realise his long-planned £130 million project to turn the derelict Bankside power station into

Tate Modern. Clearly, to justify such expenditure, London needed to be regarded as a vibrant capital city with a cutting-edge international art scene. The creation and promotion of Young British Art was integral to that ambition. Without Serota's backing it is doubtful that Young British Art would have achieved the success it did, but, conversely, would Tate Modern have been built without Young British Art?

But what exactly is (or was) Young British Art? As an umbrella term, it relies on the notion of a coherent and critical avant-garde, but, as a group, the artists involved never issued a manifesto nor claimed any alliance to the title. In fact, the term was used to cover often very indistinct and discontinuous groupings of artists, the more successful of whom now distance themselves from the label. The label suggests a false homogeneity which, as Patricia Bickers, the editor of *Art Monthly* suggests, 'subsumes the real diversity of contemporary practice'.[3] The more emblematic Young British Art is highly theatrical and relies on the provocative staging of controversial subjects such as sex and death. The freedom to express the profane pleasures of the flesh, whether alluding to pornography or paedophilia, means that the work lends itself to media coverage and public debate. It is art that is easy to have an opinion about.

Both individually and as a group, YBAs have always courted controversy. They perpetrated a particularly irreverent British urban identity that was a key factor in the international marketing of brand Britain. The collapse of the boundary between high art and popular culture that characterised some of the more infamous YBA artworks did to some extent encourage a more democratic and inclusive appreciation of the visual arts. Drawing on ostensibly 'low-brow' forms of popular culture can eliminate the belief in the need for specialist knowledge that inhibits many people from visiting galleries and museums. Furthermore, unlike the pop artists of the 1960s who appropriated and re-presented popular-culture forms within the context of the gallery, the YBAs asserted their embeddedness in popular culture as unashamed lived experience, embracing the British tabloids in works such as Sarah Lucas's 1990 collage *Sod You Gits* made up of articles and photographs from the *Sun* newspaper. YBAs emphasised the physical body (of both artist and viewer) as an indication of a new kind of subjectivity that replaced the critical distance of the aesthetic gaze. That they also made full use of the mass media by deliberately provoking tabloid outrage about both their art and their antics also testifies to the desire for and fascination with celebrity, which are hallmarks of contemporary British culture.

The democratisation of the arts, which has been central to government policy has had limited success however, and the cultural boundary needed to maintain an artwork's value in the marketplace remains
well and truly in place. The YBAs, whilst achieving some measure of
fame by performing as rebellious bohemians, were still very much part
of a knowing cultural elite. As a group of art-college graduates, they had
absorbed the implications of the free-market economics of Thatcherism
(and the concomitant decrease in public funding for the arts), and the
way in which they responded to these conditions was integral to their
success. The role the YBAs played in furthering national and corporate
ambitions to promote Britain as a world-class cultural and economic centre is particularly evident in relation to shoring up a foundering London
art market and the subsequent development of Tate Modern.

Finally, it would be disingenuous to talk about Young British Art without discussing the influence of Charles Saatchi, who, despite setbacks to
his reputation, still maintains a position in the top ten list of important
international collectors.[4] The history of recent British art would probably have been different without Saatchi, as another collector might have
focused on a different group of artists.[5] Many claim that Saatchi single-
handedly invented Young British Art and, as both a collector *and* a dealer,
he potentially has scope for manipulating the market. Certainly it is no
coincidence that Saatchi made his reputation (and his fortune) in advertising, an industry that understands the value of free publicity. But, as
the failure of his subsequent attempts to establish new contemporary-
art movements demonstrates, Saatchi could not have done it alone. For
a movement and, more importantly, for those key artists involved in it
to achieve sustained artistic success requires the coalition of a number of
congruent – and often competing – political and economic interests.

The economic context

The Arts Council of Great Britain was founded by Royal Charter in 1946
as part of the post-war project to rebuild the nation. At that time, the
arts were considered to be entirely distinct from the political realm, and,
as Rory Francis comments: 'As the civilising arm of life, it was understood that the state had a duty to support the arts though only so far as
to encourage rather than dictate terms and conditions. Political interference was seen as not only undesirable but also incomprehensible; the
arts were otherworldly, if not ultimately transcendent.'[6] Times change,

and the relationship between the Arts Council (as the conduit for government funding) and the cultural activities and organisations it supports is no longer 'arm's length'. During the 1980s, the economic agenda of the Thatcher Government called for greater accountability and scrutiny of all public institutions. This meant that for the first time the cultural sector had to justify itself in terms of value for money. Thatcher's suspicion of 'elite culture' manifested itself in year-by-year conditional funding, which was dependent on government targets being met. These included evidence of wider participation in the arts (education programmes), more efforts towards economic sustainability (shops and cafés) and the holy grail of corporate sponsorship. Whilst there was recognition that culture was good for business, the demand for public galleries and institutions to become more financially self-sufficient increasingly shifted funding for the arts from the public to the corporate sector. 'The transformation of art museums in the 1980s from purveyors of a particular elite culture to fun palaces for an increasing number of middle-class arts consumers has to be seen within the dual perspective of government policies and business initiatives.'[7] Culture is indeed 'good for business', and corporate sponsors get a lot for their money. Not only does it give them access to potential customers who tend to be richer and better educated than the general public, it also enables their executives to rub shoulders with government ministers at the private views and parties they host for blockbuster exhibitions. Moreover, as Stallabrass observes, art sponsorship also benefits companies with image problems who 'burnish their reputations with cultural munificence'.[8]

By establishing contemporary art awards, corporations such as the German beer importer Beck's, who launched the £20,000 art prize Beck's Futures in 1986, gain considerable cultural visibility while at the same time directly targeting a young ABC1 social group and becoming, as Wu describes, 'the "vin ordinaire" of the official British avant-garde'.[9] The association between Young British Art and excess was well established by such high-profile incidents as Tracey Emin appearing drunk on national television and Damien Hirst pulling down his trousers for photographers. It is also a factor in the allegedly anti-theoretical stance of the work itself. Young British Art tended to celebrate 'everyday' pleasures such as getting pissed, having a shag and watching crap television. Alcohol producers, including Beck's beer and Absolut vodka, also produced limited editions of their products with labels designed by YBAs, creating collectors' items that cemented the alliance between their product and a hip urban lifestyle. Media coverage was guaranteed, and art, or at least contemporary art as exemplified by YBA, was established as no longer the province of a 'stuffy elite' when ordinary folk could own a piece. By deploying the modes of limited production and privileged display, the coveted bottles sidestep the ubiquity of naked consumption. Traditional notions of originality, aesthetic form and artificial scarcity legitimate these products as collectible and thus contribute to what James Clifford calls *a possessive self* as an ideal.[10] The possession may not even be the beer bottle itself but rather the cultural capital that accrues from having seen, or being seen, experiencing the latest in contemporary art.

The art market

While the Conservative Government cut funding for the arts, in the 1980s, Britain (and elsewhere in the West) was enjoying a booming free-market economy in which money became increasingly global. The art market shared in the wealth, and new galleries sprang up in London, Europe and New York. If 'investment' was the key word of the times, speculating on art seemed a certainty as the finite commodity of dead artists' work could only go up in value. The art that changed hands at such dizzying prices was traditional and 'safe' in the sense that the artists were either dead or had been around long enough to receive the kind of consistent critical approval that assures posterity. Art with a capital 'A' was still safely ensconced in the world of big money and high culture. At the same time, the London contemporary art scene, largely ignored by the big dealers and collectors, was concerned with the kind of personal and intellectual issue-based practices that had grown up in the 1970s era of identity politics and the introduction into art colleges of the 'high' theories associated with French philosophy and psychoanalysis.

The challenge to the art-historical canon (as a white, middle-class, male history) initially spearheaded by feminist and post-colonial theorists, resulted in changes to arts funding, and the early 1980s was, in a sense, a golden age when previously marginalised special-interest groups were funded for specific gallery spaces and publications. These developments had no effect on the market, and, although they raised the profile of particular artists, they had little impact on the way in which the visual arts were perceived (or received) by either the elite or by the general public. By the latter part of the 1980s, increasingly sparse public funding resulted in a negative perception of issue-based art as 'victim' art, and, in a sector governed by the need for accessibility, 'high' theory was similarly rejected as elitist and obscure.

The stock market crash of 1987 triggered a gradual but relentless decline in the international art market, and, by the end of the decade, many of the new gallerists and dealers had shut up shop. But the recession that followed (and lasted well into the mid 1990s) created a huge variety of vacant industrial spaces, which were taken over by artists as studios and used for 'do-it-yourself' shows. It also meant that those dealers who were managing to survive the recession became interested in cheap local talent.

Alternative spaces

In 1985, Charles Saatchi opened his Boundary Road gallery in an old paint warehouse in St John's Wood in order to display his collection of contemporary art. The Saatchi Gallery was the first of its kind in London, and the 30,000 square feet of former warehouse space became a Mecca for London's art students. Between September 1987 and April 1988, a two-part exhibition entitled 'New York Art Now' introduced Londoners to the recent American tendency called 'neo-geo' or 'simulationism', that is, the work of Jeff Koons, Ashley Bickerton, Robert Gober *et al.* Koons, a former salesman, who even devised and starred in his own adverts and whose art celebrated American kitsch, was a favourite of Charles Saatchi. These shows were important in their impact on young British art students such as Hirst.[11]

In 1988, a group of students from Goldsmiths College, taking their cue from the Saatchi Gallery, mounted a show entitled *Freeze*, an event that was to provide the origin story of Young British Art. As Simon Ford argues, *Freeze* represents the foundational myth of Young British Art and not only connects the artists involved with the 1980s spirit of entrepreneurialism (inspired self-starters working outside of the gallery system) but also married the group to a new 1990s ethos of camaraderie rather than competitiveness.[12] Most important of all to the formulation of Young British Art as a movement, *Freeze* identified Goldsmiths College as the wellspring of new artistic talent.

Freeze, an exhibition in three parts, opened in August 1988 in the vacant Port of London Authority Building owned by the London Docklands Development Corporation. They, along with the Canary Wharf Development Corporation, sponsored the show and the publication of a full-colour catalogue. *Freeze* was conceived and curated by Damien Hirst (then a second-year Goldsmiths undergraduate) and included sixteen artists who were students or recent graduates of that college. The legendary status of *Freeze* was principally achieved through the auspices of Norman Rosenthal, the Exhibitions Secretary of the Royal Academy, who, in his catalogue essay for *Sensation* recounted how he was collected by Damien Hirst in a 'rickety old car' and driven down to Docklands to see *Freeze*. Rosenthal's story has all the elements of art-historical myth-making: the dangers and delights of slumming it with the bohemians as well as the giddy frisson of discovery. It also marked out Hirst for his drive and determination in getting the Exhibitions Secretary of the Royal Academy to see the show. Like all good myths, however, the story doesn't bear a lot of scrutiny. The accuracy of Rosenthal's account is called into question when, in an effort to demonstrate Hirst's generosity of spirit (another defining characteristic of Young British Art), he cites how Hirst insisted on also taking him to see Rachel Whiteread's *Ghost*, a large concrete cast of the interior of a Victorian room:

> Hirst was as good and skilful a publicist for his art and that of his contemporaries as he was a maker of art himself. He certainly was not promoting himself as their most significant representative as the media later claimed. At exactly the time of 'Freeze' Rachel Whiteread was showing her ambitious sculpture *Ghost* at the recently established Chisenhale Gallery in the East End. I had not heard of her at the time, but Hirst insisted that I see this and drove me there too.[13]

Whiteread's *Ghost* was showing at the Chisenhale Gallery in 1990, two years *after* the Freeze shows, demonstrating that a good origin story needs only to embody the characteristics and values of the group it defines. In this case, the YBAs (with Hirst as their figurehead) are represented as innovative self-promoters who also embrace 'softer' communal values. These act as a useful counterpoint to what could be construed as Hirst's naked ambition as, after all, art has traditionally been regarded as antithetical to commercialism. It follows on that an important part of the marketing of YBAs – as integral to a newly revitalised London – was their representation as part of a unified social scene in which the artists were all 'mates'. They attended the same college, lived in the same part of London, socialised together and eventually went on to be represented by the same handful of dealers.[14]

Exhibitions are ephemeral, but catalogues live on, and the *Freeze* catalogue is a record not only of the artworks themselves but also its staging and contextualising. As well as colour plates of the artists' works, it included an essay by Ian Jeffrey – then Head of Art History at Goldsmiths. Entitled 'Platonic Tropics', Jeffrey's essay had the tough job of elevating some of the frankly puerile individual works while at the same time offering a coherent framework for the exhibition without resorting to 'high' theory. Even so, there is no doubting the rather mannered expression of the YBAs' importance in passages such as, 'Once upon a time there were completely new starts, with yesterday a long way off, but under the new terms of reference the present comes less as itself than as the recent past re-done, re-recorded, or maybe never even away.'[15] Nonetheless, what is most interesting about the *Freeze* catalogue as documentary evidence is how little indication there is of the kind of 'shock art' that came to be associated with YBA. Nine of the sixteen exhibitors in *Freeze* were included in the infamous 1997 *Sensation* exhibition, but apart from Mat Collishaw's *Bullet Hole 1988*, which has been seen again (and again and again), there is little here that could be described as revolutionary. Damien Hirst's *Boxes* is particularly surprising given his status as the godfather of YBA. This wall piece, spread out at eye level from the corner of a room, consisted of various sized (but mostly small) painted cardboard boxes tightly arranged to form seemingly random planes. The most obvious reference is to early twentieth-century constructivism or, at best, to Frank Stella in the 1960s. There is nothing new here and certainly no foretaste of the kind of grand spectacle for which Hirst became famous. Sarah Lucas, who subsequently became known for her irreverent and seemingly offhand and provocatively sexual sculptures, showed an anodyne dented and bent aluminium tube called *Untitled*, which could best be characterised as ironic minimalism. In fact, it is the essential conservatism of the work in *Freeze* that is so fascinating, particularly in relation to the art that was to come. Clearly the importance of *Freeze* in the construction of YBA lay not in the show itself but in its exemplification of Thatcherite values. Rather than sitting around waiting to be discovered, Hirst and his colleagues located a space, obtained sponsorship, produced a catalogue and did their own publicity and promotion. In its presentation, *Freeze* replicated what they had learned from visiting the Saatchi Gallery and so they *performed* as artists – and not inward-looking, parochial British artists, but international art stars like Jeff Koons. The ultimate merit of the work itself was inconsequential because the exhibition was so well presented and the performance so impressive. As Matthew Collings writes, 'Even though they were only put on by students, or recently graduated students, they had a bold European kunsthalle look, or Soho in New York look, or the pages of *Flash Art* or *Artforum* look.'[16] This 'do it yourself' spirit was fundamental to Young British Art, and by 1990, the format of *Freeze* had been successfully replicated in other warehouse shows including *Modern Medicine, Gambler*, and *East Country Yard*. The locus of the contemporary London art scene was gradually shifting from west to east, and Hoxton and Shoreditch were hailed as major cultural quarters. A new generation of London-based galleries such as Jay Jopling's White Cube, Karsten Schubert, Victoria Miro, Interim Art and not least Charles Saatchi, were to lead the way in presenting Young British Art to a wider audience.[17]

It is difficult to pinpoint exactly when the alliance between the Eton-educated art-dealer Jay Jopling and Damien Hirst began, but it is clear that Jopling was instrumental not only in organising the warehouse shows but also in financing Hirst's more ambitious projects. The radical shift from the painted cardboard boxes in *Freeze* to the increasingly theatrical vitrines was expensive, but clearly, Jopling made a good investment. It was from *Gambler*, the show that followed *Freeze*, that Charles Saatchi acquired Damien Hirst's signature work *A Thousand Years*, a glass vitrine in which maggots feed on 'blood' (actually sugar and water) apparently from a cow's severed head. The maggots then mature, reproduce and die in an insect-o-cutor, in an endless cycle of birth and death. Hirst's preoccupation with mortality is reflected in many of the long-winded titles he gives to his works, and certainly they lend an adolescent gravitas to the works themselves. For the 1991 installation *In and Out of Love*, Hirst filled a gallery with canvases covered in pupae, which hatched out, filling the gallery with butterflies. Inevitably, the show attracted criticism from animal-rights protestors and, of course, attendant publicity. Continuing the YBAs' media flirtations, Jopling, as Hirst's dealer, boasted of his ability to manipulate the press and to provoke tabloid response to the 'new' art. No doubt this strategy prompted the *Daily Star*'s infamous photograph of their reporter standing with a bag of chips in front of Hirst's large vitrine containing a tiger shark suspended in formaldehyde under the headline: 'The World's Most Expensive Fish and Chips'. With publicity like this, the contemporary art industry was becoming as visible as pop, film and fashion. And, like those other arenas of mass culture, the personalities involved became the increasing focus of media attention.

Charles Saatchi

During the 1990s Saatchi took to visiting artists' studios in the
more marginal districts of London, especially the East End – which
hosts one of the largest concentrations of artists in the world – in
a chauffeur-driven black Lincoln Towncar on Saturday mornings
… For some obscure poverty-stricken artists his visits were
nothing short of miraculous because they offered the chance of a
transformation of their lifestyle and career prospects.[18]

Charles Saatchi has a self-confessed preference for the kind of sound-bite
art that packs an easily legible visual punch. He is not a collector in the
traditional understanding of the word because he sells as much art as he
buys and uses the profits to buy more, thus making the whole operation
self-financing. However, the advantage he had over other speculators
during the period under discussion was that his Boundary Road gallery
in the St John's Wood district of London enabled him to exhibit his pur-
chases and to promote them with glossy catalogues and erudite essays.
The conspicuous endorsement of the Saatchi Gallery thus increased the
works' status as art and consequently their monetary value, and there is
little doubt that Charles Saatchi was one of the principal players in the
London art world during that period.

In 1992, the Saatchi Gallery staged the first of the three exhibitions,
Young British Artists I–III, which gave Young British Art its name. It was
here that Hirst's shark piece, *The Physical Impossibility of Death in the Mind
of Someone Living*, made its debut. Saatchi commissioned this piece for
£50,000, and it is not difficult to imagine that someone used to working with enormous budgets for television commercials would find it
easy to arrange the sourcing of a dead shark and its suspension in a
tank of formaldehyde. Hirst's shark piece, with the help of stunts such
as the one described above, attracted a lot of publicity, but it was not
just Saatchi and Jopling who were promoting YBA as a 'movement'. In
the previous year, the Serpentine Gallery had mounted a gathering of
work by some of the Goldsmiths artists under the title *Broken English*.
The show was selected by the art critic Andrew Graham-Dixon and
signalled a new move in the art game whereby critics (as well as artists)
became curators. This overlapping of the worlds of journalism and
art further increased media attention on this new London art scene as
well as spawning a new wave of critic-curators.

Tate plc

With public galleries no longer able to purchase art on any kind of significant scale, they relied on collectors such as Saatchi for gifts and loans of important artworks. From the early 1980s through the 1990s, Saatchi was heavily involved with the Tate as a member of the Patrons of New Art whose remit was to help the Tate increase its holdings and exhibitions of contemporary art. In a 1999 article in *The Spectator*, arts editor and critic David Lee claimed that the British art establishment was effectively controlled by fourteen people, including those cited as members of the Patrons of New Art.[19] Other significant patrons at that time included Michael Craig Martin (the Goldsmiths tutor credited as 'the father of Young British Art') and the dealers Jay Jopling (White Cube) and Nicholas Logsdail (Lisson Gallery) who both represented YBAs. That all of them had a vested interest in promoting Young British Art is obvious.

One key initiative instrumental in broadening the reach of contemporary art in Britain was the 1991 relaunch of the Tate Gallery's Turner Prize. This annual award to British artists originally founded in 1984 was, until its relaunch, largely irrelevant to the contemporary art scene let alone to British society in general. The financial collapse of the US investment firm Drexel Lambert, which sponsored the award, resulted in a suspension of the competition in 1990, but a subsequent Tate 'think tank' charged with the task of getting newspapers to take contemporary art seriously came up with a revamped Turner Prize clearly aimed at capturing the youth market. An upper age limit of fifty was set for nominees, the prize money was doubled to £20,000 and the shortlist was reduced to four artists. Each of the finalists would be given space in a Tate exhibition so the public could see the work before the winner was announced, thus encouraging the notion that 'the public' had a say in the proceedings. In fact, the panel of judges, which changes annually, is made up of art insiders with Nicholas Serota as Chair. Interestingly, as David Lee points out, the same two commercial galleries have represented nine of the fourteen winners.

Press coverage of the Turner Prize fluctuated between informed interest from the broadsheets to outrage in the tabloids, particularly when there were no painters on the shortlist. The biggest coup was a sponsorship deal with Channel 4 – a network associated with youthful alternative culture – to broadcast the award ceremony and to air a series of documentaries on the individual nominees in the weeks leading up to the prize-giving. The alliance between Tate and Channel 4 marked the first truly effective marriage of contemporary visual arts with the mass media, and, as the Turner Prize gained increasing notoriety for its promotion of the kind of 'conceptual' art associated with Young British Art (Damien Hirst won it in 1995) the television coverage of the award dinner became more like the Brit Awards (for music), with celebrities such as Madonna announcing the winner.

The YBAs abroad

By the early 1990s, a host of London exhibitions focused on some variation of Young British Art as if in general acknowledgement that something revolutionary was afoot in the city. Even though, apart from Damien Hirst and latterly Tracey Emin, it has always been a slippery task to name the artists who counted as YBAs, the movement was increasingly codified as the product of a specific time and place: a subculture of artists occupying the gritty urban setting of London's East End and who came of age in Thatcher's Britain. These artists were meant to share a particularly irreverent sensibility that made little distinction between art and other forms of pop culture. Their work was easy to understand, often involving one-off visual puns. Much of the work was marked by forms of transgression and taboo-breaking, and their approach to both materials and method was eclectic, with many of the YBAs working across media as varied as photography, collage, performance, found objects, installation, sculpture and drawing.

The British Council sponsored two key exhibitions in 1995 that did much to broadcast the reputation of Young British Art abroad. *Brilliant! New Art from London* was hosted by the Walker Art Center in Minneapolis before travelling to the Houston Contemporary Arts Museum in Texas. *General Release* in Venice was not only sponsored by the British Council but was also selected by it. In both shows, attempts were made to trade on the reputation of the group, but as the 'group' as such did not really exist, the shows lacked cohesion and meaning. *Brilliant!* in particular deserves closer examination for what it can tell us about the way in which YBA was internationally staged. Both the pre-publicity and the production of the catalogue reiterated the myth of the aggressive and boundary-breaking nature of the exhibited work. But critics of the show (American and British) felt it failed to deliver, and it was left to the catalogue cover to provoke the required outrage. The catalogue, produced by the show's organiser Richard Flood, utilised the somewhat dated aesthetic of a rough-and-ready tabloid-style fanzine, and Flood selected for the cover a photograph showing the devastation caused by an IRA bomb in London with the word *Brilliant!* written in red across it. The organiser's use of such a tasteless juxtaposition was an attempt to present the YBAs as 'mad, bad and dangerous to know', but the hostile reception to the catalogue caused the British Council to distance itself from the exhibition, and none of its representatives turned up for the Houston opening. Young British Art shows always included artworks that caused public offence and controversy, and the catalogue for *Brilliant!* was a clear attempt to capitalise on this. That it backfired is not surprising as the allegedly anti-establishment stance of the group was at odds with increasing public knowledge of their blatant self-promotion. As Matthew Collings wrote in his review of the show:

> Nobody can quite sum up what they stand for. The advance publicity of *Brilliant!* presents them as cheeky cockneys and punk rockers oppressed by the Thatcher junta, dodging IRA bombs, living in squats, and making rough and ready art that screams with rage and isn't intended for pristine white gallery space, but for rough and ready warehouse spaces in London's cockney East End. In reality of course they are highly sophisticated formalists who desperately, and quite rightly, want to show in pristine white spaces like the Tate Gallery and the Walker Art Center.[20]

Sensation

Despite an increasingly bored or adverse reaction to the YBAs from both the majority of critics and the general public, the movement gained ground, reaching its zenith with the 1997 Royal Academy blockbuster show *Sensation: Young British Artists from the Saatchi Collection*. It was a surprising pairing: the cash-strapped Royal Academy, bastion of establishment art, hosting a show of brash young British artists whose work deliberately flouted artistic conventions. But the gamble paid off as controversy began before the show even opened when it was leaked to the press that the exhibition included a painting by Marcus Harvey of the Moors murderer Myra Hindley made from the stencilled handprints of children. The families of children murdered by Hindley demonstrated outside the building, and four Royal Academicians resigned in protest. 'Norman Rosenthal, the RA's head of exhibitions, was threatened with the sack and a predominantly young audience queued to get into the Academy's packed galleries.'[21] Predictably, Harvey's painting was angrily defaced, resulting in yet more publicity. Other 'sensations' drawing in the crowds were Tracey Emin's tent, entitled *Everyone I Have Ever Slept With*, in which the appliquéd names included that of an aborted foetus; Sarah Lucas's *Au Naturel*, which consisted of a grubby mattress half leaning against a wall with a bucket on its side positioned beneath two melons and alongside an upright cucumber nestled between two oranges; and Jake and Dinos Chapman's fibreglass sculptures depicting groups of naked – apart from trainers – conjoined mutant, pre-pubescent children with penises for noses and gaping mouths. Sex and violence swelled the box office, but, as was the case with most Young British Art shows, it was the loudest voices that dominated, subsuming many of the less contentious works. It is interesting to note that nearly all of the forty-two artists included in *Sensation* were born in the 1960s and were graduates of London art colleges. More than half of them were graduates of Goldsmiths. Notable exceptions were the Palestinian artist, Mona Hatoum (b. 1952) and the Australian artist, Ron Mueck (b. 1958), but as both these artists showed work that was directly concerned with the body, the age and origin of the alleged 'young British artists' was apparently overlooked.

Despite attempts to organise the show thematically according to art-historical conventions, critics of *Sensation* found it difficult to get a foothold on the art as representative of a specific movement apart from the spurious unity imposed by the Saatchi imprimatur. Kitty Hauser summed up the critical response to *Sensation* when she wrote:

> The shark it seems has been domesticated. Stamped with the approval of the Establishment (it's art!) and honoured by record numbers of exhibition visitors (it's popular!), it can now triumphantly slink back to the Saatchi archives as representative of a new(ish) kind of art; an art which is unashamedly commercial, media-friendly, pleasurable and boasts a wide audience.[22]

Sensation succeeded in establishing Young British Art's place in the history of British art while at the same time, curiously sounding its death knell. The expensively produced hardback exhibition catalogue served as a lavish PR exercise with full-colour plates and a series of essays that conformed to the kind of art history that 'fixes meaning and importance ... and lay(s) a wet blanket of consensus over the work.'[23] That the essays were as vacuous as much of the work was a fact not lost on commentators, and the academic Lisa Jardine's homage to Saatchi entitled 'Modern Medicis: Art Patronage in the Twentieth Century in Britain' attracted particular critical ire.

Sensation travelled to the Brooklyn Museum, where more scandal and controversy broke out this time over Chris Ofili's painting The Holy Virgin Mary, which features collaged images from porn magazines and balls of elephant dung as breasts. The Catholic community was outraged, and the then Mayor of New York Rudy Giuliani threatened to withdraw the museum's funding. Nonetheless, the show went ahead with predictably record attendance.

Conclusion

Sensation was the last Young British Art show to gain widespread media attention but the crowds that flocked to galleries to see it discovered that art appreciation in its contemporary context is just another form of easy consumption. The art itself is often the by-product of shopping for post-cards and meeting friends for latte, part of what Mike Featherstone calls 'the aestheticization of everyday life'.[24] In 1997, New Labour, with its social-inclusion agenda, achieved a landslide victory, and the Department of Culture, Media and Sport was born. With such an inclusive conflation of all things creative, what some termed 'Britart' was joined by Britpop and Britfashion, and, for a thankfully brief time, New Labour used the slogan 'Cool Britannia' to market itself. Since the introduction in 1998 of free entry to major museums, audiences have increased significantly (most of them children on school visits). Tate Modern opened in 2000, and, although it neither owns nor exhibits any significant Young British Art works, it continues to attract record-breaking numbers. Another 'statement' building is currently planned as an annex, and recently the Belgian artist Carsten Höller filled the enormous Turbine Hall with a giant helter skelter. Fun palaces indeed!

Despite several well-publicised attempts, Charles Saatchi has yet to create another art movement, but two of the YBAs, Damien Hirst and Tracey Emin (who didn't attend Goldsmiths and wasn't in Freeze) have achieved celebrity status: the latter with appearances on television game shows and a newspaper column to her credit, and the former by such transcultural activities as opening a (now-defunct) restaurant, writing a book and forming a band which released a single. In June 2006, Damien Hirst exhibited new paintings at the Gagosian Gallery in New York that were universally panned by critics. Despite this, works such as his diamond-encrusted skull, *For the Love of God* (2007), and *The Golden Calf* (2008), an embalmed calf with gold-plated feet and horns, are considered to be the most expensive works of art ever sold. In a BBC radio interview, Hirst claimed that his work is about 'what it is to be alive today', but as Germaine Greer points out, 'Hirst's art is marketing.'[25] Perhaps it is precisely Hirst's ability to convince the market of the value of his work that really tells us something about British culture today. If so, then it seems appropriate to leave the final words to Jean Baudrillard, who knew all about the power of simulacra:

> As long as art was making use of its own disappearance and the disappearance of its object, it still was a major enterprise. But art trying to recycle itself indefinitely by storming reality? The majority of contemporary art has attempted to do precisely that by confiscating banality, waste and mediocrity as values and ideologies. These countless installations and performances are merely compromising with the state of things, and with all past forms of art history. Raising originality, banality and nullity to the level of values or even perverse aesthetic pleasure. Of course, all this mediocrity claims to transcend itself by moving art to a second, *ironic* level. But it is just as empty and insignificant on the second as on the first level. The passage to the aesthetic level salvages nothing; on the contrary, it is mediocrity squared. It claims to be null – 'I am null! I am null!' – *and it is truly null.*[26]

Notes

1 S. Guilbaut, *How New York Stole the Idea of Modern Art* (Chicago, Ill.: Chicago University Press, 1983).

2 E. Cockcroft, 'Abstract Expressionism: Weapon of the Cold War', in F. Frascina (ed.), *Pollock and After: The Critical Debate*, 2nd edn (London: Routledge, 2000), pp. 147–54.

3 P. Bickers, 'Sense and Sensation', *Art Monthly*, 211 (November 1997): 1–6; p. 3.

4 E. Addley, 'French Tycoon Tops Art Power List', *The Guardian*, 14 October 2006.

5 R. Hatton and J. A. Walker, *Supercollector: A Critique of Charles Saatchi* (London: Ellipsis, 2000), p. 18.

6 R. Francis, 'Managing Disappointment: Arts Policy Funding and the Social Inclusion Agenda', in J. Harris (ed.), *Art, Money, Parties: New Institutions in the Political Economy of Contemporary Art* (Liverpool: Liverpool University Press, 2004), pp. 133–62; p. 140.

7 C.-T. Wu, 'Embracing the Enterprise Culture: Art Institutions Since the 1980s', *New Left Review*, 230 (July/August 1998): 28–57; p. 30.

8 J. Stallabrass, *Art Incorporated: The Story of Contemporary Art* (Oxford: Oxford University Press, 2005), p. 135.

9 Wu, 'Embracing the Enterprise Culture', p. 37.

10 J. Clifford, *The Predicament of Culture* (Cambridge, Mass.: Harvard University Press, 1988).

11 Hatton and Walker, *Supercollector*, p. 147.

12 S. Ford, 'The Myth of the Young British Artist', in D. McCorquodale, N. Siderfin and J. Stallabrass (eds.), *Occupational Hazard* (London: Black Dog, 1998).

13 N. Rosenthal, 'The Blood Must Continue to Flow', in *Sensation: Young British Artists from the Saatchi Collection* (exhibition catalogue) (London: Thames & Hudson, 1997), pp. 8–11; p. 9.

14 A. While, 'Locating Art Worlds: London and the Making of Young British Art', *Area*, 35 (3) (2003): 251–63; p. 257.

15 I. Jeffrey, 'Platonic Tropics', in D. Hirst (curator), *Freeze* (exhibition catalogue) (London: 1988), pp. 1–4.

16 M. Collings, *Blimey!* (London: 21 Publishing, 1997), p. 13.

17 While, 'Locating Art Worlds', p. 258.

18 Hatton and Walker, *Supercollector*, p. 181.

19 D. Lee, 'Conceptual Art Mafia Exposed', *The Spectator*, 30 October 1999.

20 M. Collings, cited in 'What Is It That Makes Young British Art So Different, So Appealing?', available online at http://members.lycos.co.uk/exposuremagazine/yba.html (accessed 24 October 2008).

21 A. Brighton, 'Thatcher's Artists', *Oxford Art Journal*, 22 (2) (1999), pp. 129–133; p. 130.

22 K. Hauser, 'Sensation: Young British Artists from the Saatchi Collection', *New Left Review*, 227 (January/February 1998): 154–160; p. 154.

23 Brighton, 'Thatcher's Artists', p. 130.

24 M. Featherstone, *Consumer Culture and Postmodernism* (London: Sage, 1991).

25 Interview with Mark Lawson, *Front Row*, BBC Radio 4 (15 September, 2008); G. Greer, *The Guardian*, 22 September 2008.

26 J. Baudrillard, *The Conspiracy of Art* (New York: Semiotext(e), 2005), p. 27.

12

British fashion

Just what is it that makes British fashion so different, so appealing?

In the early years of the twenty-first century, the fortunes of the ailing British clothing company Burberry were dramatically reversed as its young designer Christopher Bailey reworked its traditional motifs – beige checks and trench coats – into newly fashionable formations. Yet, although Burberry's high-profile designer was English, the chief executive responsible for poaching him in 1997 from the Italian luxury goods brand Gucci was an American, Rose Marie Bravo, and the clothes were largely manufactured overseas.[1] So how British a success story, really, was the revival of Burberry, leaving aside its history and tradition?

The question encapsulates the difficulties of defining national design in an age of globalisation. Designers such as Vivienne Westwood and John Galliano, or the late Alexander McQueen, have played with the imagery of tradition and history in their designs, creatively reinterpreting them in a modern idiom, but these are merely stylistic and iconographic indices of British identity. Their clothes are no more made in Britain than their companies are necessarily British-owned; they are more than likely to have Italian, Japanese or French backers and to manufacture in Italy or the Far East. Anachronistically, top-end Savile Row suits are still made locally, but elsewhere in Britain the manufacturing base has declined to almost nothing.

Nevertheless, the idea of Britishness has a commercial value that leads international fashion conglomerates to add quintessentially British names to their holdings: by 2001, Aquascutum and DAKS Simpson had been acquired by Japanese companies, while Church Shoes, still made by traditional methods in the company's Northampton factory, were owned by Prada, an Italian luxury brand.[2] It can seem at times as if the best customer for 'Englishness' is an overseas one, exemplified by the Japanese businessman in his Church shoes and Savile Row suit. Meanwhile, many of the fashion shops on the British high street are multinationals such as the Gap and Mango.

So just what is it that makes British fashion so different, so appealing? Although most British fashion is no longer 'made in England' (or Scotland) as the labels used to proclaim, it retains a strong profile and a distinctive identity. UK designers produce fashion that is both striking and innovative, and they are well served by the creativity of independent British fashion magazines and photographers. Fashion in the UK is part of an exceptionally wide network linking it to styling, photography, graphics and journalism, as well as to innovative retailing. Commerce has been as important as creativity, both in independent designer boutiques and in the high street. Consumers, too, have played their part in its definition. Since the eighteenth century, English dress has been associated with a high degree of eccentricity and individualism.[3] Nowadays, one can identify a particularly British way of mixing thrift-shop or vintage dressing with both high-street and designer wear. Youth and art-school culture have also played an important role, especially since the Second World War, when music, subculture and street fashion became closely connected.

To all these different elements – the emphasis on innovation and novelty, the importance of youth culture, and the high profile of the creative industries in the UK – can be added the iconography of tradition. Based on the apparently contradictory characteristics of tradition and innovation (twin sets and pearls on the one hand, punk outrage on the other), the contrasting ideals of heritage and novelty have consistently fed the imaginations of fashion designers, consumers and journalists. These powerful mythic representations of Britishness can be either recycled in a traditional vein or creatively reinterpreted in avant-garde formations.

Set against these narratives is the very real diversity of Britain and the way that its identity, even in fashion design, is rooted in multicultural variety as much as in visions of heritage. Its many ethnic communities have been involved in fashion as both producers and consumers. Fashion has long been a working-class passion just as much as it was a middle- or upper-class one; in the eighteenth century, when there was a thriving market for stolen clothes, foreigners commented on the uppityness of

British servants who aped the dress of their betters.[4] Since the Second World War, differing social groups have used fashion to stake out new social identities in a changing Britain, or to reinforce older ones; youth and subcultures have used it as a marker of difference and rebellion.[5] It is found equally in the messy vitality of the street and in the poise and control of the West End salon; and it has enthralled men as deeply as it has women.[6]

Heritage

It is hard to separate the real tradition from pastiche in British fashion. The Scottish tweeds so adored by French couturiers such as Chanel in the 1920s are no longer manufactured in Northern mills. The British textiles and manufacturing industries have dwindled to almost nothing over the past fifty years; and anyway our houses are now too warm for us to wear the thick woollens of our grandparents.[7] Yet the imagery persists, and traditional fabrics and techniques continue to exert a fascination. Shirt-making, boot-making, knitwear and woven textiles, especially tweeds and tartans, form part of the repertoire of traditional British fashion. So, too, do notions of the impeccable cut of men's tailoring over 200 years and, more recently, of the quiet good taste of English couture for women, exemplified in the pre-and post-war years by Hardy Amies and Victor Stiebel. All are open to creative recycling by contemporary designers. Not all are British, though the look is: the American Ralph Lauren has often been accused of packaging and reselling Englishness back to the English. In eighteenth-century France, fashions were dominated by 'Anglomania', the craze for all things English, and in the 1980s the French designer Jean-Paul Gaultier was strongly influenced by British street fashion. In the nineteenth century, British firms such as Redfern were established in Paris, making women's 'tailor-mades' and riding costumes for an elite clientele. And it is a cliché of fashion history that Charles Frederick Worth, the 'father of haute couture', was an Englishman, apprenticed from the age of twelve at the London department store Swan & Edgar.[8] So the idea of 'English fashion', *la mode anglaise*, has always been determined, in part, by the meaning ascribed to it by influential foreigners who themselves played a hand in establishing fashionable ideals across the world from at least the eighteenth century, and since then its allure has extended beyond France to many other countries, not least the USA and Italy.

One thing that does survive in terms of traditional manufacturing is London's Savile Row, which continues to produce its renowned bespoke men's suits locally. In 2006, despite rent increases of almost 50 per cent, the area still supported more than 500 workers, over 100 of them specialist tailors and cutters, who together produced approximately 7,000 suits a year.[9] Menswear has been paramount in the British tradition. While Paris has been associated for at least 200 years with women's fashion, over the same period the British enjoyed an unrivalled reputation for excellence in male dress, especially tailoring. Beau Brummell's dandyism, which involved the principles of sobriety, taste and discretion, hugely influenced the French dandies of the nineteenth century, and in the 1930s the ideal of the Englishman's sartorial perfectionism was exemplified in the eyes of foreigners by the Duke of Windsor's Prince-of-Wales checks, polished brogues and argyle-patterned jumpers.

Further along the spectrum from the royalty and aristocracy who patronised Worth and Savile Row, lower- and middle-class tastes were catered to by the British high street, which, since the Second World War, has dominated a far larger section of the market than in any other country. The high-street chain Marks & Spencer provided convenience, quality and value. Long before other retailers, it allowed customers to return unused goods. Innovative in its relationship to new technology, it sold the first machine-washable wools and, more recently, seamless underwear at high-street prices. Today, the high street is dominated by 'fast fashion' in the form of international brands such as H&M and Zara, but British firms such as River Island still command a substantial section of the home market, as well as franchising abroad. In general, the British high street responds imaginatively and rapidly to catwalk trends and top-end fashion, while the British consumer is equally adept at snapping up new looks only weeks after they have appeared in more elite locations. Increasingly, British high-street chains have learnt to capitalise on independent London designers' reputations by employing them to design mass-market ranges in tandem with their more exclusive, own-label designs, such as the 'Gold by Giles' capsule collection first designed by the 2006 British Designer of the Year Giles Deacon for the New Look chain in March 2007. Collaborations like this guarantee chain-store coverage in up-market fashion magazines such as *Vogue*, which, in April 2007, featured the model Kate Moss on its cover, giving advanced editorial coverage to the fashion range she had designed for the British chain Topshop.

In terms of turnover, few British designers can compete with the high street. An exception is the designer Paul Smith, who sells approximately £220 million-worth of goods a year. As well as having retail outlets worldwide, Paul Smith's wholesale business spans forty-eight countries and accounts for 80 per cent of his turnover.[10] Given the global reach of his business, his emphasis on locality and the shopping experience for his customers is striking. Paul Smith opened his first shop in 1970 in Nottingham and his first London shop in Floral Street in 1979. Floral Street has remained the base camp for his expanded empire of men's, women's and children's wear. Invoking the idea of Britain as a nation of shopkeepers, Smith's many retail outfits from Tokyo to London have lovingly recreated the look of an Edwardian gents' outfitters, in some cases reusing original shop fittings from UK shops that have gone out of business. Smith's retailing innovations echo his design strategy: the recreation of 'classics with a twist', which are neither too outrageous nor too staid to alienate the widest possible range of customers.[11]

Smith's 'ingrained sense of place' taps into the ways in which London's identity as a global fashion city has traditionally been defined by specific shopping streets such as Carnaby Street and the King's Road and also invokes the heterogeneity of Britain's many street markets and charity shops that are such rich sources of vintage and second-hand dress.[12] He has retained his first Nottingham shop as well as the London one, a nod to his Midlands roots and to the heritage of manufacturing in Britain's now largely defunct fashion and textiles industries. Smith has thus managed to build an international business on a nostalgic evocation of the working- and lower-class associations with manufacturing and shop-keeping that defined an earlier moment in British history. Other designers draw on more aristocratic and leisured ideals through the picturesque imagery of heritage, which, in 2006, was given a prominent platform in the exhibition 'AngloMania' at the Metropolitan Museum of Art in New York. Sponsored by Burberry, the exhibition sought, in the curator Andrew Bolton's words, to explore 'various normative representations of Englishness' through the lens of fashion, such as John Bull, the Hunt, Empire and Monarchy and the Gentleman's Club.[13] Set in the museum's English period rooms, the designs of Alexander McQueen, John Galliano and Vivienne Westwood were arranged in a series of vignettes that juxtaposed past and present to suggest that British fashion is characterised equally by historicism and avant-gardism. Bolton's vignettes drew upon the idea of an 'English imaginary' described by the writer Kevin Davey and were 'based on idealized concepts of English culture'.[14] In elaborating these, Bolton differentiated Englishness from Britishness:

> Englishness is a romantic construct, formed by feelings, attitudes and perceptions, as opposed to Britishness, which is a political construct, based on shared practices and institutions. Indeed, by its very definition, Britishness embraces the diverse, disparate, and diasporic character of the country (or rather countries). Englishness, however, despite social, economic and political developments, continues to suggest singularity and homogeneity. This image, of course, is a pretence, but Englishness, 'enduring Englishness', is maintained by its mythologies.[15]

Thus, in AngloMania, Bolton chose to illustrate the 'Hunt' vignette with a Burberry women's dress based on the soldier's trench coat developed in 1914 for British officers in the trenches. Reinterpreted in pale silk faille, rather than the traditional beige gabardine, it was ornamented with fox fur on the cuffs and skirt and lined in scarlet silks which recalled the 'hunting pink' of the red riding coat traditionally worn at the British Hunt. In the one garment, Christopher Bailey, the designer, thereby managed to combine references to the traditional masculine attributes of hunting and fighting and to regender them as a chic, feminine, coat dress for the modern, metropolitan woman.

Diversity, youth culture, innovation

Bolton's evocation of 'the diverse, disparate, and diasporic character of the country' suggests, however, a more heterogeneous model of British, as opposed to traditional English, fashion culture. As the manufacturing base began to disintegrate in post-war Britain, something else began to surface: youth culture. While American youth culture was always allied to mainstream consumer culture, British youth culture, with its strong affiliations with the 'caff' (the café) and the street, with popular music and, from the late 1960s, with emerging drug cultures, tended to be more oppositional in both style and content. The dress of teddy boys, for example, was a working-class parody of an upper-class Edwardian revival in tailoring. Post-war subcultural styles ranged from 1950s teds and rockers to 1960s mods and skinheads and 1970s punks. Each subculture generated its own sartorial codes and unique style of dress through which it defined itself in opposition to the dominant culture. Despite their meticulous attention to dress, subcultures were not designer-led, although Vivienne Westwood and Malcolm McLaren's King's Road shop 'Sex' sold the punk bondage trousers and pornographic T-shirts designed by the couple and worn by the band McLaren managed, the Sex Pistols. Most subcultures were associated with a specific genre of pop music, and the close relation of music to fashion is peculiarly British. While much mainstream fashion originated from London designers, subcultural groups had a lively and varied presence across the UK. In the 1970s, Northern soul had its own distinctive dress codes, while in the late 1980s rave culture, sartorially characterised by baggy clothes and smiley logos, had emerged from Manchester alongside bands such as the Happy Mondays and the Stone Roses.

Dick Hebdige argued in the 1970s that the history of post-war white subcultures reflected the history of race relations in the UK, citing as an example the way that Jamaican rude-boy style became incorporated into skinhead style in the 1960s.[16] Since then, black subcultures have achieved greater mainstream visibility, hybridising and mixing looks such as American hip hop, Jamaican dance-hall style, and sharp, East End London tailoring.[17] Great Britain's historical trading strength and its empire have contributed to its multicultural nature in a post-colonial age. There have long been tangible connections between immigrant populations and British fashion production. Exiled from France, Huguenots settled in London's Spitalfields in the eighteenth century and established silk-making communities, while East End tailoring in the nineteenth century was largely dominated by Jewish workers from Eastern Europe. The multicultural nature of modern Britain in the twenty-first century contributes both to the heterogeneity of its youth culture and the vibrancy of its fashion culture; many London designers have come from overseas, either as children – John Galliano and Hussein Chalayan from, respectively, Gibraltar and Cyprus – or as students who came to study and stayed to work: Rifat Ozbek from Turkey, Peter Jensen from Denmark, and Sophia Kokosolaki from Greece are just a few.

The association of British fashion with youth culture is one of the sources of a widely held belief that it is more creative but less commercial than fashion in any other country. Industry insiders will comment that fashion shows in Milan or New York are more geared to business and industry, whereas London shows foreground creativity and innovation and have a different audience, which includes students and creative practitioners from other fields. The youth-oriented nature of British fashion in the 1960s was identified in *Time* magazine's renowned article on 'swinging London', and in 1967 Jonathan Aitken wrote in *The Young Meteors*:

> The fashion revolution is the most significant influence on the mood and *mores* of the younger generation of the last decade ... Fashion ... binds the entire younger generation with a new sense of identity and vitality. Britain's capital has been given a completely new image at home and abroad.[18]

The 'youthquake' of the 1960s cut across several fields: retail, design and fashion publishing, and also popular culture and social mores. In fact, many of the innovations of the 1960s, especially what was to become a strong tradition of innovative fashion publishing, had their roots in the 1950s. *Queen* magazine in the late 1950s, *Nova* (1965–75), *The Face* and *i-D* magazine from 1980 and, in the 1990s, *Dazed and Confused*, all provided a platform for innovative and independent fashion photography, styling and journalism, unconstrained by the commercial considerations that dominated mass-market fashion publishing. While none had huge circulations, all were read by an influential elite of taste-makers and industry insiders and, in due course, exerted a considerable influence on the mainstream.

In the 1960s, an emerging generation of fashion designers broke all the rules of retail with chutzpah, often out of sheer ignorance. The young Mary Quant, who at the age of twenty-one in 1955 opened her first boutique, Bazaar, was, she claimed, so ignorant of the protocols of dressmaking that, unaware that she could purchase cloth wholesale, she bought all the materials for her earliest designs at Harrods and made them up with pure silk linings from amended Butterwicks paper patterns.[19] Quant herself dressed in short gingham skirts, knee socks and sandals; her husband and business partner Alexander Plunkett Greene wore shantung silk pyjama tops over his mother's slim-fitting trousers. Both looked so outlandish that many conventional rag-trade people would not deal with them. Like Barbara Hulanicki, whose shop Biba opened in London in 1965, Quant ran her early business like a cottage industry from her home, often running up clothes on her kitchen table overnight when the boutique stock had sold out.

Such cheerful chaos and uncommercial lack of forward planning continued to characterise the way many young British designers worked over the next forty years. Dedicated to frenetic clubbing and social life, many were more interested in creating an interesting and innovative shop where people could hang out than in establishing a business. Their shops were social spaces as much as retail ones; the club atmosphere extended to the catwalk in wild dancing and vamping in Quant's shows of the 1950s, Ossie Clark's of the 1970s and BodyMap's of the 1980s. Above all, the do-it-yourself ethic of punk rock in the late 1970s promulgated a sense that, in street fashion and club culture, anything was possible. The charity shop aesthetic of 1980s fashion stylists was reflected in the cut-and-mix layouts of 1980s magazines such as *i-D*, whose vox-pop coverage turned the streets of British cities into a catwalk, documenting the eclectic styles of their young residents in the magazine's 'Straight Up' pages. In 1984, the BodyMap designer Stevie Stewart wrote, 'There is a new generation emerging throughout England today, particularly from London which is now looked upon by the rest of the world as a focal point of creative energy in fashion, film, video, music and dance.'[20] She identified a number of features that typified London fashion then as it does today: a vibrant, small, independent press that reported on new talent and was read worldwide; the importance of social life, clubs and music to generate innovative fashion; the traditional association of the city with youth and subculture; the interaction of fashion and music; and, finally, the way that financial necessity required individuals to work in more than one field, crossing over between fashion, club promotion, DJing, modelling, film-making and making and selling accessories.

This toing and froing in what Angela McRobbie dubbed the 'culture society' is due, as she asserts, to the fact that 'fashion design is a highly disorganized and disintegrated economy'.[21] In reality, such designers work for very little, and their wish to do so is part of the economy of modernity. The flexibility it requires typifies the sort of professional mobility and social fluidity that the French academic Gilles Lipovetsky has characterised as intrinsic to the 'fashion person': the flexible modern subject so required in post-industrial society that, Lipovetsky argues, fashion, with its emphasis on constant change, trains us up to become.[22]

It has only been more recently that small-scale London designers have thought it 'cool' to combine commerciality with cutting-edge design. In the late 1990s, McRobbie argued that independent British designers' willingness to work for nothing derived from the art-school basis of British fashion education in which fashion became allied with art rather than popular culture.[23] Recent shifts, however, suggest the larger economic context has altered this, in particular the way that the so-called 'fast fashion' of global high-street brands such as Mango and Zara have issued a challenge to the independents as much as the growing success of international top-end luxury conglomerates such as Gucci and LVMH, owners of Dior, Louis Vuitton and Marc Jacobs. Small independent British fashion designers now have to struggle against the culture of cheap fashion more than ever before. In Paris, a young person who considered themselves fashionable might buy a vest in Zara, but not a head-to-toe look. While British fashion is often strongly individualist and eclectic, with a huge breadth of reference, British consumers are unconstrained by the Italian pursuit of the *bella figura* – the desire to present an immaculate and monied appearance, even if one has very little money – or by French ideals of *chic* and propriety. Rather, as the fashion journalist of *The Independent* newspaper, Susannah Frankel, has observed, 'people in Britain appear to take a certain amount of pride in wearing a bargain!'[24] And the Italian designer Giorgio Armani has written that, while

> the stylish among the English are among the most fashionable in the world ... in England I sometimes think there is an inverse snobbery at work – that the wealthier you are, the less well you dress. The Italians don't really have a cult of cool scruffiness, whereas I think the English possibly do.[25]

London designers on the world stage

The 'cult of cool scruffiness' that characterises British ideals of fashionability, far removed from ideals of sleek grooming, encourages its designers to take risks on the catwalk. And because London fashion is seen as youth-driven and experimental, it is common for young designers to move their shows to Paris, New York or Milan once they become established. Four of the most noted were Vivienne Westwood, John Galliano, Alexander McQueen and Hussein Chalayan, who, together, were largely responsible for the increased global attention given to British fashion in the 1990s.

The eclecticism of British fashion design is one of its driving forces. The designer Vivienne Westwood, herself untrained, forms a bridge between street fashion and the high profile celebrity designers turned out by art schools in the post-war period. Westwood has, from the 1980s, produced postmodern fusions in designs that recycle traditional British motifs, such as barathea wool jackets in hunting pink with little velvet collars, and berets like royal crowns made from Harris tweed in jewelled colours. Her punk collections from 1976, produced in partnership with Malcolm McLaren, had been predicated on outrage: inside-out seams, a 'Cambridge rapist' T-shirt, and bondage trousers connected with a strap between the knees. Yet from her 1979 'Pirate' collection onwards Westwood began to plunder the imagery of the past, and from the mid 1980s her designs shifted into a less provocative mode as she reworked motifs from English and French dress history, as well as from the history of art.[26] For all the apparent nostalgia of her evocations of an aristocratic past, Westwood's designs always retained a polemical edge, for example when wilfully appropriating Scottish tartans, or when she regendered the male codpiece as a decorative rosette for women in a single ensemble that mixed hunting pink with punk bondage and eighteenth-century stays. Throughout the 1990s she led swashbuckling raids on the past, looting the historical dressing-up box to recreate spectacular and flamboyant personae.

John Galliano, too, who debuted in 1984 London with a collection based on French revolutionary dress, has consistently rummaged through the historical wardrobe. His collections combined cultures, continents and centuries, juxtaposed African beading and European corsetry, and mixed the imagery of Oriental exoticism, pearly kings and queens, the Weimar Republic, early cinema and the Belle Époque. Galliano's skill as a postmodern *pasticheur* was balanced by his theatrical showmanship and lead to his appointment in 1995 as principal designer at Givenchy and then, in 1996, at Christian Dior, where he remains today. Galliano, Alexander McQueen and Hussein Chalayan spearheaded an explosion of dramatic and spectacular London fashion shows in the 1990s. Furniture morphed into clothing, catwalks burst into flames, rain showers drenched the models, and mechanical dresses mimicked aeroplanes on the runway. Their dramatic narratives and show-stopping excess were more akin to performance than to commercial fashion. The phenomenal cost of these twenty-minute exhibitions made them a kind of bonfire of the vanities, a view into a designer's mind which did not necessarily translate into hard sales but which made striking images that were immediately circulated around the world through magazines and new media.

Much was made of the convergence of art and fashion in this period. Yet the more prosaic reason for these dramatic British shows was the lack of infrastructure in the UK fashion industry. Designers had nothing to lose from such extreme tactics and no other means to attract global press coverage and financial backing. They were, as McQueen's contemporary Fabio Piras said, 'fashion desperadoes'.[27] For the lucky few, it worked. French conglomerates such as LVMH, owner of Christian Dior and Givenchy, were well aware of the commercial value of these spectacular shows, and both Galliano and McQueen were recruited to major French couture houses in the 1990s. In 1997, Stéphane Wagner, Professor of Communications at the Institut Français de la Mode, observed that the English were 'the best by far' at generating maximum media coverage through spectacular fashion shows.[28]

McQueen's darkly dystopian designs from the 1990s brought sex, death and commerce into a *danse macabre* on the catwalk. His 1996 'Dante' collection was designed in a mourning palette of mauve, black and bone beige and featured jet-encrusted headpieces and a lace top that extended over the model's face like a hangman's hood, held in place by a skeleton's hand reaching across her face. McQueen's aesthetic of cruelty surfaced too in the razor-sharp cutting techniques of his distinctive tailoring whose seams traced the body's contours like surgical incisions. Yet McQueen was an astute operator as well as a visionary designer who knew when to ratchet down the shock value of these shows, and once he had secured the requisite backers his shows became less extreme, maintaining just enough of the old McQueen shock value as a signature. In due course he moved to Givenchy as principal designer, while still producing his own label, and on leaving Givenchy at the end of 2000, McQueen sold a majority shareholding of his own label to the luxury goods conglomerate Gucci. By this stage, McQueen, Westwood and Galliano had all moved their shows to Paris and were manufacturing in Italy, yet all maintained a distinctive and high profile as 'British designers'.

Unusual in remaining independent through the 1990s, the London-based Hussein Chalayan pioneered a very different aesthetic. Infamous for burying his first fashion collection with iron filings, only disinterring the rusty fabric after six weeks, Chalayan's work was thoughtful, minimal and modernist. Inspired by atypical themes such as exile and migration and incorporating new technology and avant-garde music ensembles, Chalayan's shows played sophisticated visual games on the boundary of real and virtual space. In his 1998 show 'Panoramic', his models wove mesmerically in and out of a mirrored set until their images were no longer distinguishable from their presence in real space.

In his 2001 'Ventriloquy' collection, the real-time actions of the models on the catwalk echoed the computer animation that had opened the show, with wire-frame architectural figures, inspired by Japanese manga comics, ruthlessly destroying each other. Often collaborating with technologists and product designers, Chalayan embroidered dresses with the flight paths of aeroplanes, wired a skirt hem with a 'memory' and designed a paper dress that folded into an airmail envelope to be sent in the post. As a Turkish Cypriot, British-educated designer, who worked from London but showed in Paris and manufactured in Italy, Chalayan's design impetus highlighted the complexities and contradictions of modern, multicultural identity in a world of increasing mobility and globalisation.

The paradoxes of British fashion

Such designers have significantly contributed to a global sense of what British design is; they have undoubtedly been innovative as creators and will enter the history books as such. In that sense, their influence has been huge and can obscure the fact that the British fashion industry is actually very small indeed, especially compared to those of Italy, France and the USA. Only Burberry, now a public limited company, is comparable to the 'billion-dollar scale of an Armani or a Ralph Lauren'.[29] In 2004, British designers took £700 million wholesale, as opposed to $12 billion made by the American fashion industry.

London's Fashion Week remains tiny compared to those of Milan, New York and Paris, and many overseas buyers simply miss it out. In 2002, the UK trade journal *Drapers Record* published the results of a survey that showed that one third of the forty-two British-based designers showing in London Fashion Week had fewer than eight stockists worldwide (although three – Jean Muir, Jasper Conran and Ronit Zilkha – declined to disclose their figures). This excluded designers such as Chalayan and McQueen who by then had moved their shows to Paris. In London, the designers who were doing best were not the up-and-coming younger generation who had at that stage only been in business for a few years but the more senior ones with a track record of longevity. The designer with the largest number of stockists worldwide was Paul Smith Women (not the menswear for which he is more famous), with 496 stockists, including seventy-seven in the UK and 419 overseas. The designer with the largest number of stockists in the UK market alone was Nicole

Farhi, with 320 in the UK, followed by the Irish designer Paul Costelloe, with 150. These figures illustrated, as *Drapers Record* commented, 'the chasm between the established mainstream British names and the newer generation'.[30] Other evidence tends to show that even big-name designers may have huge cultural capital but very little economic capital. In 2000, for example, Hussein Chalayan was named UK Designer of the Year for the second time, his work was chosen to feature in the Millennium Dome and in international exhibitions, and he received worldwide press accolades. Yet in the same year he put his company into voluntary liquidation.

It is in this sense that British fashion is chimerical: it is hugely influential in terms of design and innovation yet negligible in its economic impact. Like conceptual fashion, it verges on trickery: it is real, but often invisible. Its supporting areas, of photography, graphics and journalism, are innovative too, and these combine with youth culture and art to generate powerful myths of British fashion that feed back into the reality, in the way it is written up and portrayed in independent London-based magazines. Such magazines are part of the sub-cultural, street and designer fashions they document and report. They are closed networks, and this is how British fashion works to create an impression of vibrancy, a buzz; but while the chic Paris store Colette in the rue Saint Honoré stocks a vast range of expensive London 'micro-zines', the photographers whose work features in them may not even be able to afford to buy a copy for the 'tear sheets' they need for their portfolios.

So London fashion exports successfully as both myth and material reality. Ideas such as 'swinging London' or the Britart and Britpop of the 1990s have a global reach. At the same time, British fashion-design graduates go and find work elsewhere. It is not unusual for the design teams at large American fashion labels such as Donna Karan and Calvin Klein to be composed entirely of British, or British-trained, designers. In 2003, 80 per cent of designers at Louis Vuitton were British-trained, 65 per cent at Levi's, and 40 per cent at Givenchy. British-trained students are also influential in the sportswear and sports-footwear industries. In 2003, around 80 per cent of global sportswear labels' design teams were from UK colleges, as were two of Nike's footwear design directors and the entire Reebok apparel design team.[31]

This may be partly due to British fashion's unique identity in a global industry, but it is also in large part due to its strong tradition of fashion education. Britain produces a huge number of trained fashion students who find employment worldwide. British fashion-degree courses are usually situated within art schools and offer a different type of education from the more skills-and-business-oriented courses of other countries, with a high premium placed on creativity and independence.[32] This type of training, combined with the individualism fostered by British fashion, may be the clue to what drives it. Patrick McCarthy, editor of American *Women's Wear Daily*, has made the point that in the past Britain, unlike Italy and the USA, 'just didn't have the infrastructure and the belief in fashion' to develop its industry, and its great textile companies such as Courtaulds and ICI, he argued, 'never supported fashion'.[33] So, while some bemoan the domestic fashion industry's recent decline, they forget that it was never that huge. It may, however, be this very poverty that galvanises British fashion, with its 'have-a-go' ethic that forces young designers to extreme postures to get attention in a country that lacks any industrial infrastructure. There are more young designers in London than in any other fashion capital. By contrast, in other fashion capitals, Tokyo for example, it is not considered acceptable to set up alone as a designer, while in France and Italy, with their more hierarchical education systems, lengthy apprenticeships and a more conservative in-house ethos, it is very hard for young designers to establish themselves.

If, however, one looks at British fashion across the board, rather than as a production line for star designers, a different picture emerges. The relationship to retail is never far below the surface. Many of the most innovative post-war British designers from Quant to Westwood started out not as designers but as shopkeepers. Today, retail innovation comes in the form of Topshop, owned by the Arcadia group. Using its flagship store in London's Oxford Circus as a laboratory for the rest of the chain, Topshop's just-in-time production methods enable it to trial small runs made in London factories which, if successful, can later be mass manufactured overseas in slightly cheaper fabrics. Changing styles every week, rapidly recycling international designer looks, introducing bands, cafés, vintage clothing and young designers in its stores, Topshop has tapped into the British desire to mix high-street, vintage and designer fashion in one look rather than looking too obviously 'designer'.

The contradictions of British fashion are many. It is fast-burning, and some of its high-profile designers are given to spontaneous combustion. Its youth-driven nature has often meant originality and innovation are valued above commercial success, something foreigners have both admired and deplored in equal measure. Britain may be a nation of shopkeepers, and much fashion innovation has been in retail, but as a fashion capital London remains small fry in global terms. Many lament the passing of the manufacturing base but fashion is no different than the rest of British industry in this respect. On the positive side, fashion in Britain continues to be networked to a wider field of cultural production than in any other country: pop music, subculture, visual art, graphics, photography and magazine publishing have all fed into it and contributed to its profile. So too have its heritage of myth and its history of textiles and tailoring. Above all, it is predicated on a number of paradoxes: between tradition and innovation, between designer and street fashion, and between its economic and cultural capital. Indeed, in an information age, it may be this last paradox that is the secret of its continuing visibility worldwide.

Notes

1 A. Goodrum, *The National Fabric: Fashion, Britishness, Globalization* (Oxford: Berg, 2005).
2 Retail Knowledge Bank (R. Clark, C. Grant and P. Leech), *International Retailers in the UK: The Future of UK Retailing?* (London: Emap Retail, 2001).
3 A. Ribeiro, 'On Englishness in Dress', in C. Breward, B. Conekin, and C. Cox (eds.), *The Englishness of English Dress* (Oxford: Berg, 2002), p. 20.
4 B. Lemire, 'The Theft of Clothes and Popular Consumerism in Early Modern England', *Journal of Social History*, 24 (2) (1990): 255–76.
5 S. Hall and T. Jefferson (eds.), *Resistance through Rituals: Youth Subcultures in Post-War Britain* (London: Hutchinson, 1976).
6 C. Breward, *The Hidden Consumer: Masculinities, Fashion and City Life, 1860–1914* (Manchester: Manchester University Press, 1999).
7 See HMSO, *Working Party Report on the Light Clothing Industry* (London: HMSO, 1947).
8 D. De Marley, *Worth: Father of Haute Couture* (London: Elm Tree, 1980).
9 See Westminster City Council, *Bespoke Tailoring in London's West End* (London: Westminster Council, 2006).
10 Goodrum, *The National Fabric*, pp. 81–6 and 159–68.
11 D. Jones, *Paul Smith True Brit* (London: Design Museum, 1995), p. 74.
12 Goodrum, *National Fabric*, p. 161.
13 A. Bolton, *AngloMania: Tradition and Transgression in British Fashion* (New Haven, Conn.: Yale University Press, 2006), p. 13.
14 K. Davey, *English Imaginaries: Six Studies in Anglo-British Modernity* (London: Lawrence & Wishart, 1999), p. 13.
15 Bolton, *AngloMania*, p. 13; Ribeiro, 'On Englishness in Dress'; C. Steedman, 'Englishness, Clothes and Little Things', in C. Breward, B. Conekin, and C. Cox (eds.), *The Englishness of English Dress* (Oxford: Berg, 2002), pp. 29–44.
16 D. Hebdige, *Subculture: The Meaning of Style* (London: Methuen, 1979).
17 C. Tulloch, 'Check It: Black Style in Britain', in C. Tulloch (ed.), *Black Style* (London: Victoria & Albert, 2004), pp. 1–5; p. 1.

18 *Time*, 15 April 1966, p. 32; J. Aitken, *The Young Meteors* (London: Secker & Warburg, 1967), p. 34.

19 M. Quant, *Quant by Quant* (London: Cassell, 1966), p. 43.

20 S. Stewart, 'Mapping the Future: Talking 'bout My Generation', in L. Johnston (ed), *The Fashion Year* (London: Zomba Books, 1985), Vol. III, p. 104.

21 A. McRobbie, *In the Culture Society: Art, Fashion and Popular Music* (London: Routledge, 1999), p. 13.

22 G. Lipovetsky, *The Empire of Fashion: Dressing Modern Democracy* (Princeton, NJ: Princeton University Press, 1994).

23 A. McRobbie, *British Fashion Design: Rag Trade or Image Industry?* (London: Routledge, 1998); McRobbie, *In the Culture Society*.

24 Susannah Frankel to the author (25 September 2005).

25 G. Armani, 'The Show Must Go on', *The Independent*, 21 September 2006.

26 R. Arnold, 'Vivienne Westwood's Anglomania', in C. Breward, B. Conekin, and C. Cox (eds.), *The Englishness of English Dress* (Oxford: Berg, 2002), pp. 161–72.

27 Quoted in H. Als, 'Gear: Postcard from London', *The New Yorker* (17 March 1997), p. 92.

28 Quoted in S. Todd, 'The Importance of Being English', *Blueprint* (March 1997), pp. 40–43; p. 42.

29 R. Foroohar, 'No Profit Zone', *Newsweek International*, 25 July–1 August 2005.

30 Worth Global Style Network, *Worth Global Style Network Press Bulletin for Journalists* (London: WGSN, March, 2002).

31 Worth Global Style Network, *Worth Global Style Network Press Bulletin for Journalists* (London: WGSN, May, 2003).

32 C. Breward, *Fashion* (Oxford: Oxford University Press, 2003), pp. 58–61; McRobbie, *British Fashion Design*.

33 Quoted in J. Andrews, 'Fashion's Favourite: Which Centre Takes the Crown?', *The Economist*, 6 March 2004, p. 4.

13

Sport in contemporary Britain

The cult of individual improvement

For the public-school-educated amateurs of the Rugby Football Union, it was the root of all evil. For the departing members of the Northern Union, as rugby league was originally called, it was what made the world go round.

The men who ran the Northern Union had earned their money not from inheritance or landowning but from industry and business, and 'their commitment to amateurism was further weakened by their general values', observed Eric Dunning and Kenneth Sheard in their *Barbarians, Gentlemen and Players: A Sociological Study of the Development of Rugby Football*. 'That is, they were more openly achievement-oriented and acquisitive, and showed a greater tendency to place money value on social relations and personal attributes.'[1]

In 1904, nine years after splitting from its amateur cousin, rugby league changed its rules, making it possible for its players to be full-time employees of their clubs, which in turn were financially dependent on admission money paid by spectators. In effect, rugby league became a fully professional sport. It was by no means unique in this respect. Association football had been professional for almost twenty years, and prizefighters had been boxing for money since the eighteenth century. Yet the division of the two rugby codes symbolised a new age, one in which professional and amateur sports would coexist, not always easily but in a stable state that would endure for the next eighty years.

Rugby's duality mirrored social and cultural changes. Industrialism had introduced *embourgeoisement*, 'the gradual emergence of the bour-geoisie as the ruling class ... their growing control of major institutions, and the … spread of their values through society', as Dunning and Sheard describe it.[2] Social reform to ensure both the welfare and control of the industrial working class had loosened the rigidity of Britain's class structure, promoting the idea of self-improvement, or 'bettering oneself' through painstaking work and achievement. This was consistent with the ethos of modernity in the organised industrial world. As Alan Fox wrote in his *History and Heritage: The Social Origins of the British Industrial Relations System*: 'The appeal of respectability and the cult of individual improvement probably rendered many working men "vulnerable to assimilation to cultural patterns determined by the middle class"'.[3]

The enthusiasm for sport had an almost allegorical quality: it represented a transmission of imaginative ideas from higher to lower social levels. While Fox believed this was produced by a shared faith, a common belief in free trade and a distrust of landed interests, a mutual interest in sport also contributed. The 'cult of individual improvement' excited a striving among a newly aspirational working class, and this was replicated in and complemented by competitive sport.

'Fundamentally, British culture is deeply individualistic', declared A. H. Halsey in the 1986 edition of his *Change in British Society*. 'The deeply embedded cultural assumption is that ultimate values are individual, that society is in no sense superior to the sum of the people who make it up; that collectivism can only be instrumental.'[4]

Opportunities in education, industry, politics and elsewhere provided a ladder for individuals born in the lower orders to climb. Improving or bettering oneself became an active ideal to be aspired to. The achievement orientation – the individualistic will to succeed rather than simply to participate – was a dominating feature of both culture and sport that took shape in the late nineteenth and early twentieth centuries. The deeper origins date back to the Enlightenment of the seventeenth century and the attitude of mind that emphasised the power of reason, rationality and, above all, individualism. We should also point to the French Revolution of 1789, which exposed the erroneous belief that individuals were cast by nature to a station where they remain fixed for their whole lives like mice on treadmills. This change in mentality brought with it an inducement to strive for success. This is precisely the motive that came to characterise and give shape to British sport in the crucial years at the turn of the century.

The achievement orientation became more pronounced in sport as the twentieth century progressed. Ends superseded means as the purpose

of sporting competition. Amateur rugby's resentment of professionalism was as much to do with values and attitudes as money. The very
word 'amateur' derives from the Latin *amatorius*, for love, and its import
is clear: participants were motivated to compete by the affection they
felt towards and the joy they took from sport. Competition itself was a
respectful order in which players exerted themselves unsparingly, yet
not only to win. The idea was to bring all participants to their peak. The
disgrace was not in losing but in not trying one's absolute best. Holding
back was a violation of fair play as it denied a rival the opportunity to
test his mettle. (I use the pronoun 'his' deliberately, of course: women
were for the most part, excluded from competitive sports, as we will
discover.)

Craving for success

Those who regarded sport in this way were appalled by the achievement-
oriented Harold Abrahams, whose Jewish background guaranteed him
marginal status in the early twentieth century, but whose uncommon
zeal for winning drove him to an extraordinary policy. After a mediocre
performance at the 1920 Olympic Games, the Bedford-born sprinter
was so determined to make amends that he sought the services of Sam
Mussabini, a coach, referee, journalist and publisher, who was active
in billiards and cycling as well as track. In 1896, he had been hired by
Dunlop to train the tyre company's professional cycling team. It was not
unusual for cycle and equipment manufacturers to sponsor their own
teams (as is the case today).

Mussabini had studied the work of Eadweard Muybridge who
exploited the potential of the relatively new technology of photography
to document physiologically precise records of sports action using the
most technically efficient means. Yet his prescience in training methods
was anathema to amateurs, for whom the very idea of preparing for a competition was a corruption of the Corinthian ideal. Worse still, Mussabini
had taken money for his services. While the film *Chariots of Fire* (1981) docu-
mented Abraham's ultimately successful pursuit of the 100 metres gold
medal at the 1924 Olympics, it downplayed the shame engendered by hir-
ing Mussabini. At the time, there were about 250,000 Jews in Britain, and
they generally embraced their integration into the wider culture; the anti-
Semitism prevalent in other parts of Europe met with opposition from
the British working class. Yet, being a minority-group member probably

fortified Abrahams in his hazard-strewn practice of training with a professional. Mussabini, as the film shows, was not even allowed in the stadium to observe his charge's moment of glory and listened to a radio commentary in a nearby hotel room. Abrahams himself was not remunerated and so protected his amateur status. His triumph was something of a rebuke to athletics' governors: not only had he employed a coach but he also adopted an approach towards winning that contrasted with that of many of his rivals. They might have found gratification in competing; his joy was in winning.

Abrahams' venture, like rugby's split, highlighted the tension between amateurism and professionalism in British sport during the early twentieth century. Association Football had allowed the payment of players since 1885, and several other sports, including cricket, pedestrianism (as athletics were then known) and, of course, prizefighting allowed professionals. All had, in some measure, moved away from their original values. 'It was the educated classes who developed and articulated an ethical code governing the way in which games in general should be played', wrote Tony Mason in his *Association Football and English Society, 1863–1915*. 'It was in essence based on aristocratic notions of chivalry'.[5]

> After 1885, the conduct of some professional players fell a good way short of the sportsmanship ideal ... intentional infringements of the law became an increasingly accepted part of the game. Neither did the predominantly working-class crowd, which watched the games, manifest signs that they had imbibed the sportsmanship ethic. Winning was all, or almost all, and the opposition were there to satisfy the craving for success.[6]

Odd as it may seem from the vantage point of the twenty-first century, the achievement orientation was a relatively new and, to many, alarming development that did not just undermine amateur ideals but replaced them with principles and standards we now recognise as commonplace. In retaining a professional coach, Abrahams disclosed a self-interest and singularity of purpose that, for many, aligned him with the rugby league and football players who competed with the sole purpose of winning. Would crowds have been interested in watching competitors do anything but?

The answer is, probably not. There was little satisfaction in watching an activity that was intrinsically rewarding to the participants. The transformation of sport from a participant activity to a mass spectator entertainment form did not just coincide with the arrival of the achievement orientation. And, while it might not have been a case of cause and effect, the two were linked as if by molecular chain. People became engaged with sport as spectators rather than contestants when the players started to compete for something clear, tangible and familiar.

The activity they watched was a microcosm of the world they knew, a world in which initiative, labour, perseverance and self-improvement were exalted and in which achieving as much as one's ability allowed was regarded as a virtue; idleness was discouraged in the industrial society of Britain. The principles that supported and gave purpose to what we now recognise as sport were part of a wider moral code that guided conduct towards individual attainment.

Ruling the roost

Asserting one's predestined superiority and natural right to rule is not action expected of a colonial power, at least not at the height of empire. England did not boast or display arrogance but rather took pride and expressed satisfaction in its role as an agent of civilisation and progress. 'Empire', as Antoinette Burton observes, was 'a fundamental part of English culture and national identity … [it] entered the social fabric, the intellectual discourse and the life of the imagination.'[7]

Only in the late nineteenth century in the midst of imperial scramble when their power began to wane did the English manifest the bravado, grandeur, nationalism and racist condescension typically associated with the rulers of the Empire. In the nineteenth century, the English and, more generally, the British came to see themselves 'as an 'elect nation', called to carry out a particular, God-given mission in the world'. This is the argument of Krishan Kumar, who in *The Making of English National Identity* suggests that, as their global influence dissipated, the English turned 'inwards towards themselves, and began to ask themselves who they were'.[8] This was a spur to the kinds of nationalistic belligerence we witness, often in sport, today. As Kumar puts it, 'if others reject you, it is natural to play up your strengths, and to take pride in precisely those things that distinguish you from those others.'[9]

The English answer to the question of identity was crisp and clear: they were special people, blessed by an inheritance and a mission in the world. England was charged with the momentous responsibility of remaking the world in its own image. 'Englishness modulated into Britishness', wrote Kumar, meaning that, as the English began to emphasise their distinctive place, role and identity, so the other British nations clung to their national identities 'as a kind of compensation for, or counterweight against, the predominant role of the English in the United Kingdom'.[10] Great Britain became something of a theatre, or a stage big enough for several players.

In 1904, seven European nations came together to form the Fédération Internationale de Football Association (FIFA). This was an initiative scoffed at by England's own Football Association (the FA). After all, the FA was the original governing organisation, founded in 1863 to codify rules, formalise the sport's governance and generally oversee the development of what was to become the world's most popular sport. Three of FIFA's founding nations – France, Spain and Sweden – did not even have organised leagues, and the other members – Belgium, Denmark, the Netherlands and Switzerland – were nowhere near England in terms of the sport's advancement. British settlers were responsible for exporting the sport to these and several other countries anyway. Only Italy claimed the sport had separate origins in the renaissance game *calcio*.

British nations had been playing international representative games since 1872 when England faced Scotland. England's mastery of its own game and superiority in all facets of its administration had not been in doubt, and the very concept of an international 'federation' – the term itself connoting an association of independent and equal units – was, to the English, an impertinence.

When Kumar wrote of the English, 'ruling the roost, they felt it impolitic to crow', he might also have been referring to England's FA, which demurred at the fledgling federation without feeling either the need to join or put pressure on it.[11] In fact, within two years, the English FA decided to affiliate but, with the other home nations, withdrew after the First World War when FIFA recognised nations that had been enemies during the war. The FA rejoined in 1924, by which time FIFA had become the organiser of the Olympic football event. The 1924 summer Olympics in Amsterdam staged the first international soccer tournament, won by Uruguay, a country that wished to celebrate the centenary of its independence by hosting the first professional world championships.

'Broken-time' payments were monetary compensations for ostensibly amateur players who took time off from work to play for their clubs. The FA abandoned any pretence of amateurism and legalised full and open professionalism in 1885. As organisers of the Olympic tournament, FIFA decided to admit broken-time payments, a decision the FA believed would reintroduce the abuses and hypocrisy it had removed from the English game. Stung by FIFA's refusal to follow its example, the English FA withdrew its membership. The first world championship was won by Uruguay, though, as Dennis Brailsford writes in his *British Sport: A Social History*, 'the conviction that British football was bound to be the best in the world was not to be disturbed ... by such new-fangled trumperies as a World Cup.'[12]

The English in particular saw themselves engaged in a larger enterprise 'as creators of a worldwide system in which they as it were gigantically replicated themselves, carrying with them their language, their culture, their institutions, their industry', as Kumar put it.[13] The growth of an organisation purporting to represent the global interests of football and staging World Cups in four-yearly cycles posed little threat to English hegemony. At least not until after the Second World War. But, by 1950, when England eventually agreed to participate in the World Cup competition, the swirling winds of change were gathering. India's independence in 1949 served notice that the Empire was disintegrating, and Britain's hitherto unquestioned leadership was open to challenge. England's suffering in its World Cup debut seemed consistent with its struggles elsewhere.

Unsportsmanlike?

Both the practical and emotional imperatives of the imperial mission depended on the will to succeed rather than just participate in a venture, a feature which was also reflected in the achievement orientation. Imperialism (from the Latin *imperium* for command) is perhaps too utilitarian: it was inspired by the belief in the desirability of acquiring colonies and dependencies. In his *Culture and Imperialism*, Edward Said distinguishes between this and colonialism, which was a specific form of imperial expansion based on the practice of implanting settlements on distant territories.[14] In this respect, England's mission was predicated on progress (one of the organising motifs of the period) rather than acquisition alone. The English were to supervise and promote the advancement of non-European peoples.

Sport was an instrument in this service. It inducted colonial subjects into a sphere where rules were of paramount importance and discipline was essential and in which a single arbiter was vested with unchallengeable authority. If they were to advance, they should remain obedient to their imperial masters. The events precipitated by the formation of FIFA in 1904 are most beneficially understood against this background. Yet it was cricket that provided the most dramatic compendium of the English response to the social and political changes erupting in the inter-war period.

Australians could perhaps be forgiven for thinking Armageddon had broken out in 1932. The visit of the English touring side was quite different from anything that had gone before. This was a team motivated not, it seemed, by the resolve to instruct by example, or even to compete with pluck and spirit, but by an uncharacteristically keen achievement orientation. Known for competing with a straight bat and a stiff upper lip, the English were faced with the indomitable batsman Donald Bradman, who had led the Australians to victory in 1930. Perhaps the memories were still fresh when England's captain Douglas Jardine instructed his fast bowlers to aim at the batsmen's bodies. While the tactic was within the laws of the game, it contravened its spirit in a way that outraged not just the Australian players but also administrators, fans and even politicians.

The Australian Board of Control for Cricket complained to England's governing organisation, the Marylebone Cricket Club (MCC), describing the 'bodyline' approach as 'unsportsmanlike'. Jardine demanded a retraction, prompting an escalation, which eventually involved Australia's Prime Minister. For a while, the dispute appeared to be developing into a diplomatic incident. An apology followed. Several Australian players finished the series with injuries. The English had played a functional, effective cricket that betrayed their purpose: to win (which they did) rather than to conduct themselves in the dignified manner traditionally associated with the colonial masters. The series was deemed a travesty by the MCC, which disciplined the bowlers involved. But it signalled a change in the imperial relationship, at least as it manifested in sport.

As imperial rulers, the English were unused to losing, whether in cricket, football or any other kind of sport. After all, they were originators of the ennobling practice which had proved to be of great utility in cultivating values and ideals among the subject nations. The paradox of having those subject nations rear themselves up and snap back defiantly, albeit in a symbolic way, was both an affront and a surprise. England's retort redefined sport in a way that we recognise today.

The notion of entering a competition with a rationale that did not include winning is difficult to countenance. Clearly, the point of sport is to try to win. But not the whole point; at least not until the 1930s. Part exhibition, part spectacle, sport was a demonstration too: it showcased virtues and qualities that were integral to a ruling elite. With struggles for independence revealing opposition to colonial rule, the English were discovering their pre-eminence in sport was under challenge too. The response was to change orientation in a way that conferred honour on trying to win and, crucially, respectability on the methods most appropriate to winning.

Surging popularity

The 100,000 people who attended the first World Cup Final in 1930 were not only spectators, they were also people gathered for the purchase of a commodity – a market. The English were aware of the demand for football: as early as 1897, the FA Cup Final had drawn a crowd of 50,000, revealing interest of a scale unsuspected twenty-four years before when the FA was created. Of course, professional sport has always been predicated on the concept of market demand: if no one was willing to pay to watch sport, whether at the event or on television, there would be no money available to players. But the rising numbers of people flocking to some events invited the prospect of converting what were once leisurely activities played in a spirit of camaraderie, recreation and fun principally for the gratification of the competitors into something that resembled a business. Cricket rivalled soccer in its widespread appeal, though its traditional bifurcation of gentlemen amateurs and professional players precluded an unobstructed commercialisation.

Not so with speedway: strongly supported by working-class fans, the sport – a new but authentic sport, incorporating the kind of machines people habitually used – featured professional riders and attracted five-figure crowds, including a record 93,000 in 1938. 'Greyhound-racing, too, leapt into sudden popularity in the early 1930s', notes Brailsford. 'It was a sport which lent itself to rapid expansion. The competitors themselves could be bred and trained quickly and the capital investment needed to set up meetings was relatively modest.'[15] Crowds exceeding 25,000 regularly attended greyhound racing, the source of the attraction lying with the gambling opportunities it offered. Betting on sport had been regulated by legislation in 1906 and 1921, and the 1960 Betting and Gaming Act introduced street betting shops (though these had existed illegally for many decades before the legislation). The fascination with wagering on animals seems to have persisted since the blood sports of the eighteenth century and earlier. There was also enthusiasm for betting on horse racing, and, since the 1890s, football, suggesting that the growth of mass spectator sport in the early twentieth century was influenced by a keenness to gamble with discretion and judgement. Horse and dog racing were dependent on followers who were thrilled less by the competitors, more by the gambling. This in itself indicates a growing awareness of the logic of competition. Spectators familiarised themselves with the importance of environmental conditions, injuries and other factors that could influence outcomes. Crowds became knowledgeable. There was some irony in the fact that it was not only self-appointed moral guardians who disapproved of betting but also, as Jeffrey Hill points out, 'the leaders of most of the sports around which betting occurred.'[16] Football, for example, tried to ban the very pools betting to which it owed some of its surging popularity in the 1930s.

Some sports drifted uncertainly towards commercialism while others headed full-tilt for a business model. Tennis, for example, was traditionally associated with affluent classes and valued its amateur status. Its popularity was widened in the 1930s, especially after Fred Perry's three Wimbledon titles and his contributions to Britain's four Davis Cup triumphs. A nascent professional tennis circuit enticed Perry away from the amateurs, starting a trend that effectively denied Wimbledon, and, indeed, the amateur sport, its premier players. It stayed this way until 1968, when the first 'open' Wimbledon admitted both amateurs and professionals.

Other sports accommodating a coexistence included cricket, though Australian media magnate Kerry Packer, in 1977, launched his own World Series Cricket and heralded what we might call the modern era of cricket. Televised matches, some played under floodlights, with well-paid professional players wearing varicoloured flannels (i.e. trousers) suggested an alternative to the old English game of yore. In his *Moving the Goalposts: A History of Sport and Society since 1945*, Martin Polley calls this a 'symbolic moment' and argues that the embrace of professionalism and the assimilation of overtly commercial imperatives both 'need to be seen in the context of developments in media coverage of sport, particularly the growth of television from the 1950s'.[17]

Tempted by the money

Rugby union, 'a game that had seemed for long the quintessence of amateurism', as Hill describes it, was one of the last mass spectator sports to embrace professionalism. Hill explains: 'faced with the competition of both rugby league and association football, and tempted by the money of television companies looking for dramatic sporting action, rugby union emerged by the end of the [1990s] decade as a professional game.'[18]

By the start of the twenty-first century the amateur ethos that had once inspired the competitive pursuits had disappeared from popular sports. Amateur sport was useful preparation for a professional career, but not a legitimate alternative. Sport was synonymous with professional sport. And, of course, the spirit of fair play that once guided sport had given way to a more ruthless win-at-all-costs tendency that was consistent with the achievement orientation.

The change had made it possible for sport to become entertainment. This is not intended to be a critical observation, nor is entertainment meant to connote crassness or theatricality – though, at times, sport has purveyed both. Sport became something that was produced and performed exclusively for an audience. Spectators derived pleasure from watching and perhaps vicariously participating. In return, they were prepared to pay. The infernal article regarded contemptuously by old rugby purists was, by the late twentieth century, the currency of sport. What was once a way of reinvigorating workers after five and a half days of labour or a character-building exercise for the future rulers of empire was part of the entertainment industry, subject to the same vagaries of demand as the cinema, the theatre or even theme parks.

In the late twentieth century, there were several emblematic events that illustrated the changing character of sport. The formal abandonment of what had become a spurious distinction between amateurs and professionals in cricket in 1963 was one. The example was soon followed by tennis and, later, athletics (which, in 1982 instituted a system of subventions to disburse payments to competitors). In 1962, the removal of the maximum wage for footballers created great earnings potential for valuable players and gave football what Arthur Marwick called 'the veneer of classlessness to be found in other branches of the entertainments industry'.[19]

While no single event represents the changes perfectly, football's astonishing deal with Sky television in 1992 presents a serviceable motif for the transformation wrought by the media in the late century. Since its decade of rapid growth in the 1950s, television had been regarded by sport with mistrust, the view of sport being that, given the choice of watching at home or actually going to a competition, many would choose the former. On the other hand, television was growing into such a popular medium in the 1960s that it offered a kind of shop window for sport. An estimated 10 million viewers watched English football's FA Cup Final on BBC television in 1953, over 100 times the number of fans who actually attended the game.

BBC's cosy relationship with football was disrupted in 1960, when the commercial channel ITV – five years after its launch – audaciously bid to broadcast 'live' football. In spite of an agreement with the FA, the clubs themselves protested, and only one game was shown. On reflection, it was an opportunity lost: football slid into a long and seemingly terminal decline. Britain itself had undergone something of a transformation. The traditional industrial, working-class heartlands lost the special economic significance they had held up to the 1950s. A combination of, first, global processes and, from the 1970s, government policies had hastened the decline of manufacturing centres. The impact was many-sided: the character of work, family life and leisure activities all changed – as did football. Writing in 1986, the historian James Walvin mournfully chronicled: 'the game in recent years has plunged deeper and deeper into a crisis, partly of its own making, partly thrust upon it by external forces over which football has little or no control.'[20]

Violence, racism, decaying stadiums, an indifferent population and two full-scale tragedies had contributed to football's degeneration. In 1989, when yet another calamity visited the sport in the form of the Hillsborough Disaster, football's crisis deepened. (Hillsborough was the name of the stadium in Sheffield where ninety-six soccer fans died after 658 too many spectators were admitted.) Sky television had its own crisis: having launched its telecommunications satellite in 1989 and started transmission, it endured punishing losses, speculated to be about £2 million per month. Its acquisition of the rights to televise 'live' games from the newly organised Premier League for a barely believable £304 million seemed suicidal. Yet, its subscription rates grew and the money filtered through to clubs, which, in turn, recruited high-ranking overseas players. By 1995, football had metamorphosed into an all-star family entertainment – with a new market. Encouraged by its success, BSkyB continued to pay often exorbitant fees for the rights to football and added rugby league, which it converted into a global competition, cricket, golf and boxing to its roster.

Football became an exemplar for market-oriented sport: it fashioned a commodity, created a new demand for it and offered it for sale. Many of the players acquired the status and the earnings power of show-business celebrities. Sponsors, emboldened by the new-found popularity of football, paid to have their names associated with either the clubs or the competitions. Advertisers paid – often dearly – to persuade celebrity athletes to endorse their products: in 2005, Gillette paid David Beckham a reported £35 million ($60 million), in a transaction that rivalled Tiger Woods' $100 million contract with Nike.

Realising the growing popularity of sport in the late twentieth century, manufacturers brokered licensing agreements to produce merchandise bearing the imprimatur of famous athletes or their clubs. Clothes, food, kitchen utensils and practically any article that could be affixed with a name began to display sport-related names or logos. This commodification of sport was regarded by some to be the reason for sport's cultural shift. 'Why has sport moved from the periphery to the centre of popular culture?' asked John Horne in his *Sport in Consumer Culture*, answering in three ways: 'one explanation is the increasing commercialisation and commodification ... A second refers to the increasing concerns about embodiment and the care of the body ... A third approach considers the focus on celebrity.'[21] The first and third answers are linked directly to the treatment afforded sport by the media, especially commercial television. Our changing understanding of the body has heightened appreciation of the manner in which others use their bodies, though this too has been affected by the media's coverage.

At the start of the twentieth century, money was, for many, a pestilence that would destroy the core value of fair play. By the start of the twenty-first, it could be argued that this was an accurate assessment. Practically every professional sport – and all major sports were professional by this time – had been embroiled in corruption, doping, violence and other activities that despoiled sport's central precept. All had their sources in money. Yet money is arguably the prime mover behind every single development in contemporary sport.

The potential of the sport market was realised in a way that not one of the 100,000 people watching the 1930 World Cup final could have imagined. Instead of gathering the spectators to the events, the market was diffused and the events were taken to the spectators. And the beauty of the arrangement was that they still paid.

More like that of a man

For most of its history, sport has been a macho maelstrom, a large and aggressive whirlpool in which a generation of men rediscovered their foundering masculinity. Organised sport appeared at a time when the factory system seemed to be replacing men with machines. By the late 1800s, industry was mechanised to the point where the physical labour once performed by men, while still required at some stages in the production process, was largely superfluous. Patriarchal arrangements were based in part on the physical capacities of men to toil in a way women could not. So when those capacities were no longer integral to productivity, men created and refined other pursuits in which to exhibit their physical prowess and so validate their manhood. This is hardly a formal history of sport, but it does present an enlivening subtext: sport as an authenticating apparatus for men alarmed at the prospect of impending emasculation.

The perpetual motion of sport's early development in Britain precluded earnest reflection. No sooner had the main governing organisations appeared than debates about professionalism filled the air. Then the big international competitions brought nationalism into sport. By the 1930s, sport's power to draw the masses had alerted two sorts of people to sport's potential: entrepreneurs and politicians. Both exploited sport. So, by the mid twentieth century, sport had almost developed into the form we recognise today. But there were notable absentees: women.

Pierre de Coubertin established something of a model for modern sport when he introduced the modern Olympic Games in 1896. 'No matter how toughened a sportswoman may be', he famously announced, 'her organism is not cut out to sustain shocks.' Sport was an 'exultation of male athleticism … with female applause as a reward', according to the visionary Frenchman. Women were later admitted to the Olympics, though only in certain events. Their participation was reflected in other sports, such as golf, tennis and motor racing, none of which involved physical contact or collision. As such they were considered appropriate for 'ladies'. Violet Percy ran a three hour, forty minute and twenty-two second marathon in 1925, but no further records were kept until 1964. When Percy ran, only 10 per cent of married women in Britain went to work; by the time record-keeping, began this had risen to 38.08 per cent.[22]

It is a popular though misleading argument that women were forcibly excluded from sports for most of the century. This is partly true, but women themselves expressed little desire to enter. There were sound reasons for this. First, females in sport were often regarded as tomboys or hoydens and thought to lack femininity. Helen Lenskyj records that they were seen to represent a moral degeneracy in society. Second, 'too much activity in sports of a masculine character causes the female body to become more like that of a man', as Lynda Birke and Gail Vines put it.[23] Third, menstruation was regarded as a disabling prohibition: the 'eternal wound', as Patricia Vertinsky called it, handicapped women to the point that entering sport would tax them biologically, possibly harming their reproductive organs. With these cautions circulating in the scientific as well as in everyday discourse, it is hardly surprising that women were not clamouring to cross the threshold into sport.

As these kinds of belief receded, women, perhaps bolstered by their physical efforts during the Second World War, began to demand entry into major sporting events. In the USA, Kathrine Switzer's illicit but iconic marathon in 1967 portended major changes: women were at the time prohibited from competing in marathons, but entering as 'K. V. Switzer', the twenty-year-old Syracuse University student completed the Boston course and so ended the myth of women's frailty. Over the next twenty-five years, women participated in every sport, even combat sports such as boxing, which had been something of a final taboo.

Switzer's run symbolised wider changes affected by and affecting women around the world. Legislation permitting legal abortion, and the availability of oral contraception complemented the legal prohibition of sexual discrimination and mandates for equal pay. More women entered higher education and went on to professional, managerial and entrepreneurial careers, suggesting symmetry between sport and the occupational world. While there was a suspicion that curmudgeonly males were interested only in aesthetically pleasing female athletes, British sportswomen such as Denise Lewis, Kelly Holmes and Paula Radcliffe demanded recognition for their achievements rather than their looks.

For most of its history, sport has remained a male domain. This is understandable: I suggested earlier that its raison d'être was to validate masculinity. But cultural changes have been reflected in and perhaps precipitated by the encroachment of women onto hitherto male preserves. Female self-determination manifests on several levels. A woman in an Arsenal shirt, or in boxing gloves, or breaking the tape after over twenty-six miles are all rebuttals of mid-twentieth-century cultural mores. In a sense, they are all doing things learned men once warned were not as nature intended. Horne has argued that women's presence in sport 'helps confirm and reinforce their role and position in society. It offers both liberation and constraint.'[24] The same could be said about sport itself: in some ways, it has provided a means through which marginal groups can find the release that comes with expression and recognition. Yet Horne is mindful that sport constrains, turning us all into consumers of a product that can be bought and sold. This is very far from the ambitions of sport in Britain during the nineteenth century.

Conclusion: why?

Sport, as we have seen, has transmuted from a playful endeavour, an agreeable recreation and a source of intrinsic reward into a tradable commodity. The Corinthian ideal of participation has been in retreat since the 1920s (before that in professional sports), leaving the baser instincts of sponsorship deals and win-at-all-costs to assume an importance that would have seemed monstrous a century ago. In the process, sport has strengthened its power to fascinate, the alliance with television proving both crucial and irresistible: many sports are now genuinely global in their appeal. They magnetise spectators, participants and gamblers, though only one does so uniformly: soccer, of which there are about 3.5 billion devotees globally. This is reflected in Britain where association football attracts 30 million 'live' spectators per year and is played competitively by 3 million men and women.

Cricket is also popular in Britain, as it is in several nations that were once part of the Empire: in total, about 3 million people play or watch cricket. Once regarded as a sport of the affluent, tennis is Britain's third most popular participation sport, though its spectatorship is seasonal, reaching its peak during the Wimbledon fortnight when BBC television viewing figures often reach a cumulative 562 million – over four times the typical television audience for the annual US Super Bowl. For comparison, soccer's four-yearly World Cup Final game draws 1.7 billion television viewers from around the world.

While football is Britain's single most popular participation sport for both men and women, competitive fishing, or angling as it often known, is also popular, as is golf. Gambling is legal in Britain, and betting volume is an index of a sport's popularity. Horse racing, once known as the Sport of Kings because of its association with royalty, consistently heads the list, though the advent of online betting has vaulted soccer into second place. Greyhound racing remains popular with bettors: as with dog racing in other parts of the world, a parimutuel form of betting (in which those backing the first three places divide the losers' stakes) is popular among gamblers.

Sport is live theatre, and its place in British culture is alongside other subdivisions of the entertainment industry, all of which have been subject to corporate power. The influence of corporations over economic and institutional resources has been supported by a strengthening of sport's power to shape popular attitudes and beliefs.

Dr Johnson's comparison of the lady preacher with a dog walking on its hind legs left him wondering not how well the dog was doing, but why it was walking that way at all. We could ask the same question of sport. Why? It has no purpose, save for the suspiciously implausible character-building function, and it has no obvious benefit to the myriad fans who are parted from ever-greater quantities of their hard-earned cash. The days are long gone when sport was a preparation for military conflict, less still a preparation for life in civil society. There again, sport's place in contemporary British culture is not assured by what it fulfils but by what it avoids: crassness and predictability. Sport is now incontrovertibly part of the entertainment industry, and it is a well-made, effectively distributed and often dramatically staged commodity that delivers something that no other form of entertainment can: an incalculable result. We never know what is going to happen. That alone guarantees its permanence.

Yet it would be a mistake to see continuity and tradition where there has been brokenness and change. Sport's relationship to the activities of the late nineteenth and early twentieth century is tenuous. The competitions resemble each other, but the organisation, structure and status are completely different. British sport is a labour of love turned into a commercial project. It is animated by the desire to achieve and the will to conquer, both elemental features of British culture in the twentieth century, and both characteristic of business endeavours. Given the compatibility, an alignment was perhaps inevitable. Had it not developed into an industry, sport might have retained some of its emotive power, but it would have remained on the cultural periphery, as Horne called it.[25]

Is it possible to be passionate about sport and stay – perhaps uncomfortably – aware that one is conniving with an enterprise founded on misogynist principles and based on selfishness, which reflects an unswerving historical mission to dominate and is now controlled largely by global corporations? Today's ruthlessly competitive pursuits have no place for humility, altruism, compassion or many other qualities we admire. This might be a harsh evaluation, as the British have often shown sympathy for doughty losers, whatever their nationality,

and have, in some sports, become accustomed to taking defeat with honour: an imperishable enthusiasm for sport remains, despite the paucity
of global champions in cricket, tennis and football. Yet the belligerent,
one-sided nationalism of soccer fans is not typically evident among followers of boxing, rugby, motor racing, track and field, snooker or other
sports in which the British have world champions or contenders. Our
enthusiasm for sport and the central place we allow it remind us that we
represent the less admirable aspects of culture more faithfully than we
dare recognise.

Notes

1 E. Dunning and K. Sheard, *Barbarians, Gentlemen and Players: A Sociological Study of the Development of Rugby Football* (Oxford: Robertson, 1979), p. 203.
2 Dunning and Sheard, *Barbarians, Gentlemen and Players*, p. 306.
3 A. Fox, *History and Heritage: The Social Origins of the British Industrial Relations System* (London: Allen and Unwin, 1985), p. 143.
4 A. H. Halsey, *Change in British Society*, 3rd edition (Oxford: Oxford University Press, 1986), p. 2.
5 T. Mason, *Association Football and English Society, 1863–1915* (Brighton: Harvester, 1980), p. 255.
6 Mason, *Association Football and English Society*, p. 256.
7 A. Burton, 'Who Needs the Nation? Interrogating "British History"', in C. Hall (ed.), *Cultures of Empire: Colonizers in Britain and the Empire in the Nineteenth and Twentieth Centuries* (Manchester: Manchester University Press, 2000), pp. 137–53.
8 K. Kumar, *The Making of English National Identity* (Cambridge: Cambridge University Press, 2003), p. 196.
9 Kumar, *English National Identity*, p. 200.
10 Kumar, *English National Identity*, p. 187.
11 Kumar, *English National Identity*, p. 187.
12 D. Brailsford, *British Sport: A Social History* (Cambridge: Lutterworth Press, 1997), p. 112. (Trumperies are showy but deceptively worthless items.)
13 Kumar, *English National Identity*, p. 189.
14 E. W. Said, *Culture and Imperialism* (London: Chatto & Windus, 1993).
15 Brailsford, *British Sport*, p. 116.
16 J. Hill, *Sports, Leisure and Culture in Twentieth Century Britain* (Basingstoke: Palgrave), p. 39.
17 M. Polley, *Moving the Goalposts: A History of Sport and Society Since 1945* (London: Routledge, 1998), p. 67.
18 Hill, *Sports, Leisure and Culture*, p. 40.
19 A. Marwick, *British Society Since 1945* (Harmondsworth: Penguin, 1982), p. 156.
20 J. Walvin, *Football and the Decline of Britain* (London: Macmillan, 1986), p. vi.
21 J. Horne, *Sport in Consumer Culture* (Basingstoke: Palgrave Macmillan, 2006), p. 80.
22 Halsey, *Change in British Society*, p. 107.

23 L. Birke and G. Vines, 'A Sporting Chance: The Anatomy of Destiny', *Women's Studies International Forum*, 19 (4) (1987): 337–47; p. 340.

24 Horne, *Sport in Consumer Culture*, p. 154.

25 Horne, *Sport in Consumer Culture*, p. 80.

14

British sexual cultures

[T]here are areas in which the State, or the community, no longer has a role or, if it does have one, it is a role that is completely different. It is not for the State to tell people that they cannot choose a different life-style, for example in issues to do with sexuality.[1]

Companions to a national culture, such as this, rarely include any sustained discussion of sexuality, sexual cultures and sexual practices; perhaps readers are not thought to require information about a nation's private pleasures. While sexuality may be acknowledged as an important part of an individual's sense of self, its relation to the body politic or nation-state is seemingly not important enough to warrant discussion. Yet this sidelining of the sexual sphere is a part of the fiction, espoused by Tony Blair in the above quotation, that the sexual exists separate from popular culture, national identity, politics and the social more generally. Perhaps it is difficult to accept that sex is closely tied to community and questions of national identity, but that is what this chapter will attempt to say. That is not to claim that there is something that can be identified as *the* British sexual character although many people have tried to define it. One-time producer of British sex films, Stanley Long summed up the British and sex: 'Until the 1960s there had been such a suppression of all things sexual. I think it was a hangover from the Victorian era and this country suffered from terrible inhibitions. I think it's a national trait that we aren't very good at being erotic. The Italians pinch bums, the French have mistresses and we're not very good at either!'[2] Hazy references to French kissing, the English vice of corporal punishment, German efficiencies and kinkiness and Scandinavian free love, which still surface in popular culture are outmoded stereotypes rather than evidence of any particular national preferences; as are the often racist ascriptions of disease and peculiar practices to other nations. However, Long may have it right; traditionally, the British are characterised, at home and abroad, as rather sexually inept, in possession of a rather obsessive and puerile sexual humour and a lack of sophistication in their pursuit of the passions. Britain also has a general reputation for being rather stoical – our British stiff upper lip – but we are also characterised as rather reserved, if not straightforwardly puritanical. Sex and sexuality are integral to discourses of regulation and policy – health, education and economics – especially where the designations of appropriate and inappropriate lifestyles, attitudes and relationships are key to a 'British way of life'. The nation's public face and its most intimate secrets are closely bound. Despite this, this chapter begins from the premise that the British and sex aren't just a national joke or a matter for policing; instead, diverse sexual identities, practices and values make up the British nation.

Increasingly, sex is a matter of intense commercialisation and individualisation in the UK (as it is in most Western nations). New technologies and rising affluence have impacted on 'the British way of life' and the British way of sex. Not only have commercial sex services expanded exponentially at home but also Britons of all social classes travel to the European Continent and further afield in pursuit of hedonistic pleasures. Sexual practices include forms of technologised interactions with like-minded individuals across the globe. Sex has been increasingly consumerised, with the rise of sex shops and other spaces in which to purchase the accoutrements to a good sex life if not the actual sex itself. Therapeutic eroticism is offered everywhere: good sex is *de rigueur*. Print media, television and books exhort Britons to improve their sex lives, to get better sex, to get more sex and to keep on having sex even after marriage, including a number of reality-TV expert programmes, such as Channel 4's *Sex Inspectors*, advising viewers how to reignite their sexual passions. The importation of the television confessional show format from the USA has been important in bringing out into the open the myriad pleasures of sexual hedonism as well as the problems of playing with the boundaries of 'normal' sexual relations: 'television discourses about sexuality are increasing not only in quantity but also in the range of moral and ideological positions from which events and issues are debated and evaluated.'[3] Socio-sexual identities have emerged, including 'new femininities', characterised by 'sexual and social confidence, aspiration and career ambition'; homosexuality has shaken off the pathologised and medicalised definitions of the 'sad young man' to embrace gay pride and the pursuit of an open and pleasure-focused lifestyle; sexual minorities (gay, trans-sexual, transgendered and sado-masochist) claim citizenship rights and the same privileges as 'normal' heterosexuals.[4] Visibility – the seizure of the public arena and the refusal to limit one's sexual identity to the private domain – has been a key feature of claims to sexual citizenship, and some of the foundational moments in recent British gay history will be discussed in this light later in this chapter.

While Tony Blair might claim that the state should stay out of the bedroom, his New Labour has, like governments before it, agonised over marriage breakdown, teenage pregnancies, rising rates of promiscuity, sexual infections, child abuse and domestic violence. These home-grown problems are not the only ones the UK Government finds itself dealing with: the effects of 'leaky' borders cause increasing anxiety to the legislature – Britain is an island state under siege. Currently, sex trafficking into Britain is a particular cause of concern: the Government's research suggests that whereas ten years ago 85 per cent of women working in brothels were British, now 85 per cent are from outside the UK, and the majority of them are believed to be working in what amounts to a 'modern-day slave trade'.[5] The Internet has ensured that Britain is no longer an island able to prevent what many see as 'the tide of pornographic filth from abroad'; cyberspace knows no national boundaries and has no care for an Obscene Publications Act which has, since its passing in 1959, acted as the main bulwark against images that would 'deprave and corrupt' the British populace.[6] In the latest Criminal Justice and Immigration Bill 2008 (which came into force in January 2009), the British Government once again sought to deal with prostitution and to limit the newer threat of cyberspace and its dissemination of the curiously and vaguely titled 'extreme pornography'. Fears of the effects of cyber-sex are regularly rehearsed in the media, alongside debates about the necessity of sex education for schoolchildren and the forms and content such education should take given the ease with which the curious child is able to access information online. Thus sexuality is of significant importance to modern British culture, as a matter of political interest and, consequently, of multiple strategies of regulation, improvement and engineering. As Michel Foucault argued, the regulation of sexuality is fundamental to the production of the modern state, and, in Britain, the meanings and materialities of sexual identities, desires, pleasures and practices have gone through significant change. Moreover, in the past fifty years, it is a history of liberalisation and commercialisation of sexuality that has been fundamental to the production of contemporary Britain.

This short chapter cannot cover all the intersections between sexuality and state or the myriad socio-sexual formations of modern British culture. What I offer here are a number of brief and therefore somewhat out-of-focus snapshots of contemporary British sexualities: my account will consider the liberalising moment of the 1960s and the legislative moves that have focused on same-sex relationships as well as some of the sexual amusements enjoyed by the British.

Keeping up appearances: a British way of sex

Does it really matter what these affectionate people do – so long as they don't do it in the streets and frighten the horses![7]

In that response to the gossip that an older actor in a production showed too much affection for the leading man, *grande dame* of early twentieth-century theatre, Mrs Patrick Campbell, neatly encapsulates one of the particular tendencies of the British national character when it comes to sex: the maintenance of the division between public and private – a division upheld by forms of self-regulation and adherence to codes of respectability. Above all else, the British have, historically, taken a pragmatic view of sexual relations, recognising that appearance is all and that a strict preservation of a public façade of continent behaviour is just as important as actually achieving it. So long as respectability has been maintained, the British state has refrained from openly intervening between husband and wife, lovers, punters and 'working girls and boys'.[8] That is not to say that the legal system did not play a key role in the regulation of morality and the demarcation of privacy in the UK, but a comprehensive history of British sex would have to recognise the complex interactions between medicine, religion, class and public debate that have shaped the nation's sexual morality and its practices: a nation whose favourite sexual position is restraint. Moreover, it may not be the case that legislation plays the leading role in the policing of sexuality in the UK. More often it seems that government lags behind other concerned groups when it comes to sexual matters; the legal system is really a 'moral thermometer' rather than the single driver of changing sexual mores.[9]

Vernacular histories of twentieth-century Britain and sex highlight the rapid changes of the last half of the century and, in particular, the changes wrought in the 1960s. The 'sexual revolution' saw the development of new codes of sexual behaviour that rejected the strict morality of state-sanctioned heterosexual marriage. Home Secretary Roy Jenkins is credited with responsibility for the permissive legislation of the period that saw relaxation of the divorce laws (1971), the abolition of theatre censorship (1968) and the private members' bills for the legalisation of abortion (1967) and the decriminalisation of homosexuality (1967). Although the Labour Government oversaw these legislative changes, Prime Minister Harold Wilson was not particularly sympathetic to them, and many others saw 'permissiveness' (a term coined by its opponents) as a harbinger of doom.

In less than thirty years, from the end of the Second World War to the beginnings of the 1970s, so the story goes, Britain moved from Victorian prudery to sexual liberation. In these histories, Britons of the 1940s and 1950s took sexual morality very seriously, their sexual behaviours were, apparently, entirely limited to heterosexual and married activity. '[T]he moral world of 1950s Britain, at least as far as the statute book was concerned, was barely altered from that of a century earlier' and consumed by 'overriding terror of almost literally unspeakable, but hugely potent horrors'.[10] The changes that came in the 1960s were nothing less than a revolution. If the author George Mikes could poke fun at the British with his one-line chapter 'Continental people have sex lives; the English have hot-water bottles' in 1946, by the end of the 1960s the British were brandishing their contraceptive pills, their free love and the dead and bloody remains of Victorian morality.[11]

This history isn't entirely false, but it is something of an exaggeration. Earlier decades of the twentieth century had their own share of sex outside marriage, and, anyway, 'the ideals [of continence and chastity] had never been more than declarations of intent.'[12] Sales of diaphragms, condoms and sex manuals throughout the 1920s to 1960s suggest that hot-water bottles weren't the only thing the British took to bed with them in the dark days before the sexual revolution. Surveys show that 'nearly half of the women born between 1924 and 1934 admitted that they had engaged in pre-marital intercourse'.[13] This doesn't mean to say that people thought sex before marriage was morally right, but it does suggest that 'even in the supposedly tedious, terrified 1950s many people could not resist breaking their own moral codes.'[14] That the 1950s and the decades before them were not as repressed as some have claimed does not, however, alter the fact that the 1960s was a period of change in relation to sex.

In 1954, Lord Wolfenden headed a committee charged with examining the twin 'problems' of prostitution and homosexuality. Despite its author's own committed belief in the sanctity of marriage, the Wolfenden Report, published in 1957, opined that 'private morality or immorality was a private affair' and that the state's role was 'the preservation of public order and decency' not interference in the behaviour of consenting adults in private.[15] So, 'while the report reflected the moral anxieties of the fifties, it dealt with them in a novel way, suggesting that the state had no place suppressing private vice.'[16] Thus, the principle that underpins the modern attitude to sex and the state, the founding principle of the 'permissive' legislation of the 1960s and the sexual revolution, is actually a product of the supposedly repressive 1950s. That Tony Blair claimed, in 2006, that the state 'no longer has a role' in the nation's bedrooms is an indication that the sexual revolution is still not wholly won, it is an 'unfinished revolution'.[17]

From Wolfenden to Section 28 and beyond to civil partnerships

Wolfenden's Report was ignored at first; labelled a 'Pansy's Charter', it didn't receive widespread support until the late 1960s. Wolfenden may have insisted that a man's activities in his own home were his own affair (no one seems to have been interested in women in this regard), but the place of homosexuality in British culture and society did not change significantly during the early years of the 1960s, and the law, introduced by Leo Abse, was not approved until 1967. The principle of privacy enshrined in the law that decriminalised homosexuality was not intended to establish homosexuality as a 'proper' sexual choice – as David Owen (a supporter of the Bill) said in parliamentary debate, 'no Hon. Member, whatever viewpoint he or she put forward, has condoned homosexual behaviour.'[18] The age of consent was set at twenty-one years rather than the sixteen for heterosexuals, and Scotland and Northern Ireland were exempted. (Scotland passed its own law in 1980 and Northern Ireland in 1982.) The age of consent remained at twenty-one until 1994 when it was lowered to eighteen; in 2001, sixteen-year-olds won the right to consent to sexual relations with a member of their own sex. The 2003 Sexual Offences Act finally removed any legal distinction in the criminal law between heterosexual and homosexual activity.

The above might suggest that Britain has become increasingly tolerant, and certainly it is unlikely that any MP would now claim, as George
Brown did in 1967, that:

> This is how Rome came down. And I care deeply about it – in
> opposition to most of my Church. Don't think teenagers are able
> to evaluate your liberal ideas. You will have a totally disorganised,
> indecent and unpleasant society. You must have rules! We've gone
> too damned far on sex already. I don't regard any sex as pleasant. It's
> pretty undignified and I've always thought so.[19]

However, it would be a mistake to view subsequent decades as following an uninterrupted path to more liberal, tolerant and accepting attitudes. British social-attitudes surveys throughout the 1970s and 1980s
found that the majority still regarded homosexuality with suspicion if
not downright disgust. There is no simplistic association between tolerance and liberalisation; instead, ways of thinking and talking about
sexuality are intensely relational.[20] For example, while the seventeenth
British Social Attitudes Survey found that attitudes were more accepting towards sexual content in cinema and television, the picture is more
complicated.[21] Overall, the survey results suggested that attitudes to
representations of same-sex activity were shifting. However, viewers
required that sexual content be essential to the plot of the drama and
felt that regulation should still attempt to balance freedom to see sexual
content and the need to protect the vulnerable. Thus, the shift in attitudes had not changed viewers' and readers' beliefs that certain kinds
of images could do damage to the 'young and vulnerable'. Viewers were
more tolerant of 'appropriate' forms of same-sex relationships (those
which most nearly replicated heterosexuality in terms of monogamy
and romance), but this was not the same as a widespread tolerance of gay
men and their actual presence in social spaces. The limits of British tolerance are perhaps best demonstrated by the passing of legislation under
Margaret Thatcher's Government (1979–90).

Section 28 of the Local Government Act 1988 was inspired by the
tabloid tales of the 'vile' book *Jenny Lives with Eric and Martin* being used
in schools to 'promote homosexuality', although there seems to have
been very little evidence that the book was ever widely used (indeed, the
Pink Paper claims that the only evidence of its being in an educational
establishment was the one copy held at the Inner London Education
Authority Teachers' Resource Centre).[22] Nevertheless, the outcry against

the publication, which told the story of a little girl living with her father and his gay partner, was exacerbated by the general homophobic climate that linked homosexuality with immorality and disease, particularly AIDS. The legislation forbade local authorities from 'intentionally promot[ing] homosexuality or publish[ing] material with the intention of promoting homosexuality'. In the public consciousness the clause was firmly linked with children's sex education, the promotion of 'pretended families' and the need to 'protect children'; the effects of the clause were far-reaching even though no successful prosecutions were ever brought: 'Section 28 has ... had an affective life and a symbolic importance of far more importance than its legal, institutional power ... The public perception has certainly been, as a *Daily Telegraph* leader put it approvingly, that Section 28's aim has been "to keep proselytising homosexual literature out of the classroom".'[23] Under the guise of 'protecting' children, sex education in Britain has been based on ensuring that sexual activities in general are regarded as private but, more importantly, that certain behaviours are not to be spoken of (that they are *intensely* private). Further, some information should be withheld as only appropriate to certain age groups – with a clear implication that too much information promotes and normalises 'bad' behaviours. Indeed, earlier parliamentary acts, for example, the Education (No. 2) Act 1986 insisted that sex education be 'given in a manner as to encourage those pupils to have due regard to moral considerations and the value of family life' (Section 46). In various directives, the Department for Education and Skills made very clear that there should be no teaching that presented homosexuality as the 'norm' or that encouraged 'homosexual experimentation'. However, Section 28 was not simply about sex education in schools: by banning local authorities from 'promoting homosexuality' in any of its publications, there was an attempt to make information inaccessible to adults as well as children. Local councils withdrew their support for gay and lesbian groups, libraries removed gay and lesbian publications from their shelves, and Section 28 fulfilled the wider remit of ensuring that homosexuality was recognised as tolerable only in private and amongst adults.[24]

While there were many religious and parental groups in favour of the legislation, opposition to the anti-gay clause was vociferous and often dramatic. In 1988, as the Section was passing through the Houses of Parliament, a lesbian group abseiled into the House of Lords and also successfully disrupted a prime-time BBC TV news broadcast. Disparate gay-rights groups and individuals were galvanised by their opposition to Section 28 and, while they were unsuccessful in preventing its passing, formed a united front for further activism throughout subsequent decades. The Section passed into law in May 1988. Tony Blair's New Labour came to office in 1997 with a gay-friendly face and an election promise to repeal the Section. While New Labour made significant inroads to some of the glaring inequalities facing same-sex couples (for example in November 2002 adoption legislation gave gay couples the right to adopt), Section 28 proved difficult to remove. Conservative hardliners and religious groups argued that the act protected children from predatory homosexuals and the latest bête noire of the tabloid press, the paedophile. Opposition in the House of Lords meant that the Bill to repeal was defeated twice in 2000, and the Section was not removed from the statute books in England until 2003. (Scotland removed it in 2000.)

The battles over Section 28, expressed in rhetorical flourishes of hell and damnation, demonstrated that for many Britons homophobia was alive and kicking. Even so, the new millennium saw Lord Lester introduce a private member's bill – The Civil Partnerships Bill – to the House of Lords. The Bill recognised the entitlement of gay and lesbian couples to most of the various rights and responsibilities of inheritance, next of kin, etc., accorded to married heterosexuals. To ministers it was a case of recognising the stability of many gay and lesbian relationships, as Meg Munn, Equality Minister, put it: 'We know there are people who have been together maybe 40 years and have been waiting for the chance to do this kind of thing, because of the important differences it makes to their lives.'[25] The first registrations for civil partnership were allowed on 19 December 2005, and there was extensive media coverage of the first partnership ceremonies: especially when these celebrated the union of celebrities such as Elton John. Within a year, 18,059 civil partnerships were formed.[26] Civil partnerships could be claimed as the last step on the necessary journey to sexual equality in the UK; how far that statement can be sustained is a matter for future analysis. There is no doubt that even as partnership ceremonies are very popular, civil unions have not been welcomed by all gay activists – for example, OutRage! activist Peter Tatchell has been very critical of the law as creating a form of 'sexual apartheid' which does nothing to change sexual politics: 'Instead of legislating a second rate version of marriage for gays only, the government could have created a truly modern system of partnership rights for everyone – gay and straight – covering all relationships of mutual care and commitment.'[27] The legitimisation of non-normative relationships will require further activism and claiming of rights to public visibility.

Greatest scandal waits on greatest state: sex and reputation

Publicity is a key element in another favoured British pastime. Apparently many Americans believe the British to be particularly good at scandals, especially when it comes to the potent mixture of sex and rank.[28] Recent decades have certainly had their share, but with the decline of the Cold War scandals have seemed less potentially cataclysmic than the Profumo Affair of 1963, which saw the then Secretary of State for War engaged in sexual shenanigans with the call-girl consort of a Russian spy.[29] Since that heyday, political sex scandals have acquired a rather ridiculous hue, none more so than the botched murder plot hatched by Liberal leader Jeremy Thorpe to silence claims of a homosexual affair during the 1960s (when homosexuality was still criminal) and which resulted in the shooting of the intended victim's dog. The details of the sexual relationship were splashed across the papers for months and ensured Thorpe's resignation.[30] Other scandals have been less bloody – through tales of David Mellor, Tory Minister for Media and Culture, bonking his mistress in a Chelsea football strip to the alleged three-hour sex romps of the most unlikely couple (Edwina Currie and Prime Minister John Major) and the claims of 'looking for badgers' trotted out by Welsh Secretary Ron Davies when caught in a 'moment of madness' on Clapham Common (a notorious 'cottaging' or pick-up site for gay men), British political sex scandals of the past thirty years have been the subject of rather more humour than outrage.[31] The tales of a five-month extra-marital affair by Liberal Democrat leader Paddy Ashdown gave rise to the memorable headline 'It's Paddy Pantsdown!' neatly summing up the particular mixture of humour, outrage and delight characteristic of British tabloid newspapers' responses to the revelation of yet another indiscretion on the part of the great and good.[32]

Yet perhaps there is more to the scandal than the cheeky headlines and puerile delight in the detail. David Mellor's antics had particular resonance because of his attempt to curb the excesses of the British press in 1989, warning that the 'gentlemen of the press were drinking in the last chance saloon'.[33] The discovery of his affair with an actress in 1992 effectively undermined any moral high ground he had claimed and sounded the death-knell for Prime Minster Major's 'Back to Basics' family-values campaign. Throughout the 1990s it seemed that members of the Conservative Government were constantly caught in priapic excesses, but this might all have been forgiven if they had not been so sanctimonious about the necessity for good behaviour and sexual prudence on the part of the electorate. The other major political parties were not scandal-free, but their scalps remained intact, perhaps because they had not espoused the imposition of a moralist code of family values on the British public. The key issue was not so much the infidelities or indiscretions but the fact that the Conservative Government behaved as if there was one law for them and another for everyone else – their sexual behaviours clearly said something about the lack of probity at the highest office and the hypocrisy of the party as a whole.

Fitness for office also came into question with various royal scandals including Squidgygate (1992) and Camillagate (1992) that broke as part of the general 'War of the Waleses'. With the break-up of Prince Charles's marriage to Princess Diana in the early 1990s, various revelations about the causes of friction and the indiscretions in their marriage began to be made public. Camillagate and Squidgygate revealed rather more about Charles and Di than most UK citizens wanted to know. Both scandals revolved around the publication of transcripts from taped telephone conversations the royal pair enjoyed with their respective lovers: Camillagate revealed that Charles wished he was a tampon so that he could get ever closer to his then mistress Camilla Parker-Bowles; Squidgygate – the revelation of Diana's affair with James Gilbey – exposed the farce of the royal marriage and Diana's own duplicity in its break-up and the attendant publicity it enjoyed in the tabloid press. The mystique of royalty was well and truly tarnished by the details of childish squabbles and extra-marital sex. Speculation about the Wales's marriage still occupies significant acreage in the tabloid newspapers ten years after Diana's death, alongside a recurrent republicanism that questions whether a divorced adulterer now married to his former lover is fit to assume the role of Head of State and Church. That many marriages in the UK end in divorce (and, for some, remarriage) is not sufficient cause, it seems, to forgive Charles his previous sins, and where there might be a proper debate about the need for a monarchy in the twenty-first century, the question is asked in relation to his intimate relationships. This may be a key feature of sex scandals in the press:

> these [kinds of] stories share a common dynamic and common
> themes: the discussions of sexual 'misbehavior', which kick each

story into gear, are rapidly edged out by themes of inauthenticity, and by suggestions that hypocrisy, risk, or disloyalty are facilitated by the man's particular institutional environment. Sex scandal stories, rather than remaining stories of individual sexual transgression, are transformed into institutional morality tales.[34]

Even so, sex scandals are not always about the politics of institutions, just as often the British tabloids do a very good job of presenting the salacious story with little or no particular justification. The leading tabloid in Britain, *The Sun*, has always had sex at its centre, from the Page Three girl feature (a topless model who smiles in sweet invitation to readers to join in the 'fun in the Sun') to stories (not all of them true) featuring celebrities and ordinary members of the public caught in flagrante delicto, *The Sun* has prided itself on its 's-exclusives'.[35] Its rivals are also pleased to publish any story that has a good rich mixture of sex including celebratory articles about British prowess in the bedroom. Under headlines such as 'Fair Play to British Sex Gods: UK Blokes are World-Beaters in the Bedroom' and 'London's Men Make Lousy Lovers … But Girls Get the Hots in Hants', breathless copy recounts the results of yet another sex survey that demonstrates that when it comes to bedroom action the British are able to hold their own with Latin lovers and French romancers.[36] Or, maybe not. *Sun* reporter Jane Symons was just as pleased to tell readers that 'Brits are slackers in the sack, having less sex than just about all our European cousins.'[37] But never fear, at least the British are good at some sexual activities: 'British reserve could be to blame for our lack of action in the bedroom – we're the Europeans least likely to tell our partners what turns us on. But we're devils at do-it-yourself, coming second in the world for using a vibrator and beaten only by the Aussies, who clearly like a bit of fun down under.'[38] Even in sexual matters the British are always in competition with their Continental neighbours.

One area of British sexual prowess caused particular distress to the gentlemen of the press: British holidaymakers' penchant for sexual excess in the tourist resorts of Cyprus, Greece and Spain. Tales of wild nights in Ayia Napa and Ibiza emphasised the damage done to Britain's reputation abroad: 'Ibiza, Ayia Napa, Sodom and Gomorrah: they are mere monasteries, we are told, compared to the organised bonk and boozathon that is Faliraki, where drunken damsels from the home counties are said to roll in the street and beg for sex from men rampaging in togas.'[39] As the papers railed against 'drunken blowjobs on family beaches in Kavos' and sex shows in bars, it seems it was the unashamed publicness of the sexual hedonism that most offended the commentators.

But it took a celebrity to really bring British exhibitionism to the nation's attention.

Park and writhe: Britain gives the world dogging

In 2004, *The Sun* newspaper broke the story of an ex-professional footballer called Stan Collymore's 'dogging shame'. Collymore was caught in a classic sting operation when he confessed to a fondness for 'dogging' to two reporters posing as a couple 'looking for fun'. Dogging combines 'public sex, voyeurism and exhibitionism, "swinging", group sex and partner swapping' (not always at the same time) and takes place in secluded car parks at beauty spots or on the urban fringes.[40] Although not a new phenomenon, with a celebrity caught in the act the press had a field day – this morality tale had legs. Not only was a celebrity caught with his pants down but he was engaging in sex with unknown partners in public spaces: spaces used by 'ordinary' members of the public. As the *People* newspaper reported it, 'Park and Writhe: Car Pervs' Naked Lust Infests the Haunts of Innocents': dogging put respectable people and children at risk.[41] Collymore's admissions of guilt and shame further fuelled the morality narrative, and the limits of the British embrace of hedonism were well and truly displayed in outraged copy. This scandal was about more than one man's fall from grace. The affair demonstrated the particular role the tabloids play in British culture: in their fondness for reporting the sexual exploits of celebrities, the papers prowl the borders of the taboo; their stories of sex and fun and sex and degradation make a clear delineation between acceptable forms of sexual hedonism and those that transgress.

Since the Collymore story there have been tales of other celebrities caught in the act, an on-duty policeman found neglecting his duty – 'halfway through, the randy copper received a police radio call – but told colleagues: "I'm busy at the moment. I'll get back to you in 20 minutes"' – and lurid tales of the dangers of sexual infection for those engaging in dogging, as well as numerous scandalised articles about the breach of public space and the mess left by doggers.[42] As one Revd Rob Wykes, of Crewe Christian Concern, put it:

> All right-minded adults recognise that sexual activity is about intimacy, privacy and sensitivity and is not something that should be carried out in a public park which is there for family enjoyment.

What gives these people the right to do whatever they want in a public place? They have completely forgotten their responsibility to the wider community.[43]

But even as its detractors bemoan practitioners' failures to consider the 'wider community', dogging is a British export, via the Internet, to the rest of the world and can make its own claims as a participatory community. There are many sites on the World Wide Web using dogging as a marketing category joining the hundreds of sites selling images and videos of 'genuine amateurs' engaged in 'real' hardcore action. Such websites use authenticity claims to further emphasise the transgression involved in viewing pornography using appropriately evocative and explicit descriptions to quote one representative site. On most of these sites, the tag 'UK' or 'British' is used to guarantee a level of quality or 'realness': the authenticity of British girls in British car parks having very British fun. Other sites stress authenticity as a particular pleasure of sexual exploration. In these participatory spaces, authenticity and 'amateurism' are important markers of the desire to share: site owners post their credentials – 'We are a genuine swinging couple from the North-West' – and mix discussion of dogging or swinging practices with text and pictures about their home lives, their work, family and even changing body shape. Thus, the websites conform to what can be termed 'a broad postmodern taste for "authentica"'.[44] They may also be instances of new forms of sexual self-representation facilitating 'taste cultures' where 'sex is the focus of participatory cultures and where commerce and community are combined.'[45] Trust and responsibility are also important in these 'sex communities': to oneself and one's partner but also to other members of the community.[46] The community sites are very aware of the negative publicity dogging has garnered and thus exhort their members to: 'Always dispose of your "dogging kit" safely and properly. Areas that are left full of used condoms and other items will soon get closed down by the authorities. If you wouldn't want your kids to find it, don't leave it.' The mundane good sense of this advice underscores the ways in which dogging is not just a sexual practice but a complex negotiation of the public/private divide. Cleaning up is a means of reclaiming privacy for the act of dogging – by removing all traces of the practice the authorities may 'forget' its presence. Yet public knowledge of the practice is required to ensure it can be practised! 'The exhibitionist and voyeurist components of dogging fetishise the "thrill" and "risk" of being in public,

rather than claiming public visibility as a political act.'[47] Whether doggers will need to seek recognition of their right to party depends on
their ability to juggle their pleasures and responsibilities in order to
ensure that their freedoms are not curtailed in the name of 'Keeping
Britain Tidy'. The British desire to police those doing it in the streets
even if they don't frighten the horses, is, after all, very strong.

That the British indulge in activities such as dogging or plain old
adultery does not mean that Britain has finally decided that sex is a matter for celebration. There is plenty of evidence of rising concerns about
the supposedly perverse activities of the British, with addiction to pornography a current favourite theme across media formats. The Sun's agony
aunt Deidre Sanders recently referred to a survey into online pornography describing Britons as suffering from a 'net sex epidemic' threatening to destroy marriages.[48] Documentaries have focused on 'the dark side
of social networking sites', 'addiction to online pornography' and the
inadequacies that rise to the surface as a result of 'too much' online sexual activity. These fears of cyber-sex have found their apotheosis in the
passing of legislation against the downloading and possession of certain
kinds of pornography with, first, the Sexual Offences Act 2003 widely
criticised for its heavy-handedness and lack of clarity, and then the more
recent clauses in the Criminal Justice and Immigration Act 2008 (mentioned earlier in this chapter) that have made the possession of 'extreme'
pornography illegal. Images of sado-masochistic practices seem most
likely to be caught within this term, but, as the parameters of offence will
probably only be decided once a case is brought to court, there are real
fears that many thousands of adults could be criminalised by the legislation for possessing images of their private and consenting pleasures.

The legislation cements the popular conception that there is something particularly suspect about people who take their sexual pleasures
from images, activities and expressions which do not fall within the narrow range of 'normal' sexual practices. More problematically, it gives the
state the right to decide what are appropriate fantasies: previous legislation required that individuals were guilty of actually practising proscribed
sexual acts; with the provisions of the Criminal Justice and Immigration
Act, a jail sentence is possible for merely possessing an image of them. That
the situation will be confused and confusing is perhaps the best indication
that despite the claims of permissiveness, sexual liberation and increasing
sexualisation of British culture, British attitudes to sex and sexual pleasure
are still defined by a continuing tension between freedom and restraint.

Notes

1 T. Blair, 'Our Nation's Future' (5 September 2006), available online at www. number-10.gov.uk/output/Page10037.asp (accessed 27 September 2008).

2 Quoted in S. Sheridan, *Keeping the British End Up: Four Decades of Saucy Cinema* (London: Reynolds & Hearn, 2007), p. 10.

3 J. Arthurs, *Television and Sexuality: Regulation and the Politics of Taste* (Maidenhead: Open University Press, 2004), p. 2.

4 E. Ticknell, D. Chambers, J. Van Loon and N. Hudson, 'Begging for It: "New Femininities," Social Agency, and Moral Discourse in Contemporary Teenage and Men's Magazines', *Feminist Media Studies*, 3 (1) (2003): 47–63; p. 47.

5 T. Branigan, 'Crackdown Pledged on Sex with Trafficked Women', *The Guardian* (18 July 2007), available online at www.guardian.co.uk/crime/article/0,2128881,00.html (accessed 18 September 2007).

6 Available online at www.opsi.gov.uk/Acts/acts1959/PDF/ukpga_19590066_en.pdf, p. 6 (accessed 26 February 2010).

7 Quoted in A. Dent, *Mrs. Patrick Campbell* (London: Museum, 1961), p. 78.

8 Janet R. Walkowitz, *Prostitution and Victorian Society: Women, Class and the State, Part II* (Cambridge: Cambridge University Press, 1980); H. Cook, 'Sexuality and Contraception in Modern England: Doing the History of Reproductive Sexuality', *Journal of Social History*, 40 (4) (2007): 915–32.

9 F. Mort, *Dangerous Sexualities: Medico-Moral Politics in England since 1830* (London: Routledge, 1987).

10 J. Green, *All Dressed Up: The Sixties and the Counter-Culture* (London: Jonathan Cape, 1998), p. 311.

11 G. Mikes, *How to Be An Alien: A Handbook for Beginners and Advanced Pupils* (London: Penguin, 1958).

12 P. Ferris, *Sex and the British: A Twentieth Century History* (London: Mandarin, 1994), p. 121.

13 D. Sandbrook, *White Heat: A History of Britain in the Swinging Sixties* (London: Abacus, 2007), p. 484.

14 Sandbrook, *White Heat*, p. 484.

15 Sandbrook, *White Heat*, p. 487; L. J. Moran, *The Homosexual(ity) of Law* (London: Routledge, 1996).

16 Sandbrook, *White Heat*, p. 487.

17 J. Weeks, *The World We Have Won* (London: Routledge, 2007), p. 7.

18 Cited in Sandbrook, *White Heat*, p. 497.

19 George Brown, quoted in Sandbrook, *White Heat*, p. 497.

20 M. Foucault, *The History of Sexuality: An Introduction* (New York: Vintage, 1990); J. Weeks, *Making Sexual History* (London: Polity, 2000).

21 R. Jowell, J. Curtice, A. Park, K. Thomson, L. Jarvis, C. Bromley and C. Stratford (eds), *British Social Attitudes Survey: The 17th Report: Focusing on Diversity* (London: Sage, 2000).

22 Reported in J. Moran, 'Childhood Sexuality and Education: The Case of Section 28', *Sexualities*, 4 (1) (2001): 73–89.

23 Moran, 'Childhood Sexuality and Education', p. 74.

24 Weeks, *The World We Have Won*.

25 BBC, 'Gay Weddings Become Law in UK', BBC Online, available online at www.news.bbc.co.uk/1/hi/uk/4493094.stm (accessed 23 June 2007).

26 'Civil Partnerships: over 18,000 Formed by December 2006', available at www.statistics.gov.uk/cci/nugget.asp?id=1685 (accessed 23 June 2007).

27 P. Tatchell, 'Civil Marriages Are Divorced from Reality', *The Guardian* (19 December 2005), available online at www.guardian.co.uk/world/2005/dec/19/gayrights.planningyourwedding (accessed 2 January 2007).

28 J. Wolcott, 'Why Are British Scandals So Much Better Than Ours?' *Vanity Fair* (February 2007).

29 A brief overview of this is available online at www.news.bbc.co.uk/onthisday/hi/dates/stories/june/5/newsid_2660000/2660375.stm (accessed 12 January 2008).

30 For detail see www.bbc.co.uk/dna/h2g2/A2430091 (accessed 12 January 2008).

31 Details of these scandals are available in C. Moncrieff, 'A Journalist Looks at Political Scandal', in J. Garrard and J. Newell, *Scandals in Past and Contemporary Politics* (Manchester: Manchester University Press, 2006), pp. 61–76.

32 *The Sun* (4 February 1992).

33 A. Bingham, '"Drinking in the Last Chance Saloon": The British Press and the Crisis of Self-Regulation', *Media History*, 13 (1) (2007): 79–92.

34 J. Gamson, 'Normal Sins: Sex Scandal Narratives as Institutional Morality Tales', *Social Problems*, 48 (2) (2001): 185–205; p. 185.

35 P. Holland, 'The Page 3 Girl Speaks to Women Too', *Screen*, 24 (1983): 84–102.

36 *Daily Record*, 8 August 2006, p. 18; D. Rowe, *Sunday Mirror*, 28 April 1996, p. 24.

37 J. Symons, *The Sun*, 10 October 2007.

38 Symons, *The Sun*.

39 J. Gerard, 'Welcome to Faliraki: Twinned with Sodom and Gomorrah', *The Sunday Times*, 24 August 2003.

40 D. Bell, 'Bodies, Technologies, Spaces: On Dogging', *Sexualities*, 9 (4) (2006): 387–407; p. 388.

41 *The People*, 11 September 2005.

42 'PC Lumber Is Sacked for Dogging on Duty: Cop in Threesome Told Colleagues: "I'm Busy"', *Daily Record*, 15 September 2006, p. 33.

43 J. Roberts, 'Park's Sex Shame', *Crewe Chronicle*, 17 March 2004, available online at http://iccheshireonline.icnetwork.co.uk/0100news/0100regionalnews/content_objectid=14061799_method=full_siteid=50020_headline=-Park-s-sex-shame-name_page.html (accessed 13 August 2006).

44 R. Barcan, 'Home on the Rage: Nudity, Celebrity and Ordinariness in the Home Girls/Blokes Pages', *Continuum: Journal of Media and Cultural Studies*, 14 (2) (2000): 145–6.

45 F. Attwood, '"No Money Shot"? Commerce, Pornography and New Sex Taste Cultures', *Sexualities*, 10 (4) (2007): 441–56; p. 442.

46 K. Jacobs, 'The New Media Schooling of the Amateur Pornographer: Negotiating Contracts and Singing Orgasm', available online at http://molodiez.org/ocs/mailinglist/archive/341.html (accessed 21 September 2007).

47 Bell, 'Bodies, Technologies, Spaces', pp. 402–3.
48 D. Sanders, 'In the Grip of a Net Sex Epidemic', *The Sun*, 17 March 2008, available online at www.thesun.co.uk/sol/homepage/news/article924883.ece (accessed 25 September 2008).

15

British popular music, popular culture and exclusivity

This chapter explores some of the ways in which popular music, within the larger arena of popular culture, is mediated, used and experienced, focusing particularly on the rise and fall of Britpop in the final decade of the twentieth century. Not least I am concerned with the ways in which the history of popular music is used to give credibility to such national sentiments as 'Cool Britannia', why such a history is selective in its choice of representative events, and the ways in which these relate to who is included and who is excluded from the sentiments associated with the national flag. It is no real surprise, for example, to find that the guitar-led bands of 1990s Britpop are predominantly male – how many British women lead guitarists can most people name? Nor is it surprising to hear the influence of such iconic bands as the Beatles, the Kinks, the Small Faces and the Smiths. If, as the argument goes, Britpop was a deliberate attempt to oust grunge and reinstate Britishness into rock, then such reference points are significant in establishing a recognisable musical identity.

The relationship between musical family trees and their relationship to genre and gender is explored further in a brief discussion of Glastonbury's 2007 headline acts, Arctic Monkeys and Björk, the Who and Shirley Bassey, so raising the question of how popular music functions ideologically and, more specifically, why the everyday reporting of British popular culture resonates with the need to explore and interrogate its often hidden agendas. How one interprets popular music is therefore important. As Richard Middleton explains, 'there is no one scientifically true account of the music, but rather a sense of *complicity*: is this story plausible, is *my* story plausible?'[1]

Meaning in popular music is produced at many different levels. A textual analysis of the lyrics and musical style provides one important methodological trajectory, but meaning also depends on our experience of similar songs. As John Covach writes:

> Listeners organize new musical experiences in terms of previous ones: any new song is heard in terms of other songs the listener knows or has at least heard. In the simplest cases, a new song that shares many musical characteristics with a number of other already known songs is easily assimilated ... Such commonly held characteristics are traditionally regarded as central to the identification of musical styles.[2]

Add to this the significance of image, sexuality and gender and, significantly, the ideological interests that support dominant interpretations, and it is apparent that how one 'tells' the story is crucial to a song's interpretation. Several Oasis songs, for example, include Beatles references. 'Take Me Away' quotes 'I'd like to be under the sea' from 'Octopus's Garden' with the addition 'but I'd probably need a phone'; the words 'Tomorrow Never Knows' appear in 'Morning Glory'. There is thus a sense of dialogue between the real bands and between the songs: 'Supersonic' includes the offer 'You can ride with me in my yellow submarine', and the title of 'Wonderwall' is taken from a film soundtrack album by George Harrison. The fact that Oasis appeared on the British pop scene when a historical consciousness about pop had developed is thus important and reflects the ways in which the interpretation of a musical text is both socially and historically situated and contextualised.[3] As Middleton notes, 'it works through dialogue – echoes, traces, contrasts, responses – both with previous discursive moments and, at the same time, with addressees real or imagined', so raising the question of whether it is possible to hear Oasis – or indeed Britpop more generally – without cross-reference to an earlier 'golden age' of popular music and whether this constitutes pastiche or plagiarism.[4] As Derek B. Scott observes,

> 'Don't Look Back in Anger' (from (*What's the Story) Morning Glory?*) can serve as a useful warning about making too facile a link to the Beatles: the opening piano figure may remind us of 'Golden Slumbers' or John Lennon's 'Imagine', but the chords are those of the Pachelbel Canon, or Handel's 'Arrival of the Queen of Sheba', or Ralph McTell's 'Streets of London'.[5]

It is thus suggested that *how* one interprets music in popular culture depends largely on the issues under investigation, that 'the story the analyst tells, though specific in its origins and tone, is one among many'.[6] For example, while the 1990s can be stereotyped by, for example, an increasing identification with celebrity culture (reality and conflict TV, pop idols, fame academy and confessional journalism), how this is 'unpacked' largely depends on the way(s) in which it is theorised. As a social sign, celebrity status carries cultural meanings and ideological values, and stardom, with its penetrating focus on personal identity, invites identification and controversy, gossip and rumour. As such, 'meaning is always *at issue* but always *real* (not arbitrary)'.[7] A similar observation could be made about the interpretation of the 1990s obsession with retro culture. For some critics it signalled a 'pop cultural revivalism – the imagery of modern culture as a data base and dressing up box', exemplified in such statements as 'we haven't had any new popular culture in the 1990s, we've simply had the recent past again, focusing on a selective memory of the 1980s', the 1970s and, most famously perhaps, the 1960s.[8]

For the analyst of popular music, the whole notion of retro brings to the foreground debates surrounding authenticity versus parody and pastiche and their relationship to postmodernism. For rock enthusiasts recovering from the death of Nirvana's iconic guitarist and vocalist Kurt Cobain (who had committed suicide at the age of twenty-seven on 5 April 1994), the emergence of Britpop signalled a welcome return to *British* guitar-based bands and a more optimistic agenda. It also promised a respite from the dominance of techno and trance evidenced by the commercial success of previously underground groups, the Chemical Brothers, the Prodigy, the Orb and the Shamen – whose controversial hit 'Ebeneezer Goode' (E's are Good) had shaken the walls of the establishment in 1992 in its celebration of the drug ecstasy, whilst signalling a betrayal of rave culture through commercialisation.[9] For others, more versed in the wiles of the media, Britpop (a collective name coined by the music press rather than a musical genre) stimulated speculation about the whys surrounding national optimism, pride in Britishness and the kudos of being part of a 'Cool Britannia' under a New Labour government. For musicologists there was a sense of déjà vu in the catchy melodies and often acute social observation, such as in Blur, *Modern Life Is Rubbish* (1993), *Parklife* (1994) and Oasis (*What's the Story) Morning Glory?* (1994). Obvious influences from the Beatles and other 1960s groups (as in Oasis's 'Wonderwall' [Lovin Spoonful's 'Summer in the City']; Oasis's 'Don't Look Back in Anger' [Manfred Mann's 'Pretty Flamingo']) suggest pastiche (a light-hearted cultural nostalgia for groups whose music inflected social commentary in an upbeat rock style), and with songs as diverse as Pulp's 'I Want to Live Like Common People', and their controversial 'Sorted for E's and Wizz', and Supergrass's pop slogan 'We are young! We are free!' this sense of nostalgic reverence was important in giving Britpop a musical DNA that transcended often disparate musical styles. Above all, it seemed to echo the heady optimism of early to mid 1960s.

> Suddenly Geri Halliwell's snappily saucy micro-dress and Noel Gallagher's guitar could be Union Jack triumphalist … And yet only a few years before, it had been more or less a crime against the People, in pop and media terms, to dally with the Union Jack. So what had happened to make it alright again? One answer might have been that this sudden targeted mediation of Imperial Nineties London saw a kind of affectionately ironic Retro Cool in the Union Jack as a primary emblem of Imperial Sixties London – of pop Art, sourcing from Elton Entwistle's Union Jacket or the original Union Jack sunglasses from Gear boutique.[10]

This discussion by Bracewell of Britpop and its relationship to the 1960s is well argued and convincing, yet, for the cultural historian, it raises several issues that necessitate further investigation and discussion.[11] His highlighting of the flag, for example, situates his comparison within the Swinging London of 1964–7, Carnaby Street, love-ins and flower power. As the epicentre of European fashion, art, design, music and theatre, London was 'the place to be seen', with Allen Ginsberg, Julie Christie, Mick Jagger, Michael Caine and David Bailey, to name but a few celebrities, frequenting the most glamorous restaurants and nightclubs. Captured by Peter Whitehead in his documentary *Tonite Let's All Make Love in London* (1967) and in the American weekly magazine *Time*, which, in 1966, dedicated an entire issue to 'The Swinging City', London was eulogised as the epitome of modern urban culture, a paean to pleasure; the Union Jack presented throughout as a symbol of national identity, past and present.

Semiotically, the flag is a signifying construct of potential meanings operating on a number of levels, not least the ideological. Flag is linked to nation, connoting both pride in country and, more problematically, a body of people marked off by common descent, language, culture or historical tradition. For fans of the Beatles, the release of the *Sgt. Pepper's Lonely Hearts Club Band* album (1967) was further proof of British supremacy, not least within the field of popular culture. Merging good-time music hall with fairground nostalgia, modal melodicism with the sounds of sitar, dilruba and tambour, setting suburban sentimentality against the tangerine trees and marmalade skies of psychedelica and including an outro that suggested anarchy and devastation, the Beatles drew on English musical traditions while giving voice to a more general-ised feeling that the old ways were out, so setting the agenda for cultural and political change. 'It was a decisive moment in the history of Western Civilisation ... for a brief moment the irreparably fragmented conscious-ness of the West was unified, at least in the minds of the young.'[12]

Even at the time, it was apparent that the Beatles held a privileged position within the pop world, that they were able to voice opinions on current situations and be heard by their thousands of fans worldwide. They had become, in effect, the socio-political zeitgeist for their gener-ation, and this is reflected in Peter Blake's pop-art design for the record sleeve, which shows the Beatles as the Sgt. Pepper Lonely Hearts Club Band, surrounded by life-size cut-outs of famous figures past and pre-sent: philosophers, artists, painters, writers, film stars, comedians and, at Harrison's request, a number of Indian gurus.[13] Waxwork figures of the Beatles (borrowed from Madame Tussaud's) confirm their celeb-rity status and hint at their historical significance; they 'had not only changed pop music, but transformed how we perceived that music, and, in a very literal sense, how we perceived ourselves' – British and proud of it![14] Even so, there is an underlying seriousness in the final song and its cacophonous outro. 'A Day in the Life' 'depicts the "real world" as an unenlightened construct that reduces, depresses, and ultimately destroys', aligning the Beatles with the hippy philosophy of 'make love not war' and so offering a more controversial interpretation of 'the flag', one that challenged the hedonistic moniker of 'swinging London', draw-ing attention – like Roland Barthes's earlier analysis of the Tricoleur – to 'whose flag are we talking about?'[15] Who is included, who is excluded?

By the late 1960s, the anti-war movement had swept across Europe with uprisings in Paris, Rome, Berlin and Czechoslovakia. British stu-dents had acquired a reputation for extremism, with many supporting the North Vietnamese in their war with the USA, and in July 1968, 3,000 Vietnam Solidarity Campaign militants charged the US Embassy in London's Grosvenor Square, the demonstration turning into a riot after an eighteen-year-old girl became trapped underneath a police horse. As Mick Jagger sang in 'Street Fighting Man', 'summer's here and the time is right for fighting in the street', a reference to his presence at Grosvenor Square and his tussle with identity politics, 'But what can a poor boy do / Except to sing for a rock 'n' roll band?' The 1960s connection of rock with politics, 'as concerning political parties, the government, the state and so on' was also reflected in the Beatles 1968 song, 'Revolution':

> We all want to change the world
> But when you talk about destruction
> Don't you know that you can count me out.[16]

Their solution ('change your head ... free your mind' and the import-ance of love as empowering change in 'All You Need is Love' [1967]) relates both to contemporary hallucinogenic drug culture, the meta-physical and flower power, a slogan used by hippies in the late 1960s and early 1970s as a symbol of their non-violence ideology, rooted in their opposition to the Vietnam War. But, then, as Tom McGrath wrote before leaving the *International Times*, 'the new approach is to make posi-tive changes wherever you are, right in front of your nose. The weapons are love and creativity – wild new clothes, fashions, strange new music sounds ... The new movement is slowly, carelessly constructing an alter-native society.'[17]

While McGrath's observation refers to the counter-culture's antag-onism towards the establishment and its focus on transforming soci-ety through universal love, the years 1965–7 had already seen dramatic changes in British society.[18] Symbolised by the death of Winston Churchill, who had been politically active since the Edwardian era and, although controversial, had proved an inspirational leader during the war years, his state funeral, on 30 January 1965, seemed in retrospect to herald a new age: the end of the Empire and the end of Britain as a world power. Deference towards the aristocracy was also under attack, not least by the Beatles, whose widely reported wit was in evidence when they were invited to perform at the televised Royal Command Performance in November 1963. John Lennon prefaced 'Twist and Shout' with 'Would the people in the cheaper seats clap your hands, and the rest of you [looking at the Queen and her entourage] ... just rattle your jewellery!' Lennon's famous wit also punctured the formalities of the 1964 Royal Variety Show. Having been presented with the Variety Club Silver Heart Award by Labour Prime Minister Harold Wilson, his 'Thanks for the purple heart – sorry silver heart!' (an allusion to a popular recreational drug of the time) and Ringo's 'Good old Mr Wilson should have one!'

was another indication that the age of blind deference was coming to an end. Nevertheless, the award of Member of the Order of the British Empire (MBE) in 1965 was considered by many inappropriate, with some existing MBEs returning their medals. Lennon's response, that the award was 'for exports' can be interpreted both as an astute recognition of the Beatles' very real economic value to the country and a refusal to acquiesce to the somewhat patronising endorsement of their artistic merit. Either way, it was the first step into today's world where celebrities are rewarded for their services to Queen and Country and an indication that the separation between high culture and popular culture was on the wane.

Wilson's recognition of the Beatles reflected his belief that economic growth should be built on a meritocracy based on technology and modernity. Epitomised by London's Post Office Tower landmark, high-rise flats, wonder plastics, nylon and the mini and bolstered by the heady optimism surrounding Carnaby Street culture and superstar groups such as the Beatles, the Rolling Stones, the (UK-based) Jimi Hendrix Experience, Cream and Pink Floyd, Britain's trendy profile was nevertheless compromised by the onset of economic recession. The Labour Party had inherited huge debts – including a massive war loan from the USA – and the period of growth promised by Wilson's government proved untenable. By the end of the 1960s, a wage freeze, cuts in public expenditure, union disputes, a seaman's strike and a move to more coercive and punitive measures in the sphere of industrial relations led increasingly towards a harsh 'control culture'. This, in turn, was accompanied by a series of measures directed against the rising tide of permissiveness characterised partly by an emerging drug culture and a so-called increase in sexual promiscuity.

The 'Union Jack as symbol of imperial sixties London' also reveals more fascistic overtones.[19] 'Imperial Sixties London', with its connotations of Empire, was now home to a growing number of immigrants. 'In 1961, 66,000 arrived from the West Indies, 23,750 from India, and over 25,000 from Pakistan … By 1968 the total number of immigrants for the year was 66,700. Of these fewer than 5,000 were from the West Indies, 15,000 from Pakistan and 28,000 from India', the majority settling in London and its suburbs, the West Midlands, Manchester, Bradford, Sheffield, Cardiff and Glasgow.[20] With ethnic concentration came problems: poor working conditions, substandard housing, high unemployment, criminal exploitation and colour prejudice.[21] Not least, racial discrimination was inflamed by the strain of economic recession and strikes, with the blame conveniently placed on immigrant communities who were marginalised to the edge of the law. Problems were further exacerbated by the rhetoric of Conservative MP Enoch Powell's 'Rivers of Blood' speech in April 1968, which had stressed that unless immigrants were repatriated the streets would overflow with blood like the river Tiber of Ancient Rome. By the mid 1970s, it seemed to many that the national flag had become synonymous with a racist ideology, that its association with the National Front had given it an exclusivity that mitigated against the concept of a multicultural nation-state. The use of 'stop and search' powers by the police escalated, with raids on Afro-Caribbean clubs and frequent passport and immigration checks. The treatment of carnival and other cultural events as threats to public order culminating in the inner-city riots, which took place in the Toxteth district of Liverpool and the Brixton district of London.

Inner-city tensions were further exacerbated by the advent of British punk. The adoption of the swastika as a shock signifier was interpreted by the tabloid press as indicative of neo-Nazism. The 1976 release of The Sex Pistols' 'Anarchy in the UK' to coincide with the Queen's Silver Jubilee further challenged the hegemony of the national flag. By 1978, growing waves of racist attacks had led Rock Against Racism (founded in 1976) to organise two festivals with the Anti-Nazi League, one in East London and one in Birmingham – both racist hotspots. A further concert was organised in 1979: the flag's earlier status as a national symbol of stability and belonging had been largely superseded by its association with racism and privilege, exploitation and the establishment. Calls for the devolution of power to Wales and Scotland and the uncomfortable fact that the numbers living abroad under the Union Jack were less than the population of Milton Keynes further served to reinforce the point that the relevance of the flag changes with different generations, not least in relation to national identity, culture and ethnicity – a point highlighted above in Bracewell's discussion of Britpop as a celebration of exuberant nationalism.[22]

The problems surrounding the national flag and its relationship to 'the People' had been given a particular focus in Morrissey's infamous singles, 'Bengali in Platforms', and 'The National Front Disco', which was performed live in London's Finsbury Park on 8 August 1992 to support the reformed Madness, one of the most prominent two-tone ska bands of the late 1970s. The figure of Morrissey, bedecked in a Union Jack against a stage backdrop of a grainy photograph of two skinheads, attracted immediate controversy. At one level, the song criticises the tactics of the politically extreme-right British National Party against a background of rising Nazi sympathies in mainland Europe. 'Morrissey's objective was to explore the vulnerability of a young suburban boy' seduced by the nationalistic sentiments of the British Nationalist Party, as implied in his characterisation of the boy's parents and lines such as 'Where is our boy? We've lost our boy!'[23] It was, however, the contentious line, 'England for the English', that provoked concern. Asian indie-rock band Cornershop burned a picture of Morrissey outside the London offices of his record label EMI in protest against the singer's supposed flirtation with far-right nationalist sentiments. Their act attracted the attention of the media, and the popular music magazine *New Musical Express* (NME) was quick to attack, interpreting Morrissey's performance as an endorsement of racism and white supremacy.[24] This was not the first time that they had accused Morrissey of racism. 'Asian Rut' from his 1991 album *Kill Uncle* had told the story of a 'Tooled-up Asian [school]boy [who] has come to take revenge / For the cruel, cold killing of his very best friend.' With its refrain of 'Oh Asian Boy, what are you on?', 'Asian Rut' was one of the songs at the centre of a campaign run by the *NME* in 1992, alleging that Morrissey had a racist agenda, although such lines as 'they may just impale you on the railings / Oh English boys, it must be wrong – three against one?' suggest that the agenda was more likely *NME*'s. Years later, in an interview with the music magazine *Mojo*, Morrissey commented,

> and then in the early '90s, they accused me of everything from extreme racism to other extremes, which has always been crap. And you can't really go cap in hand to people and say, 'Oh please accept me – not racist, really.' It just doesn't work. So you have to retain your dignity and step away.[25]

It was, however, Morrissey's earlier career with the Smiths that was to influence Suede (or the London Suede, as they are known in America), a sexually ambiguous band from Haywards Heath, Sussex, who were among the first to be labelled Britpop. Coupled with the undoubted prowess of Johnny Marr's guitar (with its emphasis on melody and texture), Morrissey's stark and often brutal imagery (which had locked into the social and cultural divide caused by Thatcherism, focusing attention on domestic violence, child murder, animal rights and bullying) resonated with Suede's somewhat depressing council-house-kitchen-sink lyrics and Bernard Butler's melodic guitar. Their trademark sound was also influenced by David Bowie and other glam rockers, and, together with their androgynous appearance, and the fact that one of their founder members (Justine Frischmann, rhythm guitar) was a woman, Suede seemed set apart from the super-lad persona of Britpop's superstar groups, Oasis, Blur, Supergrass and Pulp. Maybe sexual ambiguity didn't quite fit with the media's foregrounding of Britain's cultural heritage or 'the born-again maleness of laddism nouveau'.[26] It is also possible that by selectively invoking the sounds and sensibility of English popular culture of earlier eras, Britpop managed to erase the troubling reminder that Britain is a multi-ethnic society. As Paul Gilroy pithily quoted from the racist lexicon, *There Ain't No Black in the Union Jack*, an observation that seems particularly apt for Britpop's imperialistic nostalgia.[27] His sentiment was reiterated by Asian singer-songwriter Sonya Aurora Madan, founder and frontwoman of Echobelly, 'a Deborah Harry sing-alike, a female Morrissey, our first Asian pop star ... who has been known to wear a Union Jack T-shirt with "My Country Too" scrawled across it'.[28] Equally political, her guitarist Debbie Smith, an Anglo-Caribbean tomboy lesbian, wore a Queer T-shirt on stage. In a cultural climate that 'revived archaic notions of gender and sexuality', it seemed that one of Britpop's problems was how to accommodate its female groups, not least when they refused the dubious accolade of 'ladettes'.[29] Certainly, the media focused more on the regional rivalry between Oasis and Blur, stressing a musical family tree which was rooted in territorial fraternalism. As such, its female bands, Elastica, Echobelly and Sleeper could only be relegated to second-division players if Britpop was to retain its identity.

What is evident in the media's construction of Britpop is that it was a very 'white' and arguably macho affair. It 'didn't challenge ... it didn't threaten blokes; it catered instead to lad fantasy' and coincided with television shows such as *Men Behaving Badly* and male oriented magazines such as *Loaded*.[30] Women were once again relegated to the 1960s status of dolly-birds and sex-objects, to be partially rescued by the Spice Girls' girl-power fun feminism, albeit tempered by their admiration for the Conservative Prime Minister Margaret Thatcher. Not least, by selectively invoking the sound and sensibility of English popular culture of earlier eras, Britpop managed to avoid the ambiguities and complexities of multi-accented ethnic identities. Rather, it constructed a version of Englishness that was rooted in a thoughtless and hedonistic imperialism, with the moniker 'Cool Britannia' suggesting a pun on the patriotic song 'Rule Britannia', so raising yet another question mark over Bracewell's identification of the Union Jack as celebrating 'exuberant nationalism'.

As my discussion shows, the significance of the flag as symbolic of national identity, the 'what goes without saying', is underpinned by a self-identification of inclusion and exclusion. By the mid 1990s, it signified a resurging pride in football, which had culminated in England hosting the UEFA European Football Championship in 1996 and the anthem 'Football's Coming Home'; for others it related to both Britishness and/ or Englishness and a competitive regionalism vested in the popularity of Oasis (Manchester), Blur (London), Pulp (Sheffield), Supergrass (Oxford) and the Lightning Seeds (Liverpool). It is evident, however, that the flag, so proudly sported by Geri Halliwell and Noel Gallagher was *exclusive*, and Bracewell's identification of 'the affectionately ironic Retro Cool in the Union Jack as a primary emblem of Imperial Sixties London' is more loaded than it might at first seem.[31] The British national flag works at different levels, signifying inclusion and exclusion according to political status (including ethnicity, gender and sexuality), patriotism, social and cultural allegiance or, more simply, a desire for your national sports team to win. It is also evident that popular culture, popular music, structured within what Stuart Hall termed the opposition between the power bloc and the people can, as my discussion shows, work effectively to challenge and subvert the meaning of the flag and its relationship to identity politics. The year 1982, for example, had seen the Falklands War, which had started after the Argentine invasion of the Falkland Islands on 3 April. It stimulated a revival of the old ideas of Empire represented by the Union Jack and was arguably the single most important event for Margaret Thatcher and her government in stirring up patriotism and support for the Conservative Party. The 1985 Morrissey-written 'Margaret on the Guillotine' suggests a personal response to her politics ('When will you die? … Make the dream real') and, like the title song of his album, *The Queen Is Dead*, is a witty and erudite critique that momentarily disrupts the power of the status quo.

What, then, of contemporary Britain, contemporary popular culture and its relationship to popular music? To what extent have we moved on from the exclusivity of Britpop and its male-dominated musical agenda? My discussion here is focused by that most British of popular-music institutions, the Glastonbury Festival of Contemporary Performing Arts.

Glastonbury was founded by local farmer and site owner Michael Eavis and has its roots in the free-festival movement of the late 1960s and early 1970s, retaining its idealism through the donation of profits to such bodies as Oxfam, Greenpeace and Live Aid.[32] First held at Worthy Farm (Pilton Festival, 1970) with Tyrannosaurus Rex (later T-Rex) as the headline group, the three-day festival is timed for the weekend nearest to the summer solstice (21 June), and, since 1981, has become an 'almost' annual event showcasing rock, world, electronic, reggae, hip hop, jazz and folk as well as theatre, comedy, circus, cabaret and dance. There have been years when the festival hasn't run, for example in 2001, when the organisation worked on a strategy to prevent gate-crashing and in 2006 when the Julien Temple documentary *Glastonbury*, containing live footage, was shown instead. This follows the precedent of taking one 'fallow year' in every five to allow villagers and the surrounding areas a rest from the annual disruption caused by the festival. It is also interesting to note that Glastonbury is not simply a live event. Acts are televised, performers interviewed, and viewers are 'directed' to both major acts and fringe performers. Thus, while the significance of performance lies in its unique presence for the audience to see, hear and enjoy, Glastonbury, like Britpop, is not a single entity. Rather, it is a multiplicity of symbols and signs, to be understood as signifying different ideas, experiences and moments. As such, who is seen and heard, who is performing and where is significant, not least in the triple context of venue (with the Pyramid being the most prestigious stage), time of performance and gender.[33]

Headlined acts in 2007 included Amy Winehouse (appearing on both the Pyramid and the Jazz Stage), Lily Allen (the Pyramid Stage), Martha Wainwright (the open-air Park Stage), Beth Ditto of Gossip (John Peel Stage for up-and-coming artists), Corinne Bailey Rae (the Jazz Stage) and Dame Shirley Bassey (the Pyramid Stage, albeit at 5.15 p.m. on Sunday, before the main bands of the evening: the Who, the Kaiser Chiefs and the Manic Street Preachers). Icelander Björk was programmed against the Arctic Monkeys as the opening night's headline acts, but it seemed in one reviewer's mind that there was 'no contest there, surely?' Björk's image – 'equal parts Fisher Price, extra-terrestrial and fairy dust' – extended to the description of her performance as playful and bonkers, and, as such, she was considered no real threat to the Arctic Monkeys, the most popular and populist guitar-led indie band since Oasis, whose rock lineage includes Heaven 17 and the Human League through to Pulp and Moloko, so inscribing them within a historical musicscape that includes Britpop, the Beatles and the Kinks.[34]

This distinction between the fraternity of rock and the errant individualism associated with such whimsical female performers as Björk is significant in perpetuating deeply embedded assumptions about femininity and masculinity and their relationship to popular music. Björk, like Amy Winehouse, is unpredictable: there is undoubted talent but all too often attention has been directed at her eccentricity, elfin image and other-worldly vocals.[35] In the case of Winehouse, it is her drinking and drug abuse, which together with her improbable hairstyles, retro sailor tattoos and achingly soulful warble situate her as lying outside the norms of femininity. Both extremes remind us that the codes we live by (not least those concerning sex, sexuality and gender) are neither natural nor innocent. Femininity is all-too-often inscribed within the common sense of stereotype and cliché, so relating it to its historical construction as caring, nurturing, supportive, gentle and tender: feminine. What is evident, however, is that there is no one definition of femininity; it is never constant. Rather, it shifts with the cultural norms surrounding gender, race and ethnicity and is all too often a site of conflict, tension and vulnerability (as evidenced, for example, by the increasing number of anorexic teenage girls who aspire to the size-zero dimensions of such celebrity icons as Victoria Beckham, ex-Spice Girl and wife of footballer David Beckham). Thus, despite their very real musical talent, both Björk's and Winehouse's performances came across as unstable and emotional and, as such, can be associated with the untamed extremes of women's sexuality. They are both unpredictable and tempestuous and, as the old saying goes, 'too damned independent for their own good!' In contrast, the Who are secure in their role as founding fathers of Mod culture and are pivotal to the continuing history of rock, having established the mood of the 1960s fixation on youth with their guitar-smashing anthem 'My Generation'. They featured as the progenitors of the younger bands who followed them on the last night of the festival: the Kaiser Chiefs and the Manic Street Preachers. They spoke both to the enduring relevance of rock culture as well as the importance of Glastonbury as the world's most important rock festival. Their pedigree was impeccable.

The interconnectedness of music and gender is long-standing. Rock's lineage is masculine, with a family tree that charts the development of bands back to the founding fathers of style and image. This dynastic framework is rooted in tradition (blues, country and folk), and the emphasis on originality and self-expression has traditionally provided a larger-than-life arena for its heroes. Pete Townshend, lead guitarist and songwriter for the Who, is equally famous and valued for his controversial showmanship ('axe and amp thrashing') and big ideas.[36] Appearing with Roger Daltrey (lead singer and co-founder of the Who) on the prestigious Pyramid Stage, their performance opened against a video screen showing the red, white and blue circles associated with the British spitfire, symbolic of their status within mod culture and the underlying connotation of wild boys at play – a dangerous lifestyle, living on the edge. As founding fathers of the stylistic conventions of the rock culture they embody, their credibility is authenticated by a performance of their anthemic songs set against footage of their cult movie, *Quadrophenia*, featuring the famous battle between mods and rockers on Brighton seafront. Fronted by Townshend's high-frequency guitar solos and characteristic windmill gestures (which were to inform generations of air guitarists) and with the band's trademark song 'Who Are You?' (which introduces the US crime series, *CSI*), there is little doubt about their international pedigree. It is also present in 'Pinball Wizard' (from Townshend's rock musical, *Tommy*) and his anthem of political disillusion 'Won't Get Fooled Again'. Like Shirley Bassey (also on Sunday's Pyramid Stage), this was the Who's first Glastonbury, albeit as a reformed and resurrected band, but here the musical similarities both begin and end.

Shirley Bassey's appeal lies in her exoticism, and the fact that her most ardent fans are gay somehow sets her aside from the vigorous heterosexuality that characterises both rock culture and Glastonbury. She is a star who is remembered for such hits as 'Goldfinger' and 'Hey Big Spender', and, as the reviews stated, it was probably her first and last appearance at Glastonbury. At seventy, she was glamorous but a festival curiosity. Reputedly fulfilling a lifetime's dream by performing at the festival, she retained her image as an exotic diva, emerging from a helicopter landing and combating the mud in diamond-monogrammed wellington boots. The Who seem equally indestructible (with Daltrey and Townshend in their early sixties) – an integral part of the continuing history of Britrock. What is obvious, however, is that both can be identified as representing the 'best of British', metaphorically draped in the Union Jack that once heralded the emergence of both 'Swinging London' and Britpop. In the case of the Who, their Englishness resides in their above-mentioned contribution to mod style and their iconic standing within the fraternity of rock, Pete Townshend's MBE a recognition of his service to his country. Shirley Bassey's status as a Dame of the British Empire is an even higher accolade. Confirmed by her pedigree as an international artist who is the only singer to have recorded more than one James Bond theme song ('Goldfinger' [1964]; 'Diamonds Are Forever' [1971]; 'Moonraker' [1979]) and the popularity of such songs as 'Let's Get the Party Started', she combines glamour with composure: the embodiment of mythical Britishness, the grand dame of pop, dressed in a pink Julien Macdonald dress, drenched in rain and smiling in the face of adversity. It is, as discussed previously, the way in which the story's told that is important!

It is also interesting to note, within the context of my earlier discussion of the flag, that unlike the overt nationalism associated with sport, Glastonbury's stages are bordered by banners that underpin its philosophy of world peace, free water for all and Oxfam, linking it with such charitable interventions as Live Aid as well as with the earlier ideals of the 1960s counterculture and so forming an ideological bridge between 'the world as it is and the world as it should be'.[37] It is a sentiment that is both idealistic and problematic. Charity may relieve suffering, 'but what it does not do is change the causes of suffering', and the final night's performance by Tinariwen, whose guitar inflected desert blues and haunting songs are dedicated to 'Peace, tolerance and development in the Sahara and in the world of the oppressed' returns the reader to the question, 'Whose flag are we talking about?'[38] Who is included? Who is excluded? Originating from the desert oasis of Tamanrasset, southern Algeria, Tinariwen write songs about modern Touareg youth, 'no longer lording over the desert on their camels, but living the clandestine life far from home, surviving by any means necessary, longing for friends and family, dreaming of retribution, of freedom, of self-determination'.[39]

Postscript

For the analyst of popular music, meaning is a place of tension involving both a possible explanation of the ways in which music is produced, diffused and listened to, and the need to address the music itself.

Approaches to textual analysis are exemplified in such texts as Richard Middleton's *Reading Pop*, Martin Clayton, Trevor Herbert and Richard Middleton's *The Cultural Study of Music*, Brian Longhurst's *Popular Music and Society* and my own *Too Much Too Young: Popular Music, Age and Gender*, which, in turn, draw on similar methodological and theoretical paradigms to those discussed in John Storey's *Cultural Studies and the Study of Popular Culture*.[40] My concern, in discussing the relationship between contemporary popular music and popular culture in Britain has been to focus on specific pop moments, teasing out how they function ideologically and, more specifically, why the everyday reporting of popular music resonates with the need to explore and interrogate the often hidden agendas, which affect the connotations brought into play.

Notes

1 R. Middleton (ed.), *Reading Pop: Approaches to Textual Analysis in Popular Music* (Oxford: Oxford University Press, 2000), pp. 13–14.
2 J. Covach, 'Pangs of History in Late 1970s New-Wave Rock', in A. F. Moore (ed.), *Analyzing Popular Music* (Cambridge: Cambridge University Press, 2003), pp. 173–95; p. 180.
3 D. B. Scott, '(What's the Copy?) The Beatles and Oasis', in Y. Heinonen, M. Heuger, S. Whiteley, T. Nurmesjärvi and J. Koskimäki (eds.), *Beatlestudies 3: Proceedings of the Beatles 2000 Conference*, University of Jyväskylä, Research Reports 23 (University of Jyväskylä, 2000), pp. 208–10.
4 Middleton, *Reading Pop*, p. 13.
5 Scott, 'Beatles and Oasis', p. 204.
6 Middleton, *Reading Pop*, p. 12.
7 Middleton, *Reading Pop*, p. 13.
8 M. Bracewell, *The Nineties: When Surface Was Depth* (London: Flamingo, 2003), pp. 56, 204.
9 A. Melechi (ed.), *Psychedelia Britannica: Hallucinogenic Drugs in Britain* (London: Turnaround, 2007).
10 Bracewell, *The Nineties*, p. 224.
11 Bracewell, *The Nineties*, pp. 13–20.
12 Kenneth Tynan, cited in D. Taylor, *As Time Goes By* (London: Abacus, 1974), p. 45; Taylor, *As Time Goes By*, p. 55.
13 See S. Whiteley, 'The Beatles as Zeitgeist', in K. Womack (ed.), *The Cambridge Companion to the Beatles* (Cambridge: Cambridge University Press, 2009), pp. 203–16.
14 W. J. Dowlding, *Beatlesongs* (New York: Simon & Schuster, 1989), p. 152.
15 I. MacDonald, *Revolution in the Head: The Beatles' Records and the Sixties* (New York: Henry Holt, 1994), p. 181; See J. Storey, *Cultural Studies and the Study of Popular Culture*, 2nd edn (Edinburgh: Edinburgh University Press, 2003), pp. 104–7.

16 B. Longhurst, *Popular Music and Society*, 2nd edn (Cambridge: Polity Press, 2007), p. 106.

17 T. McGrath, *New International Times*, 13 March 1967.

18 See S. Whiteley, *The Space Between the Notes: Rock and the Counterculture* (London: Routledge, 1992).

19 Bracewell, *The Nineties*, p. 224.

20 P. Oliver (ed.), *Black Music in Britain: Essays on the Afro-Asian Contribution to Popular Music* (Milton Keynes: Open University Press, 1990), pp. 83–4

21 Oliver, *Black Music in Britain*, pp. 83–4.

22 *The History of Imperialism*, UK History Channel, 26 June 2006; Bracewell, *The Nineties*, p. 17.

23 S. Hawkins, *Settling the Pop Score* (Aldershot: Ashgate, 2002), p. 88.

24 R. Hyder, *Brimful of Asia: Negotiating Ethnicity on the UK Music Scene* (Aldershot: Ashgate, 2004), p. 7.

25 Cited in Hawkins, *Settling the Pop Score*, p. 89.

26 Bracewell, *The Nineties*, p. 15.

27 P. Gilroy, *There Ain't No Black in the Union Jack: The Cultural Politics of Race and Nation* (London: Unwin Hyman, 1987).

28 A. Raphael, *Never Mind the Bollocks: Women Rewrite Rock* (London: Virago, 1995), p. 34

29 Bracewell, *The Nineties*, p. 15.

30 Raphael, *Never Mind the Bollocks*, p. xxv.

31 Bracewell, *The Nineties*, p. 17.

32 For further discussion of Glastonbury and the origins of pop-festival culture, see G. McKay 'Unsafe Things Like Youth and Jazz', in A. Bennett (ed.), *Remembering Woodstock* (Aldershot: Ashgate, 2004), pp. 90–110.

33 Full details of Glastonbury and its various stages can be accessed on www. glastonburyfestivals.co.uk/performance.aspx?id=529 (accessed 18 September 2008).

34 See Christine Glue's review of headline acts, available online at www. soundgenerator.com/news/glastonbury2007 (accessed 24 June 2007).

35 See S. Whiteley, *Too Much Too Young: Popular Music, Age and Gender* (London: Routledge, 2005), pp. 104–15.

36 Whiteley, *Too Much Too Young*, p. 174.

37 J. M. Golby and A. W. Purdue, *The Making of a Modern Christmas* (Athens, Ga.: University of Georgia Press, 2000), p. 45.

38 J. Storey, 'The Invention of the English Christmas', in S. Whiteley (ed.), *Christmas, Ideology and Popular Culture* (Edinburgh: Edinburgh University Press, 2008), pp. 4–5.

39 Available at www.tinariwen.com (accessed 26 February 2010).

40 Middleton, *Reading Pop*; M. Clayton, T. Herbert and R. Middleton (eds.), *The Cultural Study of Music: A Critical Introduction* (London and New York: Routledge, 2003); Longhurst, *Popular Music and Society*; Whiteley, *Too Much Too Young*; Storey, *Cultural Studies*.

16

British newspapers today

In America journalism is apt to be regarded as an extension of history: in Britain, as an extension of conversation.[1]

Whenever a 'we' gets underway, there is an ideology at work.[2]

Introduction

In Britain, national newspapers contribute substantially to the supposedly shared sense of what it means to be 'British' in a global environment. This is particularly the case in Britain since unlike in other contexts such as the USA almost all the major British newspapers operate and are distributed at the national level. Yet sales of British newspapers are in long-term decline. On this basis, it is commonly supposed that their influence is similarly on the wane. The diminution of the power of the newspaper in Britain and worldwide seems all the more plausible when we take account of the development of alternative news-delivery platforms. The past 100 years or so brought first radio and then television as speedier disseminators of news and information, which, many have subsequently argued, enabled consumption practices that fit readily with the communal activities of the household.[3] More recent decades have seen the Internet emerge as a force in the production and distribution of news, emphasising a form of news delivery that thus far appears to have more in common with the imagery of television than the typography and organisation of the newspaper page, coupled with the more direct threat of daily 'free sheet' newspapers distributed to morning commuters. However, what this chapter will try to show is that, in the British case at least, the position of purchased newspapers is more complex than an assessment based solely on technology and reception might lead us to suppose. Indeed, a number of key social, political and cultural distinctions in the British civil realm have such an intimate relation with a set of terms associated with the character and content of British newspapers that understanding the continuing role of the press is central to coming to terms with contemporary British culture.

In setting about this task, I will say a little on the history of the British press and how it has come to be in its present form. This will involve reflecting upon the role of the press as a 'fourth estate' of the British realm and its establishment as a key institution in the setting of British politics. As indicated, however, I will also reflect upon the extent to which the press has a part in maintaining divisions of culture and class within this established democratic arrangement. That is, since markers of social positioning – such as the accent differences discussed by David Crystal in this volume – continue to permeate British culture, our concern is with how these distinctions are intertwined with practices of newspaper consumption. So even as the sales and marketing power of the newspapers decreases, their political and cultural influence remains steadfast.

The British press and political allegiance

Whenever any government or state establishment is confronted with a mass-media platform, its instinct tends to be to seek to curtail the activities of the media within a framework of political responsibility. While our immediate concern is with the press, all forms of mass media have their own implications for the democratic state and are therefore matters of governmental concern. Former Prime Minister Margaret Thatcher saw 'how to handle television' as an increasing concern for her election strategists, and a number of critical accounts have examined this developing relationship between the political establishment and the broadcast media.[4] However, we should be aware of an important difference between television and the press, such that whereas much of the broadcast media is subject to regulatory demands for even-handedness in their coverage of political parties – in particular at election time – the press remains free to apportion coverage how it pleases and to champion the cause of one party over another. This has allowed the newspapers to put in place an advocacy-based form of political engagement, in which a political communion is cultivated with a section of the newspaper-reading market. In order that political and commercial interests are able to masquerade as dearly held principles, this often manifests as performed

Table 16.1. *The political allegiance of British newspapers.*

Newspaper	1992 election	2005 election
Daily Express	Conservative	Conservative
Financial Times	Labour	Labour
The Guardian	Labour	Labour
The Independent	No endorsement	Labour/Liberal Dem
Daily Mail	Conservative	Conservative
Daily Mirror	Labour	Labour
Daily Record	Labour	Labour
The Sun	Conservative	Labour
Daily Telegraph	Conservative	Conservative
The Times	Conservative	Labour

Source for 1992 figures: M. Harrop and M. Scammell, 'A Tabloid War', in D. Butler and D. Kavanagh (eds.), *The British General Election of 1992* (London, Macmillan, 1992), pp. 181–2.
Source for 2005 figures: J. Bartle, 'The Press, Television and the Internet', *Parliamentary Affairs*, 58 (2005): 704.

sincerity and righteous indignation on the part of the newspapers. In discussing the development of the politically engaged press, Matthew Engel remarks 'it did not actually matter whether what you said was right or wrong, as long as you said it with conviction and élan.'[5]

Driven as much by the need to establish a place in the market as by genuine political resolve, what therefore emerged over the nineteenth and twentieth centuries were a series of editorial attachments between newspapers and political parties, which have served as informal political alliances. As a snapshot of how these alliances have developed over the past decade or so, Table 16.1 shows which newspapers opted for which parties in the 1992 and 2005 general elections. Some of these alliances are longer and more firmly established than others. The *Daily Mail*, for example, has supported the Conservative Party since the beginning of the twentieth century and has such an historical attachment to right-wing causes that it expressed support for a number of the fascist European governments of the 1930s. Also, high-circulation Scottish paper the *Daily Record* (absent from most analyses of British election coverage) is a stalwart supporter of the Labour Party, to the extent of routinely acting as effective propagandist. Third, the *Daily Mirror* has offered electoral support to the Labour Party with relative consistency since 1945.

Even in those newspapers where political compliance is relatively strong, these relationships are to some extent conditional on developments in policy and leadership style, meaning that unqualified support will not always be offered during the period between election campaigns. For example, the *Daily Mirror* voiced opposition to UK involvement in the war on Iraq instigated during a Labour administration, and many of the Conservative papers have been sharply critical of former Conservative Party leaders deemed to be ineffectual. On other occasions, these allegiances between newspaper and party can shift altogether. *The Sun* newspaper shifted its support from the Conservatives to the Labour Party for the 1997 general election, where it remained for the 2005 election, while over the same period the traditionally Conservative *Daily Express* switched to Labour for the 1997 and 2001 elections, before changing back to the Conservatives for the 2005 election.[6]

The press as a fourth estate

While dependent on the extent of difference between the policies of the main parties, this arrangement engenders some degree of political diversity in the print media. Even a relatively critical dynamic between newspapers and the major political parties means that a significant minority of the national newspapers will be editorially hostile to the sitting administration. This is true of the *Daily Mail* and *Daily Telegraph* when the Labour Party is in government, and is equally the case of the *Daily Mirror* and *The Guardian* when the Conservatives hold power. As I will go on to discuss, it is a matter of debate whether readers necessarily acquiesce with the political line of their chosen newspapers. Even so, this political engagement on the part of the papers can be optimistically viewed as the behaviour of a 'public watchdog': each newspaper scrutinising political conduct and policy on behalf of what they perceive to be the interests of their readership. At its most effective, this can mean that newspapers normally sympathetic to a political party have a deeper sense of public duty that allows them to become more censorious on particular issues.

This is an attitude towards the newspaper industry that understands the press as a 'fourth estate' of the realm: an expression that has a particular resonance in British culture. In his history of the English constitution written in the mid nineteenth century, William Stubbs gives the first three estates as the 'Lords Spiritual' of the clergy, the 'Lords

Temporal' in the upper house of parliament and the members of the 'Commons' elected to the lower house.[7] As long ago as 1752, Henry Fielding proclaimed the emergence of a fourth estate as a barb at the press's self-regard and pomposity, but it was Thomas Carlyle who used it in an optimistic flourish on the potential of the press, observing in 1840 that, 'In the Reporters' Gallery yonder there sat a fourth estate more important far than they all. It is not a figure of speech, or a witty saying; it is a literal fact.'[8] In their different ways, Fielding and Carlyle simply acknowledged a widespread view that unelected journalists were becoming as powerful as Parliament itself, and from the middle of the nineteenth century the fourth estate has offered a pointed metaphor that supposes a shift of power from the three traditional estates to the institutions of the press. On the basis that this influence might be a productive one in which 'the press would act as an indispensable link between public opinion and the governing institutions of the country', the idea of the fourth estate enshrines within the press a significant role in holding the administration of the day to account.[9]

On the other hand, of course, it might be argued that newspapers exercise authority without the legitimacy of a democratic mandate, such that journalists are not liable to be voted out of office in the manner of politicians. In an often quoted but still cutting phrase, former British Prime Minister Stanley Baldwin noted that British newspapers enjoy 'power without responsibility – the prerogative of the harlot throughout the ages'.[10] Even now, British political figures reflect with some regret that this fourth estate has taken up the role of politicians in influencing government policy.[11] So in an arrangement that continues to provoke controversy within the political establishment, the press is seen as both overseer and broker of political influence.

Wooing newspaper owners and winning elections

While their political pedigree gives the press an important role in directing political arguments at sections of the electorate, anyone interested in British newspapers should be wary of assuming that such institutions nurture a political conscience stemming from their appreciation of an onerous democratic responsibility. Evidence that more pragmatic forces are at work in these political alliances is provided by a brief survey of who owns which papers and how this translates politically. Both the *Daily Mirror* and the Scottish *Daily Record* are owned by Trinity-Mirror group, and are both stalwart Labour supporters at election time. Similarly, the long-term political preferences of both the *Daily Express* and the *Daily Mail* have been coincidental with determinedly Conservative owners (Richard Desmond and United respectively). This proprietorial influence is perhaps most pronounced in the case of the News International-owned titles *The Times* and *The Sun*, which temporarily switched political allegiances from Conservative to Labour, before turning back to Conservative: all at the behest of owner Rupert Murdoch.

The true effectiveness of the political authority that newspapers exercise over their readers is questionable at best. The newspapers themselves would often have us believe they can make the difference between electoral triumph and political oblivion. *The Sun*, in particular, claimed to have a material influence on the outcome of the 1992 general election referred to in Table 16.1. In a context in which the opinion polls veered between forecasting a narrow Labour victory, then led by Neil Kinnock, and a hung parliament, the front page of the election-morning edition carried the headline 'If Kinnock Wins Today Will the Last Person to Leave Britain Please Turn Out the Lights?' In the event, the Conservatives were to emerge with a sufficient majority to retake office, and the next day's front page immodestly declared 'It's the *Sun* Wot Won It.' Labour Party campaign managers were later to claim that they saw the opinion polls begin to turn against them the previous week, while acknowledging the likely accumulation of the several years of ridicule and political distortions directed at Labour and its then leader by *The Sun* and other Conservative-supporting papers. Nevertheless, in spite of the mixed and complex evidence, later leader of the Labour Party and future Prime Minister Tony Blair saw it as a priority to get the support of the national press where he could and immediately set about courting the approval of the above-mentioned head of News International, Rupert Murdoch. At the cost of what many have argued were a series of concessions of principles and policy, an accord has developed in which both News International titles *The Times* and *The Sun* have supported the Labour Party in every general election since 1997. This has been allied to the development of strategies of press management in the governing Labour Party in which systems of threats with occasional rewards of 'exclusives' are used to secure favourable coverage.[12] Taming the public watchdog of the press has become perceived as a key component of successful government.

It is tempting to consider the shifting allegiances of *The Sun* and *The Times* as a direct response to the efforts of the 'New Labour' project of the

1990s – of which the more ruthless approach to press management was a part – that moved Labour away from the traditional left. In these terms, the 1990s saw a strategic alliance between a number of instinctively right-wing papers and a realigned Labour Party, which lasted until the revival of the Conservative Party in the late 2000s under the leadership of David Cameron. However, David Deacon and Dominic Wring argue that what we have could be more accurately described as a 'partisan dealignment' between the parties and the press.[13] An overall shift in the attitude of parties from the ideologies of left and right in favour of centre-ground politics and pragmatism – the emergence of New Labour from the left and Conservative 'modernisation' from the right – has cracked the foundations of the old allegiances between newspapers and political parties. Emerging hand in hand with the current centrism in the political establishment is an adaptable attitude amongst newspapers with regard to their relationships with the political parties. In plain terms, there was little to gain for right-wing newspapers in advocating the election of a Conservative Party that has little chance of victory, so long as there was a stronger Labour Party willing to follow much the same policies. Most notably in the case of *The Times* and *The Financial Times*, this meant editorial support is given to a political party opinion surveys suggest meet with the disapproval of a substantial proportion of readers. While the political power of the press will remain for as long as the political establishment covets newspaper approval, the zeal of the watchdog is often matched by the adaptability of the chameleon.

British newspapers: a ready taxonomy of British culture

There is also an important cultural dimension to the composition and readership of British newspapers. To take the right-wing press as our example, any temporary withdrawal of support from the Conservative Party should be seen in the context of these newspapers' continued devotion to what may be broadly defined as 'conservative values', drawing on a creative fusion of individual responsibility and the free market, mixed with national belonging and hostility to foreigners. Temporary support for the Labour Party, when it is offered, is explicitly conditional upon that party's willingness to uphold the 'timeless' and 'common sense' standards of the political right. While it might therefore be the case that much of the press is instinctively conservative, this conservatism may be as much a commitment to a form of culture as to specific political institutions. So although there is merit in explaining the conversion of British newspapers from party allegiance to convenient politicking in terms of their response to a new, utilitarian political culture, it is also worth reflecting upon the newspapers' more established relationship with forms and distinctions in British culture as a whole.

The suggestion is that the role of newspapers in British culture is primarily a symbolic one but that they are no less important for that. Indeed, in terms of what they are seen to represent, the division and organisation of British newspaper readerships offers one of the best examples we might conceive of the link between culture and politics. This correspondence between the cultural and political associations of the press is so much a part of what Stuart Hall, in another context, describes as 'the common sense of the age' that it routinely passes without critical reflection.[14] The following lines from a 1987 episode of the BBC sitcom *Yes, Prime Minster* rehearse as common knowledge the political positions of newspapers and the character of their readers:

> The *Daily Mirror* is read by people who think they run the country; *The Guardian* is read by people who think they ought to run the country; *The Times* is read by people who actually do run the country; the *Daily Mail* is read by the wives of the people who run the country; the *Financial Times* is read by people who own the country; the *Morning Star* is read by people who think the country ought to be run by another country, and the *Daily Telegraph* is read by people who think it is. [...] *Sun* readers don't care who runs the country, as long as she's got big tits.[15]

Although this punchline-driven comedy would be out of place in more recent BBC political satires, the list retains its ring of plausibility. Even though it has now taken to advocating political parties, *The Times* continues to be regarded as the newspaper of record, read by members of the establishment. For its part, the *Daily Telegraph* is generally thought to be purchased by those in political and cultural communion with the establishment but with the paranoia that attends the reactionary political ideologue (the above passage implies that *Daily Telegraph* readers live under the delusion that Britain is infiltrated by agents of the Soviet Union). That all such representations are to some extent gendered is apparent by the nomination of the *Daily Mail* as the paper for Conservative women. In parallel, the common political upstarts said to read the *Daily Mirror* are mocked alongside the politically apathetic and sexually puerile readers of the *Sun*. Importantly, the strict accuracy of these individual representations hardly matters. The passage succeeds in its humour because of those recognisable prejudices that attach particular newspapers with various social and political types.

However, there is another crucial element in the differentiations between the various newspapers, and that is the division between the 'tabloid' and the 'quality' or 'broadsheet' papers. Along with the American phrase 'dumbing down', tabloid journalism and 'tabloidisation' are terms which have been adopted internationally and across media platforms to mean a form of news coverage that eschews complex and reflective coverage in favour of an approach to journalism driven by sensationalism, sentimentality and entertainment.[16] In the case of the British press, 'tabloid' has become interchangeable with the 'popular press', a development in the composition and marketing of newspapers that Raymond Williams attributes to the emergence in the nineteenth century of the Sunday paper (the daily papers are supplemented by a set of Sunday titles, often under the same ownership) and to a concern to mix miscellany with news.[17]

In his introduction to a light-hearted book on the press, Fritz Spiegl traces this use of 'tabloid' to the registered name for a product of the pharmacists Burroughs, Wellcome & Company, who devised a form of medicine packaged in a small and easily dispatched capsule.[18] Subsequently, the word came to be incorporated into the popular lexicon to denote anything in that comes in miniature or which is smaller than might be expected. Accordingly, Sir Thomas Sopwith's diminutive and sprightly fighter plane became known as the 'Sopwith Tabloid'. However, the most resilient application proved to be the new and more compact newspaper page. And as the association between 'tabloid' and smaller newspapers became established, the term's employment in other situations began to recede. In time, tabloid's establishment in the vocabulary of news production saw its scope of meaning extended to cover the miniature newspapers' other characteristics: what is perceived to be a less serious approach to journalism and news. While this judgemental meaning is a contested one – at least two of the tabloid newspapers could be more accurately described as 'mid-market' titles – it is to be found in the recent versions of the narratives of media malaise that have persisted since the end of the nineteenth century.[19]

There is a compelling twist to this tale. While 'tabloid' set out as a medicine designed for ease of ingestion, before going on to refer to anything that is re-presented in a smaller format, the term's development in reference to media coverage has reverted, metaphorically, to its original meaning: a form of news that will be simple to swallow. In the event, this transformation of meaning has been an appropriate one in other ways too, as the association between the 'quality' newspapers and the larger, broadsheet format has itself begun to recede. In a process beginning in 2003 with *The Independent*, a number of former broadsheets began to produce their papers in the tabloid format, on the basis of its ease of handling, although all were anxious to stress that a reduction in size would not lead to a corresponding diminution of journalistic standards. Editor of *The Times*, Robert Thompson, for example, found it necessary to reassure readers that a compacted *Times* would continue to 'bring the values and the content of the broadsheet to its new shape'.[20] Trying another tactic, one paper – *The Guardian* – has even opted for a size in between (calling it 'the Berliner'). For all that, the pejorative distinctions rendered by the terms 'tabloid' and 'quality' remain in place, and Table 16.2 shows how this division impacts upon those newspapers we looked at above. Both the newspapers and their advertisers assume some relationship between the readership of these groups of newspapers and such attendees of social class as financial standing, where popular tabloids have a greater reliance on those in manual work with lower incomes and diminished spending power. In order that the raw figures of newspaper readership can take account of these distinctions of consumer type, an organisation known as the National Readership Survey (NRS) is commissioned to research readership demographics.[21] The NRS is a commercial organisation run for the benefit of the publishing industry as a whole, and it provides subscribers with information on 'the demographic and lifestyle characteristics' of the readers of a given publication for the purpose of selling advertising space. Through the NRS, readers are allotted to one of six 'social grades' ranging from 'A' (including higher managerial occupations) to 'C2 and D' and 'lowest grade workers' (including those on state pension and the unemployed).

In moving beyond the sheer numbers of readers that newspapers attract towards establishing what social and occupational types these bodies of readers represent, the activities of the NRS demonstrate the importance of establishing and maintaining a market position within focused income and lifestyle groups. Crucially, this is not a matter of newspapers grappling for the few most affluent readers that enjoy social prestige and limitless spending. Just as consumer products and services

Table 16.2. *British newspapers according to market sector.*

Quality	Mid-market tabloid	Popular tabloid
Financial Times	*Daily Express*	*Daily Mirror*
The Guardian	*Daily Mail*	*Daily Record*
The Independent		*The Sun*
Daily Telegraph		
The Times		

are designed for a range of incomes and regimes of taste so is the advertising through which these products are sold. Thus, the readership of *The Sun* – with a relatively lower average income but likely to make a markedly different set of consumer choices – is of interest to many advertisers to whom the more affluent readers of the *Daily Telegraph* or *The Times* would be deemed irrelevant. The size and social characteristics of a readership are therefore of key importance in the newspaper industry to enable readers to be accurately defined as consumers.

Essex men, Worcester women, Guardian readers

However, such practices of division have been applied more widely, and with more far-reaching implications. Recent decades have seen the vocabularies and methods of the marketing sector enter into the strategies of British politics.[22] British political parties have taken up the US practice of dividing the electorate into categories said to reflect given sets of concerns and interests. Using the rationale that the most effective election campaigns are directed at undecided voters in marginal constituencies, the names of these categories often derive from the names of towns or areas generally seen to be crucial to winning British general elections. Amongst the more prominent to emerge have been 'Essex man', 'Worcester woman' and 'Basildon man'. While these stem from the perceived importance of the electoral outcome in these constituencies, the descriptions symbolise the political type in question more than the residents of the particular area. The designation 'Worcester woman', for example, refers broadly to 'the archetypal floating female voter in a marginal constituency'.[23] This emphasis on the individual voter profile more than where they live is perhaps clearer in those alternative forms of description that draw upon more determinedly cultural categories, such as the preferred choice of transport of 'Mondeo man' or by the daily routine of 'school-gate mother'.

It is important to acknowledge that there is an element of playfulness in the production of these categories. In the same way as the suffix 'gate' is applied to any object that has given rise to a political scandal – after the Watergate affair – a new raft of ever-more creative voter categories emerges with each election. There are occasions in which their invention is driven as much by a sense of parody as political insight, such as with a short-lived embodiment of the left-of-centre middle-class Scot as 'Byres Road man' (named after a street in the heart of Glasgow's prosperous west end). It is also easy to detect light-hearted competition between commentators on political strategy, with each trying to be the first to define a new voter type, so that a visit by then Prime Minister Tony Blair to an Asda supermarket was said to betray his electoral vulnerability to 'Asda woman'.[24]

There are a parallel set of categories that draw upon the names of newspaper readers in a correspondingly symbolic manner. There are links between these sets of descriptions, of course, and one of the qualities habitually ascribed to Essex man was that he was a reader of *The Sun*. A former editor of *The Sun*, Kelvin MacKenzie, described the typical reader of his paper with a peculiar sort of affection. He is 'the bloke you see in the pub – a right old fascist, wants to send the wogs back, buy his poxy council house, he's afraid of the unions, afraid of the Russians, hates the queers and weirdos and drug dealers.'[25] While the description is a pejorative one, in common with other tabloid newspapers *The Sun* is keen to connect with its racially specific and gendered vision of the life-blood of the British nation: the white working-class man, in a manual or semi-skilled occupation. The difference is in how particular newspapers wish to portray this target readership. In the case of *The Sun*, the image of the working class is wedded to conservative and reactionary values and is motivated by economic self-interest. It is interesting to compare this with the embodiment of the working class coveted by the mid-twentieth-century *Daily Mirror*, who even before its conversion to the political left preferred to embody its concerns within a more reflective reader: 'The *Mirror* was the intelligent chap leaning on the corner of the bar: not lah-de-dah or anything – he liked a laugh, and he definitely had an eye for the girls – but talking a lot of common sense.'[26]

Importantly, then, both *The Sun* and the *Daily Mirror* are occupied in fashioning a version of the working class, with their own political priorities in mind. These representations are based neither on a rigorous understanding of their own readerships, nor, as an analysis led by Stuart Hall demonstrates, even on some of the content of the newspapers themselves.[27] While it may be too much to dismiss the need for any correspondence between the discourse of a newspaper and its constructed readership, Mark Pursehouse highlights a fundamental incoherence in the composition of *The Sun* that sees a 'fun' based emphasis on sex operate alongside the maintenance of 'a sterner moral code' based on the family. Contradiction also straddles the bar-room sage embodied by the early *Mirror* and the patronising and 'blistering' style favoured by the editorial writers.[28] Yet a relationship between the newspaper and its readers has to be maintained. While emphasising the capacity for readers to demur from the paper's excesses, Pursehouse points out that the right-wing populism of *The Sun* is constantly renegotiated to accommodate the shifting political interests of the readership.[29]

Similar oppositions are to be found between those titles contesting middle-class readerships, which feed a parallel symbolic battle over the political and cultural character of this broad economic grouping. Over the 1990s, 'the Guardian reader' has developed as an offshoot of the left-liberal stance of the newspaper itself and is used to denote a mythical breed of self-styled intellectual committed to such left-wing totems as the public-service sector and criminal reform; a figure jokingly described by social anthropologist Kate Fox as 'a woolly, lefty, politically correct, knit-your-own-tofu sort of person'.[30] Indeed, in 2006, the *Guardian* produced a self-parodying wall-chart outlining various forms of reader, complete with mock-Latin names. The 'Daily Mail reader', conversely, has become a short-hand term for a sector of the middle-class population held to share that newspaper's concern with such matters as taxation and property prices, as well as the *Mail*'s hostility towards immigration and the influence of the European Union over British political policy.[31] This latter point, in particular, offers a further insight into the undercurrents of race and national belonging that attends many of these outwardly economic interests. Similar attributes may be attached to 'the *Telegraph* reader', although from the perspective of the upper middle and upper classes, and from a determinedly masculine position.

In broad terms, it therefore seems that there are sets of descriptions and expectations that readily attach themselves to the readerships of particular newspapers. It is important to note, however, that any relationship between newspapers on the one hand and the forms of class identification and political ideas that predominate amongst the reading public on the other hand is an extremely complex matter and is unlikely to be a simple relationship of political influence. We have already heard doubts cast upon such claims as that of *The Sun* when it asserts its own pivotal role on the Conservative election victory of 1992. Indeed, the reverse argument is often made, that newspapers such as *The Sun* merely pander to the shifting views of their readership. There are even occasions of seeming contradiction, such as the support of both *The Times* and the *Financial Times* for the Labour Party even while the greater proportion of their readers remained loyal to the Conservatives.[32]

However, there may be some merit in focusing on the symbolic relationship between the press and a broader conception of 'cultural politics' in Britain. The political editorialising of newspapers is important, but so too are the assumptions that lie behind newspaper discourse and what they are able to tell us about culture and prejudice. Our stress on the symbolic importance of the newspapers means that just as it isn't necessary that 'Essex man' be a resident of Essex, or a man for that matter, it needn't be that the middle-class reactionary conservative designated as the 'Daily Mail reader' should be someone who actually reads the *Daily Mail*. Within the hierarchy of symbolic distinction described by French sociologist Pierre Bourdieu, British newspapers operate as vital markers of class and taste.[33] In setting out particular markets and forms of subjectivity based on political and cultural difference, British newspapers therefore participate in the symbolic reproduction of a set of cultural distinctions. While we can reassure ourselves that British culture has many more dimensions than the opposing forces of the press might lead us to suppose, the newspapers themselves continue to act as prominent signifiers that long-standing divisions stay in place, at least at the level of political and cultural rhetoric.

Conclusion

This chapter has examined the active engagement of the press as a significant component in the development of contemporary British democracy. The suggestion has been that the press in Britain has been a key expression of British culture outside of formal politics, such that it informs practices of distinction in British society that extend beyond its actual readership. The picture that has emerged is one in which newspapers are participants in the ongoing processes of negotiation and settlement between culture and politics. Thus, the cultural politics of *The Sun* are addressed to a right-wing working class, just as a left-wing middle class operates in parallel with the positions of *The Guardian* and *The Independent*. Contrary assumptions concerning the relationship between class and politics are to be found in the *Daily Mirror*'s and *Daily Record*'s portrayal of a left-wing working class, just as they are in the right-wing middle class addressed by the *Daily Express*, the *Daily Mail* and the *Daily Telegraph*. Included within this articulation of culture and class, moreover, are parallel discourses of race, gender and national identity. All the while, one might wryly add, those holding the capital and the power continue to read *The Times* and the *Financial Times* and work alongside governments of whatever political hue.

We should therefore understand the newspapers in Britain as conduits of cultural and political power. The tabloids, in particular, engage what they see to be a politically apathetic readership behind causes of shared concern, using emotive language and drawing upon cultural motifs, even when the form of action instigated appears illiberal. While this has developed from a tradition of allegiance between newspapers and political parties, these relationships are becoming less clear-cut. The result is that the relatively arbitrary correspondences that newspapers fashion between socially and culturally based groupings and political traditions appear increasingly adrift from the institutions of traditional party politics. Yet, as politics develops, so too does both the discourse of the newspapers and their relationship to one another. Just as successful political parties are obliged to draw upon dominant cultures of race, gender, class and nation, so do newspapers assume a central, and often illiberal, role in shaping those cultures. Added to this, there is the dynamic relationship between the newspapers themselves, and the possible longer-term reconfiguration of hierarchies brought by the conversion of most of the broadsheet newspapers to the smaller format. Outwardly, traditional boundaries of political allegiance may be lowering both amongst newspapers and in the population as a whole, but the newspaper seems likely to continue to express the cultural divisions that remain.

Acknowledgements

Thanks to Angela Smith, Martin Montgomery and Kerry Moore for their suggestions on earlier drafts.

Notes

1 A. Sampson, *Anatomy of Britain* (London: Hodder & Stoughton, 1962), p. 128.
2 R. Debray, *Critique of Political Reason* (London: New Left Books, 1983), p. 140.

3 S. Moores, *Media and Everyday Life in Modern Society* (Edinburgh: Edinburgh University Press, 2000), pp. 42–56.

4 M. Thatcher, *The Downing Street Years* (London: Harper Collins, 1993), p. 286; B. Franklin, *Packaging Politics: Political Communications in Britain's Media Democracy*, 2nd edn (London: Arnold, 2004).

5 M. Engel, *Tickle the Public: One Hundred Years of the Popular Press* (London: Victor Gollancz, 1996), p. 92.

6 J. Bartle, 'The Press, Television and the Internet', *Parliamentary Affairs*, 58 (4) (2005): 699–711; p. 705.

7 W. Stubbs, *The Constitutional History of England: In its Origin and Development*, 2 vols. (Oxford: Clarendon, 1874), vol. 1, p. 583.

8 T. Carlyle, *On Heroes, Hero Worship and the Heroic in History* (London: Chapman & Hall, 1840), p. 194.

9 G. Boyce, 'The Fourth Estate: The Reappraisal of a Concept', in G. Boyce, J. Curran and P. Wingate (eds.), *Newspaper History: From the 17th Century to the Present Day* (London: Constable, 1978), pp. 19–40; p. 21.

10 J. Curran and J. Seaton, *Power without Responsibility: The Press and Broadcasting in Britain*, 6th edn (London: Routledge, 2003), p. 42.

11 J. Paxman, *The Political Animal: An Anatomy* (London: Michael Joseph, 2002), p. 285.

12 Franklin, *Packaging Politics*, p. 63.

13 D. Deacon and D. Wring, 'Partisan Dealignment and the British Press', in J. Bartle, R. Montimore and S. Atkinson (eds.), *Political Communications: The General Election Campaign of 2001* (London: Frank Cass, 2002), pp. 197–211.

14 S. Hall, *The Hard Road to Renewal: Thatcherism and the Crisis of the Left* (London: Verso, 1988).

15 'A Conflict of Interest', *Yes, Prime Minister*, BBC, 1987.

16 S. Barnett, 'Dumbing Down or Reaching Out: Is It Tabloidisation Wot Done It?' in J. Seaton (ed.), *Politics and the Media: Harlots and Prerogatives at the Turn of the Millennium* (Oxford: Blackwell, 1998), pp. 75–90; p. 76.

17 R. Williams, *The Long Revolution* (London: Chatto & Windus, 1961), pp. 175–6.

18 F. Spiegl, *Keep Taking the Tabloids* (London: Pan, 1983), p. 7.

19 Barnett, 'Dumbing Down or Reaching Out', p. 75.

20 Quoted in C. Byne, '*Times* Goes Tabloid', *The Guardian*, 21 November 2003, available online at www.guardian.co.uk/media/2003/nov/21/pressandpublishing.uknews (accessed 26 February 2010).

21 National Readership Survey, available at www.nrs.co.uk/lifestyle.html (accessed 2 March 2010).

22 H. Savigny, *The Problem with Political Marketing* (London: Continuum, 2008).

23 D. Smith, 'Women Flock to Cameron', *The Sunday Times*, 24 December 2006.

24 M. Riddle, 'Why Asda Woman Matters to Tony Blair', *The Observer*, 4 March 2007.

25 A. Marr, *My Trade: A Short History of British Journalism* (London: Macmillan, 2004), p. 115.

26 Engel, *Tickle the Public*, p. 161.

27 S. Hall, C. Critcher, T. Jefferson, J. Clarke and B. Roberts, *Policing the Crisis: Mugging, the State and Law and Order* (London: Macmillan, 1978), p. 337.

28 Engel, *Tickle the Public*, p. 162.

29 M. Pursehouse, 'Looking at the *Sun*: Into the Nineties with a Tabloid and Its Readers', in T. O'Sullivan and Y. Jewkes (eds.), *The Media Studies Reader* (London: Arnold, 1997), pp. 196–207.

30 K. Fox, *Watching the English: The Hidden Rules of English Behaviour* (London: Hodder & Stoughton, 2004), p. 223.

31 P. Cole, 'Why Middle England Gets the *Mail*', *Media Guardian*, 20 August 2007.

32 Bartle, 'Press, Television and Internet', p. 707.

33 P. Bourdieu, *Distinction: A Social Critique of the Judgement of Taste* (London: Routledge, 1984).

17

The struggle for ethno-religious equality in Britain: the place of the Muslim community

Introduction

Some decades ago, 'race' and gender became objects of equality struggles in Britain, as in many other places. For example, racial equality and sex-equality legislation was passed in the 1960s and 1970s. On the other hand, legislation in relation to religious discrimination and equality in the UK (outside Northern Ireland) has only been enacted in the past few years. This chapter considers how religious equality, and in particular the civic status of Muslims, has become a central feature of community relations and equal rights in Britain in the twenty first century. This involves considering the evolving and complex political and legal conceptions of racial and ethnic equality and how extending these conceptions to Muslims has created dilemmas for liberal egalitarians. Moreover, it is clear now that the political accommodation of Muslims and other post-immigration religious groups does not involve simply a commitment to religious pluralism but rethinking the nature and limits of secularism in the British context.

Multi-faith Britain

Britain has long been a multi-faith society characterised by an internal plurality that has been supplemented by the migration of different religious groups over the past two centuries. Indeed, and in spite of maintaining an 'established' Church of England, the superior status of the dominant Anglican Church has consistently been challenged by other Christian denominations, not least in Scotland where the religious majority is not Anglican but Presbyterian, and which led to the creation of an alternative 'establishment' in Scotland. Elsewhere in England and Wales, Protestant Nonconformists have been vocal; and issues such as education have in the past encouraged many of these groups to 'stand out against the state for giving every opportunity to the Church of England to proselytize through the education system'.[1] In addition to these more established faith groups, the cycles of nineteenth-century migration from Ireland to London, Glasgow and the North of England have considerably expanded the Roman Catholic presence in Britain. The turn of the twentieth century, meanwhile, witnessed the arrival of destitute Jewish migrants fleeing the pogroms and economic deprivation in Russia. Both groups have suffered racial discrimination and civil disabilities on the basis of their religious affiliation but in due course have come to enjoy some of the benefits initially associated with 'establishment' (the identification of the Church of England with the British state). This includes state funding for Catholic and Jewish, alongside Anglican and Wesleyan, schools from the mid-nineteenth century and then, in the 1944 Education Act, to opt into the state sector and to receive similar provisions to those enjoyed by members of the 'established' Church.

The most recent and numerically significant addition to this plurality include those Hindus, Muslims and Sikhs who have arrived through processes of chain migration, family reunification and social reconstruction over a period of fifty years. Indeed, these former Commonwealth citizens have now established themselves, with varying degrees of success, as part of the 'new cultural landscape' of Britain.[2] This is evidenced in several spheres but is made strikingly visible in what has been described as the 'new "cathedrals" of the English cultural landscape'.[3] This refers to the creation of Muslim *masjids*, Hindu *mandirs* and Sikh *gurdwaras* which have emerged though a process of dialogue between minority faith groups and British city-planning authorities. One of several points of interest in the creation of these places of worship is that out of the 1,000 or so that exist a majority are in fact conversions of disused chapels, churches and other such premises previously devoted to other faith groups.[4] This is partly as a result of a decline in collective worship amongst Christians (more precisely, white Christians, because attendance at black-led churches is booming) but also because all migrant and newly settled groups are more religious (sometimes much more religious) than the natives, both in terms of collective identification and in terms of participation.[5]

Anglo-American equality movements

Simultaneously, the presence of these new population groups has made manifest certain kinds of racism to which anti-discrimination laws and provisions may not be geared to redress. Initially influenced by American thinking that took the grounds of discrimination to be that of 'colour' rather than ethnicity or religion, religious-minority assertiveness only became a feature within these frameworks from around the early 1990s. Prior to this, the racial equality discourse of British equality movements was dominated by the idea that the post-immigration issue was 'colour racism'. This led to the idea in the 1970s and 1980s that all potential victims of 'colour-racism' should be conceived of as a single 'black' group, though it is doubtful whether most South Asians ever shared this view and certainly they did not do so by the late 1980s; indeed, for South Asians, religious identities seem to be more pervasive than 'racial' ones.[6] Nevertheless, one consequence of the official approach is that the legal and policy frameworks still reflect the conceptualisation and priorities of a black–white racial dualism.[7]

The initial development of racial equality in Britain was directly influenced by American personalities and events. Just as in the USA the colour-blind humanism of Martin Luther King Jnr. came to be mixed with an emphasis on black pride, black autonomy and black nationalism as typified by Malcolm X, so too the same process occurred in the UK. Indeed, it is best to see this development of racial explicitness and positive blackness as part of a wider socio-political climate which is not confined to race and culture or to non-white minorities. Feminism, gay pride and the revival of a Scottish identity are some prominent examples of these new identity movements, which have become an important feature of British politics, especially as class politics have declined in salience. This is of course not unique to Britain; the emphasis on non-territorial identities such as black, gay and female is particularly marked among anglophone countries. In fact, it would be fair to say that what is often claimed today in the name of racial equality, again especially in the English-speaking world, goes beyond the claims that were made in the 1960s. Iris Young expresses well the new political climate when she describes the emergence of an ideal of equality based not just on allowing excluded groups to assimilate and live by the norms of dominant groups but on the view that 'a positive self-definition of group difference is in fact more liberatory'.[8]

This significant shift takes us from an understanding of 'equality' in terms of individualism and cultural assimilation to a politics of recognition – to equality as encompassing public ethnicity. While the first generation of racial-equality campaigners in the 1960s emphasised that we are all the same under our varied colour skins and that each person should be valued as an individual, by the 1980s a prominent political movement in, for example, the trade unions and the Labour Party were emphasising the distinct needs of black people and were calling for autonomous forms of group representation, such as the 'Black Sections' movement in the Labour Party.[9] Moreover, in this political and intellectual climate, what would earlier have been called 'private' matters, such as personal relationships and sexual orientation, had become sources of equality struggles. It is in this American-inspired climate that religious minority assertiveness emerged as a British domestic political phenomenon quite different from that in the USA. At least in Britain, the advances achieved by anti-racism and feminism (with its slogan 'The Personal Is the Political') acted as benchmarks for later political group entrants. While religious minorities raise distinctive concerns, the logic of their demands often mirrors those of other equality-seeking groups.

Religious equality in Britain

So, one of the current conceptions of equality is a difference-affirming equality, with related notions of respect, recognition and identity – in short, what is meant by political multiculturalism.[10] What kinds of specific policy demands, then, are being made by or on behalf of religious groups when these terms are deployed? These demands have three dimensions, which get progressively 'thicker' – and are progressively less acceptable to radical secularists.

No religious discrimination

The very basic idea here is that religious people, no less than people defined by 'race' or gender, should not suffer discrimination in job, or other, opportunities. So, for example, a person who is trying to dress in accordance with his or her religion or who projects a religious identity should not be discriminated against. The issue of the Sikh turban illustrates this effectively.

Whilst early Sikh migrants discarded the ostentatious markers of traditional dress, this strategy changed as their numbers swelled and contributed to a greater self-confidence to uphold symbols of communal identity. The first campaigns for the right to wear turbans revolved around issues of employee uniforms and arose intermittently in the 1960s. These were ultimately settled by making compromises in terms of matching turbans with stipulated uniform colour schemes. A further turban campaign affected the national policy level in amending Section 32 of the Road Traffic Act (1972) safety guidelines. The 1972 Act enforced the requirement of protective headgear when travelling on a motor-cycle and was amended in The Motor-Cycle Crash Helmets (Religious Exemption) Act (1976) which declared that it 'shall not apply to followers of the Sikh religion while he is wearing a turban'.[11] An MP who supported the Bill described it as being 'based on religious tolerance and that, too, is an important and vital part of our society ... if Parliament concludes that in this case religious tolerance outweighs road safety and equality, the Government will accept the decision.'[12]

It is interesting to note that at this stage the exemption was conceived in terms of religious tolerance. It is a view that can be contrasted with the rationale behind a further turban campaign that succeeded on the grounds that equal treatment encompassed the right to cultural identification. This occurred when the headmaster of a private school in Birmingham refused to enrol as a pupil to the school an orthodox Sikh boy (who wore long hair under a turban) unless the boy removed the turban and cut his hair. The eventual House of Lords ruling in favour of the boy stated that

> It is obvious that Sikhs, like anyone else, 'can' refrain from wearing a turban, if 'can' is construed literally. But if the broad cultural/historic meaning of ethnic is the appropriate meaning of the word in the 1976 Act, then a literal reading of the word 'can' would deprive Sikhs and members of other groups defined by reference to their ethnic origins.[13]

This famous ruling effectively included Sikhs alongside Jewish minorities under existing race-relations Acts, an inclusion that has eluded Hindu and Muslim religious minorities, on the grounds that the former but not the latter consist of persons of the same ethnicity. This is an odd assumption since the Jewish diaspora is white, brown and black and so clearly not mono-ethnic – an important distinction that seems to have escaped the English courts. Nor were Muslims and Hindus in Britain protected by the legislation against religious discrimination that did exist in one part of the

UK, namely in Northern Ireland; legislation confined to that province and designed explicitly to protect Catholics. After some years of arguing that there was insufficient evidence of religious discrimination outside the context of Northern Ireland, the hand of the British Government was forced by Article 13 of the European Union (EU) Amsterdam Treaty (1999), which includes religious discrimination in the list of the forms of discrimination that all member states are expected to eliminate. Accordingly, the British Government, following a European Commission directive that it played a key role in drafting and that many member states have been slow to implement, outlawed religious discrimination in employment, with effect from December 2003. This was, however, only a partial 'catching up', with the existing anti-discrimination provisions in relation to race and gender. For, unlike the race-relations Acts, it did not extend beyond employment to discrimination in provision of goods and services, until further legislation was introduced in 2007. Even so, it still did not create a duty upon the public sector to take steps to promote equality of opportunity, as the new Race Relations Act (Amendment) 2000 did. This anomaly was remedied in the Single Equalities Act (2010), which brings together, and 'equalises' the various and differential anti-discrimination legislation that the recent Commission on Equalities and Human Rights has been created to implement. Hence, in less than ten years, the Government moved from arguing that there was no evidence of religious discrimination (making legislation unnecessary) to religious discrimination legislation that was beyond EU directives or indeed anything found in Europe (except Northern Ireland).

Even-handedness in relation to religions

Many minority-faith advocates interpret equality to mean that minority religions should get at least some of the support from the state as longer-established religions. Muslims have led the way on this argument, particularly through the example of the state funding of faith schools.[14] After a long-standing campaign, the Government has agreed in recent years to fund a limited number of Muslim schools, as well as a Sikh and a Seventh Day Adventist school, on the same basis enjoyed by thousands of Anglican and Catholic schools and some Methodist and Jewish schools.

Some secularists are unhappy about this and its implications for the continuing relationship between religion and the British state. While they accept the argument for parity, they believe this should be achieved by the state withdrawing its funding from all religious schools. Most religious minorities reject such a form of equality, which they see as the privileged losing something but the underprivileged gaining nothing. More specifically, the issue between 'equalising upwards' and 'equalising downwards' here is about the legitimacy of religion as a public institutional presence and so is a political rather than theoretical question.[15] 'Equalising downwards' only seems reasonable when combined with the presumption that religion in general, and not just minority religions, is a private matter and should, therefore, be proscribed from public institutions such as the education system. This assumption that religion should be kept separate from public institutions is quite prevalent in a moderate or radical form in contemporary British culture and seems to have been exacerbated by the efforts of some groups, especially Muslims, to accentuate faith identities, not to mention political militancy and violence motivated by religious groups and causes.

Another example of unequal treatment of religions by the state was incitement to religious hatred. This was unlawful only in Northern Ireland, while the offence of incitement to racial hatred, which extended protection to certain forms of anti-Jewish literature, did not apply to anti-Muslim literature. Muslims, at the time of the protests against the controversial novel by Salman Rushdie, *The Satanic Verses* affair, having failed to get the courts to interpret the existing statute on blasphemy to cover offences beyond what Christians hold sacred, came to demand an offence of incitement to religious hatred, mirroring the existing one of incitement to racial hatred. The British Government inserted such a clause in the post-9/11 security legislation, in order to conciliate Muslims, who, along with others, were opposed to the new powers of surveillance, arrest and detention. As it happened, most of the security legislation was made law, but the provision on incitement to religious hatred was defeated in Parliament. The Government continued to have difficulties getting support for legislation on incitement to religious hatred, not least from their own supporters, inside Parliament and outside it, where it especially provoked resistance from comedians, intellectuals and secularists, who feared that satire and criticism of religion was at risk. The latter were mindful of not just Muslim campaigns but also a recent case in Birmingham where Sikh protests against the controversial Gurpreet Kaur Bhatti play *Bezhti* had led to some violence and the cessation of further performances.[16]

Finally, Parliament passed a Bill in early 2006 to protect against incitement to religious hatred. Yet it was only passed after members of both houses of Parliament, supported by much of the liberal intelligentsia, lobbied the Government to accept amendments that weakened its initial proposals. Unlike the incitement to religious hatred offence in Northern Ireland, and the incitement to racial hatred offence in the UK, mere offensiveness was not an offence, and, moreover, the incitement must require the *intention* to stir up hatred. Nevertheless, a controversy shortly after this Bill was passed, involving the publication of a number of cartoons of the Prophet Muhammad, showed that the British media was voluntarily restraining itself. The cartoons, originally published in the Danish newspaper *Jyllands Posten*, were opposed by some Muslims who believed they were derogatory of the Prophet Muhammad and racist in implying that Muslims were terrorists. At the height of the controversy in early 2006 they were reprinted in several leading European newspapers but not by any major newspaper or periodical in Britain, suggesting there was a greater understanding in Britain than in some other European countries about anti-Muslim racism and about not giving gratuitous offence to Muslims.[17]

Positive inclusion of religious groups

The idea behind the positive inclusion of religious groups in Britain is that religion should be a category by which the inclusiveness of social institutions may be judged, as they increasingly are in relation to race and gender. For example, employers should have to demonstrate that they do not discriminate against religious minorities by explicit monitoring of their position within the workforce, backed up by appropriate policies, targets, managerial responsibilities, work environments, staff training, advertisements, outreach and so on. Similarly, public bodies should provide appropriately sensitive policies and staff in relation to the services they provide. For example, the BBC currently believes it is of political importance to review and improve its personnel practices and its output of programmes, including its on-screen 'representation' of the British population, by making provision for and winning the confidence of women, ethnic minority groups and young people. The argument from the point of view of religious equality would be that organisations like the BBC should also use religious groups as a criterion of inclusivity and have to demonstrate that it is doing the same for viewers and staff defined by religious community membership.

Although there is no prospect at present of religious equality in this full sense catching up with the importance of employers and other organizations give to sex or race, there was an early significant step in this direction when the Government agreed to include a religion question in the 2001 Census. The question was voluntary, but only 7 per cent did not answer it and so it has the potential to pave the way for widespread 'religious monitoring' in the way that the inclusion of an ethnic question in 1991 had led to the more routine use of 'ethnic monitoring'.

A retreat to a liberal public–private distinction

These prospects for the development of the status of religion in Britain no doubt seem odd within the terms of, say, the French or US 'wall of separation' between the state and religion and may make secularists uncomfortable in Britain too. But, actually, any such developments more or less mirror existing anti-discrimination policy provisions in the UK. Nevertheless, if the emergence of a politics of difference out of and alongside a liberal assimilationist equality created a dissonance, as indeed it did, the emergence of religious-minority identities out of and alongside ethno-racial identities have created an even greater set of tensions. Philosophically speaking, an increase in religious-minority identities should create a lesser dissonance, for a move from the idea of equality as sameness to equality as difference is a more profound conceptual shift than the creation of a new identity in a national culture already crowded with minority identities. But secularism is one of the defining features of British political culture, and commitment to it is particularly strong amongst the centre-left, the very same people amongst whom support for equality politics is most likely. While black and related ethno-racial identities were welcomed by – indeed were intrinsic to – the rainbow coalition of identity politics, this coalition is particularly unhappy with a heightened Muslim consciousness. While for some this rejection is specific to Islam, for many the rejection is directed towards politicised religious identities more broadly. What is most interesting is that this latter objection, if it is taken at its face value, appeals to a public–private distinction in respect of religion that advocates of identity politics have spent two or three decades demolishing in respect to gender, race and sexual orientation. Thus, secular multiculturalists routinely argue that the sex lives of individuals – traditionally, a core area of liberal privacy – is a legitimate feature of political identities and British public discourse and seem to generally welcome the sexualisation of culture, while on the other hand religion – a key source of communal identity in traditional, non-liberal societies – is regarded as a private matter, perhaps as a uniquely private matter.

This betokens a complex relationship between religion and culture in which Muslim identity is seen as the illegitimate child of British multiculturalism. Indeed, the controversy surrounding Rushdie's *The Satanic Verses* made evident that the group in British society most politically opposed to (politicised) Muslims was not Christians, or even right-wing nationalists, but the secular, liberal intelligentsia. Similarly, the large Fourth Survey by the London-based Policy Studies Institute found that nominal Christians and those without a religion were more likely to say they were prejudiced against Muslims than those Christians who said their religion was of importance to them.[18] Just as the hostility against Jewish minorities, in various times and places, has been a varying blend of anti-Judaism (hostility to a religion) and anti-Semitism (hostility to a racialised group), so it is difficult to gauge to what extent contemporary British Islamophobia is 'religious' and to what extent 'racial'. Even before 9/11 and its aftermath, it was generally becoming acknowledged in Britain that of all groups Asians face the greatest hostility today, and Asians themselves feel this is because of hostility directed to Muslims.[19] These matters are not at all easy to disentangle, only now being researched at all, and anti-Muslim racism has only recently come to be acknowledged by anti-racists. Simultaneously, however, it is important to acknowledge a need for analytical space for forthright criticism of aspects of Muslim doctrines, ideologies and practice in Britain, without it being dismissed as Islamophobia – this being a parallel problem to, say, distinguishing anti-Zionism and anti-Semitism.

It has been argued here in this chapter that minority religious assertiveness in general and those of political Muslims in particular in the 1990s emerged in a climate of multiculturalism. Moreover, Muslim identity politics have stimulated a resistance because of the powerful position that secularism came to have in twentieth-century Britain. Of course, in the twenty-first century, with terrorist events such as those of the attacks in the USA on 9/11, and the London bombings on 7 July 2005, and with the emergence of a 'clash of civilisations' discourse, the political opposition came to focus on Islamism. Yet, my argument is that the initial opposition appealed to secularism, and, moreover, this strand of opposition remains central and has divided the centre-left. This opposition is misplaced because the kinds of secularism associable with democratic polities (as opposed to, say, the Soviet Union) have been designed historically to accommodate organised religion (albeit not necessarily treating all religions equally). I want to illustrate the problematic status of this hostility towards Muslim identity politics in the case of Britain. However, in order to show that Britain is not exceptional in this regard, I will briefly compare Britain to two countries that are commonly regarded by British and other commentators to be exemplars of secularism.

Secularism: different public–private boundaries in different countries

At the heart of secularism is a distinction between the public realm of citizens and policies and the private realm of belief and worship. While all Western countries are clearly secular in many ways, interpretations and the institutional arrangements diverge according to the dominant national religious culture and the differing projects of nation-state building.

For example, the USA has as its First Amendment to the Constitution that there shall be no established church, and there is wide support for this. In the past few decades there has been a tendency amongst some academics and jurists to interpret the church–state separation in radical ways.[20] Yet, as is well known, not only is the USA a deeply religious society, with much higher levels of church attendance than in Western Europe, there is also a strong, Protestant, evangelical fundamentalism that is rare in Europe.[21] This fundamentalism disputes some of the new radical interpretations of the 'no establishment clause', though not necessarily the clause itself and is one of the primary mobilising forces in American politics to the extent that it is widely claimed that it decided the presidential election of 2004. The churches in question – mainly white, and mainly in the South and Midwest – campaign openly for candidates and parties, raise large sums of money for politicians and introduce religion-based issues into politics, such as positions on abortion, HIV/AIDS, homosexuality, stem-cell research, prayer at school and so on. It has been said that no openly avowed atheist has ever been a candidate for the White House and that it would be impossible for such a candidate to be elected. It is not at all unusual for politicians – in fact, for former President George W. Bush, it was most usual – to publicly talk about their faith, to appeal to religion and to hold prayer meetings in government buildings.

On the other hand, in Britain, the Anglican Church is the 'established' religion. Bishops sit in the upper chamber of the legislature by

Table 17.1. *Religion vis-à-vis state and civil society in three countries.*

	Relationship between religion and state	Religion in civil society
England/Britain	Weak establishment	Weak but churches can be a source of political criticism and action
USA	No establishment	Strong and politically mobilised
France	Actively secular but offers top-down recognition/ control	Weak; rare for churches to be political

Adapted from T. Modood and R. Kastoryano, 'Secularism and the Accommodation of Muslims in Europe', in T. Modood, A. Triandafyllidou and R. Zapata-Barrero (eds.), *Multiculturalism, Muslims and Citizenship: A European Approach* (London: Routledge, 2006), pp. 162–78.

right, and only the senior archbishop can crown the monarchal head of state as king or queen; a king or queen who serves as 'Defender of the Faith' and Supreme Governor of the Church of England. Yet British politicians rarely talk about their religion. Indeed, it was noticeable that when the then Prime Minister Tony Blair went to a summit meeting with President Bush to discuss aspects of the Iraq War in 2003, the US media widely reported that the two leaders had prayed together. Yet Blair, one of the most openly professed and active Christians ever to hold that office, was reluctant to answer questions on this issue from the British media on his return, saying it was a private matter. The British state may have an established church, but the beliefs of the Queen's first minister are his own concern.

France draws the distinction between state and religion differently again. Like the USA, there is no state church, but, unlike the USA, the state actively promotes the privatisation of religion. While in the USA, organised religion in civil society is powerful and seeks to exert influence on the political process, French civil society does not carry expressions of religion. Yet, the French state, contrary to the USA, confers institutional legal status on the Catholic and Protestant Churches and on the Jewish Consistory. These different national manifestations of secularism are expressed in Table 17.1.

So what are the appropriate limits of the state? Everyone will agree that there should be religious freedom and that this should include freedom of belief and worship in private associations. Family too falls on the private side of the line but the state regulates the limits of what is a lawful family – for example, polygamy is not permitted in many countries – not to mention the deployment of official definitions of family in the distribution of welfare entitlements. Religions typically put a premium on mutuality and on care of the sick, the homeless and the elderly and so forth, and while religions set up organisations to pursue these aims, so too do states.

It is clear then that the 'public' is a multifaceted concept and in relation to secularism may be defined differently in relation to different dimensions of religion and in different countries. We can all be secularists, then, all approve of secularism in some respect, and yet have quite different ideas, influenced by historical legacies and varied pragmatic compromises, of where to draw the line between public and private. It would be quite mistaken to suppose that all religious spokespersons are on one side of the line and all others are on the other side. There are many different ways of drawing the various lines at issue. In the past, any boundaries set have reflected particular contexts, themselves shaped by differential customs, urgency of need and sensitivity to the sensibilities of the relevant religious groups.[22] Exactly the same considerations are relevant in relation to the accommodation of religious minorities today. To some extent this can be seen in the actions of the New Labour government that was in power 1997–2010, which has not only extended existing provisions, such as public funding to approved faith schools to the new minority religions but has also shifted the public–private boundary. As noted above, a religion question was included in the 2001 Census, the first time a question about religion has been included in the Census since it began in 1851. This was despite the protests that faith is a private matter, though, in concession to that point, the question was not compulsory. Another example is the manner in which faith and faith communities have been made integral to the work of a government department, namely the Department of Communities and Local Government, which is represented in the cabinet.[23]

Pluralising moderate secularism in Britain

Multicultural equality, then, when applied to religious groups, means that secularism *simpliciter* appears to be an obstacle to pluralistic integration and equality. But secularism pure and simple is not what exists in the world. The country-by-country situation is more complex and, indeed, far less inhospitable to the accommodation of religious minorities than the ideology of secularism might suggest – or, for that matter, the ideology of anti-secularism.[24] All actual practices of secularism consist of institutional compromises, and these can be extended to accommodate religious minorities. The institutional reconfiguration varies according to the historic place of religion in each country, and today the appropriate response to the new Muslim challenges, for example, is pluralistic institutional integration rather than an appeal to a radical public–private separation in the name of secularism. As these accommodations have varied from country to country, it means there is no exemplary solution, for contemporary solutions too will depend on the national context and will not have a once-and-for-all-time basis.

An example is the development of a religious-equality agenda in Britain, including the incorporation of some faith schools on the same basis as those of religions with a much longer presence. It also includes a recommendation of the Royal Commission on the Reform of the House of Lords, given in 2000, that alongside the Anglican bishops who sit in that house by right as part of the Anglican 'establishment' should sit senior representatives of other Christian and non-Christian faiths.

Moreover, the British political system is less corporatist and less statist than many of its EU partners such as France and Germany. It is a politics in which civil society plays a greater role, and it is therefore more comfortable with there being a variety of voices, groups and representatives. Different institutions, organisations and associations can seek to accommodate religious minorities in ways that worked for them best at a particular time, knowing that these ways may or ought be modified over time and other pressure groups and civic actors may be continually evolving their claims and agendas. Within a general understanding that there should be an explicit effort to include religious minorities (and other marginal and under-represented groups), different organisations – like the earlier example of the BBC – may not just seek this inclusion in different ways but would seek as representatives those that seemed to them most appropriate associates and partners, persons who would add something to the organisation and who were not merely delegated from a central, hierarchical body such as a church or religious council.

While the state may seek to ensure that spiritual leaders are not absent from public forums and consultative processes in relation to policies affecting their flocks, it may well be that a model of community representation based on the Board of Deputies of British Jews offers a better illustration of a community–state relationship. The Board of Deputies, a body independent of, but a communal partner to, the British state is a federation of Jewish organisations which includes not only synagogues but also other Jewish community organisations, and its leadership typically consists of lay persons whose standing and skill in representing their community is not diminished by any absence of spiritual authority. It is most interesting that while at some local levels Muslim organisations have chosen to create political bodies primarily around mosques (for example, the Bradford Council of Mosques), it is the Board of Deputies model that seems to be more apparent at a national level. This is certainly the case with the single most representative and successful national Muslim organisation, the Muslim Council of Britain (MCB), whose office-holders and spokespersons are more likely to be chartered accountants and solicitors than imams. The MCB became the chosen interlocutor of the New Labour Government, and, as domestic and international crises affecting British Muslims became more frequent and rose up the political agenda, it came to have more regular access to senior (up to the very top) policy-makers across Whitehall than any other organisation representing a minority – religious, ethnic or racial, singly or collectively. Such relationships are at the mercy of political expediency, and the MCB's pre-eminence began to suffer from the mid 2000s, as it grew increasingly critical of the invasion of Iraq and of the so-called War on Terror. At this point, the Government started accusing the MCB of failing to clearly and decisively reject extremism and began to look for alternative Muslim interlocutors. The Government played an active role in encouraging the formation and the promotion of alternative national Muslim organisations on the grounds that they were more moderate and representative, especially the Sufi Muslim Council and the British Muslim Forum. With the realisation that no single Muslim organisation was fully reflective of non-*jihadi* Muslims, the Government seems to have readmitted the MCB back into the fold but now as only part of a plurality.

So, multicultural representation has been most productively borne by the multitudinous institutions of civil society that constitute the public space, the public interactions and the plural, public identities of Britain. Incitement to religious hatred is another issue on which one might want to prudently and pragmatically combine legal statist and non-legal strategies. For it is a case in which the British experience suggests that some legislation is necessary but what one needs to achieve goes beyond the practical scope of law, which can be a blunt instrument endangering freedom of speech. Most countries recognise that legal intervention is necessary when there is a serious risk of incitement to hatred or when the 'fighting talk' is likely to inflame passions and risk public order; or when it is likely to reinforce prejudice and lead to acts of discrimination or victimisation. (Eleven countries of the EU punish Holocaust denial by imprisonment.) But such intervention still falls short of the fostering of a mutual and democratically necessary mood of respect. For this, it is necessary to rely on the sensitivity and responsibility of individuals and institutions to refrain from what is legal but unacceptable. Where these qualities are missing one relies on public debate and censure to provide standards and restraints. Hence, where matters are not or cannot easily be regulated by law, one relies on protest and empathy, though it will take time for dominant groups to learn what hurts others. This is how most racist speech and images and other free expressions (such as the use of golliwogs as commercial brands or the 1960s and 1970s BBC TV series *The Black and White Minstrel Show*) have been censured (rather than censored) away, and it is how the British media – in contrast to most others in Western Europe – responded to the Danish Cartoons Affair, recognising that they had the right to republish them but that it would be offensive to do so.

Conclusion

In certain ways, the minority politics described in this chapter have been joined by foreign policy and security concerns from around the time of the terrorist attacks of 9/11, and especially after the invasion of Iraq in 2003 and the London bombings of 7 July 2005. These events have certainly not led to the 'death' of multiculturalism in Britain as many discerned they might.[25] But that the Muslim-equality agenda has got as far as it has is because of the liberal and pragmatic political culture of Britain concerning matters of religion, as opposed to a more thoroughgoing secularism that requires the state to control religion. A more fundamental ideological reason is that Muslims utilised and extended previously existing arguments and policies in relation to racial and multicultural equality. By emphasising discrimination in educational and economic opportunities, political representation and the media, and 'Muslim-blindness' in the provision of health care and social services; and arguing for remedies that mirror existing legislation and policies in relation to sexual and racial equality, most politically active Muslims in respect of domestic issues have adjusted to and become part of British political culture in general and British multiculturalist politics in particular. Indeed, it could be said that they achieved a significant measure of political integration. Most of this progress has taken place under the administration of a Labour government. Cynics have argued that the success of the Muslim agenda is because the Government has had to placate Muslim anti-Iraq-War anger. A longer-term analysis, as offered here, shows that Labour's attentiveness to that agenda precedes the war or even 9/11. As part of its effort to advance racial and religious equality, the Government has consciously, although sometimes grudgingly, pursued policies that did not exist before 1997 – such as the funding of Muslim schools, the creation of Muslim peers, legislation to prevent religious discrimination and hatred, and the introduction of the religion question in the 2001 census. Critically, this chapter has showed that the inclusion of religion and religious identities is a necessary constituent of integration. While this inclusion runs against certain interpretations of secularism; as with most European countries, with the partial exception of France, it is not inconsistent with what secularism means in practice in Britain.

Acknowledgement

I am grateful to Nasar Meer for research and editorial assistance.

Notes

1 G. Skinner, 'Religious Pluralism and School Provision in Britain', *Intercultural Education*, 13 (2) (2002): 171–81; p. 174.
2 C. Peach and R. Gale, 'Muslims, Hindus, and Sikhs in the New Religious Landscape of England', *The Geographical Review*, 93 (4) (2003): 487–8.
3 Peach and Gale, 'Muslims, Hindus, and Sikhs', p. 469.
4 Peach and Gale, 'Muslims, Hindus, and Sikhs', p. 482.
5 T. Modood, R. Berthoud, J. Lakey, J. Nazroo, P. Smith, S. Virdee and S. Beishon, *Ethnic Minorities in Britain: Diversity and Disadvantage* (London: Policy Studies Institute, 1997), pp. 291–308.
6 Modood *et al.*, *Ethnic Minorities in Britain*, pp. 291–7.
7 T. Modood, *Multicultural Politics: Racism, Ethnicity and Muslims in Britain* (Minneapolis, Minn. and Edinburgh: University of Minnesota Press and University of Edinburgh Press, 2005).

8 I. M. Young, *Justice and the Politics of Difference* (Princeton, NJ: Princeton University Press, 1992), p. 157.

9 K. Shukra, *The Changing Pattern of Black Politics in Britain* (London: Pluto Press, 1988).

10 T. Modood, *Multiculturalism: A Civic Idea* (Cambridge: Polity, 2007).

11 S. Poulter, *Ethnicity, Law and Human Rights: The English Experience* (Oxford: Clarendon Press, 1998), p. 297.

12 Kenneth Mark, MP, quoted in Poulter, *Ethnicity, Law and Human Rights*, pp. 295–6.

13 See *Mandla* v. *Dowell Lee House of Lords*, transcript available online at www.hrcr.org/safrica/equality/Mandla—DowellLee.htm (accessed 4 June 2009).

14 N. Meer, 'Muslim Schools in Britain: Challenging Mobilisations or Logical Developments?' *Asia-Pacific Journal of Education*, 21 (1) (2007): 53–69.

15 T. Modood (ed.), *Church, State and Religious Minorities* (London: Policy Studies Institute, 1997).

16 On the latter, see R. Grillo, 'Licence to Offend? The *Behzti* Affair', *Ethnicities*, 7 (1) (2007): 5–29; more generally, see N. Meer, 'The Politics of Voluntary and Involuntary Identities: Are Muslims in Britain an Ethnic, Racial or Religious Minority', *Patterns of Prejudice*, 42 (5) (2008): 71–80. Also see Chapter 9 in this book.

17 T. Modood, T. R. Hansen, E. Bleich, B. O'Leary and J. Carens, 'The Danish Cartoon Affair: Free Speech, Racism, Islamism, and Integration', *International Migration*, 44 (5) (2006): 3–57; see also the special issue on the Mohammed Cartoon Affair, *Ethnicities*, 9 (3) (2009).

18 Modood *et al.*, *Ethnic Minorities in Britain*, p. 134.

19 Modood *et al.*, *Ethnic Minorities in Britain*, pp. 132–5.

20 M. Sandel, 'Review of Rawls' Political Liberalism', *Harvard Law Review*, 107 (May 1994): 1765–94; P. Hamburger, *Separation of Church and State* (Cambridge, Mass.: Harvard University Press, 2002).

21 A. Greely, 'The Persistence of Religion', *Cross Currents*, 45 (spring 1995): 24–41.

22 T. Modood, 'Establishment, Multiculturalism and British Citizenship', *Political Quarterly*, 65 (1) (1994): 53–73; T. Modood (ed.), *Church, State and Religious Minorities* (London: Policy Studies Institute, 1997).

23 See the website of the Department of Communities and Local Government, www.communities.gov.uk/communities/racecohesionfaith/faith (accessed 4 June 2009).

24 T. Modood and R. Kastoryano, 'Secularism and the Accommodation of Muslims in Europe', in T. Modood, A. Triandafyllidou and R. Zapata-Barrero (eds.), *Multiculturalism, Muslims and Citizenship: A European Approach* (London: Routledge, 2006).

25 See Modood, *Multiculturalism*; N. Meer and T. Modood, 'The Multicultural State We Are in: Muslims, "Multiculture" and the "Civic Re-balancing" of British Multiculturalism', *Political Studies*, 57 (3) (2009).

Guide to further reading

Anderson, B., *Imagined Communities*, new edn (London: Verso, 2006).

Apple, M., *Educating the 'Right' Way: Markets, Standards, God and Inequality* (London: Routledge, 2006).

Arts Council of England, *The National Policy for Theatre in England* (London: Arts Council England, 2000).

Arthurs, J., *Television and Sexuality: Regulation and the Politics of Taste* (Maidenhead: Open University Press, 2004).

Ashby, J. and Higson, A. (eds.), *British Cinema: Past and Present* (London: Routledge, 2000).

Ball, S., *The Education Debate: Policy and Politics in the Twenty-First Century* (Bristol: Policy Press, 2008).

Bennett, A. (ed.), *Britpop and Englishness* (Aldershot: Ashgate, 2010).

Bertram, V., *Gendering Poetry: Contemporary Women and Men Poets* (London: Pandora Press, 2005).

Billig, M., *Banal Nationalism* (London: Sage, 1995).

Bolton, A., *AngloMania: Tradition and Transgression in British Fashion* (New Haven, Conn.: Yale University Press, 2006).

Breward, C., Conekin, B. and Cox, C. (eds.), *The Englishness of English Dress* (Oxford: Berg, 2002).

Breward, C., Ehrman, E. and Evans, C., *The London Look: Fashion from Street to Catwalk* (New Haven, Conn.: Yale University Press, 2004).

Broom, S., *Contemporary British and Irish Poetry* (Houndmills: Palgrave Macmillan, 2006).

Brown, M., *A License to Be Different: The Story of Channel 4* (London: BFI, 2007).

Connor, S., *The English Novel in History, 1950–95* (London: Routledge, 1996).

Cook, M., Mills, R., Trumbach, R. and Cocks, H. G., *A Gay History of Britain: Love and Sex between Men since the Middle Ages* (Oxford: Greenwood World Publishing, 2007).

Cooke, L., *British Television Drama: A History* (London: BFI, 2003).

Crisell, A., *An Introductory History of British Broadcasting* (London: Routledge, 2002).

Crystal, D., *The Stories of English* (London: Penguin, 2004).

　The Fight for English (Oxford: Oxford University Press, 2006).

Curran, J. and Seaton, J., *Power without Responsibility: The Press and Broadcasting in Britain*, 7th edn (London: Routledge, 2009).

Dowson, J. and Entwistle, A., *A History of Twentieth-Century British Women's Poetry* (Cambridge: Cambridge University Press, 2005).

English, J. (ed.), *A Concise Companion to Contemporary British Fiction* (Oxford: Blackwell, 2006).

Evans, C., *Fashion at the Edge: Spectacle, Modernity and Deathliness* (New Haven, Conn.: Yale University Press, 2003).

Ferris, P., *Sex and the British: A Twentieth-Century History* (London: Mandarin, 1994).

Fountain, T., *Rude Britannia* (London: Pheonix, 2009).

Gilroy, P., *After Empire: Melancholia or Convivial Culture?* (London: Routledge, 2004).

Goodrum, A., *The National Fabric: Fashion, Britishness, Globalization* (Oxford: Berg, 2005).

Harvie, J., *Staging the UK* (Manchester: Manchester University Press, 2005).

Haslam, D., *Manchester, England: The Story of a Pop Cult City* (London: Fourth Estate, 2000).

Haste, C., *Rules of Desire: Sex in Britain, World War 1 to the Present* (London: Vintage, 2002).

Hatton, R. and Walker, J. A., *Supercollector: A Critique of Charles Saatchi* (London: Ellipsis, 2000).

Higgins, M., *Media and Their Publics* (Maidenhead: Open University Press, 2008).

Hogg, R. and Denison, D. (eds.), *A History of the English Language* (Cambridge: Cambridge University Press, 2006).

Holmes, S. and Jermyn, D. (eds.), *Understanding Reality Television* (London: Routledge, 2005).

Horne, J., *Sport in Consumer Culture* (Basingstoke: Palgrave Macmillan, 2006).

Hunt, L., *British Low Culture: From Safari Suits to Sexploitation* (London: Routledge, 1998).

Jones, K., *Education in Britain: 1944 to the Present* (Cambridge: Polity Press, 2003).

Jones, K., Cunchillos, C., Hatcher, R., Hirtt, N., Innes, R., Johsua, S. and Klausentitzer, J., *Schooling in Western Europe: The New Order and its Adversaries* (Basingstoke: Palgrave Macmillan, 2008).

Kavanagh, D., Richards, D., Geddes, A. and Smith, A., *British Politics*, 5th edn (Oxford: Oxford University Press, 2006).

Kumar, K. *The Making of English National Identity* (Cambridge: Cambridge University Press, 2003).

Lenskyj, H., *Out of Bounds: Women, Sport and Sexuality* (Toronto: Women's Press of Canada, 2003).

Leonard, M., *Britain™: Renewing Our Identity* (London: Demos, 1997).

Martin, A. and Bartlett, H., *Implementing the National Policy for Theatre in England: Baseline Findings* (London: Arts Council England, 2003).

Mason, T., *Association Football and English Society, 1863–1915* (London: Routledge, 1980).

McNair, B., *News and Journalism in the UK*, 5th edn (London: Routledge, 2009).

McRobbie, A., *British Fashion Design: Rag Trade or Image Industry?* (London: Routledge, 1998).

Modood, T., *Multicultural Politics: Racism, Ethnicity and Muslims in Britain* (Edinburgh: Edinburgh University Press, 2005).

Modood, T., *Multiculturalism: A Civic Idea* (London: Polity, 2007).

Morley, D. and Robins, K. (eds.), *British Cultural Studies* (Oxford: Oxford University Press, 2001).

Mugglestone, L. (ed.), *The Oxford History of English* (Oxford: Oxford University Press, 2006).

O'Brien, S., *The Deregulated Muse: Essays on Contemporary British and Irish Poetry* (Newcastle upon Tyne: Bloodaxe, 1998).

Parekh, B., *Rethinking Multiculturalism: Cultural Diversity and Political Theory* (Basingstoke: Macmillan, 2000).

Polley, M., *Moving the Goalposts: A History of Sport and Society Since 1945* (London: Routledge, 1998).

Runnymede Trust, *The Future of Multi-Ethnic Britain: The Parekh Report* (London: Profile, 2000).

Seabrook, J., 'The End of the Provinces', *Granta*, 90 (2005): 225–41.

Sensation: Young British Artists from the Saatchi Collection, exhibition catalogue (London: Thames & Hudson, 1997).

Shaffer, B. (ed.), *A Companion to the British and Irish Novel, 1945–2000* (Oxford: Blackwell, 2005).

Shellard, D., *Economic Impact Study of UK Theatre* (London: Arts Council England, 2004).

Singh, G., 'British Multiculturalism and Sikhs', *Sikhs Formations*, 1 (2) (2005): 157–73.

Spalding, F., *British Art since 1900*, 2nd edn (London: Thames & Hudson, 2002).

Stallabrass, J., *Art Incorporated: The Story of Contemporary Art* (Oxford: Oxford University Press, 2004).

Street, S., *British National Cinema* (London: Routledge, 1997).

Temple, M., *The British Press* (Maidenhead: Open University Press, 2008).

Tomaney, J., 'Keeping a Beat in the Dark: Narratives of Regional Identity in Basil Bunting's *Briggflatts*', *Environment and Planning D: Society and Space*, 25 (2) (2007): 355–75.

Vertinsky, P. A., *The Eternally Wounded Woman: Women, Doctors, and Exercise in the Late Nineteenth Century* (Champaign, Illinois: University of Illinois Press, 1994).

Waugh, P., *Harvest of the Sixties: English Literature and its Backgrounds, 1960–1995* (Oxford: Oxford University Press, 1995).

Weeks, J., *The World We Have Won: The Remaking of Erotic and Intimate Life* (London: Routledge, 2007).

Werbner, P., 'The Predicament of Diaspora and Millenial Islam: Reflections on September 11, 2001', *Ethnicities*, 4 (4) (2004): 451–76.

Whiteley, S., *The Space Between the Notes: Rock and the Counter-Culture* (London: Routledge, 1992).

Women and Popular Music: Sexuality, Identity and Subjectivity (London: Routledge, 2000).

Williams, K., *Get Me a Murder a Day: A History of Mass Communications in Britain,* 2nd edn (London: Bloomsbury, 2009).

Womack, K. (ed.), *The Cambridge Companion to the Beatles* (Cambridge: Cambridge University Press, 2009).

Index

Lightning Source UK Ltd.
Milton Keynes UK
UKOW04f0620220614

233785UK00001B/60/P